# Almost Midnight

# Almost Midnight

Richard David Thompson

New Wine Press

New Wine Ministries
PO Box 17
Chichester
West Sussex
United Kingdom
PO19 2AW

ISBN 978-1-905991-22-8

Typeset by CRB Associates, Reepham, Norfolk
Cover design by CCD, www.ccdgroup.co.uk
Printed by Creative Print & Design, Abertillery, UK

*"Jerusalem will be trampled on by the Gentiles until the times of the Gentiles are fulfilled."*
(Luke 21:24)

# Contents

## PART 3: Israel and the Roman Empire

# Introduction

This book examines the much-misunderstood period, which Jesus called *"the times of the Gentiles"*, and the main issues associated with it. We will look at how the establishment of the State of Israel in 1948 has opened the way for the development of the EU and the start of other end-time events. In the next few years, this will culminate in the Great Tribulation with the entrance of the Antichrist and the reinstitution of Temple sacrifice. We will also see what the Scriptures have to say regarding Roman Catholicism and Islam, and their roots.

In His last days of teaching in Jerusalem, Jesus prophesied some of the events that would happen shortly after His departure and those that would occur in the last years leading up to His return. The central scripture of the whole study is:

> *"They* [the Israelites] *will fall by the sword and will be taken as prisoners to all the nations. Jerusalem will be trampled on by the Gentiles until the times of the Gentiles are fulfilled* ... *When these things* [the end-time events described by Jesus] *begin to take place, stand up and lift up your heads, because your redemption is drawing near."*
>
> (Luke 21:24, 28)

Also presented is a biblical over-view of key points revealing God's perspective on current and future events. We know in our own personal lives it is impossible to understand what the Lord has done and is doing unless we receive instruction and light from the Bible explained to us by the Holy Spirit. Likewise, a biblical insight is essential to understand how God is moving in the world today. We live in difficult but exciting times when the above scripture and many others concerning Jerusalem are in the process of being fulfilled before our very eyes!

There are two main views amongst Bible believers as far as Israel is concerned. These have become known as "Replacement" and "Non-replacement" theologies. I shall seek to show the errors on both sides of the debate and the correct aspects of each in order to harmonise them. The Church can then move forward together to support and pray for Israel and the return of her King, the King of kings.

Jesus said that these events would be terrible but He encourages us to look to Him in confidence, knowing that God is in overall control and will bring all things to a wonderful conclusion at His return. The Bible records how our loving Father has been drawing all men back to Himself over the millennia. He desires a living relationship with each individual throughout the earth but has given us the awesome freedom to say "no" to Him, whilst clearly warning us that refusing His forgiveness means eternal damnation. Although He is working within the various time frames He has set, He never violates our free will, but wants to bring that life-changing relationship with Himself to all who say "yes" to His Lordship.

As I have studied, meditated and prayed about the Scriptures, my views have changed and developed, giving me a deeper understanding of how God views the world situation and consequently a clearer idea of how to pray for the issues covered in this study. This, I trust, will also help the Church. We will look first at Israel and then some relevant aspects regarding the Church, Europe and the Middle East. Scripture shows the increasing power and influence of the European Union and how it will affect Christians not only in Europe but throughout the entire world. But, hallelujah, it also means we are approaching Jesus' glorious return!

This all sounds very grandiose, and it is, but I sense an increasing urgency in my spirit that the whole Church should understand what God is saying today about Israel and related matters. We can then pray and work with God more closely to bring this age to His conclusion.

First, some personal details. At the age of thirty, about 7.45 p.m. on Sunday 4th February 1973, I put my trust in the Lord Jesus Christ and turned from being an ardent atheist to a committed born-again believer. I soon became interested in Israel, and my desire to know more about this nation accelerated in early 1977, when God spoke to me about visiting the country. That September I flew to Israel on a Christian tour, and during the two weeks met Judith, who later became my precious wife. Where would I be without her? She has been a tremendous help to me in my personal life and with this study, as have several other people. Thank you all so very much.

While in Israel, God gave me a vision of two long lines, like a flattened X, one gradually descending and crossing a gradually ascending one. He said the downward slope, from top left to bottom right, represented the process of concluding His hard but just judgment on the nation of Israel for her sins. The gradual upward line, from lower left to upper right represented the increasing restoration of Israel through His wonderful mercy, grace and faithfulness towards her, even though most of her people still reject His Son, Jesus.

But why should God restore the nation of Israel and in our lifetime and not before? I have searched the Scriptures for over thirty years and through them the Lord has, little by little, answered these questions to which the crossed lines refer. It is because the *"times of the Gentiles"*, the phrase Jesus used to describe Israel's punishment, are being concluded as I will explain. Through the centuries there have always been Jews who have believed in Jesus, but Israel has never been a predominantly Christian nation. Now, at the end of this pro-tracted judgment, God is raising up an ever-increasing army of

Christian intercessors to pray that He might bring about the remaining promises made to her thousands of years ago.

One of the many scriptures that speaks of His immeasurable love, mercy and grace to Israel is found in Psalm 102:

> "But you, O LORD, sit enthroned for ever;
>    your renown endures through all generations.
> You will arise and have compassion on Zion [Jerusalem];
>    for it is time to show favour to her;
>    the appointed time has come.
> For her stones are dear to your servants;
>    her very dust moves them to pity.
> The nations will fear the name of the LORD,
>    all the kings of the earth will revere your glory.
> For the LORD will rebuild Zion
>    and appear in his glory.
> He will respond to the prayer of the destitute;
>    he will not despise their plea." (Psalm 102:12–17)

During my visit, I distinctly experienced something of the Lord's compassion for her very stones and even her dust.

The Lord has given me several prophetic words and visions over the years, for my direction and encouragement in continuing with this study. In 1977, during a communion service held in the Garden Tomb in Jerusalem, the likely place of Jesus' burial, a Christian minister on our tour received a vision of me standing on the walls of Jerusalem. I was looking out into the distance to see what was approaching the city in order to warn the people inside her walls. The minister explained that the Lord was saying He had called me to be a watchman of His word, to inform the people in the city of what is approaching. He encouraged me to find a place in Him to learn how to handle the word, which I have been seeking to do against severe opposition. A few years later, a sister in Christ had a picture of me standing on a rock overlooking a very large flock of sheep, with a range of mountains behind. I believe these depict the mountains of Israel, an encouragement and a confirmation of the previous vision. Some years later, a leader at a conference prophesied that God was going to make me a trumpet in the Church. More recently, a sister at our regular Sunday morning meeting saw me standing with a flaming torch in my hand. The Lord was saying I should run with the vision given to me and not be deterred by the negative faces of people who do not understand. On another occasion at a conference in 2005, the retired head of a Bible College prayed for me. He received a picture of a transmitting mast and said that God wanted me to broadcast what He had put in my heart. Finally, in the spring of 2006, another sister had a vision of a scroll with a seal, which He broke. Holding one end, He unrolled it onto the floor and said I should share what has been revealed to me from the Scriptures. So, I am seeking to speak out as a watchman of His word from the walls of Jerusalem, similar to Habakkuk's statement:

> "I will stand at my watch
>     and station myself on the ramparts;
> I will look to see what he will say to me,
>     and what answer I am to give to this complaint [that the
>         righteous are devoured by the wicked].
>
> Then the LORD replied,
>
> 'Write down the revelation
>     and make it plain on tablets
>     so that a herald may run with it.
> For the revelation awaits an appointed time;
>     it speaks of the end
>     and will not prove false.
> Though it linger, wait for it;
>     it will certainly come and will not delay.' "          (Habakkuk 2:1–2)

During Daniel's captivity in Babylon some 500 years before Christ, he received some amazing visions of the end times. The angel Gabriel gave him the following instructions regarding these:

> *"But you, Daniel, close up and seal the words of the scroll until the time of the end. Many will go here and there to increase knowledge."*
>
> (Daniel 12:4)

> *"Go your way, Daniel, because the words are closed up and sealed until the time of the end."* (Daniel 12:9)

Travel has increased and statisticians say that natural understanding of our world is doubling every two years! The angel said Daniel's unexplained visions would be opened up at the end of the age when these things were happening. This would indicate we are now in the last days, or the minutes before midnight, when our precious Lord will return – hence the title of this book.

> *"At midnight the cry rang out, 'Here's the bridegroom! Come out to meet him!' Then all the virgins woke up and trimmed their lamps. The foolish ones said to the wise, 'Give us some of your oil; our lamps are going out.' 'No,' they replied, 'there may not be enough for both us and you.'"*
>
> (Matthew 25:6–9)

Throughout the Bible it is clear that God does not bring about any major event without first speaking of it through His prophets, whether to bless or to judge. Amos states:

> *"Surely the Sovereign LORD does nothing*
> *without revealing His plan*
> *to his servants the prophets."* (Amos 3:7)

In the most significant events, timings are stated as well. For instance, God warned Abraham that his descendants would spend 400 years in a foreign land – the length of time they were in Egypt (Genesis 15:13). He said the nation of Judah would be exiled in Babylon for seventy years (Jeremiah 25:11). The greatest event of all was foretold by Daniel in chapter 9:26, namely the 483 judgment years from the decree made by the Persian King, Artaxerxes, that the Jews should return from Babylon and rebuild Jerusalem, to the Anointed One being *"cut off"*, i.e. the crucifixion. This is part of Daniel's famous seventy weeks prophecy, which I fully explain in chapter 9. Why should God change His ways and not inform us of the events leading up to the return of His Son? What's more, Jesus calls us sons and friends because He wants and requires us to understand and be involved in His plans:

> *"I [Jesus] no longer call you servants, because a servant does not know his master's business. Instead, I have called you friends, for everything that I learned from my Father I have made known to you."*
>
> (John 15:15)

As mentioned, Daniel discovered from Jeremiah's writings that the exile would last seventy years and so he knew it was near completion (Daniel 9:2). His reaction could have been that of many Christians today, "God has said it, so it will happen – who needs to bother understanding or praying about it." Daniel's response, however, once he was aware of God's timing, was to seek Him, fast, confess the sins of the people and pray that their release would come about! Fasting, of itself, does not cause God to act but it does help undermine our unbelief, which releases the faith given to us through the revelation of His word, allowing the Holy Spirit to bring the word to pass through prayer spoken in faith.

God has given mankind authority to rule the earth and He will not overrule our freewill. Consequently, He requires our agreement to move in this world. For instance, He required Pharaoh's permission to let the Israelites leave Egypt before He could lead them out through the Red Sea. He is calling us to respond like Daniel, to study the Bible and find out what is in His heart for us today. Some say we must concentrate solely on the gospel and not be distracted by end-time prophecies. Indeed, our central mission is to make disciples of all men but it will greatly help us if we have a correct and clear understanding of these scriptures in order to achieve this commission. It will markedly sharpen our evangelistic cutting edge, and we will then be in a position to explain clearly to people what is happening in our world and where we are in the end-time events. It will also be a source of great encouragement for believers who have to live through the last-day tribulations, to understand what is happening from the certainty of the Bible and how long the events will last. At the moment the Church is largely ignorant and confused by these scriptures. The apostle Paul said:

> *"All* [biblical] *Scripture is God-breathed and is useful for teaching, rebuking, correcting and training in righteousness, so that the man of God may be thoroughly equipped for every good work."*
>
> (2 Timothy 3:16–17)

Yes, this includes end-time prophecies as well! In fact they become more vital as we approach the last years of outreach by the Church throughout the world! Jesus said He would send His Spirit to help us:

> *"When he, the Spirit of truth, comes, he will guide you into all truth. He will not speak on his own; he will speak only what he hears, and he will tell you what is **yet** to come."*        (John 16:13, emphasis added)

In the process of the study, I have also unravelled the overall time sequence of events of the Jewish nation. So, I pray that this book will help to open up God's word on these issues and bring understanding about the final days leading up to the momentous return of the King of kings and Lord of lords.

# PART 1

## *Israel – Her Place in History and the Future*

# Does Israel Remain Unique Before God?

The whole Church accepts that Israel played the central role in God's plan up to the appearance of Jesus. But what of today? Has she forfeited her privileged position? To find out let's begin by considering Jesus' denunciation of the Jews in His day for their lack of understanding of the times in which they lived. He said:

> *"Hypocrites! You know how to interpret the appearance of the earth and the sky. How is it that you don't know how to interpret this present time?"* (Luke 12:56)

We, too, are very skilled at forecasting the weather for most eventualities, but God also expects us to diligently seek out the truths in the Bible to understand the times in which we live. Few of the Jewish leaders recognised their Messiah walking amongst them. The teachers of Israel should have recognised Him from His teaching and miracles. We are in a similar situation today where many ministers are not aware of what the Holy Spirit is currently doing in Israel. Nor do they understand the Devil's schemes in Europe, though the Scriptures clearly foretell these things.

Much confusion has arisen because many make an invalid assumption that all the scriptures on the end times in Daniel, Revelation and elsewhere should be treated symbolically and not be taken literally. I believe Scripture shows there is a mixture of the two and one has to discern, with the guidance of the Holy Spirit, which is which. There is symbolism in the Old Testament prophecies regarding Jesus' first advent, but there are also many specific scriptures, which He fulfilled to the letter. The account of the crucifixion in Isaiah 53 was excruciatingly real to Jesus, not symbolic! God is about to complete many of the outstanding prophecies in like manner. For instance, it clearly says in Revelation 11:3 that there will be two witnesses in Jerusalem who will proclaim the truth about Jesus. Some believe these represent two groups, namely the Church and the Jews. However, verse 5 says that anyone who harms them will be killed by fire coming out of the mouths of the two ministers! I do not see from the rest of Scripture that all who come against the Church and the Jewish nation will be burnt to death by their breath! Nor is it likely that the whole Church and the Jews who are alive at that time will all die and then be simultaneously raised from the dead three and a half days later, as chapter 11 informs us will happen to these two!

The apostle Peter, before going to Cornelius' house, as recorded in Acts 10:9–48, also had an incorrect doctrinal mindset that barred the Gentiles from salvation. It took a dramatic vision of a large sheet being let down from heaven, with the command to eat the many unclean animals that were on it, to persuade him to alter his viewpoint. A similar thing is happening in the Church today. What will it take for believers to clearly see God's involvement in the current return of the Jews to the land of Israel?

The Spirit quickened Daniel's spirit regarding Jeremiah's word in Daniel 9:1–3, which gave him faith to pray so that God could bring about the return of the Jews to Jerusalem that very year. In the same way, God has chosen to involve the Church in prayer and fasting to bring the return of Jesus. It is for this very reason that the Spirit is now opening up the end-time scriptures in the Bible to believers. Some evangelical Bible colleges have a big problem in this area. Many of their textbooks on the subject were written before God started to reveal these things to the Church.

They, like Peter, find it difficult to change their thinking but thankfully God is determined to help us renew our minds.

Jesus explained his public ministry to the Jewish nation in pictorial form by telling them a parable:

> *"A man had a fig-tree, planted in his vineyard, and he went to look for fruit on it, but did not find any. So he said to the man who took care of the vineyard, 'For three years now I've been coming to look for fruit on this fig-tree and haven't found any. Cut it down! Why should it use up the soil?' 'Sir', the man replied, 'leave it alone for one more year, and I'll dig round it and fertilise it. If it bears fruit next year, fine! If not, then cut it down.' "*     (Luke 13:6–9)

This described how He and the Father viewed Israel's hardness of heart to their Messiah. The timing refers to Jesus' spectacular public ministry, which lasted three and a half years. The Jews were also likened to figs in Jeremiah 24. The obedient were described as very good figs and the unbelieving as very bad ones.

Jesus foresaw the catastrophic consequences of their national rejection:

> *"When you see Jerusalem being surrounded by armies, you will know that its desolation is near. Then let those who are in Judea flee to the mountains, let those in the city get out, and let those in the country not enter the city. For this is the time of punishment in fulfilment of all that has been written. How dreadful it will be in those days for pregnant women and nursing mothers! There will be great distress in the land and wrath against this people. They will fall by the sword and will be taken as prisoners to all the nations. Jerusalem will be trampled on by the Gentiles until the times of the Gentiles are fulfilled."*     (Luke 21:20–24)

This violent death, destruction and second dispersion came through Titus in AD 70, when the ruthless Roman army levelled the city of Jerusalem and many towns in Israel. Please note that the New Testament never refers to Israel as Palestine. It was the

Roman Emperor Hadrian, of wall-building fame, who later tried to wipe out all traces of the Jews from the land, renaming it Palestina, and Jerusalem, Aelia Capitolina. The fig tree had been violently "cut down". However, God's grace and mercy to Israel is expressed in the second half of verse 24, where Jesus says their loss of self-government would not last forever but would one day be restored.

Israel was already under God's judgment during Jesus' earthly ministry, as shown by the Roman occupation. This subjection to foreign powers was originally brought about by her wilful and persistent sin in the times of their kings, which initially led to the exile of the northern tribes to Assyria and later the southern tribes to Babylon. After the return of the two southern tribes, they remained under various rulers until 1948 when Israel regained sovereignty over part of her land. I will explain this in much greater detail in subsequent chapters.

Matthew 24 warns that many will turn away from the Christian faith and that the end-time traumas will be worldwide, though centred around Jerusalem, with the Antichrist setting himself up in the Holy Place of the Temple! I give more details on this in chapter 9.

> "When you see standing in the holy place 'the abomination that causes desolation', spoken of through the prophet Daniel – let the reader understand – then let those who are in Judea flee to the mountains."
>
> (Matthew 24:15–16)

Jesus explained that the restoration of Israel would see a time of increasing disturbance in the heavens and the earth, culminating in catastrophic events at His return. In the immortal words of American commentators just before the grand finale, "You ain't seen nothin' yet!"

> "There will be signs in the sun, moon and stars. On the earth, nations will be in anguish and perplexity at the roaring and tossing of the sea.

*Men will faint from terror, apprehensive of what is coming on the world,
for the heavenly bodies will be shaken. At that time they will see the Son
of Man coming in a cloud with power and great glory. When these things
begin to take place, stand up and lift up your heads, because your
redemption is drawing near."* (Luke 21:25–28)

In His summary of these final upheavals, Jesus included a parable
describing the world situation in terms as different types of trees
coming to leaf in the spring:

*"Look at the fig-tree and all the trees. When they sprout leaves, you can
see for yourselves and know that summer is near. Even so, when you see
these things happening, you know the kingdom of God is near. I tell you
the truth, this generation will certainly not pass away until all these
things have happened. Heaven and earth will pass away, but my words
will never pass away."* (Luke 21:29–33)

Was Jesus referring to the replanting of Israel in 1948 in this
parable? It looks so, as why else would He single out the fig tree?

One day, on His way to Jerusalem to teach in the Temple
during His last week, Jesus was hungry and searched for fruit on a
fig tree by the roadside but found none. This spoke to Him of
Israel's lack of a fruitful response to the truths He taught and His
identity. Jesus cursed the fig tree, prefiguring the judgments that
Israel brought on herself for her hardness of heart in crucifying
Him. Fortunately, Jesus still loved them and amazingly asked
the Father to forgive them, even while the Roman soldiers
hammered those cruel iron nails through His hands and feet. God
only knows what other horrors the Jews would have endured, on
top of the genocides they have experienced, had not Jesus asked
the Father to forgive them (Luke 23:34). The narrative goes on to
say it was not the season for figs (Mark 11:12–14). Why then did
the Lord speak to it so harshly? Wasn't that unreasonable?

I do not believe it was. We discover why in the Song of
Solomon 2:13, where it refers to the season for early figs. The

spring fruit comes in Israel around Passover time. These first small figs grow together with the new leaves. The later fruit, the main crop, consists of larger figs filling out and ripening through the heat of summer. Early figs can be delayed or even destroyed by drought or heavy frost in spring. Jesus was making a point. He equated the lack of early fruit to the scarceness of true faith in Israel as a nation, particularly in her leaders. If they had believed in God, the drought and frost of unbelief would not have overcome the faith God had given them through the words of His prophets. The Jewish leaders mainly had an intellectual understanding, not one of faith in the heart. Consequently, what they offered to God was largely lip service. Are we, the Church, guilty of the same?

The Lord is still searching for fruit in Israel, that the people may come to Christ and produce godly works through faith in Him. Just as the strong heat of summer ripens the fruit, He will use the developing traumatic situation to bring the whole Jewish nation to the point where they humble themselves, seek God and so have their eyes opened to their Messiah. God, in His foreknowledge, has seen that the vast majority who survive the end-time traumas will be saved (Romans 11:26). Jesus said that He would be looking for faith when He returns (Luke 18:8), that is, faith in Him. At long last He will find the harvest of large ripe figs He has been searching for in Israel and be fully satisfied.

The British Mandate in Israel ended and the last British troops withdrew. The following day the State of Israel was declared on 14 May 1948. In Jesus' terminology the fig tree was replanted. The day after the declaration the surrounding Muslim nations attacked Israel with the sole objective of annihilating the fledgling nation. Most governments around the world assumed she would only last a few weeks, if that, but far from being killed at rebirth, and in spite of being hugely outnumbered, Israel miraculously survived because God is with her. The nation has grown significantly over the last fifty plus years but Satan is continually trying to counter God's plans. We saw this when he tried to murder Jesus as a baby by inciting King Herod to kill all under the age of two. She has been increasing ever since, but despite her gains, Gentiles are still trampling her capital city, particularly in the Temple area. Why is this?

During their exile in Babylon, God gave the following powerful promises to the descendants of Israel:

> *"Though I completely destroy all the nations*
> *among which I scatter you,*
> *I will not completely destroy you."*     (Jeremiah 30:11)

> " *'Only if these decrees* [that the sun and moon continuing
> in their courses] *vanish from my sight,'*
> *declares the* LORD,
> *'will the descendants of Israel ever cease*
> *to be a nation before me . . .*
> *Only if the heavens above can be measured*
> *and the foundations of the earth below be searched out*
> *will I reject all the descendants of Israel*
> *because of all they have done.' "*     (Jeremiah 31:36–37)

These promises are as true today after Christ, as they were before His first advent. The heavenly bodies still move in their orbit with amazing consistency. The universe has certainly not been fully explored and there is much we still don't know about the centre of our beautiful planet. We can therefore be confident from these scriptures alone that, despite all the attempts by Satan to annihilate her, Israel will remain as a nation before God.

It is obvious to an increasing number of Christians that Israel is the most significant place in the world today, but why are Muslims so incensed at her presence? It is because Satan knows that Jesus cannot return until God has fulfilled all His promises to Israel, and their restoration to the whole land is one of them. Satan knows that he will be bound in the bottomless pit at the return of Jesus (Revelation 20:1–3), so if he can stop the Jews repossessing the land he can avoid this and his subsequent casting into the lake of fire (Revelation 20:10). Satan, therefore, continually lies to Muslims that the Jews should not be there!

Currently the Temple area, the centrepiece of Jerusalem, has the Muslim Dome of the Rock very significantly built on or near the original site. King David had designated this place for the building of the Lord's Temple before he died (1 Chronicles 22), and commissioned his son to build it:

> *"Then Solomon began to build the temple of the LORD in Jerusalem on Mount Moriah, where the LORD had appeared to his father David. It was on the threshing-floor of Araunah the Jebusite, the place provided by David."*                              (2 Chronicles 3:1)

Mount Moriah was the probable site where, 1,000 years before David, Abraham received the instruction from God to sacrifice his son Isaac (Genesis 22:2). He was living in Beersheba at that time. Jerusalem is about forty miles north-east of Beersheba, so this distance fits, as it took them just over two days to travel there (Genesis 22:4). Abraham told his son that God would provide the offering. After God saw Abraham's obedience in being willing to sacrifice his son, an angel stopped him from plunging the knife into Isaac's heart. God never intended that Isaac should die and even if Abraham had disobeyed God his son would have lived. Abraham then saw a ram in the thicket – an adult male sheep (Genesis 22:13). Another 2,000 years of triumph and defeat for Israel would follow before God could send Jesus to die for the sins of the world, not only the fully mature male in His prime at age thirty-three, but also the innocent and perfect Lamb of God. Abraham himself was a picture of God the Father and Isaac a type of God the Son. Praise the Lord, an angel did not withhold Rome's hand when Jesus willingly went to the cruel cross, purchasing the totally unmerited forgiveness of sins and healing for us all!

The Muslim Dome of the Rock has, as its central feature, the exposed rock where the sacrifice of Isaac traditionally took place. The Muslims believe it was Ishmael who was to be slain by Abraham and that being the eldest the inheritance is through him. They believe that the Jews deceitfully altered the Scriptures to say it was through Isaac. However, Hagar, Ishmael's mother, was only a maidservant and not Abraham's wife and the inheritance rightly passed to Isaac. Calvary was outside the city wall and is Latin for the Aramaic name Golgotha, meaning "a skull". There are two main possible sites in Jerusalem. The traditional one is the Church of the Holy Sepulchre and the other, discovered more recently in 1883, is Gordon's Calvary with the adjacent Garden Tomb, where the "standing on the walls of Jerusalem" vision was given to me. General Gordon, a devout Christian man stationed in Jerusalem, discovered the tomb and the adjacent Roman execution site after careful study of the Gospel narrative and the city history. The cliff face on which the site is situated has the features of a skull, but now overlooks an Arab bus station! Many historians still believe the Holy Sepulchre is the authentic site, but it contradicts an important scripture found in Leviticus, where Moses gave the instructions for the whole burnt offering:

> *"If the offering is a burnt offering from the flock, from either the sheep or the goats, he is to offer a male without defect. He is to slaughter it at the north side of the altar before the Lord."*　　　(Leviticus 1:10–11)

All the Old Testament sacrifices point to Jesus' death as the perfect sacrifice. He was indeed the Lamb of God slain for the sins of the entire world and was entirely consumed in the fire of obedience to His Father – the whole burnt offering. The Garden Tomb and Gordon's Calvary are both situated to the north of the Temple area, where God told Solomon to build the altar of sacrifice. The Holy Sepulchre is to the west, which apparently contradicts this positional instruction.

After the return of the two southern tribes from Babylon to Jerusalem, Zechariah gave this prophecy:

> *"I am going to make Jerusalem a cup that sends all the surrounding peoples reeling. Judah will be besieged as well as Jerusalem. On that day, when all the nations of the earth are gathered against her, I will make Jerusalem an immovable rock for all the nations. All who try to move it will injure themselves. On that day I will strike every horse with panic and its rider with madness."* (Zechariah 12:2–4)

When the Jews returned from Babylon, the Persians became the new rulers of Israel, followed by the Greeks, and then the Romans. The Jewish Maccabean uprising in the latter years of the Greek empire was short lived, as they soon came under Roman control. After the latter's demise, the Muslims took over, followed by a short period of nearly 100 years of Roman Catholic domination during the Crusades and lastly the British governed Israel from 1917 to 1948. None of these powers found Jerusalem an "immovable rock" – quite the contrary. However, we have seen a dramatic reversal in Israel's military fortunes against the various invasions from 1948 onwards. Why is this? I will fully explain in later chapters; but suffice to say at this point, it is because God's punishment of Israel as a nation is over and He is once again able to move towards her in mercy and grace rather than judgment. It is crucial to see this point in order to understand the present-day situation. God has an ever-increasing army of believers praying for her and He is now defending Israel's borders but if her government decides to give up land, as in the recent withdrawal from Gaza, He will not stop this. It is vital that the leaders of Israel and very importantly Messianic Jews and Gentile believers, all need to understand the scriptures spoken by her prophets, stand on them, watch and pray to see her enemies repulsed and the land fully brought under Jewish control. The debatable success of Hizbulla in August 2006 in Lebanon was due to a lack of resolve and preparedness by the

Israeli authorities, but all who now violate her borders will suffer severe loss, as we have entered the Zechariah 12:2 period quoted above.

Verse 2 says the surrounding nations will besiege her. These are the Muslim countries encircling her and we have already seen the wounds they have received in their efforts to take Jerusalem over the last sixty years. Verse 3 speaks of all the nations surrounding and coming against her, which we will see during the next few years.

Zechariah continued:

> "*Then the leaders of Judah will say in their hearts, 'The people of Jerusalem are strong, because the* LORD *Almighty is their God.'*"
>
> (Zechariah 12:5)

The Sanhedrin in New Testament times did not think like this and were overrun by Titus in AD 70, confirming these words were not fulfilled then. He went on to say:

> "*And I will pour out on the house of David and the inhabitants of Jerusalem a spirit of grace and supplication. They will look on me, the one they have pierced, and they will mourn for him as one mourns for an only child, and grieve bitterly for him as one grieves for a first-born son ... On that day a fountain will be opened to the house of David and the inhabitants of Jerusalem, to cleanse them from sin and impurity.*"
>
> (Zechariah 12:10, 13:1)

The Holy Spirit was indeed first poured out on the 120 disciples at Pentecost after Jesus physically returned to heaven. Peter preached the gospel and 3,000 souls were saved. They were the first-fruits, but Jerusalem as a whole did not mourn Jesus' death, so this is also yet to happen. The prophet went on to say:

> "*The* LORD *will go out and fight against those nations, as he fights in the day of battle. On that day his feet will stand on the Mount of Olives, east*

*of Jerusalem, and the Mount of Olives will be split in two from east to*
*west, forming a great valley, with half of the mountain moving north and*
*half moving south."*                                    (Zechariah 14:3–4)

We did not see this either! But soon Jesus will stand on the Mount once again – praise God.

In Matthew 24 Jesus warned of many horrible tribulations in the world, which would increase as we reach the end of the age. Zechariah 12:2–4 quoted above predicts that the world's leaders will turn against Israel to bring the "final solution" to the Jewish problem, that the world might live in peace! Satan wove the same thoughts into the German mind in the 1930s – that their problems were mainly because of the Jews. He is perpetrating identical lies in Muslim communities today, which are spreading out into the rest of the world.

These last chapters of Zechariah are full of amazing insights into what is shortly to take place and should be studied. We are witnessing the beginning of the fulfilment of these and other outstanding prophecies from the Old and New Testaments that refer to Israel, both glorious and horrendous.

I trust this has helped you see that God still singles out Israel as a unique nation. To Him, the Church and Israel are the two leading players on the world stage! The next chapter shows how they relate to each other.

# Israel and the Church

Has the Church replaced Israel? I, together with a growing number of Christians, believe the answer is "No", but let me explain this position for those who say "Yes", and for those who have never even considered this point. Because Israel as a nation rejected Jesus, some of the Christian church believe God has rejected her and written off all the outstanding promises made to her, such as the restoration of the Jews to the land and the restoration of Jerusalem. They correctly apply God's dealings and words to Israel in the Old Testament to the Church because we have become sons of Abraham through faith in Christ, but they incorrectly remove her special status as a nation. The system of belief surrounding this has become known as "Replacement Theology". Further study reveals that this cannot be correct. Paul writes:

> "I ask then: Did God reject his people [Israel]? By no means!"
>
> (Romans 11:1)

> "Again I ask: Did they [Israel] stumble so as to fall beyond recovery? Not at all! Rather, because of their transgression, salvation has come to the Gentiles to make Israel envious [jealous]. But if their transgression means riches for the world, and their loss means riches for the Gentiles, how much greater riches will their fullness bring! I am talking to you

*Gentiles. Inasmuch as I am the apostle to the Gentiles, I make much of my ministry in the hope that I may somehow arouse my own people to envy and save some of them. For if their rejection is the reconciliation of the world, what will **their acceptance be but life from the dead**? If the part of the dough offered as firstfruits is holy, then the whole batch is holy; if the root is holy, so are the branches."*

(Romans 11:11–16, emphasis added)

*"Israel has experienced a hardening in part until the full number of the Gentiles has come in. And so **all Israel will be saved**."*

(Romans 11:25–26, emphasis added)

The first quote says God has not rejected Israel. The second informs us that *"their [the Jews'] transgression means riches for the world"* and *"their [the Jews] rejection is the reconciliation of the world"*. Both statements are speaking of the Jews' rejection of God and not God's rejection of them. If the Jews had received Jesus on a national scale during New Testament times the reverse would have happened – riches for Israel. Their prosperity would have made the world jealous, bringing multitudes of Gentiles to Christ plus avoiding their second dispersion with its terrible consequences. Paul goes on to say that Israel's return to God will be *"life from the dead"*, meaning the new birth in Christ for both Jew and Gentile. As we know the former rejected Him, but as Paul says in the third quote *"all Israel will be saved"*. They will eventually receive Christ on a national scale and will be added to the born-again Church. This will culminate in the return of Jesus.

The joining of believing Jews to the body of Christ was taught by Paul in the olive tree analogy, where he says:

*"And if they [unbelieving Jews] do not persist in unbelief, they will be grafted in, for God is able to graft them in again ... how much more readily will these, the natural branches, be grafted into their own olive tree!"*                                                (Romans 11:23–24)

Although the New Testament refers only to born-again believers as children of God, this does not mean that the outstanding promises made to Israel as a nation have been cancelled. If they had been rescinded through disobedience, God would have been equally justified in doing the same with the Church! Thankfully, our God does not break His word but remains faithful to the Jews and the Church. The former remain a special people because of the gracious covenant God made with Abraham and the grace God also worked in Isaac and Jacob (Genesis 17). Paul wrote:

> *"But as far as election is concerned, they* [natural Israel] *are loved on account of the patriarchs, for God's gifts and calling are irrevocable."*
> (Romans 11:28–29)

Romans 11:16 says, *"if the root is holy, so are the branches"*. Paul is saying here that the unbelieving Jews of today remain holy and separated to Him for His purposes because of the faithfulness of the Patriarchs. This holiness, through being joined to Abraham, is similar to the unbelieving marriage partner who is sanctified or made holy by being joined to a believing partner (1 Corinthians 7:14). The individual is not saved, however, until he or she believes for themselves. Since the introduction of the New Covenant every Jew needs to put his trust not only in God the Father but also in His Son, Jesus, to be saved.

Paul explained that the Mosaic Covenant did not nullify the earlier promises made to Abraham:

> *"The* [Mosaic] *law, introduced 430 years later* [than Abraham], *does not set aside the* [Abrahamic] *covenant previously established by God and thus do away with the promise."* (Galatians 3:17)

There were several promises in the covenant with Abraham. Firstly, he would be the father of many nations – this has happened through Gentiles accepting Jesus Christ and becoming

Abraham's sons through faith. Secondly, all the families of the earth would be blessed through him – God gave the Jews the Law and then the new birth through Jesus with the resultant good works of the Church salting the world. Thirdly, the land would be given to his descendants as an everlasting possession.

> *"I will establish my covenant as an everlasting covenant between me and you and your descendants after you for the generations to come, to be your God and the God of your descendants after you. The whole land of Canaan, where you are now an alien, I will give as an* **everlasting possession to you** *and your descendants after you, and I will be their God."*                    (Genesis 17:7–8, emphasis added)

There are several points to make here regarding the land. Firstly, the Lord said Canaan was given to the Jews *"as an everlasting possession"*, which means it is still theirs. Secondly, God put no conditions on their ownership, so it belongs to them unconditionally. In Leviticus 26 we read that if they deliberately defied God He would remove them from the land for a specified time but, because of the covenant, it would remain theirs during the exile. After the stipulated period of punishment, He would then restore them back to it. Even if the Jews were to break it in the most rebellious way possible, which they have done, God would still fully honour His promise to them! The Psalmist explained the Lord's mind on the matter:

> *"If they [Jews] violate my decrees*
> *and fail to keep my commands,*
> *I will punish their sin with the rod,*
> *their iniquity with flogging;*
> *but I will not take my love from him [them],*
> *nor will I ever betray my faithfulness.*
> *I will not violate my covenant*
> *or alter what my lips have uttered."*                    (Psalm 89:31–34)

This is extremely good news for us as well under the New Covenant!

The inheritance passed to Isaac, then to Jacob and on to his descendants. Although the whole world is the Lord's, He allotted one small piece of it to His special people, the Jews. He also made it clear that the children of Israel were only tenants in the land, not landlords!

> *"The land must not be sold permanently, because the land is mine and you [Israel] are but aliens [pilgrims] and my tenants. Throughout the country that you hold as a possession, you must provide for the redemption of the land."* (Leviticus 25:23–24)

Replacementites say the land is not mentioned in the New Testament, but this is not so. Paul said to the Galatians that the promises made to Abraham still stood, which includes the land given to his "seed". I first quote the verse he referred to in the Old Testament:

> *"The LORD appeared to Abram and said, 'To your offspring [lit. seed, singular] I will give this land.'"* (Genesis 12:7)

> *"The promises [one of them being the land quoted above] were spoken to Abraham and to his seed. The scripture does not say 'and to seeds', meaning many people, but 'and to your seed', meaning one person, who is Christ."* (Galatians 3:16)

Not only was Paul saying from these two scriptures that the land remained for the Jew but he was clearly shown by the Holy Spirit that God prophetically had one man in mind, the one seed Jesus Christ. The Father has given the Promised Land to His Son who was indeed born King of the Jews (Matthew 2:2–7). Because of the Jews' national rejection of Him, Jesus was not able to take His rightful position as their King on earth when He came 2,000 years ago. However, through grace, mercy and faithfulness, God is once again gathering the Jews back to the land of Israel to fulfil every promise made to them. This can only fully happen when, as a nation, they receive Jesus as their Messiah. In His fore-knowledge, God has seen that this glorious day will eventually occur and Jesus can return and take up His throne in Jerusalem as King of the Jews. All power and authority were given to Jesus at His resurrection, so not only is He King of the Jews now, but He is also King over every ruler in the world.

The reason for the land not being mentioned more in the New Testament is firstly, the Jews were still living there when it was written and so the issue did not arise. Secondly, God had provided enough prophecies in the Old Testament to cover the subject fully. And thirdly, their national rejection of Christ precluded God from keeping them in the land at that time, but because we near the return of Jesus, the land has come to the forefront of God's agenda. I will develop this further in subsequent chapters.

According to Replacement Theology, the land should be placed in the category of a type and shadow of Christ, just as Paul describes the tabernacle, temple and feasts in the Law of Moses. However, the land was given to Abraham and his descendants and is entirely different from the covenant with Moses and cannot be treated in like manner. Jesus came to fulfil the Law with its feasts given under the different and separate Mosaic Covenant but He never fulfilled the land! The land can, however, be seen in spiritual terms as representing Christ in that, as we grow spiritually in Jesus and possess more of Him, this parallels how the Israelites took the land little by little.

The name "Israel" occurs some seventy times and "Israelite" four times in the New Testament. Each clearly refer to physical Israel and the Jews, with one possible exception, namely:

> *"Neither circumcision nor uncircumcision means anything; what counts is a new creation. Peace and mercy to all who follow this rule, even* [Greek: *kai* literally means 'and'] *to the Israel of God."*
>
> (Galatians 6:15–16)

Here, Paul is possibly referring to the born-again Church, the new creation, as the Israel of God, i.e. spiritual Israel comprising born-again Jew and Gentile believers, or most likely he is ministering his blessing to both the Church and to natural Israel. Whichever way, he is not saying that the Church has replaced Israel. Some in replacement thinking have even gone so far as to say that the 144,000 of Revelation 7:4 refer to special Gentile believers but this cannot be taken seriously as the twelve tribes are listed. No, this latter scripture actually refers to born-again Jewish believers during the Great Tribulation, and the number may be symbolic.

Some Christians, and I was one, say from Paul's statement below, that a Gentile believer becomes a Jew through faith in Christ. However, Paul is not saying this.

> *"A man is not a Jew if he is only one outwardly, nor is circumcision merely outward and physical. No, a man is a Jew if he is one inwardly; and circumcision is circumcision of the heart, by the Spirit, not by the written code. Such a man's praise is not from men, but from God."*
>
> (Romans 2:28–29)

Paul is actually making the extremely important point that not all natural Jews are true Jews in God's sight, only those who personally trust in His word. He addressed this elsewhere:

> *"For not all who are descended from Israel* [previously named Jacob] *are Israel . . . it is not the natural children who are God's children, but it is the children of the promise* [by faith]." (Romans 9:6, 8)

> *"Those who believe are children of Abraham."* (Galatians 3:7)

> *"But Israel, who pursued a law of righteousness, has not attained it* [righteousness]. *Why not? Because they pursued it not by faith but as if it were by works."* (Romans 9:31–32)

We, the born-again Gentile Church, are included in the spiritual seed of Abraham by faith in Christ, but are never spoken of as

Jews. Paul is explaining that in Old Testament times those Jews who did not believe and obey God, even though they were circumcised, were not saved. Indeed, no one has ever been accepted by Him without faith because:

> *"Everything that does not come from faith is sin."* (Romans 14:23)

Abram was an uncircumcised Gentile when God called him. He trusted and responded to God's word to him and it was counted as righteousness. God later changed his name to Abraham and instructed him and his whole family to be circumcised as a sign of the covenant to him and his descendants (Genesis 17:11). He became the first Jew, the father of many nations, but the inheritance was only to be through Isaac and Jacob. Any Jew or Gentile who desired to follow God up until Christ came, needed circumcision and the all-important heart trust in His words to them to receive salvation.

> *"An alien living among you who wants to celebrate the LORD's Passover* [believe and partake in the Covenant] *must have all the males in his household circumcised; then he may take part like one born in the land."*
> (Exodus 12:48)

Circumcision was not enough on its own. It had to be accompanied by faith in God's word to Abraham and his descendants through Jacob. This requirement of faith goes right back to the first man, Adam. For instance, Abel offered God a more excellent sacrifice than Cain, because it was by faith and not by his own efforts alone (Hebrews 11:4).

As mentioned earlier regarding the Jewish nation:

> *"If some of the branches have been broken off, and you, though a wild olive shoot, have been grafted in among the others and now share in the nourishing sap from the olive root, do not boast over those branches ... Consider therefore the kindness and the sternness of God: sternness to*

*those who fell, but kindness to you, provided that you continue in his*
*kindness. Otherwise, you also will be cut off. And if they do not persist in*
*unbelief, they will be grafted in, for God is able to graft them in."*

(Romans 11:17–18, 22–23)

It is important to understand in this tree analogy that Jews who
lived in unbelief as far back as Abraham were broken off, but
Gentiles such as Ruth who believed in the God of the Jews were
grafted in. Many non-replacementites hold the view that all Jews
living before Christ were saved regardless of faith, and wrongly
believe that they are part of the olive tree picture. In the light of
Paul's and Jesus' teaching only Jews who believed in God's word
in their heart before Christ were saved. Please note that Jesus is
the root of the tree, as He is known at the Root of David
(Revelation 5:5; 22:16).

Since Christ, any Jew who rejects Jesus is also not saved. Some
believe that zealous Rabbis ministering the Old Covenant today
are filled with the Spirit. But how can they be? Paul wrote:

*"Brothers, my heart's desire and prayer to God for the Israelites is that*
*they may be saved. For I can testify about them that they are zealous for*
*God, but their zeal is not based on knowledge. Since they did not know*
*the righteousness that comes from God and sought to establish their own,*
*they did not submit to God's righteousness. Christ is the end of the law so*
*that there may be righteousness for everyone* [both Jew and Gentile]
*who believes."*                                            (Romans 10:1–4)

There were several very committed individuals in Jesus' time,
such as John the Baptist, who lived under the Law and were filled
with the Spirit before meeting Jesus. On seeing Him, however,
they immediately accepted Him as their Messiah because they
genuinely believed the Old Testament scriptures in their hearts.
They lived at a time of transition from Old Covenant to New, but
since the resurrection, Jews cannot be filled with the Spirit
without the new birth in Christ.

Jesus found there were many Jews who zealously prayed to God yet did not accept Him!

> *"If you believed Moses, you would believe me, for he wrote about me."*
> (John 5:46)

> *"Everyone who listens to the Father and learns from him comes to me."*
> (John 6:45)

> *"If God were your Father, you would love me, for I came from God and now am here."* (John 8:42)

From the above quotes, He also taught that they were not saved under the Abrahamic and Mosaic Covenants. If they had actually believed God's word, on hearing Jesus they would have trusted in Him, as some did. Likewise, there are numerous Gentile churchgoers today who believe and pray to God, but do not actually put their trust in Jesus. They have not received the free gift of supernatural faith, given when the Holy Spirit reveals Jesus as the Christ. The nominal believer, whether Jew or Gentile, may do many good works but without true faith he remains unsaved. John also wrote:

> *"No-one comes to the Father except through me [Jesus]."* (John 14:6)

> *"To all who received him [Jesus], to those who believed in his name, he gave the right to become children of God."* (John 1:12)

It is, therefore, a far higher priority to preach the gospel to the Jews than help them back to Israel, as important as that is. Better for them to believe in Jesus and die outside the land, than to return but die before knowing their Messiah. This is vital understanding for the "fishers" who are doing a wonderful work in blessing the dispersed Jews to "the north" and elsewhere, and assisting those who want to return. However, many in the non-replacement camp seem to believe from Ezekiel 36 and other Old Testament prophecies that they are not called to preach the gospel but just to bring the Jews back to the land. These scriptures do indeed say God will bring them back and give them a new heart, but these verses must be interpreted in the light of the New Testament. Our main priority, especially to those who are too old to return, is to bring as many to Christ as possible, so they are saved and can then help fellow Jews find their Messiah. If they refuse the gospel but agree to return, hopefully they will still be alive when God pours out the longed for revelation on the remaining Jews. Obviously, one has to be very sensitive to the Spirit's guidance in each case.

The restriction of no proselytising by the Israeli government and their hostility to Messianic Jews in Israel is a problem but not insurmountable to the Holy Spirit. My concern in making these points is that Zechariah foretold that most Jews would die even after their return to the land:

> " '*In the whole land,*' *declares the* LORD,
>    *'two-thirds* [of Jews], *will be struck down and perish;*
>    *yet one-third will be left in it.*
> *This third I will bring into the fire;*
>    *I will refine them like silver*
>    *and test them like gold.*
> *They will call on my name*
>    *and I will answer them;*
> *I will say, "They are my people,"*
>    *and they will say, "The* LORD *is our God." ' "*
>
>                   (Zechariah 13:8–9, emphasis added)

Some have said that these two-thirds perished through Hitler, but the verse refers to them being *"in the whole land"* when they die – they were nowhere near Israel in the German death camps! Others say these verses happened during Titus' destruction of Jerusalem in AD 70, but the verses say one third will be spared death and will remain in the land. These will be on fire for God and in New Testament terms would be Messianic believers. However, there were no Jews left in the land in AD 70 after the Romans put down the Jewish rebellion. Many fled the country as Jesus had advised. Josephus recorded that Titus slew at least one million in Judea alone and many more in the rest of Israel. The remainder were deported as slaves around the Roman Empire. Even if some believe they were fulfilled in the time of the Roman destruction, the first verses of the following chapter 14 have certainly not happened yet as the prophet said,

> *"I will gather all the nations to Jerusalem to fight against it; the city will be captured, the houses ransacked, and the women raped. Half of the city will go into exile, but the rest of the people will not be taken from the city."*          (Zechariah 14:2)

Tragically, this last horrendous event is definitely still to happen and could even refer to the partition of Jerusalem being negotiated by the politicians today.

However, God knows He will be able to accomplish a sound work of salvation in the remaining remnant of Jews who live at the end time, as Zechariah and Paul prophesied:

> *"I do not want you to be ignorant of this mystery, brothers, so that you may not be conceited: Israel has experienced a hardening in part until the full number of Gentiles has come in. And so all Israel will be saved."*
>
> (Romans 11:25–26)

# The Messiah and the Law

There is a progressive revelation of the Trinity throughout the Old Testament showing not only Jehovah as the Almighty God but the Messiah as His Son, and the Holy Spirit as the One who brings revelation to mankind and who works the miracles of God. The Bible says *"grieve not the Holy Spirit"* (Ephesians 4:30). A force cannot be grieved, only a person can and so the Spirit is the third Person. The concept that God was more than one first appeared in Genesis in the planning of creation and then in subsequent chapters:

> *"Then God said, 'Let us* [at least two] *make man in our image.'"*
>
> (Genesis 1:26)

> *"He* [the Christ] *will crush* [the works of Jesus on earth]
> *    your head* [Satan],
> *and you* [Satan] *will strike his heel* [Jesus on the cross].*"
>
> (Genesis 3:15)

> *"I know that my Redeemer* [Christ] *lives,*
> *    and that in the end he will stand upon the earth.*
> *And after my skin has been destroyed,*
> *    yet in my flesh* [at the resurrection] *I will see God;*
> *I myself will see him*
> *    with my own eyes – I, and not another.*
> *How my heart yearns within me!"*          (Job 19:25–27)

*"The* LORD *[the Father] says to my Lord [the Christ]:*
   *'Sit at my right hand*
*until I make your enemies*
   *a footstool for your feet.'*
*The* LORD *will extend your mighty sceptre from Zion.'"*

(Psalm 110:1–2)

*"For to us a child [the Messiah or Christ] is born,*
   *to us a son is given,*
   *and the government will be on his shoulders.*
*And he will be called*
   *Wonderful, Counsellor,* **Mighty God,**
   **Everlasting Father and Prince of Peace.**
*Of the increase of his government and peace*
   *there will be no end.*
*He will reign on David's throne*
   *and over his kingdom,*
*establishing and upholding it*
   *with justice and righteousness*
   *from that time on and for ever.*
*The zeal of the* LORD *Almighty*
   *will accomplish this."*                   (Isaiah 9:6–7, emphasis added)

We find the whole of the Old Testament peppered with the truth
that God is three Persons yet only one God. Although the word
"Trinity" is not used in either Old or New Testaments, each of
the three Persons is clearly described as God and is therefore
at the very heart of true Jewishness. Consequently, this was not a
new concept to the Jews and indeed they looked forward to the
coming of the Christ (the Greek form of the Hebrew word
*Messiah*), God's divine and anointed Son who would save them.
The leaders of Israel did not reject Jesus and call for His death on
the basis of a new doctrine, but for His blasphemy in claiming to
be the Son of God and King of Israel. This truth was revealed
to Nathanael, and Jesus accepted it:

*"Then Nathanael declared, 'Rabbi, you are the Son of God; you are the King of Israel.' "* (John 1:49)

We read the Samaritan woman's conversation with Jesus at the well:

*" 'I know that Messiah' (called Christ) [by Gentiles] 'is coming. When he comes, he will explain everything to us.' Then Jesus declared, 'I who speak to you am he.' "* (John 4:25–26)

In spite of His testimony and all the miracles, the Jews as a nation rejected Him, so Jesus declared the following judgment on them:

*"I tell you [unbelieving leaders] that the kingdom of God will be taken away from you and given to a people who will produce its fruit."* (Matthew 21:43)

This "taking" of the kingdom of God from the unbelieving Jews must not be confused with the point Jesus was making in the parable of the vineyard and its wicked tenants a few verses earlier (Matthew 21:33–41). The vineyard represented the land of Israel, not the kingdom of God. He said the tenants would be taken from the vineyard (the land) for killing the landlord's son (Jesus) and servants (the prophets), rather than the vineyard (the land) being taken from them. There were some good tenants in Israel, i.e. Jews who received Christ, but just as obedient Daniel went into exile in Babylon 500 years earlier because of the national disobedience to God during the time of her kings, so the Romans drove Messianic Jews out of the land of Israel in AD 70, along with the rebellious majority (of wicked tenants) who rejected Jesus.

We also need to look at how Jesus and His apostles regarded the Law of Moses. Paul, a Pharisee of the Pharisees, a master of

the Law, knew that since Christ there was to be a clear switch
from it to faith in Christ:

> *"Mark my words! I, Paul, tell you that if you* [Jewish and Gentile
> believers in Galatia] *let yourselves be circumcised, Christ will be of no
> value to you at all. Again I declare to every man who lets himself be
> circumcised that he is required to obey the whole law. You who are trying
> to be justified by law have been alienated from Christ; you have fallen
> away from grace. But by faith we eagerly await through the Spirit the
> righteousness for which we hope."*　　　　　　　　(Galatians 5:2–5)

The Jewish nation had utterly failed to walk with the Lord in
accordance with the Mosaic Covenant and just prior to the exile
of the two southern tribes to Babylon, God revealed His intention
to bring in the New Covenant. This was made with the Jews but
praise God, Gentiles were to be included as well:

> *" 'The time is coming,' declares the* LORD,
> 　　*'when I will make a new covenant*
> *with the house of Israel*
> 　　*and with the house of Judah.*
> *It will not be like the* [Mosaic] *covenant*
> 　　*I made with their forefathers*
> *when I took them by the hand*
> 　　*to lead them out of Egypt,*
> *because they broke my covenant,*
> 　　*though I was a husband to them,'*
> 　　　　　　　　*declares the* LORD.
> *'This is the covenant that I will make*
> 　　　*with the house of Israel*
> 　　*after that time,' declares the* LORD.
> *'I will put my law in their minds*
> 　　*and write it on their hearts.*
> *I will be their God,*
> 　　*and they will be my people.*

No longer will a man teach his neighbour,
> or a man his brother, saying, "Know the LORD,"
because they will all know me,
> from the least of them to the greatest,'
>> declares the LORD.
'For I will forgive their wickedness
> and will remember their sins no more.' "        (Jeremiah 31:31–34)

As we now know, this Covenant was made though the shed blood of Jesus and just as the Mosaic Covenant did not set aside the Covenant God made with Abraham, so Jesus says the New Covenant does not annul the Mosaic one. Jesus did not come to destroy the Law and the Prophets but to fulfil them. He said:

> "Do not think that I have come to abolish the Law or the Prophets; I have not come to abolish them but to fulfil them. I tell you the truth, until heaven and earth disappear, not the smallest letter, not the least stroke of a pen, will by any means disappear from the Law until everything is accomplished. Anyone who breaks one of the least of these commandments and teaches others to do the same will be called least in the kingdom of heaven, but whoever practises and teaches these commands will be called great in the kingdom of heaven." (Matthew 5:17–19)

Physical heaven and earth are still here and will remain until Judgment Day, when they will flee from His presence (Revelation 20:11), and are destroyed by fire (2 Peter 3:10–12). Therefore, the Law still stands today to point mankind to Christ and His exceedingly costly sacrifice on the cross. But if men choose to reject Jesus, they will have to stand before Him and be judged according to His teachings such as those found in Matthew 5–7, John 12:44–50 and every word they have spoken (Matthew 12:36–37) – a terrifying prospect without Christ. Because of man's inability to keep the Law, God included a sacrificial system to atone for their sin and keep them righteous before Him. The Levitical sacrifices and feasts were therefore an essential part, along with all the dos and don'ts, but they have now been perfectly fulfilled by Jesus through His life, death and resurrection. The Law and the Prophets contain wonderful wisdom and instruction (Romans 2:18), which is to be heeded and obeyed, not by the letter but by the Spirit and all now in the light of the New Covenant.

Jesus not only fulfilled the Law but He also taught it as God had intended. There are various scholars today who believe that by the time of Jesus, some of the oral traditions, which were summations of the written word, had bypassed the intended heart issues and reduced the Law to just externals. Because some of the teachings were no longer correct, Jesus used the phrase "you have heard it said" when referring to these, instead of "it is written". These scholars believe for example, that in Matthew 5 regarding adultery and murder, rather than introducing a new depth of obedience, Jesus was pointing out that God's intention had always been to address the wrong desires in the heart rather than just referring to the acts themselves. Also, the Old Testament had never actually said "hate your enemies", so He was correcting them on these points.

If this is so, Jesus was revealing the Law to be even more impossible than the Pharisees had come to think and had the people been truly honest with themselves, then stoning to death for adultery in their hearts would have been a regular occurrence! He mercifully said in the adulteress incident (John 8:3–11), *"If any one of you is without sin, let him be the first to throw a stone at her"* (v. 7). The Law was essentially about loving God and our neighbour as ourselves. Paul wrote:

> *"Let no debt remain outstanding, except the continuing debt to love one another, for he who loves his fellow-man has fulfilled the law. The commandments, 'Do not commit adultery,' 'Do not murder,' 'Do not steal,' 'Do not covet,' and whatever other commandment there may be, are summed up in this one rule: 'Love your neighbour as yourself.' Love does no harm to its neighbour. Therefore love is the fulfilment of the law."*
> (Romans 13:8–10)

Whether these scholars are correct or not, Jesus was about to raise the bar even higher by introducing the New Covenant with its new commandment to love as He loved us and not just to love others as we love ourselves.

During the Last Supper, after washing the disciples feet, Jesus announced the New Covenant in His blood, saying:

> *"A new command I give you: Love one another. As I have loved you, so you must love one another. By this all men will know that you are my disciples, if you love one another."*　　　(John 13:34–35)

Christ's perfect love for both His heavenly Father and mankind not only fulfilled the Law but greatly exceeded it. This new commandment is far above the Mosaic one – it requires the crucifixion of self:

> *"I have been crucified with Christ and I no longer live, but Christ lives in me. The life I live in the body, I live by faith in the Son of God, who loved me and gave himself for me."*　　　(Galatians 2:20)

This is so radical and demanding that God gives us a new heart to be able to obey it (Ezekiel 36:26), and places Christ within (Colossians 1:27). This heart desires to follow after Jesus with the aid of the Holy Spirit. It is the same Spirit who worked all the miracles through Jesus and raised Him from the dead that now also lives in the believer to do the same works and even greater! This change from the old to the new, brings about a right standing before God 24/7 through the new birth, as described by Paul:

> *"Now if the ministry that brought death, which was engraved in letters on stone, came with glory, so that the Israelites could not look steadily at the face of Moses because of its glory, fading though it was, will not the ministry of the Spirit be even more glorious? If the ministry that condemns men is glorious, how much more glorious is the ministry*

*that brings righteousness! For what was glorious has no glory now in comparison with the surpassing glory. And if what was fading away came with glory, how much greater is the glory of that which lasts!"*

(2 Corinthians 3:7–11)

Not only did Jesus fulfil the Law of Moses but Paul informs us that through faith in Christ, we automatically fulfil it as we follow the Holy Spirit:

*"He condemned sin in sinful man* [in the crucified Christ], *in order that the righteous requirements of the law* [of Moses] *might be fully met in us, who do not live according to the sinful nature but according to the Spirit."* (Romans 8:3–4)

Jesus became the sin offering for every man that has ever lived on the face of the planet. Thus the feasts, ceremonies and offerings are no longer required. They had symbolised the sacrifice that Jesus would make but could not actually remove sin themselves (Hebrews 10:4). The acceptance of Jesus' sacrificial death to God's satisfaction was confirmed when the Spirit rent the veil from top to bottom, symbolising Jesus' torn body and His resurrection. The way had been made open for believers to come into relationship and fellowship with God through the shed blood of Jesus:

*"He* [Jesus] *gave up his spirit. At that moment* [His death] *the curtain of the temple was torn in two from top to bottom."*

(Matthew 27:50–51)

*"We have confidence to enter the Most Holy Place by the blood of Jesus, by a new and living way opened for us through the curtain, that is, his body."* (Hebrews 10:19–20)

He was indeed the Lamb of God, as pictured by the Passover Lamb. All who believed in Jesus but had died during His earthly ministry were raised with Him at His resurrection, including the criminal on the cross who had believed (Matthew 27:52–53). This was a wonderful fulfilment of the Wave Offering, which happened in the first month of every year when the first ripe green sheaf of barley, the earliest crop, was waved before the Lord. The first Jewish month was originally called *Abib* and meant "green ears", referring to the barley harvest. (It became known as *Nisan* during the Babylonian exile.) The sheaf was presented on the day after the Passover Sabbath, the resurrection day (Leviticus 23:12), and represented a first-fruit from the harvest of believers in Christ, who would come to Him throughout the Church age over the next two millennia.

Jesus' death on the cross also fulfilled the other animal sacrifices in the feasts, for example First-fruits (Leviticus 23:12), Pentecost (Leviticus 23:18) and Tabernacles (Leviticus 23:36). He also fulfilled other aspects of both the Feast of Pentecost by baptising the Church in the Spirit and Tabernacles by living in a physical body with the Jews in the spiritual wilderness of Israel:

> *"The Word became flesh and made his dwelling* [Greek: tabernacled] *among us."* (John 1:14)

Praise God, any shortcomings by believers are now covered by His blood:

> *"If we confess our sins, he is faithful and just and will forgive us our sins and purify us from all unrighteousness."* (1 John 1:9)

> *"Therefore, there is now no condemnation for those who are in Christ Jesus."* (Romans 8:1)

We can see from the whole of the New Testament, that God never intended Christianity to be an addition to Judaism but the fulfilment of it. Christianity is faith in Christ alone, which is actually pure Judaism. God has spent the last few hundred years trying to remove Old Testament Christianity from the Gentile part of the Church and is now working to achieve the same in the Jewish part as well.

If we truly walk by the Holy Spirit we walk in the greater law, the Law of the Spirit of life in Christ Jesus, which sets us free from our selfish ways to love God and our neighbour as Christ loved the Church:

> *"Through Christ Jesus the law of the Spirit of life set me free from the law of sin and death."*                                    (Romans 8:2)

The law of the Spirit of life is like the law of aerodynamics, which overcomes the law of gravity, enabling an aircraft to fly. At the new birth, the law of sin and death is removed from our spirit (our spirit is now dead to sin because that's the part of us which was crucified with Christ and is born again [Romans 6:2]). But the law of sin and death remains in our physical body like gravity (Romans 7:23), and pulls us down unless we overcome it by faith – the *"law of the Spirit of life"*. The precious promises together with the faith given to us at the new birth, are like the wings and engine of the aircraft. The Holy Spirit is the fuel which gives us the power and ability to fly in the Spirit, live above sin and so partake of the divine nature (2 Peter 1:4; Galatians 5:16). Paul said:

> *"I myself am not under the law* [of Moses] *... but am under Christ's law."*                                    (1 Corinthians 9:20–21)

> *"For sin shall not be your master, because you are not under law, but under grace."*                                    (Romans 6:14)

> *"For we maintain that a man* [Jew or Gentile] *is justified by faith apart from observing the law. Is God the God of Jews only? Is he not the God of the Gentiles too? Yes, of Gentiles too, since there is only one God, who will justify the circumcised by faith and the uncircumcised through that same faith. Do we, then, nullify the law by this faith? Not at all! Rather, we uphold the law."*                                    (Romans 3:28–31)

*"Live by the Spirit, and you will not gratify the desires of the flesh."*

(Galatians 5:16)

From the scriptures quoted so far it is clear to see that the Law of Christ (the Law of love and serving others) has not only fulfilled the Law of Moses for Jews and Gentiles alike but by the Spirit we are able to obey the higher Law. This change in the Law now affects prophecies regarding Israel, such as those in Jeremiah, Ezekiel, Daniel etc. For instance, in Jeremiah 31:31 quoted earlier, *"I will put my law in their minds"* should now be interpreted as God putting the Law of Christ into a believer's heart, whether he be Jew or Gentile. This is why the nation of Israel has to come to Christ before God can fulfil all the outstanding promises made to her. He can only relate with a people who are right with Him. Paul said:

*"All who sin apart from the law will also perish apart from the law, and all who sin under the law will be judged by the law."*

(Romans 2:12)

As discussed, unbelieving Gentiles will have to give account for their every thought, word and deed, and unbelieving Jews the same, but for them it will be in the context of the Law of Moses, which includes the curses for disobedience:

*"All who rely on observing the law are under a curse, for it is written: 'Cursed is everyone who does not continue to do everything written in the Book of the Law.' Clearly no-one is justified before God by the law, because, 'The righteous will live by faith.' The law is not based on faith [alone]; on the contrary, 'The man who does these things will live by them.' Christ redeemed us from the curse of the law by becoming a curse for us, for it is written: 'Cursed is everyone who is hung on a tree.' He redeemed us in order that the blessing given to Abraham might come to the Gentiles through Christ, so that by faith we might receive the promise of the Spirit."* (Galatians 3:10–14)

> *"For whoever keeps the whole law and yet stumbles at just one point is*
> *guilty of breaking all of it."*                              (James 2:10)

The Law of Moses itself is not a curse, but the punishments for rebellion or falling short of its requirements are. Therefore, God continues to deal with the nation of Israel, as she rejects Christ, according to the Law with all its penalties.

The writer to the Hebrews dealt with another very important issue, the change in priesthood in the New Covenant:

> *"If perfection could have been attained through the Levitical priesthood*
> *(for on the basis of it the law was given to the people), why was there still*
> *need for another priest to come – one in the order of Melchizedek, not in the*
> *order of Aaron* [a Levite]? *For when there is a change of the priesthood,*
> *there must also be a change of the law. He of whom these things are said*
> *belonged to a different tribe, and no-one from that tribe has ever served at*
> *the altar. For it is clear that our Lord descended from Judah, and in regard*
> *to that tribe Moses said nothing about priests. And what we have said is*
> *even more clear, if another priest like Melchizedek appears, one who has*
> *become a priest not on the basis of a regulation as to his ancestry but on the*
> *basis of the power of an indestructible life. For it is declared:*
>
> > *'You are a priest for ever,*
> >   *in the order of Melchizedek.'*
>
> *The former regulation is set aside because it was weak and useless (for the*
> *law made nothing perfect), and a better hope is introduced, by which we*
> *draw near to God."*                              (Hebrews 7:11–19)

We are priests of a new order in Christ from the tribe of Judah, not Levi, which radically affects our interpretation of Ezekiel's Temple, as detailed in chapters 40–48, and the celebration of the feast of Tabernacles in the millennium (Zechariah 14:16–19). Both of these involve animal sacrifice (Leviticus 23:36), which Jesus has fulfilled. The New Testament, which includes the book of Revelation, says absolutely nothing about either, only that we will worship Jesus our King. All these future prophecies regarding Temple and Tabernacles etc. must now be interpreted in the light of the New Covenant. Changing the priesthood from Levitical to Judaic in Christ will not affect the physical division of the land between the twelve tribes in the millennium, as detailed in Ezekiel 45:1–7, nor our going up to be with Jesus in Jerusalem as prefigured by Tabernacles (Zechariah 14), though I doubt we will be sitting with Him in booths made of tree boughs!

Ezekiel saw the glory of the Lord depart from the Temple before the Babylonian exile, as recorded in Ezekiel chapters 9–11. However, we read later in chapter 43 that the glory returned to it. The Body of Christ, the Church, is now the Temple of God with Jesus as High Priest and ourselves as royal priests. The glory of God did indeed return to His Temple when the Spirit filled the New Testament Church on the day of Pentecost.

Paul taught that the Temple, which God is building today, is no longer one of stone but one of flesh and blood of believers in which He dwells.

> *"Don't you know that you yourselves are God's temple and that God's Spirit lives in you?"*     (1 Corinthians 3:16)

On their return from exile in Babylon, the Lord revealed to Zechariah His plan to amalgamate the offices of High Priest and King, which was to bring in the new order. To distinguish between the two distinct and different offices in the Old Covenant, the King wore a crown (2 Samuel 1:10) and the High Priest a turban (Exodus 28:4). The Lord said to the prophet:

> *"Take the silver and gold and make a crown* [plural, crowns in Hebrew prefiguring the many crowns on Jesus' head (Revelation 19:12)], *and set it on the head of the high priest, Joshua son of Jehozadak. Tell him this is what the LORD Almighty says: 'Here is the man whose name is the Branch and he will branch out from his place and build the temple* [now the Church] *of the LORD. It is he who will build the temple*

*of the LORD, and he will be clothed with majesty* [kingship] *and will sit and rule on his throne. And he will be a priest on his throne. And there will be harmony between the two."*                              (Zechariah 6:11–13)

God instructed Joshua, the High Priest at that time, to prophetically enact the combined role of High Priest and King, which Jesus the Branch would fulfil:

*"In those days and at that time*
*I will make a righteous Branch sprout from David's line;*
*he will do what is just and right in the Land."*          (Jeremiah 33:15)

This scripture confirms that the Branch refers to Jesus. Consequently, Peter and Paul taught that every born-again believer becomes a king and a priest with access to the Father, and has a place on the throne of God to reign in life through Christ Jesus (Romans 5:17):

*"But you are a chosen people, a royal priesthood, a holy nation, a people belonging to God."*                              (1 Peter 2:9)

*"God raised us up with Christ and seated us* [on His throne] *with him in the heavenly realms."*                              (Ephesians 2:6)

Therefore, because of Jesus, no Levite alive today or in the future will be a special priest to God, as the Mosaic sacrifices and ministry are totally null and void. A person can now only be purified by faith in Christ through the blood He shed. However, through Jesus, the High Priest, God has kept His promise with the Levites to always have a man ministering before Him and interceding on our behalf. The relevant scripture is:

*"For this is what the LORD says: 'David will never fail to have a man to sit on the throne of the house of Israel, nor will the priests, who are Levites, ever fail to have a man to stand before me continually to offer burnt offerings, to burn grain offerings and to present sacrifices.'"*
                              (Jeremiah 33:17–18)

Several years after the resurrection there were many Messianic Jews in Jerusalem who were still zealously practising the Law of Moses (Acts 21:20), along with Temple worship and sacrifice. When Paul went there at Pentecost following his third missionary journey, he did not discourage the believers from doing so but kept quiet about it. Because of this incident, some who subscribe to Non-replacement Theology believe that Paul thought Jews can continue in the Law and that only Gentiles should not participate, but this could not be further from the truth. The apostle James, together with all the elders of the Church there, were acutely concerned that the Jewish authorities would arrest Paul as he had been teaching believing Jews to forsake the Law of Moses for faith in Christ (Acts 21:21). They suggested that he at least perform a purification rite in accordance with the law. Paul felt his conscience would allow him to do this, because he did not want to aggravate an extremely sensitive situation in Jerusalem (Acts 21:23–26). However, this did not mean Paul had changed his doctrine one iota. He explained his thinking in his first letter to the Corinthians:

> *"Though I am free and belong to no man, I make myself a slave to every-one, to win as many as possible. To the Jews I became like a Jew, to win the Jews. To those under the law I became like one under the law (though I myself am not under the law), so as to win those under the law.*
>
> (1 Corinthians 9:19–20)

His expectation was that, as the Holy Spirit continued to teach on these issues, their eyes would be opened to see the Law as a schoolmaster to Christ and they would eventually graduate from it. Paul's main desire at that point was for the Jews to grow in faith and obedience to the Spirit, rather than be fully correct in seeing that the Law was now fulfilled in Christ.

> *"Now that faith has come, we are no longer under the supervision of the law ... as long as the heir is a child, he is no different from a slave, although he owns the whole estate. He is subject to guardians and*

> *trustees until the time set by his father. So also, when we were children,*
> *we were in slavery under the basic principles of the world. But when the*
> *time had fully come, God sent His son, born of a woman, born under law,*
> *to redeem those under the law, that we might receive the full rights of*
> *sons."*                                              (Galatians 3:25, 4:1–5)

Referring to the same Jerusalem visit, Acts 20:22 informs us that Paul was urged by the Spirit to go to the city, which he sought to reach by Pentecost. On arriving, it is significant that there is no mention in the narrative as to whether he did or did not observe the feast. It is unlikely though, because observant Jews were still sacrificing animals (Leviticus 23:18). Furthermore, fifty days earlier in Philippi, Paul broke bread with believers on "the first day of the week" (Acts 20:7). The Feast of Weeks commenced each year on the Sunday, the day after the Friday/Saturday Passover, lasted forty-nine days plus the day of Pentecost, a total of fifty days. The first day of this feast, the Feast of First Fruits, was fulfilled by the Father raising Jesus and other believers (Matthew 27:52) on the day after the Sabbath. Pentecost was fulfilled when believers later received the Holy Spirit. There is no indication that Paul kept the Passover Feast, for the same reason explained in the last paragraph. The narrative only states that he broke bread on the Sunday probably in accordance with his teaching on communion in 1 Corinthians 11:20. Some of the believers had left Philippi before the seven-day Feast of Unleavened Bread ended (Acts 20:5). This shorter feast covered the first seven days of the forty-nine-day Feast of Weeks concluding with Pentecost. So, here again there is nothing to show they were observing these feast days. This group included Timothy, whose Jewish mother Eunice had brought him up in the Christian faith according to Paul's doctrine (2 Timothy 2:5).

All this indicates that the Jewish believers who were with Paul were no longer observing the Jewish festivals in the Jewish manner. His desire to reach Jerusalem by Pentecost, whether directed from the Holy Spirit or not, seems to relate more to a fixed time in the Jewish calendar that they could all relate to, rather for than for ceremonies to be observed. Keeping the feasts is never mentioned in the New Testament after the first believers were filled with the Spirit at Pentecost. There is no indication that the Church is to be involved with them. God now wants us to celebrate the reality of these, which is Christ in our everyday lives every day.

Unfortunately there are many Christians today who, in their zeal to save the Jews, are going beyond this very wise sensitivity of Paul in Jerusalem and actively encouraging Messianic Jews to continue in aspects of the Law and the feasts. They are even reverting back to parts of it themselves – the Galatians required apostolic correction for this. We are called to preach the gospel of the Kingdom of God, as the early Jewish believers did, not Old Covenant Christianity. The Holy Spirit must show us how to deal very sensitively with every situation regarding believing Jews and the Law.

Paul taught that the Law was holy and contained many spiritual principles for the Christian to understand and obey, but since Christ was crucified, a walk of faith in Him is all that is required to fulfil it and actually surpass it. Here are some examples of how Paul used the feasts in his teaching:

> *"You* [mainly Gentiles and some Jews who were reverting back to Judaism] *are observing special days and months and seasons and years! I fear for you, that somehow I have wasted my efforts on you."*
>
> (Galatians 4:10–11)

> *"For Christ, our Passover lamb, has been sacrificed. Therefore let us keep the festival* [in our lives each day], *not with the old yeast, the yeast of malice and wickedness, but with bread without yeast, the bread of sincerity and truth."*          (1 Corinthians 5:7–8)

> *"Do not let anyone judge you by what you eat or drink, or with regard to a religious festival, a New Moon celebration or a Sabbath day. These*

*are a shadow of the things that were to come; the reality, however, is*
*found in Christ."*                                    (Colossians 2:16–17)

Because Paul was a circumcised Jew, he could legally take part in
the feasts, but we never read that he did, or that he ever taught or
encouraged other Jews and Gentiles to do so. Paul only went to
synagogues to preach the gospel. He and the other apostles did
not celebrate the feasts because they had found the reality and
fulfilment in Christ. Paul said they were only shadows of things to
come. If a person's shadow appears from behind a building, for
example, it would be foolish to continue looking at it after he has
come into full view!

It is very important when interpreting Old and New Testament
scriptures not to fall into the trap of Replacement Theology,
which unfortunately has permeated many of our theological
colleges and therefore much of the Church. But we must not fall
into the ditch on the other side of the road either by thinking that
Jews need to be involved in the Mosaic Law and Feasts.

All these points are not just a matter of crossing "ts" and
dotting "is" of doctrine, but are vital in helping us work with God
to fulfil His purpose of bringing the whole Jewish nation to Christ
and helping them to live by the Spirit. We will then all grow
together into full maturity in Him, free from the supervision of
the Law but upholding, fulfilling and exceeding it. God desires us
to live free from religious spirits that can cause the Law to be
handled wrongly. Paul wrote regarding his time in Antioch:

*"When I saw that they* [Peter and other Jews] *were not acting in line*
*with the truth of the gospel, I said to Peter in front of them all, 'You are a*
*Jew, yet you live like a Gentile and not like a Jew. How is it, then, that*
*you force Gentiles* [fellow Gentile believers] *to follow Jewish customs?*
*We who are Jews by birth and not 'Gentile sinners' know that a man is*
*not justified by observing the law, but by faith in Jesus Christ. So we*
[Jewish believers], *too, have put our faith in Christ Jesus that we may*
*be justified by faith in Christ and not by observing the law, because by*

*observing the law no-one will be justified* [because we cannot keep it without sacrifice and God has made the Levitical priesthood defunct]. *If, while we seek to be justified in Christ, it becomes evident that we ourselves are sinners* [going against God's changes], *does that mean that Christ promotes sin? Absolutely not! If I rebuild what I destroyed, I prove that I am a law-breaker. For through the law* [which led me to Christ] *I died to the law so that I might live for God. I have been crucified with Christ and I no longer live, but Christ lives in me. The life I live in the body, I live by faith in the Son of God, who loved me and gave himself for me. I do not set aside the grace of God, for if righteousness could be gained through the law, Christ died for nothing!"*

(Galatians 2:14–21)

Only the power of the unadulterated gospel of mercy and grace by the revelation of the Holy Spirit is going to turn the Jews as a nation to Christ. May God raise up the ministries to achieve this – the two witnesses in Jerusalem will be central characters in the final evangelistic push of this age (Revelation 11:3).

Another issue requiring explanation concerns Paul's desire that the believing Gentiles should make the Jews jealous:

*"Again I* [Paul] *ask: did they* [Israel] *stumble so as to fall beyond recovery? Not at all! Rather, because of their transgression, salvation has come to the Gentiles to make Israel envious. But if their transgression means riches for the world, and their loss means riches for the Gentiles, how much greater riches will their fullness bring! I am talking to you Gentiles. Inasmuch as I am the apostle to the Gentiles, I make much of my ministry in the hope that I may somehow arouse my own people to envy and save some of them."* (Romans 11:11–14)

This will only be achieved through bringing the Gentile believers to maturity:

*"It was He who gave some to be apostles, some to be prophets, some to be evangelists, and some to be pastors and teachers, to prepare God's people*

*for works of service, so that the body of Christ may be built up until we all*
*[the born-again Church] reach unity in the faith and in the knowledge*
*of the Son of God and become mature, attaining to the whole measure*
*of the **fullness** [pleroma] of Christ."*

(Ephesians 4:11–13, emphasis added)

What an amazing statement! Paul used the word *pleroma* for "fullness", which describes quality not quantity, and he used it again in the following scripture:

*"Israel has experienced a hardening in part until the **full** [pleroma]*
*number of the Gentiles has come in. And so all Israel will be saved."*

(Romans 11:25–26, emphasis added)

This last verse has nothing to do with the *"times of the Gentiles"* in Luke 21:24, which refers to the period when Israel was under foreign domination. We will look at that verse in much greater detail in chapters 7, 8 and 9. A more literal and therefore a more correct translation of Romans 11:25 is found in the AV, which says *"until the fullness of the Gentiles be come in"*. Paul is explaining that when the Jews see the fullness of Christ in the Gentiles, as prophesied in Ephesians 4:11–13, quoted above, they will hopefully be roused to jealousy and be drawn to Christ. He is not meaning that when a certain number of Gentiles are saved, the Jews will come to Christ regardless of the attitude of the Gentile Church. It will be partly by the love shown to them by the Church plus revelation from the Holy Spirit that Israel will be brought to repentance and faith in Christ. Every nation needs this same love, but Paul is saying we are not to treat the Jews like other nations because they are special to God. The Church should encourage them in their uniqueness before God, because of the Patriarchs and His promises to them as a nation. However, as with the Gentiles, they still need to personally trust in Jesus as their Messiah to be saved.

If the fig tree prophecy quoted below refers to Israel, it means
that those who see her come to bud as a nation will, in their
lifetime, see all things accomplished, including Jesus' return to
set up His Kingdom on earth. The other trees would then
represent other nations. This, I hasten to add, has nothing to do
with the olive tree picture spoken of by Paul in Romans. Jesus
said:

> *"Look at the fig-tree and all the trees. When they sprout leaves, you can
> see for yourselves and know that summer is near. Even so, when you see
> these things happening, you know that the kingdom of God is near. I tell
> you the truth, **this generation** [Greek: **genea**] will certainly not pass
> away until all these things have happened."*
>
> (Luke 21:29–32, emphasis added)

The "fig tree" was uprooted in AD 70 by the Romans, but was
miraculously replanted in 1948 when the state of Israel was
declared! Her roots have since been established, the main stem
and branches have grown substantially and leaves are appearing.
It is amazing to see this miracle performed by God against all the
odds. I believe from the above scripture that because I have seen
the rebirth of Israel albeit at the age of five, and given my
expected life span, I will witness the whole remnant being
converted on a national scale – the tree will come into full leaf,
culminating in the glorious return of Jesus who will harvest a
bumper crop of full ripe figs! Praise the Lord indeed! Many cults
such as the Mormons, Jehovah's Witnesses, Christadelphians and
Unitarians have tried to predict the exact day and hour of the
Lord's return but this is in God's hands alone. (As a matter of
interest Sir Isaac Newton was a Unitarian – see Isaac Newton,
Heretic, on Google.)

Some have said that the Greek word *genea*, in bold italics in the
above verse, should be translated "this people" or "this race"
rather than "this generation". Every time the word *genea* is used
in the New Testament it is always in the context of a limited

period of time, describing a particular generation. Why should this be an exception to the rule?

And lastly in this chapter, I quote a verse referring to the end-time return of the Jews:

> " 'In those days, when your numbers have increased greatly in the land,' declares the LORD, 'men will no longer say, "The ark of the covenant of the LORD." It will never enter their minds or be remembered; it will not be missed, nor will another one be made. At that time they will call Jerusalem, The Throne of the LORD, and all nations will gather in Jerusalem to honour the name of the LORD. No longer will they follow the stubbornness of their evil hearts. In those days the house of Judah will join the house of Israel, and together they will come from a northern land to the land I gave their forefathers as an inheritance.' "
>
> (Jeremiah 3:16–18)

This clearly shows that both northern (the ten tribes of the house of Israel) and southern (the two tribes of the house of Judah) will unite and a significant number will come back from the old USSR and that area, which we have already witnessed. The desire of Jewish Rabbis to rebuild the Temple and recommence sacrifice will be surpassed by the revelation that Jesus is indeed their true Messiah. They will at last come to Christ and realise that Temple worship is redundant, which makes the way for Jesus' return. The city of Jerusalem will then indeed be called "The Throne of the Lord" as Jesus will be reigning from there.

God intended the Jewish nation to embrace the New Covenant when Jesus came the first time but despite her hardness of heart in rejecting Him, God will eventually win her. Satan knows the scriptures on this subject better than many Christians, and is doing everything in his power to stop the Church understanding and praying for the Jews. He is desperate to prevent them from being established in the whole land because he knows full well that when this happens, his 1,000-year imprisonment is imminent

(Revelation 20:2). After this he will be released for a short while before being thrown into the lake of fire, which has been created for him and his demons (Revelation 20:7–10).

# Four Thousand Years of Jewish History

After our first visit to Jerusalem in 1977, God miraculously made a way for Judith and me to return in 1992 for our fifteenth wedding anniversary. A business opportunity opened up for my company with a Jewish glass bottle factory based south of Beersheba. When the export director learned that my visit coincided with our wedding anniversary, he very generously and unexpectedly invited Judith as well, and paid for our hotel. During our visit, we saw how the country had dramatically developed since we first met there fifteen years before. The fig tree, representing Israel, had grown significantly and had formed buds of new towns etc. One could also take these buds to mean new life in Israel through the Messianic Fellowships, which are springing up in the land.

We were also able to walk along the top of the walls of Jerusalem and from David's Tower there is a spectacular all-round view of Jerusalem and the mountains surrounding the city. We happened to meet one of the leaders of Prayer for Israel whilst surveying the whole panoramic scene. I believe that was further encouragement from the Lord.

For a clearer understanding of the present situation we have to investigate both the biblical and secular history of the land in some detail. During the time of Jesus and the early Church, the country was still called Israel. As mentioned earlier, it was the Romans who later used the Latin name *Palaestina* to describe the area, purposely ignoring 1,500 years of Jewish heritage in the land. They even changed the name of Jerusalem to *Aelia Capitolina* in an attempt to obliterate any Jewish connection! Nothing has changed. Instead of the Romans trying to eradicate the Jews from Israel today we have the Muslims trying to repeat the same thing.

The Romans chose the name *Palaestina*, which some language experts think was derived from the Philistines. The latter, along with the Canaanites, lived there before the Jews conquered it in about 1500 BC. But from whom did these nations descend? We have to turn to the only sure source, the Bible. The sole survivors of the flood were Noah and his family. He had three sons, Shem, Ham and Japheth, all of whom were married (Genesis 10). After the flood, the Shemites settled south of Ararat, which is now southern Turkey, and east towards Iraq, Ur being in southern Iraq. The Hamites travelled further south to what is now Israel, and to the regions around Egypt. The Japhethites moved to areas north of Mount Ararat onto which the ark had settled. Ham had four sons (Genesis 10:6), the second being Mizraim, who fathered Caslu from whom came the Philistines (Genesis 10:14). Canaan was the fourth son of Ham from whom obviously came the Canaanites. Abraham lived in Ur with his wife Sarai and was the tenth generation from Shem (Genesis 11:10–26). This means that there is no near relation between Abraham and the two peoples of the Philistines and Canaanites, who were both descended from Ham. Hagar, the maidservant of Abraham, came from Egypt, and was also about the tenth generation from Ham (Genesis 21:9). She bore Ishmael for Abraham and later chose an Egyptian woman for him to marry (Genesis 21:20). The sons of Ishmael could possibly be descended from the Philistines, the Canaanites or even the Jebusites but they are excluded from any right to the land because God clearly passed judgment on all the indigenous nations. This was due to their detestable sins, such as child sacrifice, temple prostitution, homosexuality and bestiality (Genesis 15:16; Leviticus 18:21–30 etc.). They disqualified themselves from any right to the land, as Moses explained:

*"After the Lᴏʀᴅ your God has driven them out before you, do not say to yourself, 'The Lᴏʀᴅ has brought me here to take possession of the land because of my righteousness.' No, it is on account of the wickedness of these nations that the Lᴏʀᴅ is going to drive them out before you."*

(Deuteronomy 9:4–5)

God also excluded Hagar and Ishmael from the inheritance:

*"For the slave woman's [Hagar's] son [Ishmael] will never share in the inheritance with the free woman's [Sarah's] son [Isaac]."*

(Galatians 4:30)

I repeat the extremely important scripture mentioned in chapter 2, where God clearly gives the land to the Jews by an irreversible covenant:

*"I will establish my covenant as an everlasting covenant between me and you and your descendants after you for the generations to come, to be your God and the God of your descendants after you. The whole land of Canaan, where you are now an alien, **I will give as an everlasting possession to you and your descendants after you; and I will be their God."***            (Genesis 17:7–8, emphasis added)

This promise, therefore, stands today and He also remains the God of the Jews.

Later, Abraham's great grandsons went down to Egypt (Genesis 46). After the Israelites' sojourn there for 400 years, the Lord led them out of slavery and into the wilderness through Moses in about 1500 ʙᴄ. They were given clear instructions whilst in the wilderness, to separate themselves from all other peoples. Hence, forty years later when they entered the Promised Land, which was flowing with milk and honey, they remained a distinct nation with an entirely different identity from the other countries surrounding them. They conquered the seven nations of the Canaanites (Genesis 10:15–18), successfully possessing all except the lower western coastline (the Gaza Strip), which was populated by the Philistines.

God's judgment was to command Joshua to implement the sentence of death to all the inhabitants of Canaan. Even the children had been so utterly corrupted by their parents that they were beyond remedy. We are fast approaching a similar depth of sin in society today, which will only be dealt with in similar manner at the return of Jesus. However, a careful reading of Scripture reveals that the Israelites did not put every person from the seven clans to the sword. Substantial numbers of the Philistine nation also survived (Judges 3:1–6). The latter developed five major cities along the Gaza Strip – Gaza, Ashkelon, Ashdod, Ekron and Gath, and remained at war with Israel for many years. Eventually, the remaining Canaanites fell under the control of the Assyrian Empire, along with the ten northern tribes of Israel, the latter being unceremoniously deported to Assyria. The two southern tribes of Judah and Benjamin were later subject to Nebuchadnezzar's rule, after the Babylonians had conquered the whole Middle East.

The Philistines were eventually destroyed by the Egyptians:

> *"This is the word of the* LORD *that came to Jeremiah the prophet concerning the Philistines before Pharaoh attacked Gaza . . .*
>
> > *'For the day has come*
> > *to destroy all the Philistines*
> > *and to cut off all survivors*
> > *who could help Tyre and Sidon.*
> > *The* LORD *is about to destroy the Philistines,*
> > *the remnant from the coasts of Caphtor* [Crete]."
>
> (Jeremiah 47:1–4)

At the end of the seventy-year exile in Babylon, the Persians and Medes conquered the Babylonians and assumed rule over Israel, followed by the Greeks. The Jewish Maccabees gained brief self-rule, only to be overrun by the Romans who were in total control of Israel at the time of Jesus. It was indeed this brutal people who crucified the precious Son of God on behalf of the spiritually blind leaders of Israel. Later, in AD 70, the Romans crushed the rebellious Jews, razing Jerusalem to the ground. The Roman Empire began to be "Christianised" around AD 300 when Constantine accepted Jesus as God's Son. After the empire's demise in the fifth century, Israel was subject to various tyrants attacking it, followed by the third Caliph, an Arab named Umar, the overall spiritual leader in succession to Muhammad, conquering and occupying Jerusalem and Israel in AD 638. So, it was the Muslims who stole the land from the Jews and not the other way around! Later, the pre-Reformation Roman Catholic crusaders, with as much brutality as the Romans and Muslims, captured the city in AD 1099. However, after about 100 years the Mamelukes, a militaristic land-holding Muslim Arab aristocracy governing large areas of the Middle East, seized it back by the scimitar!

Moving on to AD 1517, the Turkish Sultan, Salim, captured Jerusalem and made it part of his Muslim Ottoman Empire. His successor Suleiman the Magnificent rebuilt the walls in the Turkish style that we see today. Under later Sultans the land became depopulated with mainly nomadic peoples and only small communities of Jews. It was poorly cultivated with eroded hills, sandy deserts and marshland. The ancient irrigation systems, towns and villages crumbled, and its forests cut down, mainly due to a Turkish tax on trees. Napoleon fought in the region around Har Megiddo in northern Israel, in 1799. Whilst standing on the hill of Megiddo, which overlooks the vast plain of Jezreel where Armageddon will be fought, he is reported to have said:

> "All the armies of the world could be assembled for battle on this plain!"

I wonder if he had read his Bible?

## Further steps in Israel's redevelopment

George Gawler, became the first governor of the newly established colony of Australia. After returning to England in 1841, he began to encourage Jewish settlements in Palestine. His experience in Australia led him to believe that uninhabited land could be settled within years. He wrote,

> "I should be truly rejoiced to see in Palestine a strong guard of Jews established in flourishing agricultural settlements and ready to hold their own upon the mountains of Israel against all aggressors. I can wish for nothing more glorious in this life than to have my share in helping them do so."

Surely, a man who heard from the Spirit of God! However, immigration was slow and in 1867, Mark Twain (Samuel Clemens) of *Huckleberry Finn* fame, visited Palestine and described the land in his book *The Innocents Abroad* as a "desolate country whose soil is rich enough, but is given wholly over to weeds – a silent mournful expanse, wherein we saw only three persons – Arabs, with nothing on but a coarse shirt – on the whole route. There was hardly a tree or shrub anywhere. Even the olive and cactus, those fast friends of a worthless soil, had almost deserted the country".

A report from the Palestine Royal Commission earlier that century confirms the state of the country at that time. It quotes an account of the Coastal Plain:

> "The road leading from Gaza to the north was only a summer track suitable for transport by camel and carts ... no orange groves, orchards or vineyards were to be seen until one reached Yavne village ... houses were all mud, schools did not exist ... The western part, towards the sea was almost desert ... The villages in this area were few and thinly populated ... and many villages were deserted by their inhabitants."

The French author, Voltaire, also described Palestine at that time as "a hopeless, dreary place". All this paints a picture of sparse population in Israel. Later in the nineteenth century, a few Jews from Yemen in the south, Russia in the north, Morocco in the west and Iraq in the east began to migrate back into the area and so the Jewish population increased. They could only purchase land at exorbitant prices from Arab landlords living in Cairo, Damascus and Beirut, who owned about 70% of the land. Approximately 80% of the Arabs living in the land worked for these landlords. They were debt-ridden peasants, semi-nomads and Bedouins.

Shortly after the fierce pogroms (organised massacres) against the Jews in Russia in 1881, William H. Hechler, an ordained Protestant pastor, became private tutor to Prince Ludwig, son of Frederick the Grand Duke of Baden, in Germany. Through his contacts of Christians in high positions, he participated in a meeting in London to consider the possibilities of settling Jewish refugees from Russia and Romania in Palestine. Hechler and Theodor Herzl were friends. The latter, a Jewish visionary who chaired the first International Zionist Conference in Basle, Switzerland in 1897. Herzl wrote prophetically, "In Basle I founded the Jewish State."

We have now reached the beginning of the twentieth century when many Bible-believing Christians, who understood God's purposes for the Jews, were praying for their restoration to the land. On studying the various key people involved in the Jewish return, one can see that just as God raised up the Persians to liberate the Jews from Babylon, so He raised up the British Empire to play a leading role in freeing them from Turkish Muslim rule towards the end of the First World War in 1917. General Allenby, a Christian, entered Jerusalem on foot realising the significance of the event. He led the British, Australian and New Zealand soldiers, and the Turkish Empire was divided into several new countries by the victorious Allied Forces.

As part of the conquering allied nations and not the instigators, Britain quite legitimately adopted the declaration formulated by

Arthur James Balfour. He had been a Prime Minister of Britain but became Foreign Secretary during the war and, very significantly, was also a Christian man. Indeed, seven out of ten in the British war cabinet were Bible believers and knew God's word concerning the Jewish return to Israel. God moved Balfour's heart, as He had done with King Cyrus over 2,000 years before, the cabinet concurred and proposed a homeland for the Jews in Palestine, with due respect being given to other peoples and religions living there. This declaration was issued on 2nd November 1917 and I quote the full statement in chapter 8. The Balfour Declaration won the approval of the United States and other Western powers. The moderate Muslim leaders also supported it because they knew Israel had been taken from the Jews by the Arab Muslims in AD 638 and it was rightfully their homeland.

When war broke out in 1914, T.E. Lawrence (later of Arabia) an intelligence officer in Cairo, met various sheikhs who were rebelling against the Turks. He galvanised them to fight a gorilla warfare against the Turkish army in Arab lands. They were headed up by the Grand Sharif Hussein, ruler of the Hashemite tribe, who controlled the religious centres of Mecca, Medina and the surrounding areas, collectively known as the Hejaz. After the war, the Allies tried to please the Arabs and meet the promises Lawrence had made to them, so the British gave Hussein the area of Hejaz and made it a kingdom. However, the Wahhabi tribe in central Arabia later overthrew him and the other tribes and set up the Saudi kingdom over the whole peninsular. Emir Faisal, one of the sons of Hussein took Damascus from the Turks and made himself king of Greater Syria, which included Lebanon, but he recognised the Jewish homeland. He met with Chaim Weizmann and other Zionist leaders during the Paris Peace Conference of 1919. Faisal signed the agreement and said regarding historic Israel:

"Mindful of the racial kinship and racial bonds existing between Arabs and the Jewish people ... the surest means of working out the consummation of their national aspiration is through the closest possible collaboration in the development of the Arab state and Palestine [as the Jewish State]."

Faisal continued,

"The Arabs, especially the educated among us, look with deepest sympathy on the Zionist movement ... We wish the Jews a hearty welcome home ... We are working together for a reformed and revised Near East and the two movements compliment one another. The Jewish movement is nationalist and not imperialist."

*Map 1.* 1920 – Palestine under the British Mandate

The Balfour Declaration and the Paris Peace Conference Agreement were ratified in 1920 in San Remo, Italy, by the League of Nations (see Map 1). The latter was set up after the First World War, the forerunner to the United Nations formed in 1946 after the Second World War. As I have said, it bore a striking resemblance to the decree made by the Persian King Cyrus after the overthrow of the Babylonian Empire, when he declared that the Jews could return to their beloved homeland in Israel. This Declaration prompted a new wave of immigration by the oppressed Jews of Europe and Russia. Very soon over 50,000 more Jews found a home to the west of the River Jordan.

The League of Nations gave Britain the Mandate to govern Israel and Trans-Jordan, and the French were given Syria and Lebanon. The French did not recognise Faisal's claim over Lebanon with her Christian majority and after much resistance removed him by force from Syria. The British cobbled together a kingdom which they named Iraq, comprising Kurds in the north, Sunnis in the middle and Shia in the south with Faisal as their King. In 1921 Sir Winston Churchill gave 70% of the mandated territory, known as Trans-Jordan to Abdulla, another son of Hussein, today the Kingdom of Jordan. Later, Faisal's son inherited the throne in Iraq but he and the entire royal family were slaughtered in 1958 by a military coup. Saddam Hussein subsequently came to power through the Ba'ath Party in 1979.

Map 2 shows the territory allocation to the Jews; their historic borders had been handed back to them by a vote of the nations of the world – a blessing on the nations!

However, a fundamental Muslim called Haj Amin al Husseini, the Grand Mufti in Jerusalem in the 1930s, stirred up the Arabs to hate both the Jews and the British. These riots saw 10,000 people killed between 1936 and 1939, comprising around 8,500 Arabs (mostly killed by other Arabs vying for control), 1,000 British and 500 Jews.

During these years the British, also fearing for their oil interests, broke International Law by severely restricting further

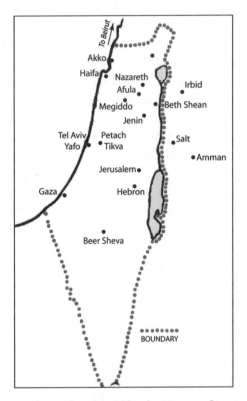

*Map 2.* 1922 – Area agreed by the League of Nations
for the Jewish Homeland

Jewish immigration to Israel, even though it was also well known that Hitler was heavily persecuting them in Europe. The British authorities imprisoned many Jews in wire-fenced compounds in Israel as they returned to the country. This was similar to the camps Hitler constructed, and which prompted some in Israel to form liberation groups to counter the illegal activities of the British government. They were putting into practice what the League of Nations had mandated Britain to do, namely settle the Jews in their own land! However, they were labelled terrorists. The Irgun were the most militant in undermining the British. They destroyed trains and their most desperate act was to blow up part of the King David Hotel in 1946 with ninety killed.

The Stern Gang was also extreme and killed some British soldiers in the conflict. But it is estimated that certainly tens of thousands, and maybe hundreds of thousands of Jews died unnecessarily in the German death camps because the British blocked the escape routes from Europe, turning their emigration ships away from Israel.

In the meantime widespread Arab migration was allowed to continue unabated into Israel from the surrounding nations, particularly Jordan, leading to a very much larger Arab population than Jewish.

In the light of this whole study you will see clearly the spiritual dimension of the situation and see that Satan was, and still is, trying to thwart God's purposes for the Jews by bringing as many Muslims into the land as possible. It is these Arab immigrants, along with their second and third generations, who form the majority of the present-day Palestinians, many of whom left in the 1948 conflict. The Arabs deliberately keep the refuge camps in poverty for political gain, refusing to use the aid to upgrade them. Also, based on the grounds of longevity of tenancy in the land, most of the Arabs living in Israel have not been there any longer than the Jewish immigrants. But Jews have lived there as their homeland from 1500 BC to AD 70, some 1,570 years, and the majority only left due to their enforced removal by the Romans in AD 70. As I have said, it was the Arab Muslims who then took the historic land from the Jews in AD 638.

The efforts of the Jews to re-establish themselves peacefully in the land, with freedom for all law-abiding Muslims, were resisted by extremists who made false accusations against them on many occasions. For instance, the Peel Commission was set up in 1937 to investigate an accusation made by the Arabs that the Jews had obtained too large a proportion of good land. It conclusively decided that this was totally unfounded, as much of the land now bearing orange groves had been sand dunes or swamp and was uncultivated when purchased.

Significantly, Haj Amin al-Husseini collaborated with Adolf

Hitler during the Second World War in their common desire to exterminate Jews. Interestingly, Haj Amin was related to Yasser Arafat through his mother, and Hitler had been brought up a Roman Catholic.

There is much more information on Israel's development from Christian Friends of Israel (see their website: www.cfi.org.uk).

## Modern history

In the second half of the last century the insoluble situation was handed over to the United Nations, who voted in November

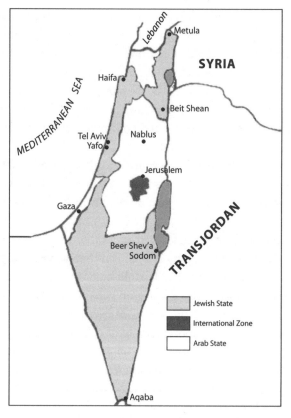

*Map 3.* UN Proposal 1947

1947 to partition the land west of the River Jordan into Muslim and Jewish areas (see Map 3).

It is important to say here that there is significant historical justification to correlate the demise of various nations and empires with their actions against Israel because God said:

> *"I* [God] *will bless those who bless you* [Abraham
>    and his sons through Jacob];
>    *and whoever curses you I will curse;*
> *and all the peoples on the earth*
>    *will be blessed through you."*        (Genesis 12:3)

Britain, for example, lost her empire by turning from Bible truths and breaking the promise made to Israel through the Balfour Treaty in 1917. This had not stipulated a two-state solution. Other empires and individuals that came against Israel have also disappeared or fallen from power. Muslim nations already suffer the curse of God for cursing and resisting Israel's legitimate existence and will be heavily implicated in the future judgment stated by Joel. The USA and EU will receive similar opposition from God, if they pursue the setting up of a Palestinian State on Jewish land in contradiction to His word.

The proposed UN borders in 1947 not only separated Jerusalem from the half allocated to the Jews but were also extremely difficult to defend as they comprised 50% desert! The Jews, however, accepted the offer, whereas the Arabs rejected it and declared war on the State of Israel in order to annihilate the Jews and take the whole of Israel. The Muslims made no attempt to build State institutions of their own but chose only violence, corruption and destruction. The day after the last British troops left, the state of Israel was declared on 14th May 1948. The five armies of Egypt, Syria, Jordan, Lebanon and Iraq immediately attacked Israel. On invasion day, Azzam Pasha, Secretary General of the Arab League, said in Cairo:

"this would be a war of extermination and a momentous massacre, which would be spoken of like the Mongolian massacres and the Crusades."

However, after much bloodshed on both sides, the little Israeli nation mainly with small arms miraculously repelled the larger Arab armies, which had larger artillery. The ceasefire left Jordan occupying the West Bank and the Egyptians the Gaza Strip. As a result of this war, initiated by the Arabs, the Israelis gained additional land and a corridor to Jerusalem. The border became known as the 1949 Green Line (see Map 4). It was a modern-day example of the David and Goliath contest, which clearly had the awesome hand of God on it.

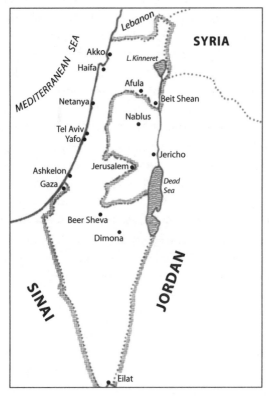

*Map 4.* Israel 1949 – after the War of Independence

Before the outbreak of war, the civilian Arabs who lived in Israel were encouraged by their Arab leadership, through loud hailers in the streets etc., to leave the country and avoid the fighting, then return after the slaughter. Some 600,000 left in haste. Thus the Arabs themselves initiated the refugee problem! Interestingly, those who fled from Israel roughly equalled the number of Jews who were forced out of the surrounding Arab countries by the Muslims during that time. Jewish property confiscated by Iraq, Syria, Libya and Egypt more than offset Arab claims of compensation for houses deserted by their own people during the War of Independence in 1948.

In 1956, President Nasser illegally broke the 100-year Suez Canal contract with Britain and France. Later, in May 1967 before the Six-Day War, he mobilised his army and instructed the UN Emergency Forces to leave Sinai and the Gaza Strip, which had acted as a military buffer. Cairo Radio announced "Egypt was preparing to plunge into total war to put an end to Israel". She imposed a naval blockade off the Gulf of Aqaba, stopping Israel's sea trade from the south and east, an Act of War under International Law and also made a military alliance with Jordan. There were military preparations by the neighbouring Arab states and Syria bombarded northern Israel with artillery and made many terrorist raids into the land. Before the Arabs mounted their full-scale attack, Israel responded by bombing Egyptian air bases, which had been the greatest military threat. To the East, Jordan attacked Israel prompting a response from them. The US offered to demand a ceasefire from Israel and a return to the pre-1967 borders but the USSR advised Egypt not to accept. Egypt had misinformed the Russians they were winning and so the latter advised the Arabs that rather than go back to the same border they could take more land, if not the whole of Israel. However, this was wishful thinking and totally back-fired on them as they were defeated. So it was the Arabs who again by default lost much land namely the Gaza strip, the Sinai Peninsula, the West Bank and the Golan Heights

*Map 5.* Cease-fire lines after 1967 Six-Day War

and threw away the opportunity to return to the 1967 borders (see Map 5).

A well known international Bible teacher, who will remain anonymous and who was praying for Israel, saw on the first day of the Six-Day War a vision of angels in heaven with a golden cord holding them back. As he watched the vision, the golden cord was drawn aside and immediately, with joy and excitement the whole throng of angels descended to earth. No prizes in guessing their assignment!

During the next conflict, the 1973 Yom Kippur War, again started by the Arabs, Lance Lambert, a well known Messianic Jew, and other Christian intercessors were in Jerusalem. Whilst praying, they saw a vision of God's hand holding back the enemies of Israel. Lance heard on the radio that while most of the Israeli tanks were in the south dealing with the Egyptians, the Syrian tanks had invaded from the north. For some naturally inexplicable reason, they stopped advancing giving the Israeli tanks enough time to cover the distance and repel them! This third major attempt by the Arabs to completely destroy the nation was again soundly thwarted.

A significant point to highlight here is the practice of nil liability employed by the Muslims. Let me explain. The Arabs rejected the will of the United Nations in 1947 and effectively decided to gamble the land allotted to them in order to gain the whole of Israel. However, this was not achieved and their action effectively removed their right to self-rule in the half offered to them. Again in 1967, the Arab nations mustered their armies to annihilate the State of Israel, but on losing, they brazenly claimed the pre-war borders once more. It was very clear from their words and actions that they had compounded their loss of right to self-governance of any territory given to them in 1947! The Arabs once again stood as defenders of the United Nations' ruling, when they had blatantly rejected it themselves by going to war. Perversely, they then cast Israel as violator of the UN and the world continues to fall for the deception.

When Germany lost the Second World War, which she had started, her leadership changed and she was occupied until she could prove her sincerity and capability in making responsible policies. This she did, and foreign troops have correspondingly been withdrawn from her territory. Unfortunately, the Palestinians have done precisely the opposite!

On the other hand, the Israelis' record is far from perfect. For instance, during their occupation of Lebanon, Israelis allowed the Lebanese so-called "Christian Militia", the Orthodox Phalange, to have access to the Palestinian refugee camps of Sabra and Shatila, when many were killed. Israeli retaliation has also been with disproportionate force on many occasions where there has been no justification for it, but their errors have no comparison to the ongoing evil perpetrated against them! The recent 34-day war in 2006 against Hamas in the Gaza, and Hizbullah in Lebanon, was in retaliation for the continual shelling of innocent civilians and their entering Israel to kill and kidnap three of her soldiers. This sparked off a major effort to render the Islamic forces inoperative. On the face of it, the Israeli's actions were disproportionate but when seen in the context of the Muslim objective to totally destroy the State of Israel, it is not. The Muslims demanded the total withdrawal of Israeli troops from Lebanon, and that happened and was reasonable, but it must be coupled with the total dismantling of Hizbullah as an independent army in Lebanon.

It is important to point out that the PLO was formed in 1964 before Israel had taken the West Bank in the 1967 war. Its main aim then was to destroy the State of Israel. Since losing the Six-Day War, the media has been fed with the story that violence against Israel is because of the occupation of the West Bank in 1967. This is just a ploy, which the West falls for not knowing or wanting to know all the facts of the situation. Even though the PLO now officially says they accept Israel's right to exist, their real objective remains to destroy the whole of Israel and establish a Palestinian State as a two-step process. Hamas only has a one-step policy!

All this is based on the Palestinians' own statements and can be checked with the relevant TV networks and the Arab national news agencies. For instance, the late Mr Arafat declared to the Western press in English that he wanted a two-state solution and had renounced terrorism. However, the Palestinian leadership continued to say in Arabic to their own people, that they did not want a Palestinian State consisting of only half the land, but one, which included all Israel with every Jew dead! This is the problem Israel faces. Arafat rejected the extremely generous terms offered by Yitzhak Rabin in 1993, and those of President Clinton and Ehud Barak in 2000 at Taba, because he wanted all Jerusalem and all Israel, not just half. The "peace process" from Oslo in 1994 sought a "land for peace" solution with a view to establishing a Palestinian State. Consequently, Israel allowed well over 90% of Palestinians to live under their own rule in the West Bank as a first step. In return for self-governance, the Palestinians agreed to give up violence. However, Arafat made no effort to stop the various warring factions from killing Jews and actively encouraged hatred towards them. Even if Israel went back fully to the pre-1967 borders, the Palestinians would not be content but would redouble their fight for the rest of the land!

Arafat made the following statement to the Palestinians on returning to Israel, after he signed the Oslo Accord on 10th May 1994:

> "This has to be understood by everybody. The Oslo Agreement, I do not consider more than the agreement which has been signed between our prophet Muhammad and Quraysh."

The Quraysh were the most powerful tribe in Mecca who initially resisted Muhammad and his teachings. It benefited him to sign a truce with them while he was weak but as soon as he became strong by the scimitar, he tore it up and proceeded to massacre them for not accepting his revelations! This is justified in Muslim eyes, because the Quran teaches that breaking a promise is permissible:

> "Freedom from obligation is proclaimed from Allah and his messenger toward those of the idolaters [Jews, Christians and other *infidels*] with whom you have made a treaty."
>
> (Part 10; Sura 9:1–14)

Hence, it is futile to sign an agreement with any fundamentalist Muslim. Arafat's deputy, Othman Abu Arbiah, also said in November 1999:

> "Every Palestinian must know clearly and unequivocally that the independent PLO-Arab State [with half the land], with Jerusalem

as its capital, is not the end of the road. The Palestinian State is a stage. After that there will be another stage and that is the democratic state in all of Palestine [meaning no Jewish State!]."

Abd-Al Malek Dahamshe, a Palestinian member of the Knesset, was interviewed on Palestinian television in September 2000. He agreed with the statement of one participant, that their problem was not a border problem but one of the existence of Israel. The Palestinian Authority representative for Jerusalem Affairs also said:

"Had the US and Israel realised, before Oslo, that all that was left of the Palestinian National Movement and the Pan Arab movement was a wooden horse called Arafat of the PLO, they would never have opened their fortified gates and let it inside their walls ... Oslo, or any other agreement, is just a temporary procedure, or just a step towards something bigger ... We distinguish the strategic, long-term goals from the political phased goals, which we are to accept temporarily due to international pressure ... Palestine, according to the higher strategy, is from the river Jordan to the Mediterranean Sea. It is entirely an Arab land of the Arab nation!"

The world press was told in 2000 that the Intifada started because Sharon had come to the El Aqsa mosque. He actually went on to the Temple mount to see reconstruction work being carried out by the Muslims, but never entered their mosque. The Minister of Communications for the Palestinian Authority said to the Palestinians on 5th May 2000:

"Whoever thinks that this Intifada of El Aqsa started as a result of the despicable visit of Sharon to El Aqsa mosque is in error. That was merely the straw that broke the patience of the Palestinian people."

They said this Intifada had been planned ever since President Arafat returned from the talks where he rejected the very generous terms brokered by President Clinton.

Israel's incursions into Palestinian towns have not been to control them but to stop terrorists from making bombs and firing rockets into Jewish communities. The Israelis have been executing known murderers of Jewish citizens because the Palestinian Authority will not arrest and judge them themselves. Had Arafat and Abbas imprisoned the terrorists for their capital offences, the killers would still be alive today, albeit behind bars! Also, the UN and Lebanese government did not implement the UN resolution in Lebanon, made a few years before, to disarm Hizbullah but have allowed it to grow unabated. If Hizbullah had been disarmed, the 34-Day War would not have happened!

The election of Hamas and their bloody and cruel occupation of the Gaza Strip has had one positive effect – they are telling the world the truth about their intentions. They are impatient zealots rather than artful politicians and through them the real issues are coming to the surface in the media.

I have quoted the words of Palestinian leaders in this study but it is also important to say that throughout the Muslim nations, the media freely broadcast a daily diet of hatred towards the Jews, portraying them as subhuman, evil and only worthy of death. This stems from Muhammad's writings in the Quran, which contains derogatory statements such as:

"We shall say unto them: 'You [Jews] shall be detested apes.' "
(Surah 2:65)

"Allah had cursed him [Jews] whom his wrath has fallen! Worse is he of whose sort Allah has turned some to apes and swine."
(Surah 5:60)

An example of misinformation from the Muslims is through a film, made in Egypt, from the book *The Protocols of the Elders of*

*Zion.* This book originally appeared courtesy of the Czarist secret police in the late nineteenth century, to subvert the Jewish position in Russia. It was among the books actively circulated in Germany, even in the schools, under the arch racist Hitler. The aim was to poison the minds of his citizens, old and young alike, so they could justify the mass extermination of the Jewish nation. This book accuses the Jewish leadership of encouraging their people to infiltrate Western society, for some to even convert to Christianity in order to rise in society and manipulate the offices of power in nations to control the world. The Lord does indeed place Jews in influential positions, like Esther, but it is for good to save the Jews and bless the nations, not for evil domination.

The Quran teaches that Muslims must physically conquer the whole world and make it bow down to Allah and the Sharia law. They teach that it is legitimate to kill those who do not believe, similar to Hitler's tactics, which is how Islam grew so quickly in the Middle East and elsewhere. Palestinians are indoctrinated in their schools with half-truths and lies, especially by the extremists, and are encouraged to become suicide bombers. This is similar to the Nazi youth rallies. The same spirit of child sacrifice, which Joshua was told to eradicate in Canaan, lives on in modern form! The Muslim is taught that if he dies in *Jihad* he will avoid standing before the great white throne of God at the end-time judgment, but will proceed straight to heaven to be with Muhammad. He will tragically find himself with Muhammad and they will both stand at the Judgement Seat of God before going into eternity together, but not to where they thought! The Bible says every man and woman will have to stand before Jesus and give a full account of his or her life – praise God we have an Advocate before God, even the same Jesus Christ, if we put our trust in Him!

In truth, Satan knows from Scripture that the Jews will eventually return to their land, come to Christ, and that Jesus will rule from Jerusalem as their King! He is twisting the truth against the Jews and filling those who do not know God's word with wrong interpretations of the Bible. Muhammad taught that the Quran is the definitive word of God and that dishonest Jews in the Old Testament and deceitful Christians in the New Testament have introduced all the differences in the Bible! All effective opposition to the Quran has to be eliminated. The biblical love and forgiveness of God are replaced by hate and death in this world to all who oppose its teachings.

Satan knows that if he can stop the Jews living in the whole land of Israel, a promise which has to be fulfilled before Jesus returns, then he can delay his own demise! The Scriptures say that Jesus will return to Jerusalem and lock Satan in the abyss. Islam's hatred of the Jews has resulted in at least 80% of Palestinians being in favour of suicide bombers and a minimum of 60% desiring the total destruction of the Jewish state! In 2006, even 10% of British Muslims were in favour of the London bombings and 20% sympathetic to their cause, but not by bombings.

All men need to heed God's word to Abraham regarding the curses so I repeat His word on the matter:

> *"I will bless those who bless you [Jews],*
>     *and whoever curses you [Jews] I will curse;*
> *and all the peoples on earth*
>     *will be blessed through you."*         (Genesis 12:3)

God has blessed, and is blessing, the whole world through Jesus, a Jew by birth. The Muslims do not accept the teachings of Jesus. They do not realise that their poverty is brought about by self-inflicted curses through words and acts of hatred towards the descendants of Abraham, Isaac and Jacob.

Paul taught that the government of a nation state is God's servant to keep law and order and punish wrong behaviour. Its army protects the citizens from outside attack and, where necessary, declares war on a rogue government, such as Hitler's.

*"For he* [the government] *is God's servant to do you good. But if you do*
*wrong, be afraid, for he does not bear the sword for nothing. He is God's*
*servant, an agent of wrath to bring punishment on the wrongdoer."*

(Romans 13:4)

We have seen this implemented in the Israeli-Arab wars, where
Muslims have suffered severe defeats for opposing what is right in
God's eyes.

Ariel Sharon handed back Gaza, contrary to God's word and
look what happened to him. When the Israelis give back land by
their own choice, the Lord is limited in what He can do. This is
different from being unlawfully attacked, where the Lord can
fight for them. The Israeli government, however, has said that
there are five or so settlements, as well as Jerusalem, which are
non-negotiable, but are we seeing a change of mind?

I have sought to report the historical situation in the Middle
East accurately, but am aware that this is diametrically opposed
to most of the propaganda put out by the Muslims and views of
the media reporters. The latter do not understand the historical
facts, let alone what the Quran or what the Bible teaches. Satan
blinds the minds of non-believers and has constructed the most
horrendous case against the Jews. Sadly, this has been their lot
throughout history, epitomised in classic literature by the
Shakespearian character, Shylock. The hatred whipped up against
them by Hitler in Germany resulted in the most horrific crime in
human history, the systematic slaughter of six million Jews. The
bid to prove German superiority took a further thirty million
Gentile lives, both German and non-German, during the Second
World War. The parallel from this most recent history is stark.
The same hatred for the Jews is being spread throughout the
Muslim world and is spilling over into the rest of the nations –
witness the Iranian president's declared intention to wipe the
Jewish State from the map! This is surely a breach of International
Law for which he should be brought to account. It is taught in
Muslim circles that the Holocaust and other atrocities against the

Jews never actually occurred. Muslims say it is only Jewish propaganda to gain sympathy from the world! Paradoxically, Hizbullah, is on record as saying that they want every Jew to return to Israel, not for God's reasons, but in order that the whole nation can be more easily exterminated! What they desire is not just a repeat of the six million Jewish holocaust but also the removal of the entire fourteen million Jews worldwide. It is racism at its worst.

Arafat was on record as calling for a million Palestinian martyrs, i.e. the whole Muslim population of the West Bank being willing to give up their lives to remove the Jews! The reason for this hatred has not changed throughout their long and torturous history, and it is because God chose Israel for Himself, to bring salvation to the world through them. In the meantime, the frightening probability is that this time the demonic hatred is likely to spill over and kill not just thirty-six million as in the Second World War but hundreds of millions of innocent people throughout the whole world in the very near future!

As one understands the monumental spiritual battle taking place over Israel's very existence, it is easy to see that she would have been overrun years ago, were it not for God laying the burden of intercessory prayer on believers' hearts! Both sides are suffering from the extremist Muslims. Had it not been for these fundamentalists there would be no Palestinian refugees, and both parties would be living prosperously in peace together, as first envisaged by the Jewish and Muslim leaders at the end of the First World War. There is an evil dimension of hatred and blood thirst that desperately needs prayer. Jesus died for both sides and they need to know God's love, acceptance and forgiveness. As Christians, we must continue to pray for the peace of Jerusalem in the light of the Scriptures.

# The Mountains
# of Israel

A look at the relief map shows that the mountains of Israel formed a large part of the territory offered to the Muslims by the United Nations in 1947, most of the area surrounding Jerusalem to the west of the Jordan river shown in white on Map 6. This is extremely significant in the light of the prophecy in Ezekiel 36.

It is important to remember that God opened the way for the Jews to have the whole land of Israel, including these mountains, in 1917. The Allied Army liberated Palestine (Israel) from the Muslim Ottoman Empire and what was then called Trans-Jordan. Israel became a British Protectorate with full rights in the land. Balfour committed the British government to a homeland for the Jews, fully endorsed by the League of Nations in 1920. Through the Muslims' attempted extermination of the Jews in 1948, 1967 and 1973, they have shown they have no desire to live at peace with them.

The land was irreversibly promised to the Jews through God's covenant with Abraham and remained theirs even when they were scattered around the world due to their rebellion. It is vital to see this and link it with Ezekiel's prophecy given during the first half of the seventy-year exile in Babylon. He said they would return and never again be deprived of the mountains of Israel. The relevant verses are quoted below. It is also crucial to see that the Lord was referring to this present time in history and not to any

*Map 6.* UN Proposal 1947

earlier or later period, which I will seek to prove from Scripture. I repeat, do not be taken in by the mass of incorrect information from the media, who do not understand the detailed history of the situation, let alone God's Word! Be under no illusion, a spiritual battle of global proportions is taking place, literally to the death. Praise God, we can read the end of the Bible and see who will win!

> " 'Son of man, prophesy to the mountains of Israel and say, "O mountains of Israel, hear the word of the LORD. This is what the Sovereign LORD says: The enemy said of you, 'Aha! The ancient heights have become our possession.' " Therefore prophesy and say, "This is

*what the Sovereign* LORD *says: Because they ravaged and hounded you from every side so that you became the possession of the rest of the nations and the object of people's malicious talk and slander, therefore, O mountains of Israel, hear the word of the Sovereign* LORD: *This is what the Sovereign* LORD *says to the mountains and hills, to the ravines and valleys, to the desolate ruins and the deserted towns that have been plundered and ridiculed by the rest of the nations around you – this is what the Sovereign* LORD *says: In my burning zeal I have spoken against the rest of the nations, and against Edom, for with glee and with malice in their hearts they made my land their own possession so that they might plunder its pasture-land." Therefore prophesy concerning the land of Israel and say to the mountains and hills, to the ravines and the valleys: "This is what the Sovereign* LORD *says: I speak in my jealous wrath because you have suffered the scorn of the nations. Therefore this is what the Sovereign* LORD *says: I swear with uplifted hand that the nations around you will also suffer scorn.*

*' "But you, O mountains of Israel, will produce branches and fruit for my people Israel, for they will soon come home. I am concerned for you and will look on you with favour; you will be ploughed and sown, and I will multiply the number of people on you, even the whole house of Israel. The towns will be inhabited and the ruins rebuilt. I will increase the number of men and animals upon you, and they will be fruitful and become numerous.* **I will settle people on you** *as in the past and will make you prosper more than before. Then you will know that I am the* LORD. *I will cause people, my people Israel, to walk upon you.* **They will possess you, and you will be their inheritance; you will never again deprive them of their children." ' "***

(Ezekiel 36:1–12, emphasis added)

The two southern tribes returned to Israel after their seventy humiliating years in Babylon, and resettled in the southern part of the mountains in Judea where Jerusalem is situated. Although they were back in their land, they continued to be under the rule of the Persians, later the Greeks, and then the Romans. The ten northern tribes never totally returned in Jesus' time. There was no seventy-year prophetic time scale for them, but a promise that God would bring them back at some stage in the future, as recorded in Jeremiah 16:14–16. After Jesus ascended into heaven, the Jews were once more separated from the mountains in AD 70, this time by the occupying Roman army! They were ruthlessly dispersed throughout the world, even further afield than in the banishments by the Assyrians and Babylonians over 500 years before. After the demise of the Roman Empire, the land was open to the four winds and Muslims captured and occupied Jerusalem in AD 638. Mainly Muslim powers took control until the British Army liberated her from Turkish rule in 1917. So, the return to Jerusalem and the mountains of Israel after the seventy years captivity in Babylon could not have been the fulfilment of Ezekiel 36, since the prophet said *"you* [the mountains] *will never again deprive them* [Israelites] *of their children"*. I believe we are witnessing today the step-by-step fulfilment of the long promised restoration of all twelve tribes to all their territory. We will look at these dispersions and returns in the next chapter.

The reason for this long and bloody delay is due to the great period of punishment visited on the Jews, called the *"times of the Gentiles"*, when foreign kings ruled her. The first stage came to an end at the declaration of the State of Israel in 1948. Jesus said:

> *"Jerusalem will be trampled on by the Gentiles until the times of the Gentiles are fulfilled."*      (Luke 21:24)

Ezekiel's prophecy, together with all other end-time words regarding Israel, could not be fulfilled until this punishment was completed. God meticulously carried it out to the exact year, as will be explained in the next three chapters.

The lengthy sentence is now ended, and the way is open for God to fulfil all the many remaining promises He made to Israel. He started by giving them the whole land in 1917 but due to Islamic militants, the illegal actions of the British Government and the biblical blindness of the UN, she was limited to only half of her land. Because we are at the conclusion of *"the times of the Gentiles"*, anyone coming against Israel now will find themselves fighting God as well as the Israelites! As already mentioned, during the many recent conflicts, Israeli soldiers have personally reported seeing angels helping to defend her. No doubt the archangel Michael is heading up this angelic army!

It must be clearly understood from this study that God is more interested in people than land and desires to bring precious Muslims and Jews to Christ and so to Himself, whilst fulfilling His promises to the descendants of Israel. He wants to reconcile all sides in Christ and will work events around so eventually the Jews will have full control of the whole land.

So, despite all we see and hear through the media, the building of settlements on the West Bank is not unjust but has actually happened through the Lord's enabling! The Israeli government needs to read and understand the Old Testament scriptures. Israel is not even in breach of any UN resolution concerning her occupation of the West Bank because there was no resolution specifying how much land she was expected to relinquish after the 1967 war. The Arabs rejected and violated the will of the UN by attacking Israel in 1948, then by amassing troops and starting to attack in 1967 and again in 1973, all aimed at her annihilation!

Ezekiel went on to say in 36:26 that the Lord would *"give a new heart"* to the Jews. This began when many Jews put their faith in Jesus, as recorded in the Gospels and the Acts of the Apostles. However, verses 28 to 38 refer to a national turning to the Lord, which has yet to be seen. These verses must be interpreted in the light of the New Covenant without discarding the long-standing promise to the Jews regarding their right of return to the land:

> " 'For I will take you out of the nations; I will gather you from all the countries and bring you back into your own land [Israel]. I will sprinkle clean water on you [washing of rebirth by the Word (Titus 3:5)], and you will be clean; I will cleanse you from all your impurities and from all

*your idols. I will give you a new heart and put a new spirit in you; I will remove from you your heart of stone and give you a heart of flesh* [the new birth in Christ]. *And I will put my Spirit in you and move you to follow my decrees and be careful to keep my laws* [Jesus fulfilled the Law for us and it is now by faith in the perfect law of Christ which gives believers freedom (James 1:25)]. *You* [Jews] *will live in the land* [Israel] *I gave your forefathers; you will be my people, and I will be your God. I will save you from all your uncleanness. I will call for the corn and make it plentiful and will not bring famine upon you. I will increase the fruit of the trees and the crops of the field, so that you will no longer suffer disgrace among the nations because of famine. Then you will remember your evil ways and wicked deeds, and you will loathe yourselves for your sins and detestable practices. I want you to know that I am not doing this for your sake, declares the Sovereign* LORD. *Be ashamed and disgraced for your conduct, O house of Israel!*

*'This is what the Sovereign* LORD *says: On the day I cleanse you from all your sins, I will resettle your towns, and the ruins will be rebuilt. The desolate land will be cultivated instead of lying desolate in the sight of all who pass through it. They will say, "This land that was laid waste has become like the garden of Eden; the cities that were lying in ruins, desolate and destroyed, are now fortified and inhabited." Then the nations around you that remain will know that I the* LORD *have rebuilt what was destroyed and have replanted what was desolate. I the* LORD *have spoken, and will do it.'*

*This is what the Sovereign* LORD *says: Once again I will yield to the plea of the house of Israel and do this for them: I will make their people, as numerous as sheep, as numerous as the flocks for offerings at Jerusalem during her appointed feasts. So will the ruined cities be filled with flocks of people. Then they will know that I am the* LORD."

(Ezekiel 36:24–38)

God is developing the situation in Israel in order to accomplish every word He has spoken to them. He intends to give the whole nation a new heart in Christ and so prepare the way for the return of His Son, Jesus, to Jerusalem!

*"On that day his [Jesus'] feet will stand on the Mount of Olives, east of Jerusalem."*                                        (Zechariah 14:-4)

*" 'Men of Galilee [Jesus' disciples],' they [angels at the ascension] said, 'why do you stand here looking into the sky? This same Jesus, who has been taken from you into heaven, will come back in the same way you have seen him go into heaven.' Then they returned to Jerusalem from the hill called the Mount of Olives."*                        (Acts 1:11–12)

*"Then I looked, and there before me was the Lamb, standing on Mount Zion."*                                           (Revelation 14:1)

It is vital to understand that this current division of the land, eternally covenanted to the Jews by God, directly contradicts His word and will result in the serious consequences spelt out by the prophet Joel. All the nations that have scattered the Jews and divided the land, including the current UN, are therefore included in this judicial warning from God:

*"In those days and at that time,*
  *when I [God] restore the fortunes of*
  *Judah and Jerusalem,*
*I will gather all nations*
  *and bring them down to the valley of Jehoshaphat [Armageddon].*
*There I will enter into judgment against them [the nations]*
  *concerning my inheritance, my people Israel,*
*for they scattered my people among the nations*
  *and divided up my land."*                              (Joel 3:1–2)

This future judgment is also mentioned in Revelation 16:

*"Then they [the demons] gathered the kings [the nations of the whole world] together to the place that in Hebrew is called Armageddon."*
                                                    (Revelation 16:16)

The Rider (Jesus) on the white horse (the Holy Spirit) returning to earth in Revelation 19:11–16 refers to the same event. Here, Jesus is called Faithful, True and the Word of God. He fights the final battle of this age against all who come against the Jews in Jerusalem and who see their annihilation as the "final solution to the worlds problems". But God has a "final solution" as well – He will eliminate all ungodliness from the face of the earth.

> *"Then I saw the beast* [the Antichrist] *and the kings of the earth and their armies gathered together to make war against the rider on the* [white] *horse and his army."*                    (Revelation 19:19)

But Jesus will triumph over all because He is King of kings and Lord of lords and His throne will be established in Jerusalem forever.

# The Jews' Dispersions and Returns

There are many very significant prophecies, which have yet to be fulfilled before Jesus returns. One is the central verse of the study dealing with the *"times of the Gentiles"* punishment, repeated below. To discover accurately when this period concludes, we have to know its beginning and duration. This chapter will cover its beginning, chapter 7 its length, chapter 8 its completion, and we will also see how the dispersions and returns fit in with her overall judgment.

> *"They* [Israel] *will fall by the sword and will be taken as prisoners to all the nations. Jerusalem will be trampled on by the Gentiles until the times of the Gentiles are fulfilled."* (Luke 21:24)

To understand this we have to look at the instructions and warnings that God gave Moses in the wilderness. There were blessings for obedience and curses for disobedience. The curses first came upon the Israelites during the period of the judges, when foreign kings ruled over them, and their crops were stolen as punishment for turning from the Lord.

> *"You will plant seed in vain, because your enemies will eat it. I will set my face against you so that you will be defeated by your enemies; those who hate you will rule over you, and you will flee even when no-one is pursuing you."* (Leviticus 26:16–17)

Whenever they came under foreign rulers, as they cried out to the Lord He raised up a leader to deliver them. The most documented example is Gideon in Judges 6.

Later, the whole Jewish nation knew great spiritual and natural prosperity under Kings David and Solomon. Tragically, Solomon disobeyed God and married many foreign women, 700 from royal birth and 300 concubines, who turned his heart to their gods. The Lord consequently divided the kingdom in two – north and south. In subsequent reigns, apart from a few revivals, both halves sank lower and lower. There was even male temple prostitution and child sacrifice to the gods of the surrounding heathen nations. The northern kingdom of Israel, comprising ten tribes, fell into major sin many years before their brothers in the south. So God punished the north first, by allowing the Assyrian army to overwhelm and deport them to Gozen in Assyria (northern Iraq) (2 Kings 17:6). The southern kingdom of Judah and Benjamin withstood these ruthless attacks because King Hezekiah sought the Lord and obeyed Him. Subsequent kings in the south prostituted themselves to foreign gods and God was forced to take drastic action by executing His righteous judgments on them, as forewarned in Leviticus 26:16–17. He raised up Nebuchadnezzar to rule over them, and eventually all but the poorest were deported to Babylon (southern Iraq) during the seventy years.

> *"The* LORD *Almighty says this: 'Because you have not listened to my words, I will summon all the peoples of the north and my servant Nebuchadnezzar king of Babylon,' declares the* LORD, *'and I will bring them against this land and its inhabitants . . . But when the seventy years are fulfilled, I will punish the king of Babylon and his nation, the land of the Babylonians, for their guilt,' declares the* LORD.*"*
>
> (Jeremiah 25:8–9, 12)

Because the Jews stubbornly resisted God during the seventy years of punishment, He extended their sentence further by imposing the great seven times punishment at the end of the exile:

> "*If after all this you will not listen to me, I will punish you for your sins seven times over.*"                                    (Leviticus 26:18)

These were some of the additional disasters they brought on themselves:

> "*If in spite of this you still do not listen to me but continue to be hostile towards me, then in my anger I will be hostile towards you, and I myself will punish you for your sins seven times over. You will eat the flesh of your sons and the flesh of your daughters. I will destroy your high places, cut down your incense altars and pile your dead bodies on the lifeless forms of your idols, and will abhor you. I will turn your cities into ruins and lay waste your sanctuaries, and I will take no delight in the pleasing aroma of your offerings. I will lay waste the land, so that your enemies who live there will be appalled. I will scatter you among the nations and will draw out my sword and pursue you.*"
> (Leviticus 26:27–33)

The phrase "*seven times*" is repeated on four occasions in verses 18, 21, 24 and 28 of Leviticus 26, but it is clear that God was referring each time to the same overall seven times punishment. He was explaining the progressive penalties within that period, if the Jews continued in their resistance to Him.

General Nabopolassar, Nebuchadnezzar's father, conquered the Assyrians and made himself king whilst establishing his new enlarged Empire – known as the Neo Babylonian Empire. Biblical and secular historians all agree he died in the year 605 BC, when his son Nebuchadnezzar came to the throne and attacked Jerusalem the same year. Cuneiform records (ancient clay tablets and cylinders inscribed with wedge-shaped writing) excavated from southern Iraq state that Nabopolassar reigned for twenty-one years. Subtracting 21 from 604 BC, the first official full year of his son's reign, brings us back to 625 BC, when Nabopolassar came to the throne. Many have incorrectly taken the twenty-one years from 605 BC, the accession year of Nebuchadnezzar.

To explain, it was the custom in Babylon not to count the first year of the new king's reign, because it was reckoned to be the last year of the previous king. It was described as the accession year of the new king, with the second year being counted as the first official one. The years of each reign could then be added to calculate how long the Empire had lasted. This is confirmed in the Bible where it records that during the third year of the Jewish King Jehoiakim, Nebuchadnezzar became king, attacked Jerusalem and carried away the first wave of Jews in 605 BC (Daniel 1:1 and Jeremiah 24:1). However, Jeremiah goes on to record that the fourth year of the same King Jehoiakim was the first year of Nebuchadnezzar, 604 BC (Jeremiah 25:1). This distinction between the accession year and the first official year is recorded on Tablet 25127, excavated in Babylon and held in the British Museum.

There were several attacks against Jerusalem by King Nebuchadnezzar. They began in his accession year and ended with the torching and final violent destruction of the beloved city in 586 BC, a period of nineteen years. The last miserable remnant of Jews were deported four years later, making twenty-three years in all.

God had instructed the Israelites, through Jeremiah, to comply with her conquerors and Nebuchadnezzar kept the Jewish King, Jehoiakim, on the throne in Jerusalem as a puppet monarch (Daniel 1:1–6). Daniel went to Babylon during the first of the seventy years, along with other nobles, skilled craftsmen and many members of the royal family, including the king's son Jehoiachin (Jeremiah 24:1). However, Jehoiakim continued to do great evil before both the Lord and Nebuchadnezzar, which resulted in further slaughter. His son Jehoiachin was returned back to Jerusalem from Babylon to replace him but he too walked in his father's evil ways.

Nebuchadnezzar replaced Jehoiachin with his uncle, Zedekiah, but he was not in the divinely ordained royal line. So, Jehoiachin was the last of the God ordained kings of Israel. Alas, Zedekiah wilfully rebelled and brought the full wrath of God upon Jerusalem (2 Kings 24:18–20; 25:1–30). This last attack in the ninth year of Zedekiah (2 Kings 25:1), was in the seventeenth year of Nebuchadnezzar, who laid siege to the city for two years. It finally fell in 586 BC, the eleventh year of Zedekiah, resulting in the utter destruction and torching of the whole capital, including the Temple (2 Kings 25:2). This was the nineteenth year of Nebuchadnezzar. As mentioned, the continued rebellion during the seventy-year punishment ensured further foreign domination, as detailed in Leviticus 26:18–39 after the Jews returned to Jerusalem in 353 BC.

The major stages of attack are listed in Table 1, and enable me to explain in subsequent chapters how the Lord has been moving in modern history to restore the Jewish nation. The dates cover the years from the enthronement of Nabopolassar in 625 BC, to the Jewish return to Jerusalem in 535 BC. We know these years very precisely, as they are all clearly recorded in the Bible in relation to the years of Nebuchadnezzar's reign. 586 BC, the year of Jerusalem's destruction, is a key starting date and accepted by every Bible scholar and secular historian alike. The verse below clearly states it to be the nineteenth year of Nebuchadnezzar, so the other events can be accurately calculated from this point. Full details of the fall of Jerusalem are found in Jeremiah 52 and 2 Kings 24.

> *"On the seventh day of the fifth month, in the **nineteenth year** [586 BC] of **Nebuchadnezzar King of Babylon**, Nebuzaradan commander of the imperial guard, an official of the king of Babylon, came to Jerusalem. He set fire to the temple of the LORD, the royal palace and all the houses of Jerusalem. Every important building he burned down. The whole Babylonian army, under the commander of the imperial guard, broke down the walls around Jerusalem."*
>
> (2 Kings 25:8–10, emphasis added; see also Jeremiah 52:12–14)

## *Table 1.* Table of dates

From Nabopolassar's reign in 625 BC to the Jews' return in 535 BC, including their seventy-year exile in Babylon.

| Years of reign by *Nabopolassar* | | | | |
|---|---|---|---|---|
| 625 BC | 0 | Accession year | | Nabopolassar conquered the Assyrians and became king of the Neo Babylonian Empire. |
| 624 BC | 1st | First official year | | |

| Years of reign by *Nebuchadnezzar* | | | Years of exile | |
|---|---|---|---|---|
| 605 BC | 0 | Accession year | 0 | Nabopolassar died. His son Nebuchadnezzar II acceded to the throne and attacked Jerusalem. Daniel, many royals, nobles, craftsmen exiled and some Temple articles taken (Daniel 1:2–6). The third year of Jehoiakim, first vassel king of Judah (Daniel 1:1). |
| 604 BC | 1st | First official year | 1 | The fourth year of King Jehoiakim (Jeremiah 25:1). Jeremiah prophesied that the exile would last seventy years (Jeremiah 25:11). Jehoiakim rebelled against Nebuchadnezzar causing him to attack a second time and deport thousands more to Babylon. |
| 588 BC | 17th year | | 17 | Final attack in the ninth year of King Zedekiah (2 Kings 25:1, 8–7). He persisted in rebellion against both God and Nebuchadnezzar, causing the latter to destroy Jerusalem (2 Kings 24:18–20) and besiege the city for two years. |

| Years of reign by *Nebuchadnezzar* (cont.) | | Years of exile | |
|---|---|---|---|
| 586 BC | 19th year | 19 | Jerusalem and Temple destroyed in eleventh year of Zedekiah (2 Kings 25:2–8). |
| 582 BC | 23rd year | 23 | Last exiles – 745 people taken in twenty-third year of Nebuchadnezzar (Jeremiah 52:30). |
| 535 BC | End of exile | 70 | King Cyrus of Persia conquers Babylon and decrees the rebuilding of the Jewish Temple in Jerusalem. First exiles return (Ezra 1:1–11; 2 Chronicles 36:22–23). |

It is worth pointing out for the historians that Archbishop Ussher calculated the year of return to the land as 536 BC, not 535 BC. He inadvertently added the seventy years to 604 BC, the official start of the king's reign, rather than to 605 BC, the year of Nebuchadnezzar's accession when the captivity began.

At the end of the seventy-year Babylonian exile, Daniel wrote and acknowledged the continued sin of his people during their captivity and, like all truly sincere and godly intercessors, identified with it himself:

> "*Just as it is written in the Law of Moses* [Leviticus 26], *all this disaster has come upon us, yet we have not sought the favour of the LORD our God by turning from our sins and giving attention to your truth. The LORD did not hesitate to bring the disaster upon us, for the LORD our God is righteous in everything He does; yet we have not obeyed him.*"
>
> (Daniel 9:13–14, emphasis added)

It was through Daniel's fervent prayer of repentance that the Lord brought about their promised return to Jerusalem, but because of their sin whilst under the Babylonians, the "seven times" punishment began in 535 BC. This stopped the Lord reinstating the royal line at that time. Instead, foreign powers continued to rule over Jerusalem for some 2,500 years.

The Jews returned under Persian rule. The Greek Empire followed, then the brief uprising of the Jewish Maccabees in 165 BC, initiated by the Hasmonean priestly family. They produced the Royal House from which came Herod the Great in the time of Jesus. However, these royals were not descended from the divinely ordained kingly line of David, as Jesus was by birth.

The Romans soon took power, bringing us to Jesus' first advent. The Jews' national rejection of God's Son and the salvation He wrought for them and all mankind, ensured continuation of the punishments of Leviticus 26:18–39. This involved the second destruction of Jerusalem and their second dispersal on a worldwide scale this time. With great compassion and grief, Jesus foresaw from the Holy Spirit that the Romans would attack, kill and scatter the Jews around the world. This second exile began when Titus attacked Jerusalem in AD 70, but the promise remained that the *"times of the Gentiles"* would eventually end. Jerusalem would then cease to be occupied and would be restored to Jewish control.

Some Jews found their way back to Israel before a large part of the Roman Empire collapsed in the fifth century. Muhammad introduced Islam to the world in AD 610. He rapidly conquered the Middle East by force with his new teachings, opposing every religion, especially Judaism and Christianity. Many were slaughtered, including at least 600 Jews in Medina and Mecca for not bowing the knee to Allah. The Muslims continued in the same spirit of death and destruction, taking advantage of the power vacuum in Israel and conquering and occupying Jerusalem and the Jewish land relatively easily.

The liberation of Palestine (Israel) by the Allied armies in 1917 was a major step in returning the Jews back and larger numbers began to return, drawn by God and driven by anti-Jewish behaviour from the likes of the Russian Czars and Hitler. Here again, God used foreign powers to free Israel and enable her people to return. Who knows what level the hatred will grow to today if the remainder of the Jews do not respond to God's word and return by their own choice? It is a big challenge for them. Living in Israel is difficult enough now, but in the years to come, returning there will become like jumping from the frying pan into the fire! However, God is at work and as their options are reduced, we will see them genuinely return to Him, resulting in their salvation in Jesus Christ! God is stirring the Church to pray for this.

God brought about an extraordinary change in the fortunes of Israel in just three years from the Nazi death camps at the end of the Second World War in 1945, to the re-establishment of the State of Israel in 1948. This second return will not only see her total re-establishment in the land but because we are at the end of the *"times of the Gentiles"* punishment it also heralds a time of glory that Jerusalem has never known before, not even under King David and King Solomon. God is making a way for Jesus her King to physically reign from there for a thousand years and bring with Him a time of unprecedented peace and prosperity!

Isaiah 11 informs us that there are two returns, namely the Babylonian one and the one we are witnessing today. A search of the Scriptures reveals there are no more than two. The current events fit all the aspects in prophecies regarding the second return, so we can be sure it is the final one. Some have thought that verse 11 *"the Lord will reach out his hand a second time"*, quoted below, refers to the return from Babylon with the first being from Egypt, but this does not stand up to investigation. God gave the whole of chapter 11 to encourage the Jewish nation that there was still hope after the devastating judgment that was about to befall them through the Babylonians conquering them and taking them into captivity:

> *"A shoot* [Jesus] *will come up from the stump of Jesse;*
> *from his roots a Branch* [Jesus] *will bear fruit.*

*The Spirit of the* LORD *will rest on him* [Jesus] –
  *the Spirit of wisdom and of understanding,*
  *the Spirit of counsel and of power,*
  *the Spirit of knowledge and of the fear of the* LORD –
*and he will delight in the fear of the* LORD . . .

**In that day** the Root of Jesse [Jesus] *will stand as a banner for the peoples; the nations will rally to him, and his place of rest will be glorious.* **In that day** *the Lord will reach out his hand* **a second time** *to reclaim the remnant that is left of his people from Assyria* [northern Iraq], *from Lower Egypt, from Upper Egypt, from Cush* [Ethiopia], *from Elam* [Persia], *from Babylonia, from Hamath* [Syria] *and from the islands of the sea* [everywhere else].

*He will raise a banner for the nations*
  *and gather the exiles of Israel;*
*he will assemble the scattered people of Judah*
  *from the four quarters of the earth."*

(Isaiah 11:1–3, 10–12, emphasis added)

It is clear from the following scripture that the root of David refers to Jesus:

*"The Lion of the tribe of Judah* [Jesus], *the Root of David, has triumphed. He is able to open the scroll and its seven seals."*

(Revelation 5:5)

And so the Root of Jesse, King David's father, in Isaiah 11:10, also refers to Jesus the Messiah:

Therefore, the verses in Isaiah 11 are all clearly speaking of Jesus and after His time on earth. This means the "second time" could not have occurred before Jesus came and so verse 10 cannot refer to the return from Babylon. Also, it was only the two southern tribes that came back from Babylon but the above verses say they returned *"from Assyria . . .", "the islands of the sea"* and *"the four quarters of the earth"*, meaning from around the world. This return we see today is from around the whole earth. These verses also say that the second return will be by all twelve tribes, comprising the ten northern tribes of Israel and the two southern tribes of Judah and Benjamin. Therefore, it is extremely clear on all counts that Isaiah is referring to the events we are witnessing.

Subsequent verses 13 to 16 also speak of events after Christ, which we are witnessing in our day. For example:

> *"Ephraim's jealousy will vanish,*
>     *and Judah's enemies will be cut off."*                      (Isaiah 11:13)

Judah would have nothing to do with Ephraim, one of the ten northern tribes, after the return from Babylon right through the time of Jesus and up to the second dispersion in AD 70, but this has now changed. The jealousy started when God tore the kingdom into two because of the disobedience of Solomon (1 Kings 11:29–40). The prophet Ahijah tore his new cloak into twelve pieces and prophesied that ten of the tribes, known as Israel, would be taken from the king and given to Jeroboam, the leader of Solomon's army.

> *"Take ten pieces for yourself, for this is what the LORD, the God of Israel, says: 'See, I am going to tear the kingdom out of Solomon's hand and give you [Jeroboam] ten tribes. But for the sake of my servant David and the city of Jerusalem, which I have chosen out of all the tribes of Israel, he [Solomon] will have one tribe [as well as Judah his own tribe].'"*
>                                                            (1 Kings 11:31–32)

Benjamin would be kept with Judah. This privileged position had nothing to do with their faithfulness but everything to do with God's faithfulness to David. Consequently, God only specifically restored the two southern tribes and their priests after the exile in Babylon. Israel had fallen into gross sin under Jeroboam, who made two golden calves to worship, so they were exiled but with no time-scale given for their return. Some of the northern tribes had come back by the time of Jesus but many from the first exile were still scattered to the north of Israel and only now are we seeing evidence of the second major regathering from the two dispersions. Jeremiah referred to the phenomenon we are seeing today – Jews from all the tribes of Israel returning not only from countries to the north but from all around the world. More and more of them are being converted today, which is the health and healing God wants the whole nation to experience in Christ and which is referred to in the following passage. God is fulfilling His Word in both the spiritual and natural realms.

> *"I will bring health and healing to it* [Jews in the nation of Israel coming to Christ]*; I will heal my people and will let them enjoy abundant peace and security. I will bring Judah and Israel back from captivity and will rebuild them as they were before. I will cleanse them from all the sins they have committed against me and will forgive all their sins of rebellion against me."*                                (Jeremiah 33:6–8)

Jews who became Christians in New Testament times dealt with their differences, as recorded in the Gospels and Acts, but it has taken many painful centuries for the jealousies to disappear from the remaining unsaved part of the nation. Unfortunately jealousy has been replaced with major divisions between Jews who are New Age, Humanist and Orthodox. Fundamental Muslims are turning up the heat against them and these diverse views among the Jews give rise to very different strategies in each group to deal with the situation. God will work everything around to fulfil His Word, resulting eventually in their widespread conversion to Christ!

We saw the beginnings of Isaiah 11:14–16 being worked out in the 1967 war, when the Israelites occupied the Gaza Strip, the West Bank and the Golan Heights. Although there has been a decision by the Israeli government to relinquish Gaza, this area was never properly conquered by the Israelites, not even by King

David! At some stage the situation will be reversed in Gaza and the land will also be taken to the east of the Dead Sea as well. Moses had given permission for the Reubenites, the Gadites and half of the tribe of Manasseh to settle there, so this may be considered as their land plus it would enable Israel to protect her borders against attacks from that region:

> *"They* [the Israelites] *will swoop down on the slopes*
>      *of Philistia* [Gaza] *to the west;*
>   *together they will plunder the people to the east.*
> *They will lay hands on Edom and Moab,*
>    *and the Ammonites* [all on the east side of the Jordan
>      and the Dead Sea], *will be subject to them."*          (Isaiah 11:14)

About two million Israelites left Egypt in the Exodus, around eighty-four thousand of the two southern tribes returned from Babylon, but nearly five million have returned in the current ingathering, with over one million alone from the former USSR. As prophesied, the Exodus has therefore been eclipsed by God drawing Jews back to their land in greater numbers in our time:

> *" 'The days are coming,' declares the LORD, 'when men will no longer say, "As surely as the LORD lives, who brought them out of Egypt," but they will say, "As surely as the LORD lives, who brought the Israelites up out of the land of the north and out of all the countries where he had banished them." For I will restore them to the land I gave to their forefathers. But now I will send for **many fishermen**,' declares the LORD, 'and they will catch them. After that I will send for many hunters, and they will hunt them down on every mountain and hill and from the crevices of the rocks.' "*          (Jeremiah 16:14–16, emphasis added)

Again, some say that the land of the north in this scripture refers to the return from Babylon, but Jeremiah says *"many fishermen"* are involved in helping them back. There were only a few men directing the two southern tribes back from Babylon, namely

Ezra, Zerubbabel and Nehemiah – a definite shortage of fisher-men, and so from this point alone it cannot relate to that time. On the other hand many people have been involved with helping the Jews return in our day.

So, in summary, because of the people's sin during the seventy-year exile, the further "seven times" punishment came into operation in 535 BC on their return from Babylon. I will explain its length of time in the next chapter. From the table in this chapter, we have a complete and accurate list of dates for the various events in the build-up of judgment, rather than the guesswork dates one normally sees in many publications. This will prove very instructive when we look at how God is working today in restoring the Jews back to the land. As a consequence of the "seven times" punishment, Israel had to continue without a king during this whole period of time. Their rejection of the lordship of Christ as a nation caused the second dispersion and as there are only two exiles and two ingatherings prophesied in the Bible, we are definitely seeing the second and last one in our day. However, there are many dreadful battles still to come before we reach the glorious conclusion of Jesus being enthroned in Jerusalem.

# PART 2

## *Israel – God's Clock*

# How Long Is a "Time"?

To understand further how God's dealings with the world revolve around Israel let us now look more closely at the duration of *"the times of the Gentiles"*. I requote the central verse of this book:

> *"They* [the Israelites] *will fall by the sword and will be taken as prisoners to all the nations. Jerusalem will be trampled on by the Gentiles until the* **times** *of the Gentiles are fulfilled."*
>
> (Luke 21:24, emphasis added)

As mentioned, many believe Jesus was describing the dispensation when Gentiles would come to a saving knowledge of God through faith in Jesus and that the word "times" has no special length. They confuse this verse with Paul's statement, which does indeed refer to the Gentiles receiving salvation:

> *"Israel has experienced a hardening in part until the full number* [literally, fullness in quality not numerical] *of the Gentiles has come in. And so all Israel will be saved."* (Romans 11:25–26)

Luke 21:24 has nothing to do with the salvation of the Gentiles. Jesus was talking about political issues and predicting that foreign occupation of the city would continue for many years, resulting in the death and dispersion of the Jewish nation. The Jews had been subject to Gentile kings since the Babylonians, with the brief exception of the Maccabean revolt against Antiochus IV, the last ruler over Israel in the twilight of the Greek Empire. The uprising produced a Jewish king but he soon capitulated to the irresistible Roman forces. Gentiles did not officially start coming to Christ until several years after His death when Peter preached the gospel to Cornelius' household.

Jesus was also clearly warning that there would be a second scattering of the Jews, necessitating a second return and restoration of Jerusalem. As discussed in the previous chapter, only two dispersions and two ingatherings are prophesied in the Old Testament, which is very important to see for today's situation, since it means they will never be scattered again!

But what does the word "time" actually mean when used in this context? The Holy Spirit first used it when He gave the Babylonian king a dream, describing him and his empire as a large and beautiful tree laden with fruit. It was to be cut down due to the king taking the glory to himself rather than accepting that it was God who had enabled him to conquer all the nations in the Middle East. Daniel had previously explained to the king that it was God who had enabled him to rule the then known world through the vision of the great statue:

> *"You, O king, are the king of kings. The God of heaven has given you dominion and power and might and glory; in your hands he has placed mankind and the beasts of the field and the birds of the air. Wherever they live, he has made you ruler over them all. You are that head of gold."*
> (Daniel 2:37–38)

God pronounced judgment on Nebuchadnezzar for his pride. The Lord said it would last for a specific period, which was described as *"seven times"*. Daniel said in the great tree vision:

> *"You, O king* [Nebuchadnezzar], *are the tree! You have become great and strong; your greatness has grown until it reaches the sky, and your*

*dominion extends to distant parts of the earth. You, O king, saw a messenger, a holy one, coming down from heaven and saying, 'Cut down the tree and destroy it, but leave the stump, bound with iron and bronze, in the grass of the field, while its roots remain in the ground. Let him be drenched with the dew of heaven; let him live like the wild animals, until* **seven times** *pass by for him.' This is the interpretation, O king, and this is the decree the Most High has issued against my lord the king: You will be driven away from people and will live with the wild animals; you will eat grass like cattle and be drenched with the dew of heaven.* **Seven times** *will pass by for you until you acknowledge that the Most High is sovereign over the kingdoms of men and gives them to anyone he wishes. The command to leave the stump of the tree with its roots means that your kingdom will be restored to you when you acknowledge that Heaven rules."*          (Daniel 4:22–26, emphasis added)

Daniel used the word *iddan* on each occasion for "times" in the phrase "seven times". He used it again in Daniel 7:25, quoted below.

*"He* [the Antichrist] *will speak against the Most High and oppress his saints and try to change the set times* [zeman] *and the laws. The saints will be handed over to him for a time* [iddan], *times* [iddanin] *and half a time* [iddanim].          (Daniel 7:25)

He used a different word *zeman* when he said "the set times". This latter word means "an appointed time or season" and refers to the Antichrist attempting to change both the religious calendar of the Jews and the Mosaic law just prior to Jesus' return. However, the same word *iddan* is employed for the phrase "time, times and half a time". *Iddan* is the singular, *iddanin* the plural, doubling the value, and *iddanim* the diminutive halving a time.

The New Testament repeats this unusual phrase in the book of Revelation. The visions given to the apostle John complement and expand many of the prophecies and pictures received by Daniel. It obviously refers to the same length of time.

> *"The woman was given the two wings of a great eagle, so that she might fly to the place prepared for her in the desert, where she would be taken care of for a time, times and half a time, out of the serpent's reach."*
>
> (Revelation 12:14)

The Greek scripture specifically states that the last part of the phrase is exactly "half a time". The length of this period is given earlier in verse 6:

> *"The woman fled into the desert to a place prepared for her by God, where she might be taken care of for 1,260 days."*

Dividing 1,260 days by three and a half shows that a "time" comprises 360 days. This is a special year, rather than the normal 365.25-day solar year. It is the first key point in understanding how God reckons times of judgment and it unlocks many scriptural conundrums. We now know from Daniel 4:24, quoted above, that Nebuchadnezzar lost his kingdom and ate grass for seven of these special 360-day judgment years, a total of 2,520 days.

The dates of Noah's flood provide more information on the length of a month during times of judgment.

> *"In the six hundredth year of Noah's life, on the seventeenth day of the second month – on that day all the springs of the great deep burst forth, and the floodgates of the heavens were opened. And the rain fell on the earth for forty days and forty nights."*          (Genesis 7:11–12)

> *"The water receded steadily from the earth. At the end of the hundred and fifty days the water had gone down, and on the seventeenth day of the seventh month the ark came to rest on the mountains of Ararat."*
>
> (Genesis 8:3–4)

These verses explain that the flood lasted five months, stated as 150 days, from the start of the rain to when the Ark came to rest on top of Mount Ararat. Each of these months was, therefore, thirty days long, which fits with the 360-day judgment year having months of thirty days, i.e. 12 × 30 = 360.

The principle of a seven times or sevenfold punishment is first seen in the Bible when God placed a mark on Cain to protect him:

> "If anyone kills Cain, he will suffer vengeance seven times over [or sevenfold]."                                    (Genesis 4:15)

Jesus continued this principle by teaching that seven more spirits would enter a man if he carried on sinning after forgiveness and deliverance.

> "When an evil spirit comes out of a man, it goes through arid places seeking rest and does not find it. Then it says, 'I will return to the house I left.' When it arrives, it finds the house swept clean and put in order. Then it goes and takes seven other spirits more wicked than itself, and they go in and live there. And the final condition of that man is worse than the first."                            (Luke 11:24–26)

This sevenfold punishment is the second point in understanding how God deals with sin. A third point regarding His perspective on time during periods of judgment is found in the "year for a day" principle. For instance, the Israelites were punished in the wilderness for forty years because they did not believe the good report that Joshua and Caleb gave. The judgment was based on a year for each of the forty days the spies were in the land.

> "For forty years – one year for each of the forty days you explored the land – you will suffer for your sins and know what it is like to have me against you."                                (Numbers 14:34)

As explained in chapter 5 God repeated four times in Leviticus that punishment for the Jewish nation would be increased sevenfold or seven times if His word was not obeyed (Leviticus 26:18, 21, 24, 28). He also judged Nebuchadnezzar for a period of seven times, which I have shown to be 2,520 days (Daniel 4). But the punishment of Israel could not have been just 2,520 days, as the Gentiles have ruled over Israel for more than two millennia. We find God actually implemented a 2,520-year punishment, using the "year for a day" principle.

The biblical principle of the punishment fitting the crime is also seen here. Jesus said it would be more bearable for Sodom and Gomorrah on the day of judgment than for those towns that rejected the power ministries of Jesus and His apostles. These people had seen God's strength demonstrated, the sick being healed and the dead being raised (Matthew 10:1–16 etc.). Likewise, the punishment of the Jews was greater than the 2,520 days of Nebuchadnezzar (Daniel 4:22–37), because they had seen far more of God's power – for example during their deliverance from Egypt, their time in the wilderness when they received daily manna from heaven, through the conquering of the promised land with the destruction of Jericho etc., as well as God's supernatural intervention down through the centuries. The Babylonian king saw Daniel's deliverance from the fiery furnace, which was relatively little compared to the amount that the Jewish nation witnessed.

To summarize:

1. God uses the period called a "time" during judgment – a 360-day year, consisting of twelve months, each thirty days long.
2. God also employs a sevenfold judgment where applicable.
3. When judgment is pronounced in terms of days, one has to ascertain from the context, whether the Lord means them to be calculated in days or years.

# How Has God Applied the Seven Times Punishment?

After much investigation, I have discovered that God used this period like a ruler of fixed length of time in His dealings with Israel. One end marks the most significant dates in the build up and execution of His judgment against her, and the other end marks a parallel series of the most important dates in her restoration. It sheds further light on the vision of the multiplication sign God gave me when I was first in Israel and started me on this study. One note of caution, however. This 2,520-year measuring rod can only be applied to events directly involving the Babylonians, which are from 625 BC when the first king Nabopolassar of the New Babylonian Empire came to the throne, to 586 BC when his son Nebuchadnezzar destroyed Jerusalem and the Temple. It was this ruthless empire which God raised up to punish Judah and Benjamin – hence my calling it the "Babylonian Time Ruler". This warning came through Habakkuk:

> "I am raising up the Babylonians,
>> that ruthless and impetuous people . . .
> O LORD, you have appointed them to execute judgment;
>> O Rock, you have ordained them to punish."    (Habakkuk 1:6, 12)

To appreciate fully how the years correlate between the punishment and restoration of Israel, it is important to remember the point made in chapter 6, namely that the Babylonians differentiated between the accession year and the first full year of each new king. I am using the table of dates established in that chapter to demonstrate the methodical way that God is restoring Israel today.

## The 2,520-Year Babylonian Time Ruler

### *Stage 1: 625 BC – accession of Nabopolassar*

**625 BC + 2,520 years = AD 1896**

Nabopolassar's reign commenced in 625 BC, starting the great Neo Babylonian Empire. Habakkuk's words, quoted above, referred to the raising up of this kingdom, and Jeremiah later confirmed them when he informed the Jews that the king's son, Nebuchadnezzar, was to attack Jerusalem:

> *"I will make you* [the High Priest in Solomon's Temple] *a terror to yourself and to all your friends; with your own eyes you will see them* [the Israelites] *fall by the sword of their enemies. I will hand all Judah over to the king of Babylon* [Nebuchadnezzar], *who will carry them away to Babylon or put them to the sword."* (Jeremiah 20:4)

> *"Therefore the* LORD *Almighty says this: 'Because you have not listened to my words, I will summon all the peoples of the north and my servant Nebuchadnezzar King of Babylon,' declares the* LORD, *'and I will bring them against this land and all the surrounding nations.'"* (Jeremiah 25:8–9)

Add the "time ruler" of 2,520 years to this date and it comes to 1896 AD. In this year, the prominent Hungarian Jewish leader, Theodor Herzl, published his book *Der Judenstaat* (*The Jewish State*). Being a socialist secular Jew, his vision was of a political rather than a spiritual solution to anti-Semitism. At least he saw that social integration into other societies would not work and that a homeland of their own was the answer. He is reported to have had a dream at twelve years of age, in which he saw an old but regal man say to him, "I have raised you up that you might be the means of bringing My people together from the ends of the earth." No doubt this helped form his answer to the Jewish dispersion. He even discussed his vision with German Emperor Wilhelm II of the Second Reich (AD 1701 – AD 1918) and Sultan Abdal Hamid II of the Ottoman Empire in Turkey, who ruled Israel at that time. Not unsurprisingly his ideas fell on deaf ears but the British government did initially suggest Uganda as a possibility! This was rejected by the Zionist Congress, which advocated Israel. Referring back to the vision the Lord gave me of the flattened multiplication sign, 1896 heralded the beginning of the restoration line commencing from bottom left ascending to top right.

### Stage 2: 624 BC – Nabopolassar's first official year
**624 BC + 2,520 years = AD 1897**
624 BC was the first full official year of King Nabopolassar. 2,520 years later, in AD 1897, came the second step in Israel's restoration when Theodore Herzl chaired the first International Zionist Conference in Basle, Switzerland. The object was to discuss how the Jews could set up a Zionist state. Herzl wrote prophetically, "In Basle I founded the Jewish State!"

### Stage 3: 605 BC – accession of Nebuchadnezzar
**605 BC + 2,520 years = AD 1916**
King Nabopolassar died in 605 BC and his son Nebuchadnezzar came to power. The first two years of his reign reveal more significant steps in the judgment and restoration of Israel. He came against Jerusalem in his accession year, capturing the initial group of Jews and took them into exile. He left King Jehoiakim as a puppet on the throne in Jerusalem.

In AD 1916, 2,520 years later, the Sykes-Picot Agreement was drawn up between Britain and France on the apportionment of the Ottoman Empire, which was finally conquered by the Allied armies a year later. It was decided that Israel would come under British rule.

### Stage 4: 604 BC – Nebuchadnezzar's first official year
**604 BC + 2,520 years = AD 1917**

604 BC was Nebuchadnezzar's first official year on the throne. Jehoiakim rebelled against the Babylonian king, who replaced him with his son Jehoiakin. 2,520 years later, in AD 1917, two major events took place in the history of Israel:

1.  The British Government made the famous "Balfour Declaration of Intent", working towards establishing a Jewish state. It stated:

    > "His Majesty's Government views with favour the establishment in Palestine of a national home for the Jewish people and will use their best endeavours to facilitate the achievement of this objective, it being clearly understood that nothing shall be done which may prejudice the civic and religious rights of existing non Jewish communities in Palestine, or the rights and political status enjoyed by Jews in any other country."

    (2nd November 1917)

2.  A month later on 11th December 1917, General Allenby of the British Army, a Christian man, led the liberation of Jerusalem and the rest of Israel from Turkish Islamic rule. The Allies also took land to the east of the River Jordan, which was later to be called Jordan. These two countries came under British jurisdiction by rightful conquest. The Turks had sided with Germany and were the protagonists, consequently forfeiting their right to the land. God had used the First World War to free Israel from Islamic domination and make her a British Protectorate.

The League of Nations ratified the Balfour Declaration in 1922 and gave Britain the Mandate to rule Israel. Although this stipulated that Jews should be free to return to their land, the

British authorities unlawfully stopped Jewish immigration for fear of their oil interests and the violence of the extreme Muslims. However, the Arabs were allowed unhindered access into Israel from Jordan and the other surrounding countries!

### Stage 5: 588 BC – last two-year siege of Jerusalem
**588 BC + 2,520 years = AD 1933**

588 BC saw the beginning of the last major attack on Jerusalem, which lasted two years. 2,520 years later in 1933 Hitler came to power as Chancellor of Germany. God used his evil anti-Semitic agenda to uproot the Jews from Europe, where they had been established for over 1,000 years. In that year, Hitler set up the first labour camps and removed constitutional protection against arbitrary arrest, thus opening the way for the Gestapo to do their worst. He began to ostracise Jews, along with other social outcasts such as gypsies and the mentally ill. A small number of Jews had returned to Israel during the few hundred years before Hitler, but nowhere near enough for God's promises about their promised return as a nation to have been fulfilled. Tragically, despite much anti-Jewishness over the centuries, the continued hardness of their hearts to God has meant that the vast majority still do not understand His word on the matter of their return to the land, let alone His salvation in Christ. Paradoxically, anti-Zionism has actually served to keep the Jews a separate and distinct people. All things are indeed servants of the Lord!

### Stage 6: 586 BC – destruction of Jerusalem
**586 BC + 2,520 years = AD 1935**

The last major step of judgment by the Babylonians came two years later when Jerusalem finally fell and was destroyed in 586 BC. The Bible very clearly states that the city, including the Temple, was torched in the nineteenth year of Nebuchadnezzar's reign (2 Kings 25:8–12). This is a pivotal date on which all the secular historians and Bible scholars agree.

2,520 years later in 1935, the Nuremberg Laws were passed

which withdrew citizenship from the Jews in Germany. This terrible unjustifiable act against the Jewish people was used by God to restore them to Israel. Hitler, guided by Satan, had meant it for horrendous evil but God used it for ultimate good. The Second World War had shaken the very foundations of Jewry in Europe and started the big push to return to Israel.

During the time of Jesus, the Jews were under the Romans but at least they were in the land. Their sins were not great enough to warrant a further exile until their rejection of the Messiah. This opened the door for further satanic attack, resulting in the overthrow of Jerusalem and the second dispersion in AD 70. As explained, the punishment period of Leviticus 26:18 was still in force and because they continued to reject Jesus, even in their exile, the punishments escalated to the eventual unimaginable diabolical tragedies of the mass extermination camps in Europe, for which Satan, his demons and human henchmen will pay dearly. The Law clearly warned the Jews of what God would do:

*"You will perish among the nations; the land of your enemies will devour you. Those of you who are left will waste away in the lands of their enemies because of their sins; also because of their father's sins they will waste away. But if they will confess their sins and the sins of their fathers – their treachery against me and their hostility towards me, which made me hostile towards them so that I sent them into the land of their enemies – then when their uncircumcised hearts are humbled and they pay for their sin, I will remember my covenant with Jacob and my covenant with Isaac and my covenant with Abraham, and I will remember the land. For the land will be deserted by them and will enjoy its sabbaths while it lies desolate without them. They will pay for their sins because they rejected my laws [Mosaic] and abhorred my decrees. Yet in spite of this, when they are in the land of their enemies, I will not reject them or abhor them so as to destroy them completely, breaking my covenant with them. I am the* LORD *their God. But for their sake I will remember the covenant with their ancestors whom I brought out of Egypt in the sight of the nations to be their God. I am the* LORD.*"*                          (Leviticus 26:38–45)

The Lord had to wait for this great Seven Times judgment period to end, but on its completion He was once again able to apply that part of the covenant made to Abraham to bring the Jews back to their land. While they were in exile, God wanted as many of them as possible to come to Christ, and some did. Today, even though they continue to reject Jesus as a nation, God remains faithful to His word, as spoken through Ezekiel:

> *"This is what the sovereign LORD says: It is not for your sake, O house of Israel, that I am going to do these things, but for the sake of my holy name, which you have profaned among the nations where you have gone. I will show the holiness of my great name, which has been profaned among the nations, the name you have profaned among them. Then the nations will know that I am the LORD, declares the Sovereign LORD, when I show myself holy through you before their eyes. For I will take you out of the nations; I will gather you from all the countries and bring you back into your own land. I will sprinkle clean water on you, and you will be clean; I will cleanse you from all your impurities* [in Christ] *and from all your idols. I will give you a new heart and put a new spirit in you; I will remove from you your heart of stone and give you a heart of flesh. And I will put my Spirit in you and move you to follow my decrees and be careful to keep my laws* [of Christ]. *You will live in the land I gave your forefathers; you will be my people, and I will be your God."*
>
> (Ezekiel 36:22–28)

We are witnessing the Lord acting on the above promise – *"I will take you out of the nations, I will gather you from all the countries and bring you into your own land."* The nations are going to see just how Almighty the Lord is through an awesome restoration of Israel, which will be for the sake of the Lord's holy name. These verses must, of course, now be read in the light of the New Covenant. It is the law of Christ, which God will put in their hearts, not the law of Moses.

Just as God took deliberate steps to judge the two southern tribes with their eventual removal from the land, so He is taking equally methodical steps to restore them back to the Promised Land. And to demonstrate His amazing ability, He has arranged for the most significant events in their judgment and restoration, to be 2,520 years apart. By grace He also included the ten northern tribes in this second restoration. God said in Daniel 12:9 that the end-time prophecies would be sealed up until they were about to happen. He is revealing them now because He is bringing world events to a conclusion.

I firmly believe all these steps of restoration are what God was referring to in the vision of the two lines crossing each other. However, I have only understood the detail as He has opened up the Scriptures to me over these last thirty years.

Although God used the Babylonian Empire to punish Judah, He still held the Babylonians accountable for their own sin and in turn brought judgment against them through the Persians. He does not forget any evil action against Israel, or any other nation, down through the centuries. All will be punished sooner or later.

### A second "Time Ruler"

The execution of God's judgment described in Leviticus 26 resulted initially in the seventy-year Babylonian captivity. Their continued rebellion even whilst under foreign rule, added the extra "seven times", or 2,520 years, to the end of the exile in 535 BC. These two periods total 2,590 years and cover all the years when foreigners ruled the Jews and gives rise to a second "Time Ruler". The empires involved in this one were the Babylonians, Persians, Greeks, Romans, Muslims from Mecca, Roman Catholic Crusaders taking Jerusalem, Muslim Turks and finally the British who liberated them. But, as previously explained, God considers lengths of judgment in years of 360 days. So, He sees each of the 2,590 solar years in terms of 360 days, not 365.24 days, which produces a period of 2,552 whole judgment years (omitting the decimal place). The calculation is:

**70 yrs under Babylon + 2,520 yrs under other kings = 2,590 yrs**
But considered by God as judgment years:

$$\frac{2,590 \times 360 \text{ days in a judgment year}}{365.24 \text{ days in a solar year}}$$

**= 2,552 whole years – the times of the Gentiles**

This 2,552 years is the total number of years, which Jesus referred to as the *"times of the Gentiles"* (Luke 21:24).

When this period is applied to the years in which the three most important judgments were brought against Judah, the three most significant dates in her restoration are revealed. The first is the initial attack on Jerusalem in 605 BC, when the seventy years of exile commenced. The second is the catastrophic destruction of Jerusalem and Temple in 586 BC. The third is the beginning of the additional 2,520 years of punishment under foreign rule at the end of the exile, in 535 BC. The calculations are:

**605 BC + 2,552 times of the Gentiles = 1948**
The exile in Babylon began in 605 BC, when Nebuchadnezzar became king and first attacked Jerusalem, deporting many of the nobles, including Daniel, and some of the Temple treasures (Daniel 1:1–2). Adding 2,552 years brings us to 1948, the year the state of Israel was reborn! Coincidence? I believe not. God knew that Israel had received all her punishments in full by the end of the First World War in 1945 and moved swiftly to keep His word and restore her to the land. This year of 1948 is of extreme importance in that it is the start of the fulfilment of Jesus' words prophesied in Luke 21:24 – that the times of the Gentiles would eventually end. The fig tree needed first to be replanted in the right soil to grow!

**586 BC + 2,552 times of the Gentiles = 1967**
Adding this same time period to the second major judgment in 586 BC, the year Jerusalem was destroyed by the Babylonians,

comes to 1967. In this year, during the Six-Day War, Israel retook Jerusalem, including the Temple site, the West Bank, Gaza and the Golan Heights – her historic borders. She also captured Sinai, but gave it back as part of the Camp David Accords in 1970. The Israeli army commander, Moshe Dayan, a secular Jew, had no problem in handing the Temple site back to the Muslims rather than hand it to the religious Jews. The government still continues to leave the everyday running of the site to the Muslims.

### 535 BC + 2,552 times of the Gentiles = 2018?

The last of the "big three" stages of punishment occurred in 535 BC when the Persians and Medes conquered the Babylonians and took over ruling the Jews, decreeing that they could return to Jerusalem. I believe it is legitimate to add the 2,552 years to 535 BC as well as the two other years, as this measuring rod includes the seventy years of Babylonian rule plus all the years the other empires dominated Israel. This raises an extremely controversial issue, namely the year of total restoration of sovereignty to Israel.

As a committed evangelical – one who takes the Bible as God's literal Word, I have wrestled with this, since I have been led to believe we do not know the year of Jesus' return. Many sects have tried and predictably failed because they are manipulated by deceiving spirits. But is this a holy cow to be slaughtered in Christian circles? His disciples asked Him when the kingdom would be restored after His resurrection:

> " 'Lord, are you at this time going to restore the kingdom to Israel?' He said to them: 'It is not for you to know the times or dates the Father has set.' "                                                      (Acts 1:6–7)

Firstly, I have discovered that the original Greek does not actually say "dates" but "seasons", which means a short number of months. Secondly, the Lord had told Daniel that believers at the end of the age would have his visions opened up to them, so they would understand the season in which they lived. This leads to the conclusion that although Jesus was speaking to His present-day disciples, He was also referring to all generations except those living in the end-times – that's us! This is confirmed by 1 Thessalonians 5:5 which says *"you are all sons of the light"*, so we are to be aware of what is happening. Thirdly, Jesus said in Matthew 24:36, that it was not for us to know either the day or the hour but He did not say we wouldn't know the year! Whichever way, I cannot in all good conscience ignore this year of AD 2018 but submit it to the saints for weighing and judging as to its significance.

> **May I stress that this date of 2018 is not a prophecy but a conclusion drawn from understanding the length of a "time", the sevenfold punishment and the "day for a year" principle and adding these to the seventy years of the exile. God meticulously applied this second time period of 2,552 years to both 605 BC and 586 BC, ending in 1948 and 1967 respectively. These two years of greatest significance confirm all the previous calculations to be correct, but will 2018 be marked with a major event?**

If 2,552 years can be legitimately added to the third major judgment date of 535 BC, the inescapable conclusion from the above argument is that 2018 is the year when all things are restored to Israel and every aftereffect of the *"times of the Gentiles"* will be removed. This must involve the end of Jerusalem being trampled on by the Gentiles. The Father has seen in His foreknowledge that the nation will eventually put her trust in Jesus as Messiah (Romans 11:26), thus enabling Him to fulfil all the promises made to her. Israel will be internationally recognised as a Messianic nation with all the land under her control and Jerusalem her capital. We will see the Son of David take the throne in Israel! This of course, is Jesus, born King of the Jews, who was raised from the dead as King of kings and Lord of lords.

This date must also be seen in the light of other scriptures which need to be fulfilled before His return, such as the Antichrist reintroducing Temple sacrifice and all the nations being reached for Christ etc., see chapter 9. If sacrifice is restarted in AD 2011, which would be the beginning of the seven-year tribulation, we will definitely know that 2018 is the year of the Lord's return. These points need to be weighed very carefully and I believe the Holy Spirit will make the scriptures crystal clear as we move into the last years.

If you would like to check the additions of the 2,520 and 2,552 year periods from BC to AD, please be sure to take into account that there is no zero year between BC and AD. Julius Caesar, in 45 BC, introduced the solar calendar from which we work today, with the start of his reign being year 1. Quite reasonably, the Catholic Church decided to take the birth of Jesus as the beginning of our dating system, but the Western world did not understand the concept of a zero year at the time of decision. The birth of Jesus was therefore set at 1 BC, rather than 0 and it remains the same to this day. So, to calculate the number of years from 568 BC to AD 1967 we have to adjust for the lack of year zero:

**Add the two periods and subtract 1 year:**
> **Step 1: 586 BC + AD 1967 = 2,553 years**
> **Step 2: 2,553 − 1 = 2,552 years**

Some Christians have a problem with taking biblical numbers literally but God is actually a stickler for detail, including numbers. You have only to look at nature to see His staggering mathematical genius in creation. He is perfect and does things meticulously and mathematically. The Bible is packed with numerical information and we even have a whole book called Numbers!

Whichever way events work out, the run up to His return will be very traumatic. It is described as Jacob's Trouble, the like of which has never been seen:

" 'This is what the LORD, the God of Israel, says: "Write in a book all the words I have spoken to you. The days are coming," declares the LORD, "when I will bring my people Israel and Judah back from captivity and restore them to the land I gave to their forefathers to possess," says the LORD.'

These are the words the LORD spoke concerning Israel and Judah: 'This is what the LORD says:

"Cries of fear are heard –
    terror not peace.
Ask and see:
    Can a man bear children?
Then why do I see every strong man
    with his hands on his stomach
        like a woman in labour,
    every face turned deathly pale?
How awful that day will be!
    None will be like it.
It will be a time of trouble for Jacob,
    but he will be saved out of it.
In that day," declares the LORD Almighty,
    "I will break the yoke off their necks
and will tear off their bonds;
    no longer will foreigners enslave them.
Instead, they will serve the LORD their God
    and David their king,
    whom I will raise up for them . . .
I am with you and will save you,"
    declares the LORD.
"Though I completely destroy all the nations
    among which I scatter you,
    I will not completely destroy you.
I will discipline you but only with justice;
    I will not let you go entirely unpunished." ' "

(Jeremiah 30:2–9, 11)

Jeremiah makes it clear in his next chapter that this will all occur in the time of the New Covenant (Jeremiah 31:31). As previously mentioned ,Zechariah says:

> *"A day of the LORD is coming when your plunder will be divided among you. I will gather all the nations to Jerusalem to fight against it; the city will be captured, the houses ransacked, and the women raped. Half of the city will go into exile, but the rest of the people will not be taken from the city. Then the LORD will go out and fight against those nations, as he fights in the day of battle. On that day his feet will stand on the Mount of Olives, east of Jerusalem, and the Mount of Olives will be split in two from east to west, forming a great valley, with half the mountain moving north and half moving south. You will flee by my mountain valley, for it will extend to Azel. You will flee as you as you fled from the earthquake in the days of Uzziah king of Judah."*                    (Zechariah 14:1–5)

Jesus referred to these tribulations in Matthew 24:21. But, praise God, it will also be a time of great supernatural blessing for believers, both Jew and Gentile, enabling them to minister the gospel and withstand the persecution even at the expense of their lives. The Body of Christ will be reaching *"maturity, attaining to the whole measure of the fullness of Christ"* by then (Ephesians 4:13). On the other hand, it will be even more terrible for unbelievers as God pours out His wrath on those who stubbornly resist His salvation in Christ.

These sums in this book are not just a mathematical nicety. They have the hallmark of the Almighty Creator woven right through them and demonstrate that God is running circles around the efforts of men and Satan to thwart His purposes, but in no way violating the absolute free will of man. The calculations confirm all the other dates and patterns shown elsewhere in this study, revealing clear and direct links between Israel's judgment and her current and final restoration by the Almighty.

# The Temple and the Antichrist

Some ask, "What on earth is the point of rebuilding the Temple? The Church is now the temple of God; it is pointless to rebuild a stone one!" I agree wholeheartedly, but the Bible does say the Temple will be there at the end time! It will, therefore, have to be rebuilt, though definitely not at God's instigation as was the case when the Jews came back from the Babylonian captivity. This requires an in-depth investigation to undermine the plethora of wrong understandings on the subject. So, let us look at the relevant verses, which also reveals more information on God's timing for the Jews in the past and in the last years before Jesus returns.

Jesus spoke about the Temple while teaching in its outer courts in the week before His crucifixion. Luke records Him saying to the crowds:

> *"As for what you see here, the time will come when not one stone will be left on another; every one of them will be thrown down."* (Luke 21:6)

He went on to say:

> *"When you see Jerusalem being surrounded by armies, you will know that its desolation is near. Then let those who are in Judea flee to the mountains, let those in the city get out, and let those in the country not*

> *enter the city. For this is the time of punishment in fulfilment of all that*
> *has been written. How dreadful it will be in those days for pregnant*
> *women and nursing mothers! There will be great distress in the land and*
> *wrath against this people. They will fall by the sword and will be taken*
> *as prisoners to all the nations. Jerusalem will be trampled on by the*
> *Gentiles until the times of the Gentiles are fulfilled."* (Luke 21:20–24)

As usual, God was giving forewarning of impending disaster to
those who would listen regarding the implementation of the
punishments detailed in Leviticus 26:25–29. Many believers in
AD 70, both Jews and Gentiles, took heed of these words and fled
after hearing the awful news that the Roman army under general
Titus was quelling all rebellion in Israel. Those who fled
mercifully escaped the sword and the destruction of Jerusalem.
However, a large number of unbelieving Jews ignored the words
of Jesus and fought to the bitter end. The city, including the
Temple, was completely destroyed in the carnage. The Leviticus
punishments had built up once more against the Jews since their
return from Babylon because of their continued national refusal
to accept Jesus as Messiah. They had even said to Pilate:

> *"Let his* [Jesus'] *blood be on us and on our children."*
>
> (Matthew 27:25)

However, Jesus asked the Father to forgive that generation who
killed Him but the next generation paid the price for it by the
Roman legions marching on Jerusalem. Luke went on to outline
the end-time events and from the same discourse Matthew also
records the Temple being levelled to the ground:

> *"I tell you the truth, not one stone here will be left on another; every one*
> *will be thrown down."*                    (Matthew 24:2)

But he referred later in the chapter to a desecration of the Temple
at the end of this age:

*"Because of the increase of wickedness, the love of most will grow cold, but he who stands firm until the end will be saved. And this gospel of the kingdom will be preached in the whole world as a testimony to all nations, and then the end will come. So when, you see standing in the holy place* [an inner court of the Temple], *'the abomination that causes desolation' spoken of through the prophet Daniel* [Daniel 9:27] – *let the reader understand – then let those who are in Judea flee to the mountains. Let no-one on the roof of his house go down to take anything out of the house. Let no-one in the field go back to get his cloak. How dreadful it will be in those days for pregnant women and nursing mothers! Pray that your flight will not take place in winter or on the Sabbath. For then there will be great distress, unequalled from the beginning of the world until now – **and never to be equalled again**. If those days had not been cut short, no-one would survive, but for the sake of the elect those days will be shortened. At that time if anyone says to you, 'Look, here is the Christ!' or, 'There he is!' do not believe it. For false Christs and false prophets will appear and perform great signs and miracles to deceive even the elect – if that were possible."*

(Matthew 24:12–24, emphasis added)

Many theologians who uphold Replacement Theology, believe that the abomination (verse 15) happened when Jerusalem and the Temple were destroyed by Titus in AD 70. Luke says the Temple would be destroyed followed by a lengthy period when the Jews would be dispersed around the world until the *"times of the Gentiles"* were concluded; whereas Matthew clearly states that the Antichrist's defilement of the Temple is near the return of Jesus. Although there was much tribulation at the time of the Roman slaughter, the unequalled distress that Matthew records in verse 21 did not occur at this time. The Jews have tragically endured further massacres since Titus, culminating in the Holocaust, when Hitler systematically murdered six million of them. The context of Matthew's account of the Temple therefore is definitely at the end time, when the gospel will be preached to all nations (verse 14), false Christs will appear with signs and wonders, and the love of most will grow cold. Verse 22 states that the last days will be shortened for the sake of the elect. The opposite actually happened in AD 70, as Titus waited for some time to give the Jews opportunity to surrender.

Josephus, a Jewish historian who lived through the destruction of Jerusalem, and who negotiated between Titus and the Jewish leaders, records that Titus razed and burnt the Temple to the ground. The Roman general had no desire to kill and destroy the whole of Jerusalem, so after demolishing the two north walls of the city, he offered an amnesty to those who would surrender. Some gave themselves up but most resisted, so he destroyed the remainder as well as the last stronghold, the Temple, with great loss of life. He records that Roman standard flags were erected outside the burning Temple and their own sacrifices were made on the Temple platform in celebration of the destruction. As Josephus was of the current priestly family, he would have made more of this, had it been the defilement of the Temple as prophesied in Daniel 9:27, and to which Jesus was referring in Matthew 24:15, quoted above. Daniel said the abomination would be set up in the Holy Place, i.e. inside the inner courts next to the Holy of Holies, not on the platform which is the outer court. Also, Titus actually stopped the Jewish Temple sacrifice, whereas Daniel 9:27 predicts the person *"to come"* will re-introduce it and then abolish it. Therefore, Matthew's Temple desecration is yet to happen.

Jesus' instructions to believers on both occasions were to evacuate the city. On the second occasion, due in the next few years, it will not only be to avoid the fighting but also the earthquake, which will split Jerusalem in two when He returns to sort the whole situation out.

> *"I* [God] *will gather all the nations to Jerusalem to fight against it; the city will be captured, the houses ransacked, and the women raped. Half of the city will go into exile, but the rest of the people will not be taken from the city. Then the* LORD *will go out and fight against those nations,*

*as he fights in the day of battle. On that day his feet will stand on the Mount of Olives, east of Jerusalem, and the Mount of Olives will be split in two from east to west, forming a great valley, with half the mountain moving north and half moving south."* (Zechariah 14:2–4)

Jesus continued explaining the events:

*"For as the lightning comes from the east and is visible even in the west, so will be the coming of the Son of Man . . . Immediately after the distress of those days*

> *'the sun will be darkened,*
> > *and the moon will not give its light;*
> *the stars will fall from the sky,*
> > *and the heavenly bodies will be shaken.'*

*At that time the sign of the Son of Man will appear in the sky, and all the nations of the earth will mourn. They will see the Son of Man coming on the clouds of the sky, with power and great glory. And he will send his angels with a loud trumpet call, and they will gather his elect from the four winds, from one end of the heavens to the other."*

(Matthew 24:27, 29–31)

The revelation of Jesus to all mankind happens at His return, along with the resurrection of the dead in Christ and the subsequent rapture. It will then be too late for those who have not believed and have the mark of the Beast.

Paul also taught that there would be a Temple at the end time where the Antichrist would enthrone himself as God! He wrote:

*"Concerning the coming of our Lord Jesus Christ and our being gathered to him, we ask you, brothers, not to become easily unsettled or alarmed by some prophecy, report or letter supposed to have come from us, saying that the day of the Lord has already come. Don't let anyone deceive you in any way, for that day will not come until the rebellion occurs and the man of lawlessness is revealed, the man doomed to destruction. He will*

*oppose and will exalt himself over everything that is called God or is worshipped, so that he sets himself up in God's temple, proclaiming himself to be God."* (2 Thessalonians 2:1–4)

Although there is no such building in Jerusalem at the moment, only the Dome of the Rock, which is certainly not God's Temple, I believe there soon will be!

Paul was raising an extremely important point that the "man of lawlessness" must first appear before Jesus Christ returns. The leaders of the Reformation, quite understandably, thought the murderous attacks by the various Popes against Christians who refused the unbiblical Catholic teachings, were what Paul was describing. They thought the Church, the spiritual Temple, had been invaded and defiled by men who accepted Catholic doctrines. They were indeed antichrists, but not the final man of lawlessness. Only true born-again believers make up the spiritual Temple of God whether they are from Catholic or Protestant ranks.

Some say the Temple in these scriptures refers to some New Age building, but as it is referred to as the Temple of God, it cannot be from a non-Jewish or non-Christian religious group. These ideas are not tenable. No, the straightforward interpretation is that it refers to a Temple made of stone, which will be rebuilt by the Jews, without God's instruction, and will be used by the Antichrist for his own enthronement! One assumes the "man of lawlessness" will initially present himself as saviour of the Jews, but his true colours will be revealed during the Tribulation. Revelation 11:1 says that there will be many Jews who will offer their worship to God in the new Temple, not understanding the true motives of the Antichrist. I believe when his actual intentions are revealed and the situation becomes clear, all Israel will turn to Christ.

*"I was given a reed like a measuring rod and was told, 'Go and measure the temple of God and the altar and count the worshippers there.'"*

(Revelation 11:1)

Jesus said in Matthew 24:15 that the desecration of the Temple referred to in Daniel 9:27, quoted on the next page, had yet to happen. Despite this, some believe that Antiochus IV Epiphanes, who ruled during the last years of the divided Greek Empire long before Jesus' birth, fulfilled the prophecy. His abomination was in 168 BC, and the previous chapter in Daniel 8:23–25 refers to it. Daniel 8:21 specifically mentions the King of Greece, who turned out to be Alexander the Great. Verse 22 says the kingdom would be divided into four, which happened after Alexander's death when the empire was split between his four top generals. One died in battle, another was assassinated, the third took Egypt and the area to the south of Israel and the fourth, Antiochus I Seleucius, took the area comprising Israel, Syria, Babylon, Susiana, Media and Persia to rule. It was his fourth generation descendant, the infamous Antiochus IV Epiphanes, who desecrated the temple in 168 BC, so fulfilling the abomination prophesied in Daniel 8:9–12. He laid siege to Jerusalem, forbidding Temple sacrifice and setting up his own god Zeus in the Holy of Holies, sacrificing unclean animals. But he never confirmed a covenant with the Jews, as required by Daniel's 9:27 prophecy.

Daniel's visions of these future empires were so amazingly accurate that secular historians are convinced that someone else must have written them after the events, and then wrongly attributed them to him! But we Christians know who the Author is and to whom and when they were revealed!

The Muslims conquered Jerusalem in AD 638 and later began building the Dome of the Rock on the Temple site, but they too did not confirm a covenant with Israel or reintroduce Temple sacrifice. Therefore, neither Antiochus, Titus nor the Muslims were the fulfilment of this prophetic word.

Knowing that there is a further Temple yet to be built helps us understand Daniel's prophecy regarding Jerusalem and the Temple. The angel Gabriel spoke to Daniel when he was in exile in Babylon and gave an overview of the complete future of Jerusalem in a time scale of seventy weeks (Daniel 9:24–27), quoted below. It starts from the year of the command to rebuild the walls of Jerusalem by the sixth Persian King Artaxerxes I, and finishes at the second advent of Jesus when we know that He will cast the Antichrist, *"the one who causes desolations"*, into the lake of fire (Revelation 19:20). The original Hebrew literally says this period spans seventy *shabua* or sevens, meaning seventy weeks, totalling 490 days. Because all these events did not happen within this number of days, God meant them to be taken on a "year for a day" basis, meaning 490 years (see Numbers 14:34).

> *"Seventy 'sevens'* [490 years] *are decreed for your people and your holy city to finish transgression, to put an end to sin, to atone for wickedness, to bring in everlasting righteousness, to seal up vision and prophecy and to anoint the most holy. Know and understand this: from the issuing of the decree to restore and rebuild Jerusalem* [the walls by Nehemiah, not the Temple by Ezra, which was before] *until the Anointed One, the ruler, comes, there will be seven 'sevens',* [49 days – 49 years] *and sixty-two 'sevens'* [434 days – 434 years]. *It will be rebuilt with streets and a trench, but in times of trouble. After the sixty-two 'sevens'* [434 days – 434 years], *the Anointed One will be cut off and will have nothing. The people of the ruler who will come will destroy the city and the sanctuary* [Temple]. *The end will come like a flood: War will continue until the end, and desolations have been decreed. He will confirm a covenant with many for one 'seven'* [7 days – 7 years]. *In the middle of the 'seven' he will put an end to sacrifice and offering. And on a wing of the temple he will set up an abomination that causes desolation, until the end that is decreed is poured out on him."* (Daniel 9:24–27)

Let us look at each verse individually:

**Verse 24**. This 490 years prophecy is divided into three parts – 49 years, 434 years and 7 years. Although the Temple was rebuilt on their return from Babylon with the prescribed sacrifices, it was not the everlasting righteousness prophesied in this verse. That would only be accomplished through the death of Christ on the cross.

**Verse 25**. It was ninety-one hard and dangerous years after the first return in 535 BC that Nehemiah asked the sixth king of Persia, Artaxerxes I, in the twentieth year of his reign if he could go back to rebuild the city walls. One of the reasons the Lord described the whole prophecy in weeks and not years is that the first part covers the time from the king's command to rebuild the walls to the actual start of reconstruction by Nehemiah, which would have taken seven weeks, i.e. forty-nine days (Nehemiah 2:1). However, in the context of the whole vision, these forty-nine days are also to be taken as forty-nine years and added to the 434 years. They fit perfectly with historical dates, which I will explain in the next chapter. After Jerusalem's restoration the *"streets and a trench"* were reconstructed. The city remained intact for many centuries, even though it experienced *"times of trouble"* particularly due to Antiochus IV in 168 BC.

Please note that the previous decree by Artaxerxes I in his seventh year (Ezra 7:13), was referring to the rebuilding of the Temple that Cyrus had earlier decreed and which had stopped through opposition, rather than to the reconstruction of the walls of the city, which Nehemiah supervised in the king's twentieth year, Nehemiah 2.

**Verse 26**. When the 434 years are added to the forty-nine years they total 483 years from the *"issuing of the decree"* to rebuild the walls of Jerusalem to the *"cutting off"* of the Anointed One. All accept this refers to the crucifixion of Jesus Christ and that *"the ruler who is to come"* is speaking of Titus. The end of his campaign against the Jews did indeed come *"like a flood"* in AD 70 with the destruction of Jerusalem. Jesus spoke of this prophecy when He said, *"not one stone will be left on another"* (Luke 21:6). The verse goes on to say that *"war will continue until the end"*, which we have seen to this day, and will continue until the return of Jesus.

**Verse 27**. This refers to events during the remaining seven years of the 490-year prophecy, which we have not yet seen. There is, therefore, an approximate 2,000-year time gap between the end of the sixty-ninth week and the beginning of the last week, which explains why the last seven years are treated separately – this is known as either "Daniel's last week" or "seventieth week". It is evident that *"he"* who confirms a covenant is not Titus, because the latter never made or confirmed a covenant with the Jews to be broken three and a half years later. Indeed, no one has confirmed or made a covenant with them that might fit the prophecy.

So, we are still awaiting the person who will *"confirm a covenant"* with the Jews. As the verse speaks of ending sacrifice and Daniel 12:11 also refers to Old Covenant Temple sacrifice, in the same end-time situation, we can conclude that some agreement will be made which includes something akin to the Old Covenant sacrificial system.

Most believe *"he"* of verse 27 is the Antichrist but there are some who say *"he"* refers to Jesus. The first view, in a nutshell, says the Antichrist confirms the Old Covenant with the Jews, introduces Temple sacrifice but stops it after three and a half years to set himself up in the Temple as God. The second interpretation says the last seven years are divided into two halves with the first part having been fulfilled by Jesus' three and a half year ministry to the Jews. His crucifixion rendered the Temple sacrifice obsolete, thus He *"put an end to sacrifice"* at the cross. Both schools of thought agree that the Antichrist's full reign of terror happens in the last three and a half years of the seven.

It does seem to me that the Antichrist view fits better with the rest of Scripture for several reasons. Firstly, Jesus confirmed or fulfilled the Old Covenant for all thirty-three years of His life, not just for the three and a half years of His public ministry. Secondly, Daniel's prophecy states that the Anointed One, the Messiah, is cut off at the end of 483 years, at the start of the last seven years and not halfway through them. Thirdly, Daniel 12:11 refers to the same abolition of sacrifice by the Antichrist and not Jesus' death on the cross. And lastly, the Jews continued to sacrifice right up to AD 70 when Titus destroyed the Temple.

We are left with the simple straightforward meaning that *"he"* who *"confirms a covenant"* refers to the Antichrist, and that he is a leader from the same empire as Titus, namely the Roman Empire. The Roman involvement continuing to the end of this age is clearly shown in Nebuchadnezzar's vision (Daniel 2) by the iron continuing down the legs and feet to the ten toes of the statue, the ten end-time kingdoms, which we will look at in chapter 12. So, this end-time individual is from the same Roman Empire.

If these conclusions are correct, then those going through the last seven years will know when it starts, as the Antichrist will set up some agreement which satisfies the orthodox Jews with Temple sacrifice. Therefore, a Temple needs to be rebuilt. We will have further evidence of this interpretation if the Antichrist breaks the covenant three and a half years later declaring himself to be God and causing abominations in the Temple and destruction in the world.

> "He [the Antichrist] *will confirm a* [the] *covenant with many for one 'seven'* [seven years]. *In the middle of the 'seven' he will put an end to sacrifice and offering. And on a wing of the Temple he will set up an abomination that causes desolation, until the end that is decreed is poured out on him."*          (Daniel 9:27)

It will, therefore, be very clear when the last seven years commence and the midpoint is reached. We will not know the exact day of the Lord's return, however, as God will shorten the end period by some unspecified period of days, for the sake of the elect, otherwise none would survive (Matthew 24:22).

I have already mentioned that Daniel 12:11 speaks of defilement and I will cover this in more detail later in the chapter, but Daniel 11:31 also refers to defilement. This needs investigating closely, as it reveals very important points regarding the Antichrist. Daniel 11:3 states that the Greeks would overthrow the Persians, a repeat of the Daniel 8 prophecy, confirming information regarding Alexander the Great and the division of the Empire.

> *"Now then, I tell you the truth: Three more kings will appear in Persia, and then a fourth, who will be far richer than all the others. When he has gained power by his wealth, he will stir up everyone against the kingdom of Greece.* Then a mighty king will appear [Alexander the Great of Greece], *who will rule with great power and do as he pleases. After he has appeared, his empire will be broken up and parcelled out towards the four winds of heaven* [Alexander's Empire divided between his generals]. *It will not go to his* [Alexander's] *descendants, nor will it have the power he exercised, because his empire will be uprooted and given to others. The king of the South* [one general became King Ptolemy I over the Egyptian area] *will become strong, but one of his commanders will become even stronger than he and will rule his own kingdom with great power. After some years, they will become allies. The daughter of the king of the South will go to the king of the North* [another general of Alexander became King Seleucius over the Syrian area, which included Israel] *to make an alliance."*          (Daniel 11:2–6)

Verses 6–30 of this chapter predicted continued warfare between the royal descendants of King Ptolemy I to the south, and King Antiochus I Seleucius to the north. Israel was caught in the middle. At one brief stage, Israel came under the rule of the southern king of Egypt, but otherwise she lived under the domination of the Greek empire to the north.

History confirms the whole chapter up to verse 35 and reveals that the contemptible king of verse 21 was Antiochus IV. He tried to remove Judaism from Israel and Hellenise the nation (introduce Greek religious ways). The verses below describe how he spiritually seduced many Jews and forced others to transgress the Old Covenant, finally desecrating their Temple in 168 BC:

> *"His* [Antiochus'] *armed forces will rise up to desecrate the temple fortress and will abolish the daily sacrifice. Then they will set up the abomination that causes desolation. With flattery he will corrupt those who have violated the* [old] *covenant, but the people* [Jews] *who know their God will firmly resist him. Those who are wise will instruct many,*

*though for a time they will fall by the sword or be burned or captured or*
*plundered. When they fall, they will receive a little help, and many who*
*are not sincere will join them. Some of the wise will stumble, so that they*
*may be refined, purified and made spotless until the time of the end, for it*
*will still come at the appointed time."*          (Daniel 11:31–35)

At first sight, verse 36 quoted below still appears to be speaking of
Antiochus or maybe his son Antiochus V, but it says that this
particular man will introduce foreign gods rather than the Greek
ones that his father had served. Secular records show that
Antiochus and his successor only introduced the Greek gods of
their ancestors, namely Zeus and his fellow demons. Verse 36
must, therefore, relate to a subsequent unsavoury and ruthless
character, who instigates many international battles in the Middle
East to bring the area under his control, and who introduces a
strange new god. As we have not yet seen this person, he must be
the man Paul speaks of in 2 Thessalonians 2:4 who will appear
before Jesus returns.

*"The king [Antichrist] will do as he pleases. He will exalt and magnify*
*himself above every god and will say unheard of things against the God of*
*gods. He will be successful until the time of wrath is completed, for what*
*has been determined must take place.* **He will show no regard for the**
**gods of his fathers** *or for the one desired by women, nor will he regard*
*any god, but will exalt himself above them all. Instead of them, he will*
*honour a god [Satan] of fortresses; a god unknown to his fathers he*
*will honour with gold and silver, with precious stones and costly gifts.*
*He will attack the mightiest fortresses with the help of a foreign god and*
*will greatly honour those who acknowledge him. He will make them*
*rulers over many people and will distribute the land at a price."*

(Daniel 11:36–39, emphasis added)

So here again we find a gap of over 2,000 years between verses
31–35 when Antiochus desecrated the Temple, and verses 36–38
when the king who exalts himself above all appears. Verse 36

must be referring to the end-time Antichrist who thankfully reigns only for a brief period. As I have shown, Daniel 9:27 indicates he will be a leader from the Roman Empire and will reintroduce sacrifice in line with the Old Covenant – see chapter 12 of this book. For him to desire this he will either be a natural Jew, a convert to Judaism or an accepted leader from the European Union arising from the current Road Map negotiations. As he finally sets himself up in the temple as God, he probably believes he is the Messiah, the Christ, the Son of God. He would thus seek to fully obey the Law. He might not declare his self-deluded identity until three and a half years later, when he abolishes the sacrifice, declares himself to be the Son of God and introduces his reign of terror. He will believe he is praying to Jehovah but we know it will actually be to Satan.

Furthermore, verses 40 and 41 state that both the current kings of the north and south will attack him. These refer to Syria and Egypt and the areas surrounding them. We see that the Antichrist invades Israel to start the end-time scenario.

> *"At the time of the end the king of the South will engage him* [Antichrist] *in battle, and the king of the North will storm out against him with chariots and cavalry and a great fleet of ships. He will invade many countries and sweep through them like a flood. He will also invade the Beautiful Land* [Israel]. *Many countries will fall, but Edom, Moab and the leaders of Ammon will be delivered from his hand. He will extend his hand over many countries. Egypt will not escape. He will gain control of the treasures of gold and silver and all the riches of Egypt, with Libyans and Nubians in submission. But reports from the east* [Iran?] *and the north will alarm him, and he will set out in great rage to destroy and annihilate many. He will pitch his royal tents between the seas at the beautiful holy mountain. Yet he will come to his end, and no-one will help him."*
>
> (Daniel 11:40–45)

Many thought Hitler was the Antichrist. He was certainly high up in the league of perpetrators of evil, murdering six million Jews and causing the deaths of a much greater number of Gentiles in the Second World War. But he did not invade Israel or set himself up as God in the Temple in Jerusalem. He promised utopia to the Germans who fell under his spell, as will the world when it comes under the Antichrist's control.

A further aspect to understand regarding this end time is where the phrase *"time, times and half a time"* fits in, as it crops up in several prophecies relating to Israel, Jerusalem and the Temple. We saw in chapter 7 that it describes a period of 1,260 days, comprising "a time (one 360-day year), times (two 360-day years) and half a time (180 days)." There are five references in the Bible to this period and all speak of the second half of the last seven years:

> *"He* [the Antichrist] *will speak against the Most High and oppress his saints and try to change the set times and the laws. The saints will be handed over to him for a time, times and a half time* [1,260 days].*"*
>
> (Daniel 7:25)

> *"The man clothed in linen, who was above the waters of the river, lifted his right hand and his left hand towards heaven, and I heard him swear by him who lives forever, saying, 'It will be for a time, times and half a time* [1,260 days]. *When the power of the holy people has been finally broken, all these things will be completed.'"*  (Daniel 12:7)

> *"Exclude the outer court, do not measure it, because it has been given to the Gentiles. They will trample on the holy city for 42 months* [42 × 30 = 1,260 days]. *And I will give power to my two witnesses, and they will prophesy for 1,260 days, clothed in sackcloth."*   (Revelation 11:2–3)

> *"The woman was given the two wings of a great eagle, so that she might fly to the place prepared for her in the desert, where she would be taken care of for a time, times and half a time* [1,260 days], *out of the serpent's reach. Then from his mouth the serpent spewed water like a river, to overtake the woman and sweep her away with the torrent. But the earth helped the woman by opening its mouth and swallowing the river that the dragon had spewed out of his mouth."*   (Revelation 12:14–16)

> *"The beast was given a mouth to utter proud words and blasphemies and*
> *to exercise his authority for forty-two months* [42 × 30 = 1,260 days].
> *He opened his mouth to blaspheme God."*                    (Revelation 13:5–6)

Some have said that 1,260 days in the above verses should be
treated on a "year for a day" basis to give 1,260 years, and this
would cover the length of time from the rise of the Catholic
Church, when darkness invaded the Church, until the Reformation. However, Constantine did not adopt Christianity until
AD 312, the earliest possible date for this period to begin, and it
was in AD 1517 that Martin Luther announced his ninety-five
theses on reforming the doctrine of the Church – a maximum of
1,205 years later, not the required 1,260 years. The dates and
theory is very nebulous and there is no need to apply the "day for
a year" principle in this case anyway, as the 1,260 days fit into the
last three and a half years perfectly – see Table 2.

There is a further scripture mentioning two very important
end-time periods:

> *"From the time that the daily sacrifice is abolished and the abomination*
> *that causes desolation is set up, there will be 1,290 days. Blessed is the*
> *one who waits for and reaches the end of the 1,335 days."*
>                                                      (Daniel 12:11–12)

We know from Daniel 9:27 that Temple sacrifice is abolished
midway through the last seven years. Revelation 13:11–18
informs us that the second beast (the false prophet) will erect
an idol of the first beast (the Antichrist) in the Temple and
from the above scripture we see that this will occur thirty days
after the second 1,260 day period has ended. During the whole
of these 1,290 days, the Antichrist will forbid worship to any
god other than himself and place his mark on all who will bow
down to him. As mentioned, the above verse supports the interpretation that *"he"* of Daniel 9:27 refers to the Antichrist
rather than Jesus because the "abolishing of the sacrifice" in

Daniel 12:11 states that the Old Testament animal sacrifice is being performed and then removed.

The 1,335 days also start from the cessation of the sacrifice and end with what is described as "the blessed end", which is Christ's return. It follows that the whole of the appalling period of 1,335 days covers the one Jesus said would be cut short in order that the elect might survive (Matthew 24:21–22). This means that there are a maximum of forty-five days, when God tolerates the idol. In His love and mercy God has given these precise timings, that believers who are alive in those days will be encouraged to know the maximum duration of the horrors. We do not know by how many days the end will be shortened, as it is in the Father's hands, but we can say that it will be sometime less than 1,335 days from the abolition of the sacrifice to the Lord's return – a blessed end indeed!

Table 2 on the next page shows these timings.

Returning to the approximate 2,000-year time period between Daniel 9:26 and 27, there are many other Old Testament prophecies which hide this same large span of time within them. I have already explained the one between verses 35 and 36 of Daniel 11. Another example is where Isaiah prophesied that the Messiah would come to declare both favour and vengeance:

> "To proclaim the year of the LORD's favour
>  and the day of vengeance of our God."          (Isaiah 61:2)

Jesus purposely omitted the last part regarding vengeance, when He read from Isaiah in the synagogue in Nazareth. Vengeance for rebellion to God was to be fulfilled at His second advent. He came first to show the favour of God. The 2,000-year gap was in the middle of one sentence in this case, not just between two verses!

The reason for these long time spans in between some prophesied events is that the Church is not revealed in the Old Testament because she is hidden in Christ. It was not until Jesus

### *Table 2.* The seven-year Tribulation

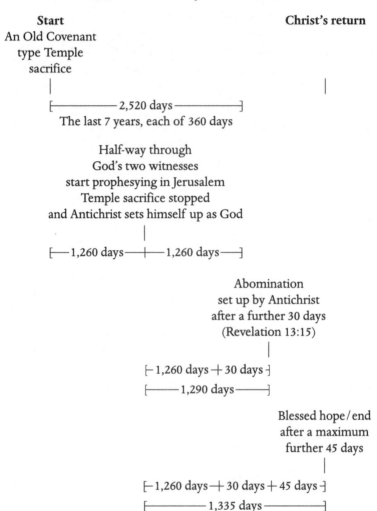

**Start**                                    **Christ's return**
An Old Covenant
  type Temple
  sacrifice

  |                                              |

⊢————— 2,520 days —————⊣
The last 7 years, each of 360 days

Half-way through
God's two witnesses
start prophesying in Jerusalem
Temple sacrifice stopped
and Antichrist sets himself up as God

                |

⊢—1,260 days—⟋—1,260 days—⊣

                        Abomination
                        set up by Antichrist
                        after a further 30 days
                        (Revelation 13:15)

                                |

        ⊢ 1,260 days + 30 days ⊣
        ⊢——— 1,290 days ———⊣

                        Blessed hope / end
                        after a maximum
                        further 45 days

                                |

        ⊢ 1,260 days + 30 days + 45 days ⊣
        ⊢——— 1,335 days ———⊣

came to earth that God through the Holy Spirit opened this
glorious truth of the Church to the believer. She remains a
mystery to Christless eyes.

It is important to see that the Temple spoken of in Revelation
11:1 is a physical temple and must therefore refer to the one yet to
be built by the Jews. This will be of stone and must not be

confused with the spiritual Temple of heaven, mentioned later in Revelation 11:19. The tabernacle and Temple were replicated on earth as pictures to help the majority of Old Testament believers, who did not have the Holy Spirit, to understand what was happening in the spiritual realm. An interesting point associated with the physical Temple in Revelation 11:8 is that the whole world will gloat over the dead bodies of the two witnesses as they lie outside it for three and a half days. The only way they could naturally be seen by everyone at the same time is by television or visual mobiles and confirms this scripture is for our day.

There are further passages to confirm that God will not be involved with the end-time Temple, but that it will be built as a result of Jewish human endeavour, prompted by Satan. Firstly, He tore the veil from top to bottom at the crucifixion of Christ:

> *"And when Jesus had cried out again in a loud voice, he gave up his spirit. At that moment the curtain of the temple was torn in two from top to bottom. The earth shook and the rocks split. The tombs broke open and the bodies of many holy people who had died were raised to life."*
>
> (Matthew 27:50–52)

This signalled that God had finished with Temple worship and replaced it with the new order in Christ. The rejection of this Man, the Branch, has fundamental consequences for non-believing orthodox Jews. Some quite rightly see that only the Messiah can rebuild the Temple, hence the need, in their eyes, for His appearance before reconstruction can commence. They quote from Psalm 127:1 *"Unless the LORD builds the house, its builders labour in vain."* However, they refuse to see that Jesus is their Messiah and Lord and so cannot see that the born-again Church has become the Temple of God. I can envisage the situation becoming so appalling in Israel that many Jews, from Kabalists to Humanists, will agree with some Orthodox leaders that rebuilding a stone Temple and sacrificing animals to obey the Law fully is the only way get the Almighty to save them! This will be orchestrated by the Antichrist who, being deceived by Satan, will believe he is the King of the Jews! As dealt with in chapter 3, the Antichrist may take the office of High Priest as well as king (Zechariah 6:12), and personally reinstitute some form of Old Covenant with *"the many"* Jews (Daniel 9:27), promising them peace with God through the sacrifices, when of course we know there is no peace now with God other than in Christ!

Jeremiah also saw the time when the stone Temple and its furniture would be made redundant. Jesus, through the New Covenant in His blood, made this possible but it will only come about when the nation comes to Christ.

> *" 'In those days, when your numbers have increased greatly in the land,'*
> *declares the LORD, 'men will no longer say, "The ark of the covenant of*
> *the LORD." It will never enter their minds or be remembered; it will not*
> *be missed, nor will another one be made. At that time they will call*
> *Jerusalem The Throne of the LORD, and all nations will gather in Jeru-*
> *salem to honour the name of the LORD.' "*          (Jeremiah 3:16–17)

It is important to see that despite all the ungodliness and rebellion, Jerusalem also remains holy (separated) to the Lord:

> *"After Jesus' resurrection they* [people who were raised with Jesus]
> *went into the **holy city** and appeared to many people."*
> (Matthew 27:53, emphasis added)

> *"They* [Gentiles] *will trample on the **holy city** for 42 months."*
> (Revelation 11:2, emphasis added)

So, we have more information on the Lord's timing of events and indeed, Jerusalem remains very much separated to God in His reckoning, contrary to the thinking of many Christians today. He is in the process of fully restoring the city to her rightful tenants with a view to bringing them to Christ.

CHAPTER

# God's Timing for the
# Jewish Nation

**10**

In the last chapter I dealt with the 490 years from the rebuilding of the walls of Jerusalem to the second return of Christ. We have seen how God specified a certain length of judgment for Israel when the Gentile nations dominated her, but there is also a divine pattern of time governing the Jewish nation in this age. To discover it, we need to understand a third way in which God calculates time during periods of judgment. Sir Edward Denning of the Plymouth Brethren published a paper in 1818, which provides the key.

He explained from Leviticus 25 that neither the sowing, reaping, pruning nor harvesting of vines was allowed during each seventh year – the land was to enjoy a Sabbath rest for the whole year. God promised such an abundance in the sixth year that the yield would see them through the seventh, to the sowing and pruning in the eighth year and until the harvest in the ninth year (Leviticus 25:1–7, 20–22). On a smaller scale, in the wilderness a double portion of manna was provided on the Friday to cover the Sabbath. Both these examples were intended to dramatically demonstrate to the Jews and surrounding nations the miraculous provision God has for His people! They are also lessons for us, as God requires Christians to live today in the supernatural provision of the indwelling Holy Spirit in order to demonstrate that He is able to provide for everyone who trusts and lays down his life for Jesus' sake.

Leviticus 25:8–55 says that the forty-ninth year, after seven of these seven-year rests, was a special one called the Jubilee. It was to be a year of restoration and rejoicing to further explain more of the glorious abundance and freedom God has for His people. Again, nothing was to be sown or harvested from the land as it was a seventh year, but in addition, if property or land had been sold, it was to be returned to the original owner. If a Hebrew had become poor and sold himself as a servant, he was released in this year. In this way tribes and families would regain their property and allotted areas of inheritance. This return of property etc. commenced on the Day of Atonement, on the tenth day of the seventh month. Jewish society and their feasts were thus set in an overall framework of forty-nine-year cycles, but sadly there is not much evidence in the Bible that all these instructions were fully and consistently carried out.

During the 1940s, Arthur Ware and Frank Paine, well known Bible chronologists in certain circles, together with a few others, carried out a detailed study of God's timing in Scripture and built on Sir Edwards' work. One of the many principles they discovered was this Jubilee cycle. They found that if the years of judgment when foreign kings ruled Israel are excluded from calculations, the history of the Jewish nation can be divided into ten forty-nine-year cycles. They called these 490 year periods Forgiveness Year Cycles because the Jews were governing their own affairs and making sacrifice for their sins.

The first cycle after Israel became an independent nation started when God delivered the Jews out of Egypt and it finished at the dedication of Solomon's Temple. With a mighty hand God had delivered Israel from the bondage of slavery through the leadership of Moses, and she began organising herself under God's direction. Moses instructed the people that there would be blessings for obedience and curses for disobedience. As explained in chapter 6, their punishment for continued defiance against Him was summed up by the following verse:

*"I will set my face against you so that you will be defeated by your enemies; those who hate you will rule over you."*          (Leviticus 26:17)

Adding the number of years from the Exodus to the dedication of Solomon's Temple comes to 621 in all. However, there were seven periods when foreign kings ruled over Israel. The actual number of years for each judgment is clearly recorded:

|              | **Years** |
|--------------|-----------|
| Judges 3:8   | 8         |
| Judges 3:14  | 18        |
| Judges 4:3   | 20        |
| Judges 6:1   | 7         |
| Judges 10:8  | 18        |
| Judges 13:1  | 40        |
| 1 Samuel 7:2 | 20        |
|              | 131       |

Subtracting 131 from the overall 621 years leaves 490 years when the nation enjoyed living in the forgiveness of God – ten Jubilee cycles each forty-nine years.

This sheds light on the opening verse of chapter 6 in the first book of Kings, where the figure of 480 years has caused some academics to say the Bible cannot be trusted as true.

*"In **the four hundred and eightieth** year after the Israelites had come out of Egypt, in the fourth year of Solomon's reign over Israel, in the month of Ziv, the second month, he began to build the Temple of the LORD."*

(1 Kings 6:1, emphasis added)

The critics correctly count 611 actual years from the Exodus to the start of building the Temple – a considerable number of years more. It took seven years to complete (1 Kings 6:37–38), and experts reckon that it would have taken Solomon another three years to furnish before it was dedicated to God – a total of ten years, giving an overall total of 621 years. 480 years from the commencement to build plus the extra 10 gives 490 years from the Exodus to the consecration of the Temple. We can now see in the above passage that the Lord was referring to the 480 forgiveness years between the two events mentioned and that the writer was recording by the inspiration of the Holy Spirit, leaving out the times of punishment, rather than just counting every actual year. This vindicates Scripture and provides one of the many glimpses in the Bible of how God sees time and judgment.

For the second cycle we need to add up the years from the dedication of Solomon's Temple to the twentieth year, in 444 BC, of the sixth king of Persia, Artaxerxes I. The years of the Persian kings are now known to within plus or minus one year from cuneiform tablets and papyri parchments excavated in Persia. So we know that there were 91 years between the decree of King Cyrus to rebuild the Temple at the end of the exile, and the decree by King Artaxerxes to rebuild the walls of Jerusalem (Daniel 9:25 quoted below and Nehemiah 2). Adding together the 399 years of the kings of Israel from the Temple dedication to the beginning of the exile, the 70 years of exile and the 91 years of the Persian kings, gives a total of 560 actual years up to the twentieth year of Artaxerxes I. Remove the 70 years of captivity in Babylon and again we find 490 years of self-governance when the Jews were back in their land making sacrifices to God for their sins.

The third and final cycle was announced in the amazing prophecy given by the angel Gabriel and discussed in detail in the previous chapter, namely the 490 year prophecy given to Daniel. This started from the decree to restore and rebuild Jerusalem made by Artaxerxes I in his twentieth year, and finishes at the end of the age:

> "*Seventy 'sevens'* [490 years] *are decreed for your people and your holy city to finish transgression, to put an end to sin, to atone for wickedness, to bring in everlasting righteousness, to seal up vision and prophecy and to anoint the most holy. Know and understand this: From the issuing of the decree to restore and rebuild Jerusalem until the Anointed One, the*

*ruler, comes, there will be seven 'sevens' [49 years], and sixty-two 'sevens' [434 years]. It will be rebuilt with streets and a trench, but in times of trouble. After the sixty-two 'sevens' [434 years], the Anointed One will be cut off and will have nothing. The people of the ruler who will come will destroy the city and the sanctuary [Temple]. The end will come like a flood: War will continue until the end, and desolations have been decreed. He will confirm a covenant with many for one 'seven' [7 years]. In the middle of the 'seven' he will put an end to sacrifice and offering. And on a wing of the temple he will set up an abomination that causes desolation, until the end that is decreed is poured out on him."*

(Daniel 9:24–27)

As discussed, verse 24 literally says it would take seventy "sevens" or seventy weeks, i.e. 490 days, to finish transgression, put an end to sin, atone for wickedness, bring in everlasting righteousness, seal up vision and prophecy and anoint the most holy. This must include putting an end to the abominations caused by the Antichrist. None of this happened when the Jews returned to Jerusalem from the exile because they only recommenced animal sacrifices for their sins. Seventy "sevens" must mean a longer period than 490 days and as God employs the "year for a day" principle in times of judgment (Numbers 14:34), He actually means it will take 490 years for the whole prophecy to be fulfilled. Some have said these 490 years ended at the cross but the dates and events do not allow for this. Even though Jesus was anointed with the Spirit at His water baptism and He brought in everlasting righteousness to all who believe, vision and prophecy were still not "sealed up" as God was to give more through the book of Revelation many years after the cross. These events are therefore still to happen.

Moving to verse 25 of the prophecy, the Jews returned from captivity but continued under foreign rule without a king of their own up to the birth of Jesus, when the majority in Israel rejected Him. God had sent Jesus to bear the promised judgment for their wickedness as well as the sins of the whole world.

The prophecy states that the crucifixion would occur 483 years (49 + 434) after the decree of Artaxerxes I made in his twentieth year. Because these years fall in the *"times of the Gentiles"*, a period of judgment, each year is 360 days long, which reduces the time span to 476 years. Academics have narrowed down the birth of Artaxerxes 1 to just three possible years, namely 465, 464 and 463 BC. The confusion is because of the difficulty in knowing how their years begin and end in relation to ours. The king's twentieth year would therefore be either 446, 445 or 444 BC. Adding 476 years to each gives us the possible crucifixion dates of AD 31, 32 or 33. So, which of these is correct?

Before we discover the answer, we need to look at why some discount the 360-day judgment year calculation in this prophecy, despite it harmonising the biblical and secular dates. They haven't understood why, earlier in Daniel 9, the seventy years of exile that Jeremiah prophesied, although a time of judgment, are treated as seventy normal years rather than being reduced to 360-day years. The reason is that God employs a further principle throughout the Bible that when a period of time is stated in years it is to be taken as a normal year, but when He describes years in the unusual terms such as days, months or a "time" during years of judgment, the 360-day year is employed.

Luke helps us to decide between the three possible years of crucifixion by recording a date showing precisely the starting year of John the Baptist's ministry and clearly linking the New Testament to the Roman Julian calendar, which we know runs from January to December:

> *"In the fifteenth year of the reign* [government] *of Tiberius Caesar . . . the word of the God came to John . . . in the desert. He went into all the country around the Jordan, preaching a baptism of repentance for the forgiveness of sins."*                          (Luke 3:1–3)

We know that Tiberius became co-ruler with Augustus Caesar in AD 13 in preparation for the latter's death. Augustus died in

August the following year and the Senate gave Tiberius full official status in September of that year, AD 14. John the Baptist would therefore have commenced his ministry fourteen years later in AD 28, the fifteenth year of Tiberius' individual reign. This is the earliest year that John could have baptised Jesus. It is clear from the Gospels that Jesus ministered for three and a half years until His crucifixion at the spring Passover (and from Daniel's prophecy this was 476 judgment years after the decree by Artaxerxes I to rebuild the walls of Jerusalem). If John had commenced his ministry early enough in AD 28 for the people from Jerusalem, all Judea and the whole region of Jordan to go out to him, Jesus could have been baptised later that summer. Three and half years later makes the earliest year of crucifixion to be AD 32. Or, He could have been baptised in the late summer of the next year in AD 29, which would mean the crucifixion would have occurred in the spring of AD 33. This is the last year that historical events allow for the death of Christ.

We have narrowed the three possible dates of Artaxerxes I decree to two but let us look at Jesus' birth to try and narrow it to one. Jesus started His ministry about the age of thirty, which would mean He was born in 1 or 2 BC. The reason for the "about" description of His age is probably due to the timing of His baptism. He is most likely to have been born at the Feast of Tabernacles in September but if He was baptised by John in August he would not be quite thirty years of age, hence the phrase. In recent times, earlier dates for the birth of Christ of between 6 and 4 BC have become increasingly accepted. This is mainly due to the mention of a lunar eclipse by Josephus, which occurred shortly before Herod's death (nothing to do with the star of Bethlehem). He only mentions one eclipse and selecting the wrong one has brought the date of Jesus' birth too far forward. These earlier dates are convincingly challenged by some very useful information on the various eclipses, together with more understanding of the historical events as put forward by John Pratt. He submitted a paper to *The Planetarium* (a journal printed in December 1990), some of which I will summarise.

Firstly, he points out that there are lunar eclipses every year or so in Israel yet Josephus only ever refers to one. Mr Pratt sets out a very good argument for 29th December 1 BC as being the eclipse Josephus referred to, rather than the one on 13th March 4 BC which is now commonly accepted. Very simply, the 29th December eclipse was the only one occurring at sunset when everyone would have been awake to see the characteristic reddening of the eclipsed portion. All the others between 6 BC and AD 1, including the eclipse of 13th March 4 BC, happened after midnight when most people would have been fast asleep, and so they would not have been noteworthy. They would have only been seen by the persistent neighbour Jesus spoke of, who badgered his friend for some bread in the dead of night! There was one exception on 15th September 5 BC, which started at 9 p.m., but this does not fit any historical events.

Secondly, John Pratt discovered that another investigator, Martin Ernest, author of *The Birth of Christ Recalculated* (Pasadena, CA: FBR Publications), had found many problems with the 4 BC date. For instance, the taxation records in 8 BC, which are used to support the 4 BC argument, only applied to Roman citizens, whereas the census in 2 BC, recorded by another historian, Orosius, covered the entire population of the Roman world. It would have taken about a year for the news to travel throughout the empire and for Joseph and Mary to travel from Nazereth to their ancestral town Bethlehem, thus fitting the Bible account and making the birth 1 BC. It was probably in the autumn at the feast of Tabernacles, as the scripture says, *"The Word became flesh and made his dwelling* [tabernacle] *among us"* (John 1:14).

Ernest also points out that Varus was governor of Syria during 6 and 5 BC, confirmed by coinage bearing his inscription and these dates. Josephus indicates that Saturninus was governor for the two years preceding Herod's death but records that Varus was actually governor at Herod's death. An inscription found near

Varus' villa describes a man who was twice governor of Syria – if this refers to Varus, it explains the apparent contradiction that he was governor at an earlier date, and supports the 1 BC date as Christ's birth. All this vindicates the Catholic Church's calculations in placing the birth of Christ in that year in the first place. Subtracting 476 years from this date, makes it most likely that the twentieth year of Artaxerxes is 444 BC

There are many other points on the subject and it is worth looking at the whole argument (www.herod.html – yet another eclipse for Herod).

We can see that there are still seven years of the 490-year prophecy remaining, each year to be taken as 360 days. This third cycle is, therefore, not simply 490 consecutive years. We find an approximate 2,000-year gap between AD 33 and the last seven years at the end of the age due to the rejection of Jesus by the Jews. This gap also explains why Daniel's prophecy singles out the last years. The 360-day judgment year principle will again operate here, as the tyrannical reign of the Antichrist in the second half of the seven years is described as lasting only 1,260 days rather than the normal three and a half years:

> *"He* [the Antichrist] *will speak against the Most High and oppress his saints and try to change the set times and the laws. The saints will be handed over to him for a time, times and a half time* [1,260 days]*."*
>
> (Daniel 7:25)

This third period of 490 forgiveness years is unique in that it is both a time of forgiveness and judgment. The Jews were back in the land after the seventy-year exile, sacrificing for their sins and receiving God's forgiveness with the promise of restoration. But they were also in the *"times of the Gentiles"* judgment with foreign kings ruling over them. Today, at the conclusion of *"the times of the Gentiles"*, we are witnessing God bringing them back to the land once again, for the long-prophesied final seven years. These years are known as "Jacob's Trouble" (Jeremiah 30:7). The nation will witness unprecedented tribulation as well as His grace, but the remnant will survive and come to Christ as a nation. We are going to see every single biblical prophecy in this age regarding Israel come to pass, hence the Jewishness of chapter 4 onwards in the book of Revelation.

In Genesis there is another of those nice little touches from God regarding the three 490-year periods of Jewish history. Together they total 1,470 years and it was no coincidence that Jacob, the father of Israel, lived to be 147 years old (Genesis 47:28). He said to God,

> *"Of all that you* [God] *give me* [Jacob] *I will give you a tenth."*
>
> (Genesis 28:22)

God has ordained that Israel will stand as a nation in forgiveness before Him for 1,470 years, so He responded to Jacob's heart's desire and gave him 147 years, one tenth of this time on earth.

So, we have discovered a further point which God employs regarding divine timing. He excludes times of judgment in His calculations. Understanding this principle is vital in making sense of some parts of the Gospel accounts surrounding the crucifixion and resurrection of Jesus. He said,

> *"For as Jonah was three days and three nights in the belly of a huge fish,*
> *so the Son of Man will be three days and three nights in the heart of the*
> *earth."*                          (Matthew 12:40)

But He said to the thief whilst they were on the cross,

> *"Today you will be with me in paradise."*          (Luke 23:43)

After dying Jesus went down into hell to proclaim to the spirits what He had accomplished (1 Peter 3:19). He did not rise for three days (Matthew 12:40, quoted above). Jesus excluded from His reckoning the three days and nights when His body would be in the tomb, because they were part of God's judgment. He therefore said that they would both be in heaven that day. The same exclusion principle was shown to Matthew:

> *"The curtain of the temple was torn in two from top to bottom. The earth shook and the rocks split. The tombs broke open and the bodies of many holy people who had died were raised to life. They came out of the tombs, and after Jesus' resurrection they went into the holy city and appeared to many people."*     (Matthew 27:51–53)

This is written as though there was no time lapse between Jesus' death and resurrection. The judgment period of three days and nights has been omitted by Matthew, inspired by the Holy Spirit, as it is not counted in God's reckoning.

The number 490 itself denotes forgiveness and is the product of seventy times seven. Jesus purposely used it when He answered Peter regarding forgiveness:

> *"Then Peter came to Jesus and asked, 'Lord, how many times shall I forgive my brother when he sins against me? Up to seven times?' Jesus answered, 'I tell you, not seven times but seventy times seven.'"*     (Matthew 18:21–22)

So, we see God is working events out in the nation of Israel in a very precise way. There are three periods of 490 forgiveness years, each comprising ten Jubilee cycles of forty-nine years. The last seven years of the third period are still to happen. These years fit in with dates in the rest of this study providing a complete chronological framework of the Jewish nation covering the Old and New Testaments. Lastly, the 483 years to the death of Christ in AD 33 were revealed by God to the Jews as a further con-firmation to them that Jesus was indeed His son and their Messiah.

# The Rapture and Beyond

Let us look again at the last seven years before Jesus returns to earth but this time from the "rapture" point of view, as well as some aspects of the millennium and the "new earth". As you may have noted, I lean to the post-tribulationist view, i.e. the "rapture" or "catching up" of the Church at the end of the seven years of tribulation. This was the traditional understanding of the Church until the early nineteenth century. The new teaching says that believers are taken at the beginning of the tribulation. So let me explain my stand-point as I believe we are about to enter this testing time very, very shortly.

The apostle John's visions in the book of Revelation states that believers will still be on earth at the very end, even after the Antichrist has performed his worst deeds and Babylon, the world's religious and corrupt commercial system, is judged. He wrote:

> *"Come out of her* [Babylon], *my people,*
> *so you will not share in her sins,*
> *so that you will not receive any of her plagues."*   (Revelation 18:4)

> *"Woe! Woe, O great city,*
> *O Babylon, city of power!*
> *In one hour your doom has come!"*   (Revelation 18:10)

If the "catching up" happens at the start of the seven years, who are those who remain at the return of Jesus? Are they a second Church or does the current Church remain until the end?

The emphasis changes after Revelation 4:1 from the then current Church to the scene in heaven and the end time, where it says, *"Come up here, and I will show you what must take place after this."* Pre-tribulationists take this to mean the Church is raptured before the Tribulation. The Jewishness of these later chapters is because the Jews will take a central role in the last years just as they did at the beginning of the Church age. We could certainly do with more ministries of the stature of Paul, Peter, James and John!

If the rapture happens before the Tribulation then nominal believers who are left would be in a state of shock at the disappearance of the born-again Christians. Many may be jolted into believing but they would probably have hardened hearts and not be the effective spiritual fighting force required to support a nation of baby Jewish believers. If the Church was removed, one assumes there would also have to be a Paul type "road to Damascus" encounter for the Jewish nation, who would then evangelise the rest of the world, as Paul did in his day. However, he required three years in the wilderness for God to teach, change and establish him in Christ before he was able to preach the gospel clearly and accurately (Galatians 1:18). Jesus also took three and a half years to prepare His apostles! There will be little time at the end as there are only seven years of tribulation. Surely, the new Jewish believers as well as the other new Gentile converts will need a mature Church all through the seven years to nurture, pray and correctly teach them during this very traumatic time.

Those who hold the pre-tribulation view believe that because the word "church" is omitted from Revelation 4:1 until Revelation 22:16 and only the words "saints" and "elect" are used in the intervening chapters, this is confirmation that the Church has been "taken away" before the last seven years begin. However, there are six other New Testament books, which do not use the words "church" or "saints", and "elect" is used for the Church throughout the New Testament letters.

Jesus said in John 14:1–4 that He was going *"to prepare a place for us"* and return that we might be with Him. Some "pre-tribbers" believe the return spoken of in this scripture refers to the secret return of Jesus at the beginning of the Tribulation, unknown to the rest of the world, when He "raptures" the Church. Jesus was indeed referring to a secret return but this happened immediately after the resurrection when He only appeared to His disciples. The spirits and souls of believers who have died since then go straight to heaven and enjoy citizenship there with Him (Philippians 3:20). Our home in heaven after death is only temporary until we all reign with Jesus on earth during the millennium. Humans were created to live in a body on the earth. Angels, who do not have a body, were made for heaven and the lake of fire was created for Satan and his demons. Tragically, those who reject Jesus effectively choose to be in Satan's camp and will join him in the eternal fire. When at last the new earth is created, believers will live there with the Father, Son and Holy Spirit forever – hallelujah!

The apostle Paul taught the post-tribulationist view, and clearly wrote in his letter to the Gentile Church in Thessalonica that they would go through the end-time tribulation and then be caught up in the air to meet the Lord. Before that is to happen, they were to see the Antichrist and no mention of a pre-rapture. He was also expecting these events to happen in his lifetime:

> *"Brothers, we do not want you to be ignorant about those who fall asleep, or to grieve like the rest of men, who have no hope. We believe that Jesus died and rose again and so we believe God will bring with Jesus those who have fallen asleep* [died in Christ] *in him.* **According to the Lord's own word, we tell you that we who are alive, who are left till the coming of the Lord, will certainly not precede** [**not be raptured before**] *those who have fallen asleep* [**died in Christ**]. *For the Lord*

*himself will come down from heaven, with a loud command, with the voice of the archangel and with the trumpet call of God, and **the dead in Christ will rise first. After that, we who are still alive and are left will be caught up** [**raptured**] together with them in the clouds to meet the Lord in the air. And so we will be with the Lord for ever."*

(1 Thessalonians 4:13–17)

It is not until the Lord's return at the end of the Tribulation (which Paul describes as the *"blessed hope"*, Titus 2:13), that Christians who have died will enter their resurrection bodies and be raised to meet Jesus in the sky. The above scripture states that the resurrection is immediately followed by the rapture of believers who are alive on the earth at that time. They also join Jesus in the air having received their new bodies. Both groups return to earth with Him and reign with Him for the millennium and forever! As the rapture is after the resurrection of dead believers, and the latter occurs at the end of the seven years when Jesus returns, the catching up must also be at the end and not before.

The scripture on the end-time Antichrist is:

*"Concerning the coming of our Lord Jesus Christ and our being gathered to him, we ask you, brothers, not to become easily unsettled or alarmed by some prophecy, report or letter supposed to have come from us, saying that the day of the Lord has already come. Don't let anyone deceive you in any way, for that day will not come until the rebellion occurs and the man of lawlessness is revealed, the man doomed to destruction. He will oppose and will exalt himself over everything that is called God or is worshipped, so that he sets himself up in God's temple, proclaiming himself to be God."*                                (2 Thessalonians 2:1–4)

So, here again, the Church is present during the Tribulation when the Antichrist appears. Very importantly, these verses also show that in the early Church, Paul had to deal with some who tried to unsettle believers with the false teaching of a secret return of the Lord, which is required by those who believe in an early rapture.

The apostle went on to teach about the Antichrist:

> *"Don't you remember that when I was with you I used to tell you these things? And now you know what is holding him* [the Antichrist] *back, so that he may be revealed at the proper time. For the secret power of lawlessness is already at work; but the one* [the Holy Spirit] *who now holds it back will continue to do so till* **he [the Antichrist]** *is* **taken out of the way.** *And then the lawless one* **[the Antichrist]** *will be revealed* [exposed to his followers as to who he is], *whom the Lord Jesus will overthrow with the breath of his mouth and destroy by the splendour of his coming."*                    (2 Thessalonians 2:5–8, emphasis added)

Paul is saying that the Holy Spirit is constraining sinful man and will only allow so much evil to occur. The Antichrist will confirm something along the lines of the Old Covenant at the beginning of the last seven years and break it half way through, taking absolute power and declaring himself to be God. True Christians will see through his guise and not receive his "mark", but those who do not want to know the truth are deceived until Jesus returns, when He captures and removes the Antichrist. The true nature of the Lawless One is then revealed to his followers and they are judged (Revelation 19:20, quoted below). Many pre-tribulationists believe that the verse *"he is taken out of the way"* refers to the Holy Spirit being withdrawn with the Church and that *"the lawless one will be revealed"* refers to the Antichrist taking up his dictatorial rule, rather than him being exposed and removed by Jesus. Paul could not have meant this, as removal of the Holy Spirit would stop any more people believing in the Lord and we know that there are believers on earth at the end of his reign (Revelation 18:4). Paul says we can only truly confess His divinity by the Holy Spirit (1 Corinthians 12:3).

> *"Then I saw the beast and the kings of the earth and their armies gathered together to make war against the rider on the horse* [Jesus] *and*

*his army. But the beast was captured, and with him the false prophet who had performed the miraculous signs on his behalf. With these signs he had deluded those who had received the mark of the beast and worshipped his image. The two of them were thrown alive into the fiery lake of burning sulphur. The rest of them* [who had received the mark] *were killed with the sword that came out of the mouth of the rider on the horse, and all the birds gorged themselves on their flesh."*

(Revelation 19:19–21)

Paul also spoke to the Corinthians on the matter:

*"We will not all sleep* [die in Christ], *but we will all be changed – in a flash, in the twinkling of an eye, at the last trumpet. For the trumpet will sound, the dead* [in Christ] *will be raised imperishable, and we will be changed* [raptured]*."*

(1 Corinthians 15:51–52)

The last trumpet sounds at the Lord's return. This final blast is also spoken of by Matthew, and he too refers to the rapture happening at the end of the seven years when Jesus comes back. This is no secret return as all will see the Son of Man appear:

*"At that time the sign of the Son of Man will appear in the sky, and all the nations of the earth will mourn. They will see the Son of Man coming on the clouds of the sky, with power and great glory. And he* [Jesus] *will send his angels with a loud trumpet call, and they will gather his elect from the four winds, from one end of the heavens to the other."*

(Matthew 24:30–31)

In Revelation we are further informed that there will be seven angels who blow their trumpets with the seventh one sounding the final blast to herald in the glorious return of Christ:

*"The seventh angel sounded his trumpet, and there were loud voices in heaven, which said:*

> *'The kingdom of the world has become the kingdom*
> *of our Lord and of his Christ,*
> *and he will reign for ever and ever.'"*          (Revelation 11:15)

Our generation lives at the conclusion of the *"times of the Gentiles"* and, as promised by the angel Gabriel to Daniel, there is the appropriate revelation of Scripture concerning the end-time events (Daniel 12:9). This is for the benefit of believers who have to live through these extremely troubled years. The battle against Israel will intensify and a mature Church is essential to help the Jews come to Christ and provide prayer cover for them through these horrendous times.

The pre-tribulationists have three further verses in their argument, none of which stands scrutiny:

> *"And to wait for his Son from heaven, whom he raised from the dead –*
> *Jesus, who rescues us from* [Greek: *ek,* 'out of or separated from'] *the*
> *coming wrath."*          (1 Thessalonians 1:10)

> *"Since you have kept my command to endure patiently, I will also keep*
> *you from* [Greek: *ek,* 'out of or separated from'] *the hour of trial that*
> *is going to come upon the whole world to test those who live on the*
> *earth."*          (Revelation 3:10)

> *"For it will come upon all those who live on the face of the whole earth.*
> *Be always on the watch, and pray that you may be able to escape all that*
> *is about to happen, and that you may be able to stand before the Son of*
> *Man."*          (Luke 21:35–36)

They say God will not allow His Bride to go through the awful events of the Tribulation and these verses show that He will take us "out of" this world before they happen. But what about the hellish persecutions and deaths over the last two millennia that many countless hundreds of thousands, of Christians have suffered? What will they think if Christians at the end time are spared this treatment? No, God's wrath is only poured out on those who stubbornly continue to reject Jesus, not on the Church, which He will keep through it. For example:

> *"They* [the demons] *were told not to harm the grass of the earth or any plant or tree, but only those people* [unbelievers] *who did **not** have the seal of God on their foreheads. They were not given power to kill them* [unbelievers] *but only to torture them for five months. And the agony they suffered was like that of the sting of a scorpion when it strikes a man."* (Revelation 9:4–5, emphasis added)

> *"Ugly and painful sores broke out on the people who had the mark of the beast and worshipped his* [the beast's] *image."* (Revelation 16:2)

> *"The fifth angel poured out his bowl on the throne of the beast, and his kingdom was plunged into darkness. Men gnawed their tongues in agony and cursed the God of heaven because of their pains and their sores, but they refused to repent of what they had done."* (Revelation 16:10–11)

And these are only some of the trials ordered by God to try and bring the lost to repentance and faith in Christ. Up until this time God has mainly tried the carrot but He will then apply the stick as well to try and save as many as possible!

We saw a similar situation in Egypt when God judged Pharaoh. There were tremendous plagues but none of the Jews were harmed. God "passed over" those who had blood on the door-posts and lintels. Because of the judgments and display of God's power, many Egyptians joined the Israelites when they left (Exodus 12:38). Similarly, we will be protected by the blood of Jesus and many will come to Christ through the demonstration of His mighty power. However, many Christians will hunger, thirst and be killed by the Antichrist but not by God's actions. Could He be allowing the deaths of the saints to prick the hearts of blind zealous religious people like Saul who consented to

Stephen's death? God used this to prepare him for his encounter on the road to Damascus.

So, reading through the book of Revelation up to Revelation 20 there is no clear scripture about the rapture. However, some "pre-tribbers" see various raptures mentioned not just at the beginning but during the seven years! Jesus also taught that those in Jerusalem at the end time should watch for the appearing of the Antichrist in the Temple (Matthew 24:15) and He clearly said that the rapture would occur at His return, not seven years before or even three and a half years before:

> *"And they knew nothing of what would happen until the flood* [Noah's] *came and took them away. That is how it will be at the coming of the Son of Man. Two men will be in the field; one will be taken and the other left. Two women will be grinding with a hand mill; one will be taken and the other left."*                    (Matthew 24:39–41)

The Lord is carefully preparing today's Church to stand through this extremely exacting time, so we can nurture the multitudes from every nation whom God will bring to Christ during these last years. The whole Church will be reaching maturity in Christ and believers will have learnt to receive by faith more and more of the provision God has already poured out on us.

Another point to raise is that some "pre-tribbers" say that God's judgments cannot come on the nations until the Church is taken but His wrath has already been seen, the most devastating being the holocaust which was caused by the Jews rejection of Jesus. There are scriptural examples such as the angel of the Lord striking Herod (Acts 12:19–23), and blindness coming on Elymas the sorcerer (Acts 13:6–12). God does not need to take the Church from the earth to reveal to mankind that He cannot be mocked.

Revelation 20:1–8 speaks of Jesus reigning on earth for 1,000 years, which some say describes the whole Church era – from the resurrection of Christ to His return. But these verses, quoted below, say Satan is bound during the millennium period, which means it cannot be the time we are living in now, as he is the accuser of the brethren today. They say that the binding of Satan was effected by Jesus when He said, *"first bind the strong man"* (Matthew 12:29), but it is an angel who binds Satan for a thousand years, not Jesus:

> *"And I saw an angel coming down out of heaven, having the key to the Abyss and holding in his hand a great chain. He seized the dragon, that ancient serpent, who is the devil, or Satan, and bound him for a thousand years* [the millennial reign of Christ]. *He threw him into the Abyss, and locked and sealed it over him, to keep him from deceiving the nations any more until the thousand years were ended. After that, he must be set free for a short time."*
>
> (Revelation 20:1–3)

If the 1,000 years is figurative, then why not the judgment seat of Christ? Why not the miracles that Jesus performed, and so on? No, the 1,000 years are yet to happen. Just as the Church is not clearly spoken of in Old Testament prophecies, so it is with the 1,000-year reign of Christ.

Revelation 20:4–8 describes the first resurrection, not the rapture, and, as I have shown, this occurs at the end of the seven-year tribulation at the return of Jesus.

> *"I saw thrones on which were seated those* [all the overcomers in Christ] *who had been given authority to judge* [1 Corinthians 6:1–4; Revelation 2:26]. *And I saw souls of those who had been beheaded because of their testimony for Jesus and because of the word of God* [some of the over-comers have special mention]. *They* [both groups] *had not worshipped the beast or his image and had not received his mark on their foreheads or their hands. They came to life and reigned with Christ for a thousand years. (The rest of the dead did not come to life until the thousand years were ended.) This is the first resurrection. Blessed and holy are those who have a part in the first resurrection. The second death has no power over them, but they will be priests of God and*

*of Christ and will reign with him for a thousand years. When the*
*thousand years are over, Satan will be released from his prison and will*
*go out to deceive the nations in the four corners of the earth."*

(Revelation 20:4–8)

This resurrection of the dead will consist of all true born-again believers who have died during the whole Church age, with martyrs from the Great Tribulation being given special mention. Here are some of the scriptures regarding these people:

*"Do you not know the saints will judge the world?"*

(1 Corinthians 6:2)

*"To him who overcomes and does my will to the end, I will give authority*
*over the nations."*                                    (Revelation 2:26)

*"But the court will sit, and his* [the Antichrist's] *power will be taken*
*away and completely destroyed forever.* **Then the sovereignty, power**
**and greatness of the kingdoms under the whole heaven will be**
**handed over to the saints, the people of the Most High.** *His kingdom*
*will be an everlasting kingdom, and all rulers will worship and obey*
*him."*                                (Daniel 7:26–27, emphasis added)

To clarify the second death, there is natural birth followed by spiritual birth through faith in Christ. There is natural death followed by the lake of fire for unbelievers, which is the second death.

The whole born-again Church will reign with Jesus during the millennium and the parable of the talents reveals how believers will be organised to reign in their respective countries around the world – those who have been obedient in their faith will have greater responsibility. The Jews would be the ones in Israel of course. Revelation 19:21, quoted previously, says that only those who have the mark of the beast are slain at the return of Jesus, but there will be many who have not received the mark or believed in

Jesus. So we are left with the situation that there will be believers in their resurrection bodies as well as others on the earth during the millennium. This would explain the reluctance of some to go up to Jerusalem to be with Jesus to celebrate the consummation of the feast of tabernacles:

> *"Then the survivors from all the nations that have attacked Jerusalem will go up year after year to worship the King, the LORD Almighty, and to celebrate the Feast of Tabernacles. If any of the peoples of the earth do not go up to Jerusalem to worship the King, the LORD Almighty, they will have no rain."* (Zechariah 14:16–17)

A similar thing happened when Jesus appeared to His disciples after the resurrection (Luke 24:13–35) when He ate, walked and talked with them but I do not believe we will be able to disappear like Jesus did, as we are not God.

As dealt with in chapter 3, since Jesus has fulfilled the Feast of Tabernacles, we will indeed go up to Jerusalem to worship Jesus and have fellowship with Him but not in the limitations of the Old Testament shadow.

After this time of unprecedented peace, incredible as it seems, there will be a rebellion at the end of those who have hardened their hearts. Because of the absence of Satan during this period, there will be swift judgment by fire on those who choose their own ways and rebel rather than looking to the Lord. Satan is used once again for the final sifting before he and the rebellious are cast into the lake of fire (Revelation 20:7–10).

After this comes the second and final resurrection, which consists of all the remaining dead, who are brought before the great white throne for judgment.

> *"Then I saw a great white throne and Him who was seated on it. Earth and sky fled from his presence, and there was no place for them. And I saw the dead, great and small, standing before the throne, and books were opened. Another book was opened, which is the book of life. The*

> *dead were judged according to what they had done as recorded in the*
> *books. The sea gave up the dead that were in it, and death and Hades*
> *[two spirits] gave up their dead that were in them, and each person*
> *was judged by what he had done. Then death and Hades were thrown*
> *into the lake of fire."*                          (Revelation 20:11–14)

The earth and sky then flee away, are burnt up by fire and disappear (2 Peter 3:7). The new heaven and earth are created for the saints to live with Jesus. The new heaven refers to the first heaven, the atmosphere around the earth. The second heaven is the universe, which is not remade, and the third heaven is the spiritual one.

So, the sequence of events will be:

1. Seven-year Tribulation.
2. The Lord returns but tarries in the sky.
3. First resurrection – the dead in Christ rise to meet Him in the air.
4. Rapture of believers still alive on the earth after the first resurrection, who join them in the air. All believers are now in their resurrection bodies as the Bride of Christ ready for the Wedding of the Lamb (Revelation 19:7).
5. All return to earth with Jesus who saves Jerusalem and overcomes the Antichrist at the battle of Armageddon (Revelation 16:16).
6. Babylon destroyed. The Antichrist and false prophet thrown into the lake of fire.
7. Satan bound for 1,000 years.
8. Jesus and believers reign on earth with Him for 1,000 years.
9. Satan loosed for a short while after millennium.
10. Last rebellion (Revelation 20:7–9).
11. Satan cast into the lake of fire.
12. Last resurrection of all the remaining dead.
13. Last judgment before the great white throne of God.
14. Earth and whole universe destroyed by fire (2 Peter 3:10).

15. New heaven and earth created without sea (Revelation 21:1) and without sun or moon (Revelation 21:23).
16. Believers from Old Testament and born-again believers placed on the new earth with Jesus (Revelation 21:2).

We will see on the new earth the names of the twelve tribes written on each of the gates of the new Jerusalem (Revelation 12:12) and the names of the twelve apostles, all Jewish, inscribed on its twelve foundations (Revelation 21:14). Praise God, the Gentile believers are included in their number.

On several occasions I have alluded to point 15 in the above list, that there will be no sun, moon or sea on the new earth. From the following words in Jeremiah, Israel will then no longer remain a separate nation and therefore the description Jew and Gentile will finally be removed. The names of the tribes and apostles will probably serve as a reminder that salvation came to the world through the Jewish nation, just as the scars in Jesus' body will remind us of His perfect sacrifice.

> " 'This is what the LORD says,
>
> *he who appoints the sun*
>    *to shine by day,*
> *who decrees the moon and stars*
>    *to shine by night,*
> *who stirs up the sea*
>    *so that its waves roar –*
>    *the LORD Almighty is his name:*
> *Only if these decrees vanish from my sight,'*
>    *declares the LORD,*
> *'will the descendants of Israel ever cease*
>    *to be a nation before me.' "*
> (Jeremiah 31:35–36)

# PART 3

## *Israel and the Roman Empire*

# What Does the Bible Say About the Roman Empire?

From Daniel 9:24–27, discussed in chapter 9, we have seen that the man of sin who causes desolation and brings abominations to the Temple will be a leading figure from the revived Roman Empire. Other verses in Daniel shed more light on how this revised empire and the Antichrist emerge. I use the words "revised" and "revived" interchangeably, because this empire has never totally disappeared. The spirits driving it, however, have very cunningly changed the costumes and the scenery for the final act.

The second chapter of Daniel gives a grand overview of events concerning Israel from the Babylonian captivity onwards. During the second year of his reign Nebuchadnezzar, King of Babylon, received a very dramatic dream of a huge and impressive statue, which troubled him greatly (Daniel 2:1). Daniel had been taken to Babylon the previous year, in the first wave of exiles, and was summoned to the king to interpret the vision. He said:

*"There is a God in heaven who reveals mysteries. He has shown King Nebuchadnezzar what will happen in days to come ... You looked, O king, and there before you stood a large statue – an enormous, dazzling statue, awesome in appearance. The head of the statue was made of pure gold, its chest and arms of silver, its belly and thighs of bronze, its legs of*

*iron, its feet partly of iron and partly of baked clay. While you were watching, a rock was cut out, but not by human hands. It struck the statue on its feet of iron and clay and smashed them. Then the iron, the clay, the bronze, the silver and the gold were broken to pieces at the same time and became like chaff on the threshing floor in the summer. The wind swept them away without leaving a trace. But the rock that struck the statue became a huge mountain and filled the whole earth.*

*This was the dream, and now we will interpret it to the king. You, O king, are the king of kings. The God of heaven has given you dominion and power and might and glory; in your hands he has placed mankind and the beasts of the field and the birds of the air. Wherever they live, he has made you ruler over them all. You are that head of gold.*

*After you, another kingdom will arise inferior to yours. Next, a third kingdom, one of bronze, will rule over the whole earth. Finally, there will be a fourth kingdom, strong as iron – for iron breaks and smashes everything – and as iron breaks things to pieces, so it will crush and break all the others. Just as you saw that the feet and toes were partly of baked clay and partly of iron, so this will be a divided kingdom; yet it will have some of the strength of iron in it, even as you saw iron mixed with clay. As the toes were partly iron and partly clay, so this kingdom will be partly strong and partly brittle. And just as you saw the iron mixed with baked clay, so the people will be a mixture and will not remain united, any more than iron mixes with clay.*

*In the time of those kings, the God of heaven will set up a kingdom that will never be destroyed, nor will it be left to another people. It will crush all those kingdoms and bring them to an end, but it will itself endure forever. This is the meaning of the vision of the rock cut out of the mountain, but not by human hands – a rock that broke the iron, the bronze, the clay, the silver and the gold to pieces. The great God has shown the king what will take place in the future. The dream is true and the interpretation is trustworthy."* (Daniel 2:28, 31–45)

Although Daniel said the head of gold represented King Nebuchadnezzar, he interpreted the silver as a subsequent empire that would come after him. The head, therefore, included all the rulers of the mighty Babylonian Empire, not just Nebuchadnezzar.

The silver chest and arms were thus the united Medo-Persian Empire under King Cyrus, who conquered the Babylonians. The belly and thighs of bronze were the Greek Empire, and the legs of iron depicted the cruel unbending Roman Empire, which divided into east and west as represented by the left and right legs. It is very important to see that the iron continues right down through the feet to the tips of the toes, albeit in a mixed form. This shows that the Roman Empire continues and finally produces ten kingdoms before the rock strikes the feet, toes included, destroying the whole statue. The rock not made with human hands represents Jesus' return. It could not depict His first advent because He did not destroy the four empires through His life, death and resurrection, and the last ten nations, shown by the ten toes, were not in existence at His death. Also, Jesus was born in the time of the full Roman Empire, in the time when there was no clay present in the iron – in the time of the legs. No, it speaks of His glorious return when *"the kingdom of the earth becomes the kingdom of our Lord and his Christ"* (Revelation 11:15). So far, we have not seen these ten end-time kingdoms, although some thought they were the ten nations that started the EEC. However, at the time of writing, there are twenty-seven countries in the EU, so we have to look further.

Some have argued that the Medes were the silver, the Persians were the bronze and the Greeks the iron. This does not fit with the picture of two arms of silver representing two empires ruling concurrently, the Persians being one shoulder and arm, and the Medes the other. Remember, Daniel 2:39 says that the silver arms came *"after"* the golden head of the Babylonians. History reveals that the Medes became established to the east of the Assyrian Empire in 816 BC under King Arbaces. This was long *before* the new Babylonian Empire emerged under King Nebopolassar who came to the throne in 625 BC whilst overthrowing the Assyrian Empire. Meanwhile, the Persians also developed to the east of the

Assyrian Empire but south of the Medes, with their first notable king, Teipes, reigning in 650 BC. It was not until Cyrus the Great of Persia conquered the Medes to his north in 550 BC, that their combined strength succeeded in overcoming the Babylonians in 535 BC. Therefore, the Medes alone could not have been the second empire, as they were conquered by the Persians before the demise of the Babylonians and not "after" as the vision states! So, the silver arms below the golden head of the Babylonians were indeed the combined Mede and Persian Empires.

God gave other visions of the same four empires to highlight additional important details about them. These are recorded in Daniel 7 and are depicted as four beasts:

> *"The first was like a lion, and it had the wings of an eagle. I watched until its wings were torn off and it was lifted from the ground so that it stood on two feet like a man, and the heart of a man was given to it.*
>
> *And there before me was a second beast, which looked like a bear. It was raised up on one of its sides, and it had three ribs in its mouth between its teeth. It was told, 'Get up and eat your fill of flesh!'*
>
> *After that, I looked, and there before me was another beast, one that looked like a leopard. And on its back it had four wings like those of a bird. This beast had four heads, and it was given authority to rule.*
>
> *After that, in my vision at night I looked, and there before me was a fourth beast – terrifying and frightening and very powerful. It had large iron teeth; it crushed and devoured its victims and trampled underfoot whatever was left. It was different from all the former beasts, and it had ten horns."* (Daniel 7:4–7)

The first vision in verse 4 likened the Babylonians to a lion with eagle's wings symbolising the strength, ferociousness and swiftness with which Nebuchadnezzar conquered the Middle East. He had been described by God as the king of kings in Daniel 2, but his wings were plucked off, referring to his humbling in the fields for "seven times". Daniel 4:24–37 records he was taken from power, driven from his people and reduced to eating grass like an animal.

The vision shows he was later given the heart of a man, which refers to Nebuchadnezzar subsequently coming back to his senses as a human being, when he acknowledged the sovereign Almighty God.

The second beast in verse 5 was a lop-sided bear. The lower shoulder on one side depicted the Medes being subject to the Persians in the combined empire, but both ruling together – a shoulder in Scripture represents authority. The three ribs, which the bear devoured, describe the three kingdoms of Babylon, Egypt and Lydia, all conquered by the Persians and Medes and included in their Empire. God moved the heart of Cyrus I, the first king, to make the famous decree enabling the Jews to return from Babylon and rebuild the Temple in Jerusalem (Ezra 1:1–2).

The third beast, verse 6, represents the Greek Empire and is described as a four-winged flying leopard with four heads. The leopard with wings refers to Alexander the Great, who ruled for a relatively brief period but who made a remarkably fast conquest of an extremely large area for those times. The four heads of the leopard represent the four generals who divided Alexander's empire between them after his untimely death. Only two of them survived the infighting amongst themselves for power and territory.

The fourth beast, verse 7, was the Roman Empire, which featured ten horns on its head! These horns refer to the same ten end-time kingdoms, shown as ten toes on the feet of the statue in Nebuchadnezzar's dream (Daniel 2).

Daniel 8 provides further explanation regarding the second empire, the united Medo-Persian kingdom, and its fall to the conquering Greeks:

> "*I* [Daniel] *looked up, and there before me was a ram with two horns* [the Medes and Persians]*, standing beside the canal, and the horns were long. One of the horns was longer than the other and grew up later.* [the larger being the dominant King Cyrus of Persia, who conquered the Medes]*. I watched the ram as he charged towards the west and the*

*north and the south. No animal could stand against him, and none could*
*rescue from his power. He did as he pleased and became great* [Cyrus also
overcame the Babylonians].

*As I was thinking about this, suddenly a goat with a prominent horn*
*between his eyes came from the west, crossing the whole earth without*
*touching the ground* [Alexander the Great, who very quickly
enlarged his Greek Empire from the west, conquering the Medes
and Persians as far as India]. *He came towards the two-horned ram I*
*had seen standing beside the canal and charged at him in great rage.*
*I saw him attack the ram furiously, striking the ram* [Medes and
Persians] *and shattering his two horns. The ram was powerless to stand*
*against him; the goat knocked him to the ground and trampled on him,*
*and none could rescue the ram from his power. The goat became very*
*great, but at the height of his power his large horn was broken off, and in*
*its place four prominent horns* [the four generals succeeding
Alexander, who died young] *grew up towards the four winds of*
*heaven."*                                        (Daniel 8:3–8)

And finally, God literally names the second and third empires
later in the same passage.

*"The two-horned ram that you saw represents the kings of Medea and*
*Persia* [the unified empire, the second empire to rule Israel]. *The*
*shaggy goat is the king of Greece, and the large horn between his eyes is*
*the first king* [Alexander – king of the third empire to rule Israel].
*The four horns* [four generals] *that replaced the one that was broken off*
*represent four kingdoms that will emerge from his nation but will not*
*have the same power."*                           (Daniel 8:20–22)

The kingdom of Greece is likened here to a shaggy goat and
significantly the Aegean Sea of Greece means the Goat Sea. At his
death, Alexander's four generals each ruled a part of his empire
but as mentioned one died in battle and another was assassinated.
Of the two survivors, one ruled Syria and the surrounding
countries including Israel, and the other took Egypt and the

surrounding areas to the south of Israel. Over the years these two squabbled and Israel passed briefly under Egyptian rule. The battles are described in Daniel 11, which I explained in chapter 9 of this book. The statue vision in Daniel 2 shows the bronze, representing the Greek Empire, started at the belly and went down the two thighs, each describing one of the two empires that grew out of the remains of Alexander's kingdom. The Antiochus Seleucius dynasty to the north, predominantly ruled Israel.

There are several crucial points to draw from all these visions. The first to note is that they describe the four empires which ruled Israel for significant lengths of time, starting with the Babylonians and ending with the Romans. There have been many other empires throughout history in the rest of the world but God only includes in the Bible those that affect Israel. Therefore, countries such as India, China and the USA do not get a mention. Some believe the woman acquiring the two wings of an eagle in Revelation 12:14 is reference to the USA protecting Israel, which we have certainly seen since Britain failed her.

The second point is that the iron in the feet of the statue continues down to the toes, indicating that the Roman Empire is still present today and will influence Israel until the Lord's return. Because the materials in the statue represent political powers, the clay must describe some other power which takes control of part of the Roman Empire and rules over Israel. It is interesting to note that in God's estimation each successive material moving down the statue is inferior in value to the previous one.

The symbolism in these visions, such as four-winged leopards, seems strange to our modern Western minds but one only has to look in museums at the art and statues of Daniel's day to see that God was communicating to them in ways they would understand. For instance, the walls of Babylon had these strange winged creatures painted on them.

Let us look more closely at the fourth beast in Daniel 7, as this is the one which affects us today.

*"In my vision at night I looked, and there before me was a fourth beast –
terrifying and frightening and very powerful. It had large iron teeth; it
crushed and devoured its victims and trampled underfoot whatever was
left. It was different from all the former beasts, and it had ten horns.
While I was thinking about the horns, there before me was another horn,
a little one,* [the Antichrist, the eleventh horn], *which came up among
them; and three of the first horns were uprooted before it. This horn had
eyes like the eyes of a man and a mouth that spoke boastfully . . . Then I
continued to watch because of the boastful words the horn was speaking.
I kept looking until the beast was slain and its body destroyed and
thrown into the blazing fire . . . As I watched, this horn was waging war
against the saints and defeating them, until the Ancient of Days came
and pronounced judgment in favour of the saints of the Most High, and
the time came when they possessed the kingdom. He* [an angel] *gave me
this explanation: 'The fourth beast is a fourth kingdom that will appear
on earth. It will be different from all the other kingdoms and will devour
the whole earth, trampling it down and crushing it. The ten horns are ten
kings who will come from this kingdom. After them another king will
arise* [the Antichrist], *different from the earlier ones; he will subdue
three kings* [three of the ten kings]. *He will speak against the Most
High and oppress his saints and try to change the set times and the laws.
The saints will be handed over to him for a time, times and half a time*
[3.5 years, each 360 days, totalling 1,260 days, the second half of
the last seven years of the great Tribulation]. *But the court will sit,
and his power will be taken away and completely destroyed for ever.
Then the sovereignty, power and greatness of the kingdoms under the
whole heaven will be handed over to the saints, the people of the Most
High. His kingdom will be an everlasting kingdom, and all rulers will
worship and obey him.' "*                          (Daniel 7:7–8, 11, 21–27)

This amazing vision reveals that the fourth beast representing the
Roman Empire, will eventually produce the little horn, which all
agree is the Antichrist. The ten horns are alternatively shown as
ten toes in Nebuchadnezzar's vision of the statue in Daniel 2 and
both represent the ten kings to come from the fourth beast. Quite

naturally, the leaders in the Reformation assumed that they were living in the last days due to the persecution from Rome by the Catholic Church. This led them to believe that the ten horns represented ten of the largest areas of power in Europe in their day. However, Revelation 17:12 quoted below states the ten are end-time kingdoms lasting for only one hour, which indicates a very short period. This traumatic time ends in the return of Jesus with His faithful followers. He overcomes the Antichrist and his army and brings this age to an end. Therefore, John could not have been referring way back to the dark ages when the Popes had absolute power over Europe. Alas, there are even darker times ahead described elsewhere as "Jacob's Troubles".

> *"The ten horns you saw are ten kings who have not yet received a kingdom, but who for one hour will receive authority as kings along with the beast* [the eleventh king, the little horn in the previous quote, the Antichrist]. *They have one purpose and will give their power and authority to the beast. They will make war against the Lamb, but the Lamb will overcome them because he is Lord of lords and King of kings – with him will be his called, chosen and faithful followers."*
>
> (Revelation 17:12–14)

This end battle is referred to again two chapters later:

> *"Then I saw the beast and the kings of the earth and their armies gathered together to make war against the rider on the horse and his army. But the beast was captured and with him the false prophet who had performed the miraculous signs on his behalf."*
>
> (Revelation 19:19–20)

From Daniel 7:8, previously quoted, three of these ten end time kings will be uprooted and supplanted by the Antichrist. One assumes he detects disloyalty to his cause. Hopefully, it means they have become believers?

It is also important to see that Revelation 13:5, Daniel 7:25 and

2 Thessalonians 2:1–4 all refer to the same final three and a half
year period when the Antichrist is allowed to utter proud words
and exercise his authority for forty-two months (3.5 judgment
years), just before the return of Jesus. The three scriptures are:

> *"The beast* [the Antichrist] *was given a mouth to utter proud words and
> blasphemies and to exercise his authority for forty-two months* [each of
> 30 days totalling 1,260 days]*."*                    (Revelation 13:5)

> *"He will speak against the Most High and oppress his saints and try to
> change the set times and the laws. The saints will be handed over to him
> for a time, times and a half a time* [1,260 days]*."*         (Daniel 7:25)

> *"Don't let anyone deceive you in any way, for that day will not come
> until the rebellion occurs and the man of lawlessness is revealed, the man
> doomed to destruction. He will oppose and will exalt himself over
> everything that is called God or is worshipped, so that he sets himself up
> in God's temple, proclaiming himself to be God."*
>                                          (2 Thessalonians 2:3–4)

The Antichrist's diabolical reign of terror occurs in the second
half of the great Tribulation. He exalts himself over everything
that is called God and even enthrones himself as God in the
rebuilt Temple. Revelation 13:11–18 enlarges on the end-time
scenario and informs us that the false prophet, the spiritual
partner in evil to the Antichrist, is probably deceived into thinking
he is Elijah (Malachi 4:5). John the Baptist came in the spirit of
Elijah but at the second coming of Christ the true prophet will be
there, probably one of the two witnesses in Jerusalem. The false
prophet forces the inhabitants of the earth to receive the Mark of
the Beast, which is the number 666, and allows only those who
have received it to buy and sell:

> *"If anyone has insight, let him calculate the number of the beast, for it is
> man's number. His number is 666."*                (Revelation 13:18)

To explain this mark, we have to understand that the New Testament is written in Greek and, like Hebrew, is unusual in that the letters of both alphabets are assigned numerical values to form their respective everyday numbering system. Alpha is 1, beta is 2, gamma is 3, delta is 4, epsilon is 5, digamma is 6, zeta is 7, eta is 8, theta is 9, iota is 10, kappa is 20, lambda is 30 etc.; then rho is 100, sigma is 200, tau is 300, upsilon is 400 and so on. To see how this numbering system works in spiritual terms, let us take the numerical value of the name Jesus, in Greek, which totals 888:

| I | iota | = | 10 |
|---|---------|---|-----|
| E | eta | = | 8 |
| S | sigma | = | 200 |
| O | omega | = | 70 |
| U | upsilon | = | 400 |
| S | sigma | = | 200 |
| | | | 888 |

The Antichrist's name in the Greek language will total 666 – the number of man is 6 and the number of new life is 8. We need to be very careful with this number as there will be many instances where it will appear. Sometimes the numerical value of a person's name in Greek or some financial system will be an expression of the spirit of Antichrist, but in other cases it will be merely coincidental. We see in the next verse that the 144,000 Jewish believers also had names on their foreheads (Revelation 14:1) and all on the new earth have it as well (Revelation 22:4). However, I believe God definitely marks us in a spiritual way but Satan will probably identify us in a carnal way, which looks like it will be with an implant of some description. The man of sin will primarily be identified by his fulfilling the various scriptures we looked at earlier and this number 666 in the Greek language is only to be a confirmation.

Returning to the fourth beast, there is further very important information concerning the Roman Empire given in Revelation 17. We read that this beast has seven heads:

> *"The seven heads are seven hills on which the woman sits. They are also seven kings. Five have fallen, one is* **(the sixth one)**, *the other* [the seventh one] *has not yet come; but when he does come, he must remain for a little while. The beast who once was, and now is not, is an eighth king. He belongs to the seven and is going to his destruction."*
>
> (Revelation 17:9–11, emphasis added)

The first point to note is that the Bible gives the seven heads two very distinct and different meanings. Firstly, they represent seven hills. Rome was the only major city in the empire built on this number of hills, and Christians in the apostle John's day definitely associated them with that capital.

Secondly, the heads also stand for seven kings of which five had previously fallen. We know the sixth king, the *"one is"*, referred to the king reigning over Israel at the time of John's imprisonment on the isle of Patmos. Imperial Rome was in power when he received the great apocalyptic vision, and Domitian was her Caesar. He was a particularly vain and deceived individual who demanded that everyone throughout the Empire acknowledge him as divine! But Domitian was about the eleventh Caesar, not the sixth! As there were over forty emperors, from Julius in 45 BC until the overthrow of the Western Empire by the Germanic Goths in AD 476, the sixth head must represent the Roman Empire as a whole, rather than individual rulers. This is consistent with the golden head of Nebuchadnezzar's dream representing all the monarchs of the Babylonian Empire, not just one.

The Daniel 2 vision of the great statue depicted four of the empires to rule Israel, but the seven empires expressed as seven heads in Revelation 17 include two previous ones and a subsequent seventh one as well. As pointed out earlier, it is vital to see that God only mentions in the Bible those nations that have a significant bearing on Israel. We find, therefore, that the first head was Egypt. Jacob and his family journeyed down to Egypt as a result of a famine. The Jews eventually became slaves to a later Pharaoh, who ruled them cruelly, but God delivered them through Moses. The second head was the Assyrians who conquered the north of Israel and exiled the ten tribes to their land. Then came the four empires previously discussed – namely the Babylonians who took the remaining two southern tribes captive, followed by the Persians and then the Greeks. The sixth head, the Roman Empire, shown in Daniel's statue as legs of pure iron, continued right down through the feet and toes, the latter being mixed with baked clay. We know from Daniel 2 statue and Daniel 7:7 beast that the Roman empire continues right up to the ten end time kingdoms shown by the iron continuing to the ten toes and the ten horns, so the seventh head must be a revived Roman Empire, but which is weakened by the clay.

The verses at the beginning of Revelation 17 provide more vital information. The seven-headed beast and its rider are both scarlet, signifying sin, but the woman also wears purple, indicating rulership. Red and purple are the colours of Rome, and gold refers to wealth. The woman rides the beast, which very importantly shows she is in control of the monster:

> " 'Come, I will show you the punishment of the great prostitute, who sits on many waters. With her the kings of the earth committed adultery and the inhabitants of the earth were intoxicated with the wine of her adulteries.' Then the angel carried me away in the Spirit into a desert. There I saw a woman sitting on a scarlet beast that was covered with blasphemous names and had seven heads and ten horns. The woman was dressed in purple and scarlet, and was glittering with gold, precious stones and pearls. She held a golden cup in her hand, filled with abominable things and the filth of her adulteries. This title was written on her forehead:*

MYSTERY

BABYLON THE GREAT

THE MOTHER OF PROSTITUTES

*AND OF THE ABOMINATIONS*

*OF THE EARTH.*

*I saw that the woman was drunk with the blood of the saints, the blood of those who bore testimony to Jesus."*                    (Revelation 17:1–6)

So, who does Mystery Babylon the mother of prostitutes represent? She speaks of spiritual prostitution – false religion, rather than sexual sin, though the latter may well be involved. She is also drunk with the blood of Christians, those that gave testimony to Jesus, so she must live after Christ came. This would cover the same time period as the first interpretation, where the woman is seated on seven hills, meaning she reigns spiritually over political Rome. The early Church clearly saw that in both interpretations of the seven-headed beast, the seven hills of the first interpretation represented the city of Rome, and the sixth head in the second interpretation represented the Roman Empire. The woman symbolised the priests of their gods in both cases. Martin Luther and the other spiritual teachers of the Reformation saw the woman had developed into the Roman Catholic Church, headed up by the Popes. God has not changed the meaning today in order to be politically correct. Revelation 17:18 says she represents *"the city* [Vatican city] *that rules over the kings of the earth"*, which is exactly what we have seen over the centuries in Europe and continue to witness around the world. The Roman Catholic Church has dominated politics over the centuries, as I will explain in the next chapter, and is still seen as the authoritive voice of Christianity, rather than Bible-based Christian communities.

In the second biblical interpretation, where the seven heads represent seven empires, the woman who rides these empires stands for the religions that have governed them – the Egyptians etc.

Revelation 17:10–12, quoted earlier in the chapter, informs us that mercifully the seventh empire will only reign for a short while, followed by an eighth king, the Antichrist, who will come from the seventh empire and reign for three and a half years. It is important to emphasise that the ten horns of this seven-headed beast of Revelation 17 represent the same ten end-time kingdoms, also shown as horns in Daniel 7:7. They, along with the final little horn of Daniel 7:8 and 20, all grow out of the seventh head of the Beast, not from the woman. This shows that the Antichrist will emerge from the political rather than the religious side. Since Satan has deceived the Antichrist into thinking he is the Messiah, there will be a strong spiritual dimension of false signs and wonders to his political and military might. He may take on the High Priest ministry as well, which would combine the spiritual with the military. He will rise to power as Hitler did, by promising every-thing and believing he is the Saviour of the world. Unfortunately, he will go much further than even Hitler was able to take things. The Antichrist will not only eliminate all opposition but also take all power by declaring himself to be God over all other gods!

In Daniel 7:20–25 and Revelation 17:12–14 the ten kings arising from the Beast are intent on making war against the Lamb and His followers (Jesus and His Church). These ten will receive authority from the Antichrist for a short time to serve his purposes.

> *"The ten horns you saw are ten kings who have not yet received a kingdom, but who for one hour will receive authority as kings along with the beast."*                          (Revelation 17:12)

Thankfully, after much persecution, the saints on earth finally triumph. Revelation 17:16 says the ten kings, which come from the beast (political), all turn on the prostitute (false religion) and destroy her!

> *"The beast and the ten horns you saw will hate the prostitute. They will bring her to ruin and leave her naked; they will eat her flesh and burn her with fire ... The woman you saw is the great city* [a large religious grouping] *that rules over the kings of the earth."*
>                          (Revelation 17:16, 18)

In the nineteenth century Napoleon (an antichrist) savagely attacked the Catholic Church and drastically reduced her power, but we are still waiting to see these infamous ten latter kings and their leader, who will turn on the religious establishment. The whole of Revelation 18 shows that the business community are seduced by the woman as well. For example:

> *"The kings of the earth committed adultery with her,*
> *and the merchants of the earth grew rich from*
> *her excessive luxuries."* (Revelation 18:3)

Therefore, the end-time scenario so far studied is – the revived Roman Empire dominates world trade, overseen by the religion of Rome. The Antichrist will arise and confirm some form of Old Covenant sacrifice. He will subsequently speak boastfully, declaring himself to be God, persecuting and killing the saints and eventually turning against the false religion of Rome. He will overthrow three of the end-time rulers he has made kings. Fortunately, from the time he declares himself to be God, there will only be around three and a half years before Jesus returns to cast him into the lake of fire. God has given these details for the direction and encouragement of believers who will have to go through these horrendous times, and very importantly, these scriptures will become a powerful tool for evangelism.

# The History of the Roman Empire

To appreciate the connection between the original Roman Empire and our day, it is essential to understand some of its history. Emperor Constantine (AD 307–337) is said to have converted to Christianity after seeing a vision of a flaming cross in the sky. He subsequently won a significant battle, which he put down to the God of Jesus. Some say he incorporated his idea of Christianity into his paganism, developing a mixture of Christian and Roman beliefs. Others say he was truly born again and tried to change what he could. Whichever way, he sought to introduce some Christian principles and while rightly allowing religious freedom, he wrongly persecuted the Jews, outlawing the Saturday Sabbath and the Passover, which exposed an anti Semitic spirit.

In AD 286, Emperor Diocletian, several Caesars before Constantine, had divided the empire into East and West for ease of governance, which Daniel 2 describes as two legs in the statue vision. He chose his general, Maximianus, as co-Emperor over the West, while he governed the East, as Constantine later did. Theodosius (AD 379–395), several rulers after Constantine, also governed the eastern side. He officially outlawed the numerous Roman gods in AD 391, and Christianity became the official religion of the whole empire. He established the scripturally-based Nicene creed, "I believe in God the Father..." and a correct biblical definition of the Trinity. He was definitely a genuine Christian.

The primacy of Rome's bishop over all the other bishops was asserted by the Council of Chalcedon, which met near Constantinople (now Istanbul), in AD 451. The Bishop of Rome, Papa Leo I, started to make decrees that were prefaced by "Peter, the apostle, has spoken by Pope Leo ... Let him be anathema who believes otherwise." This became known as speaking *ex cathedra*, i.e. when the Pope, as head of the Roman Church, is supposedly speaking the word of God. By then the doctrine of the Pope being known as Father and being sole custodian of the keys of the kingdom was developing. Understanding the new birth was slowly lost, with the consequent lack of revelation on scriptures such as Jesus' conversation with Peter:

> " 'Who do you say I am?' Simon Peter answered, 'You are the Christ, the Son of the living God.' Jesus replied, 'Blessed are you, Simon son of Jonah, for this was not revealed to you by man, but by my Father in heaven. And I tell you that you are Peter, and on this rock will I build my church, and the gates of Hades will not overcome it. I will give you the keys of the kingdom of heaven; whatever you bind on earth will be bound in heaven, and whatever you loose on earth will be loosed in heaven.' "
>
> (Matthew 16:15–19)

The Catholic Church has misunderstood Jesus' words and because Peter was a prominent leader in the newly-born Church, they believe him to be the rock on which the Church was to be built. Therefore, only he could legitimately hand the keys on to a successor. This is not what Jesus was referring to nor did it occur. The rock Jesus spoke of was the revelation from the Holy Spirit to Peter's heart that Jesus was the Christ, the Son of the living God. It is this revelation alone which, when believed in the heart, brings about the new birth and enables every true Christian to share the gospel, to bind and to loose. It is only through this experience that a believer joins the Church and upon this foundation alone that the Church is built and grows. Earlier the Holy Spirit had shown Jesus to give Simon the name Peter, meaning rock, in anticipation of this conversation. As far as handing the leadership on, Paul, for example, did not have hands laid on him by Peter to become a leader in the Church nor did Peter hand over leadership of the Church. Today, God is raising up leaders all over the world to build His Church, with no reference to the Pope.

Unlike the Popes and subsequently the local priests, when the apostle John referred to believers as "his children" in his letters, he was nurturing them as a spiritual father. He was not encouraging them to call him by this title. The apostle Paul said there were many teachers but few fathers, and he too was not teaching believers to refer to him or any other leaders by this name. Indeed, Jesus specifically taught against this,

> *"Do not call anyone on earth 'father'* [spiritually], *for you have one Father, and he is in heaven."*                    (Matthew 23:9)

The Church was obviously becoming more confused and dictatorial, witnessed by speaking in the name of Peter rather than Jesus. Although many of the major doctrinal issues agreed at the Chalcedon Council were still scriptural, man was beginning to be head of the Church rather than Jesus. Slowly, unscriptural infant christening became established as the entrance to the Body of Christ rather than new birth through personal faith.

The political intervention of Pope Leo I in AD 455 to persuade Attila the Hun, a Mongol, not to invade Rome laid the foundation for the Popes' political power.

The Pope in Rome overruled the bid by Flavian, Bishop of Constantinople, to be made Patriarch of the Church in the eastern part of the empire with equal status to Rome. The western half of the Roman Empire had ceased politically for a time when the Goths deposed Romulus Augustus in AD 476. The eastern part continued to flourish and expand, becoming known as the Byzantine Empire. From here, Justinian in AD 554 reconquered a large part of the western empire and acknowledged the supremacy of the Pope in Rome on spiritual matters rather than the eastern Bishop. The Church and state in the west became more intertwined.

In 607 AD, Pope Boniface III took on the title of Universal Bishop in Europe. The teachings of the Popes became as valid as those of the writers of the Bible, even when they contradicted Jesus and His apostles! Hence, gross errors developed. The woman clothed in scarlet and purple, representing Roman Catholicism, was now firmly in the saddle, riding the seven-headed beast – the seven hills of Rome.

The next major event in Europe was Pope Leo III crowning Charlemagne in St Peter's Basilica in Rome in AD 800, naming him Great Emperor of the Romans. He was of Teutonic descent and ruled Franconia – an area originally covering Germany and France. He conquered most of western and central Europe – roughly the western part of the original Roman Empire and became Western Europe's self-confessed Christian Kaiser (Caesar). He revived the Holy (or correctly, Unholy) Roman Empire and ordered conversion to so-called Christianity by sword point. This was the First Reich (German Rule). The king being crowned by a Pope introduced the perception that the Imperial Crown of Rome was not valid unless confirmed and overseen by the Pope, and that the kingdoms of Europe spiritually belonged to the Bishop of Rome.

In AD 962 Otto I, the next notable German king, came to the throne and revived Charlemagne's flagging empire. He was duly crowned Holy Roman Emperor by Pope John XII and tried unsuccessfully to make an alliance with the Byzantine Emperor Nicephoros II, who ruled the eastern part of the Roman Empire. This attempt to fan into flame the glory of the original Empire eventually died down and did not aspire to being known as the Second Reich.

In 1054 the Church in Constantinople broke with the Bishop of Rome, and formed the Eastern Orthodox Church. The eastern Empire declined politically but was retaken by the Roman

Catholic Crusaders in 1099. Constantinople was later captured by the Turks in 1453 and came under Muslim rule.

In the eleventh century Pope Gregory VII claimed absolute and unlimited spiritual and political dominion over all the countries in Europe (Christendom). During the next few hundred years, and despite the efforts of the Roman Catholic Church to stamp out all dissent, there were certain significant areas of Europe where learned and sincere Christian leaders, who understood the Greek and Latin versions of the Bible, taught a faithful witness to the Christ of the Scriptures. In AD 1179 the Catholic Lateran Council decided to exterminate this opposition to Papal authority. These antibiblical campaigns by the Popes in Europe were linked to the Roman Catholic Crusades in the Holy Land. Their worldly efforts to take back Jerusalem for Christ led to countless thousands of Muslims and Jews being slaughtered. They have much to answer for for the current misconception of many Muslims regarding Christianity.

A century later Count Rudolf of Habsburg, an Austrian, took the Imperial crown of Rome, which then became an hereditary title in his family. The most famous Habsburg, Emperor Charles V of Austria, built a Roman Catholic empire stretching from Vienna to Peru.

Not only were the Catholic doctrines now seriously at odds with the Bible, but also the immorality of the Popes was well known. John Wycliffe and other Bible scholars in England, who lived 100 years before Luther, declared the Popes as Antichrist. They opposed Rome with its corruption and false doctrines such as transubstantiation, prayers to Mary and the saints etc. By AD 1514 the Pope declared that all organised opposition had been eliminated. It was the zenith of papal power and to the Reformers it looked as though the "man of lawlessness" had set himself up in the Temple of God. But this was only a foreshadowing of things to come. Despite the horrendous campaign against them, the Reformation was given fresh impetus in AD 1517 when Luther, an outspoken Catholic monk and theologian, published his famous ninety-five theses against papal corruption, doctrinal error, indulgencies etc. Intensive study of the Bible convinced him that political Rome was the seventh head of the beast in Revelation 17, and that the Catholic Church was the woman riding it. It was revelation of the Scriptures that increased his faith and gave him boldness to counter the religious stranglehold over Europe. He and many others laid the foundations for the Protestant Church. Later the Pope launched an extremely strong Counter Reformation and hundreds of thousands, of sincere believers were slaughtered because they refused to accept Rome's teachings. They laid down their lives in order that biblical teachings might be upheld, free from the darkness of Rome's doctrines.

It is important to see that Henry VIII had nothing to do with altering Catholic doctrines when he set himself up as Supreme Head of the English Church. Indeed, he was strongly opposed to Luther's teaching. Although he became independent from the Pope and dissolved the monasteries – he remained a Roman Catholic in faith. The rebellion against Rome was for his own selfish marital and political plans but it did open the way and make it easier for the Reformation to succeed later in England. It was not until his death in 1547, when Edward VI came the throne, that Cranmer was able to bring in the doctrinal Reformation, consolidated by Elizabeth I (see Google Catholic Encyclopedia: Anglicanism).

The next significant ruler of Europe was Napoleon. He took the title of First Consul from the Roman Empire's hierarchical structure and kept a bust of Julius Caesar prominently displayed in his study. He dreamed of a united Europe but this time, of course, dominated by France, and in particular by himself! He declared, "I am of the race of the Caesars, and of the best of those who laid the foundations." Not content with making Pope Pius VII come to Notre Dame Cathedral in Paris to crown him, he displayed further characteristic arrogance during the ceremony, by seizing the crown from the Pope's hands and placing it on his own head! He then allowed the Pope to bless his reign, thus demonstrating his superiority over the Papacy. At the height of his power he crowned himself again with the "iron crown" of Lombardy, as worn by Charlemagne, and wrote to the Pope saying, "I am Charlemagne, the sword of the Church, her Emperor." The Austrian Habsburgs promptly relinquished the Imperial crown and the title of Holy Roman Emperor for fear of their lives. Napoleon subsequently rounded on the Roman Catholic Church and severely reduced its power; a foreshadowing of the Beast (the Antichrist) of Revelation 17:16 turning on the spiritual prostitute during the end-time Tribulation.

Napoleon said, after his defeat at Waterloo, whilst exiled on St Helena, "I wanted to found a European system, a European code of laws, a European judiciary. There would have been one people throughout Europe." His attempts were at the cost of countless tens of thousands of lives. Interestingly, Napoleon could not have children by Josephine, so he married Marie Louise, daughter of the Austrian Emperor, Francis I. She bore Napoleon a son and he called him the King of Rome.

In 1933 Hitler became Chancellor of Germany and started to build the Third Reich to impose and demonstrate the mastery of the Aryan race. Mussolini declared the resurrection of the Holy Roman Empire in Rome in 1936, claiming himself to be an Emperor of Imperial Rome. Both dictators adopted the straight-arm salute that the Roman Emperors had insisted upon when saluting Caesar, clearly displaying the same dominant spirit inherited from the Roman Empire, which manifested as Fascism in the two men. Both were Roman Catholics with many right-wing Catholics complicit in their evil activities.

It is clear from the last few paragraphs that the spirits which rule over the western half of the Roman Empire have tried to raise the seventh head on several occasions but none have succeeded in producing the end-time Antichrist as foreseen by God. Why? It is vital to see that these dark forces have not given up and are still at work today. They have an insatiable desire to take back full control over the territory of the original Roman

Empire and more if possible! What has held them back? It is none other than God! He has restrained them from coming to full power too soon, because the rise of the Antichrist, who is to rule the world through Europe, signals the return of Jesus. God desires every nation (literal Greek: *ethnos*, meaning "ethnic group") to fully hear the gospel before the end of this age (Luke 24:47), and He has the Church on target to achieve this in line with the development of the spiritual and political situation, which will produce the Antichrist. This restraining was covered in chapter 11 in the context of the rapture, but I repeat the scripture:

> *"Don't let anyone deceive you in any way, for that day* [when Jesus returns] *will not come until the rebellion occurs and the man of lawlessness* [the Antichrist] *is revealed, the man doomed to destruction. He will oppose and will exalt himself over everything that is called God or is worshipped, so that he sets himself up in God's temple, proclaiming himself to be God. Don't you remember that when I was with you I used to tell you these things? And now you know what* [the Holy Spirit] *is holding him* [the Antichrist] *back, so that he may be revealed at the proper time. For the secret power of lawlessness is already at work; but the one* [the Holy Spirit] *who now holds it back will continue to do so till he* [the Antichrist is defeated and exposed to the unbeliever and] *is taken out of the way."*                    (2 Thessalonians 2:3–7)

God will allow the Antichrist to have his reign of terror but only by His permission, as we saw in the first chapters of Job, and then Jesus will return to remove him and his followers from power and cast him into the lake of fire. Isaiah had a revelation regarding the desire by Satan to sit unopposed in the temple in Jerusalem and, as we have seen in other scriptures, this will be through the Antichrist:

> *"You* [Satan] *said in your heart,*
> *'I will ascend to heaven;*

> *I will raise my throne*
> > *above the stars* [angels] *of God;*
> *I will sit enthroned on the mount of assembly*
> > [the Temple in Jerusalem],
> > *on the utmost heights of the sacred mountain*
> > > [on which Solomon's Temple was built].'"   (Isaiah 14:13)

Since the Devil's last attempts to take power in the Roman Empire through Hitler and Mussolini, a most miraculous and momentous event has occurred, namely the formation of the State of Israel. I cannot overstate the enormity of the sea change in the spiritual realm that this has caused, and consequently we are in a totally new situation today. Satan has tried everything in his power to stop it but he is no match for the Almighty. This restoration was a major promise to the Jews, and God is working to bring about their rightful possession of the whole land. But even greater promises are yet to be fulfilled, even the revelation of Christ to the whole Jewish nation (Romans 11:26), followed by Jesus' return as King of kings!

Satan, in his delusion, continues to work for the revival of the empire with an ultimate objective of gaining absolute control over the whole earth but as usual he is just playing into God's hand! Because the Jewish state is now in existence, Satan is desperate to exterminate the whole Jewish nation, remove the State of Israel and dupe the world with a false Messiah, but God's preordained purposes will be accomplished.

# Where are the Scarlet Beast and the Woman Who Rides It Today?

First, I repeat Daniel's interpretation of King Nebuchadnezzar's dream:

> *"You looked, O king, and there before you stood a large statue – an enormous, dazzling statue, awesome in appearance. The head of the statue was made of pure gold, its chest and arms of silver, its belly and thighs of bronze, its legs of iron, its feet partly of iron and partly of baked clay. While you were watching, a rock was cut out, but not by human hands. It struck the statue on its feet of iron and clay and smashed them. Then the iron, the clay, the bronze, the silver and the gold were broken to pieces at the same time and became like chaff on the threshing floor in the summer. The wind swept them away without leaving a trace. But the rock that struck the statue became a huge mountain and filled the whole earth.*
>
> *This was the dream, and now we will interpret it to the king. You, O king, are the king of kings. The God of heaven has given you dominion and power and might and glory; in your hand he has placed mankind and the beasts of the field and the birds of the air. Wherever they live, he has made you ruler over them all. You are that head of gold."*
>
> (Daniel 2:31–38)

When Jesus came to Israel, the Romans were in full control of their empire, the iron had no clay mixed in it. Jesus brought in the kingdom of God on a spiritual level making a way for the forgiveness of sin, healing and deliverance from spiritual bondage. The Lord described the empire in terms of iron and it was indeed this cruel unbending metal that pierced Jesus' hands, feet and side. The kingdom of God today is righteousness, joy and peace in the Holy Spirit and we enter it through the new birth in Christ. One day the kingdom will come physically as well, when Jesus returns to reign. We will then be given our resurrection bodies – praise God! I do not believe we will be able to appear and disappear in them as Jesus did, because we are not God. He came the first time as a humble servant and sin-bearer, but at His second appearance He will come as the all-conquering King of kings. Jesus is the rock not hewn by human hands. He will completely destroy not only the feet, but the whole edifice – a picture of the cumulative sin, harlotry and efforts of all the empires that have ruled over Israel. This rock, describing Jesus and His Kingdom, becomes a mountain filling the whole earth – His 1,000 years reign on earth from Jerusalem.

The iron continuing down into the feet and toes of the statue shows that the Roman Empire continues until Jesus' return. So, where is it today? It is, of course, the European Union, initially the EEC, formed very significantly by the Treaty of Rome in 1957. Many continentals dreamed of a united Europe but it was the inspiration primarily of Roman Catholic thinkers and politicians such as Jean Monnet, Adenauer, Paul Henri Spaak, and Robert Schuman, to name but a few, that formed its particular style. Signed in 1957 by the six original countries, it brought the European Economic Community into being.

The failed attempts by Hitler and Mussolini were the last efforts to revive the Roman Empire by the gun, but I believe we are witnessing an extremely subtle and sophisticated re-emergence in our day. This is the seventh head of the Beast but we are told, thankfully, that it will only last for a short time. It will produce the eighth king, the evil Antichrist, whose bloody dictatorial reign will be shorter – three and a half years to be exact.

> *"Five have fallen, one is* [Rome in John's time], *the other* [the
> seventh head] *has not yet come; but when he does come, he must remain
> for a little while. The beast who once was, and now is not, is an eighth
> king* [the Antichrist]. *He belongs to the seven and is going to his
> destruction."*                    (Revelation 17:10–11, emphasis added)

After the devastation of the Second World War, Germany and
France started working towards the same age-old dream of a
unified Europe with the objective of avoiding future wars within
the continent. The politicians assured Britain that it was joining
an economic community and there would be no political Superstate! We were deceived – it was their intention all along! We are
fast moving towards their goal and have already lost much of our
sovereignty. The French and Dutch polls in 2005 demonstrated a
fundamental unease about the EU and the Euro, yet there is an air
of resignation about the inevitability of it all continuing and
growing, despite most not wanting it. Why?

The same spirits who governed the Roman Empire have tried
to regain control of the whole area and still long for this. They
have brought about the EU, run by the European Commission,
which not only creates policy but also produces legislation to
ensure it is implemented. It consists of a large number of
Commissioners from each member state, and a six-month
rotating president is chosen, soon to be changed by the Lisbon
Treaty to an elected one for a two and a half year minimum
period. Mr Tony Blair has been suggested as the first president.
He has officially joined the Roman Catholic Church, which
means he agrees with all their unscriptural doctrines and has
started an interfaith trust. In its own statement, the commissioners are to act in the interests of the Union, independent of
national governments. The Council of the European Union
comprises foreign ministers from each national government to
be headed up by an EU foreign minister. The European
Parliament still has limited powers at this stage but does have
the authority to dissolve the Commission. The European 2007

Treaty will give the Brussels Parliament proportionately more power, as the individual nations lose theirs. It is opposite to Britain, where the government mainly initiates policy and Whitehall seeks to implement its will. The foreign ministers of each member state and the European Parliament struggle to cope with the mountain of legislation presented to them by the Commission. The Commission employs 25,000 staff, roughly half the total employed by all the European institutions. A formidable juggernaut indeed, which is self-perpetuating regardless of public opinion. The elder statesmen of the enterprise are now open about their once well-veiled agenda because they believe it has reached the point of no return! They now unashamedly declare that their true objective to develop a European Superstate was there from the start. Deception is one of the foundation stones of Satan.

The Bill of Rights, the new European Legal Order, was signed in 1972 overriding British Law and superseding the Magna Carta in 1215. The new treaty currently being considered develops the new Legal Order more towards Continental law. Our fundamental position in Britain of being innocent until proven guilty, would reverse to the individual having to prove his innocence if charged. Trial by jury would also be removed, and a British citizen could be arrested in another country inside the Union for up to nine months without charge. The EU will be a single legal entity like a country. The Lisbon Treaty will enable changes to be made by majority voting rather than a unanimous agreement by all national governments. The size and role of an EU army is being formulated.

The manner in which all opposition is being disregarded with disdain in the development of the Union has the tell-tale signs of the fascist spirit re-emerging once again in Europe and the scene is being set to bring about a State where an unscrupulous individual could take dictatorial power as happened in Germany.

For Christians the economic and political arguments for or against joining the Euro currency and so on, are important but only superficial, because we are dealing with something that has all the hallmarks of a spiritual principality, namely antibiblical teaching, control, secrecy, deception, lies, lack of morals etc.

It is worth mentioning the new European Parliament building in Strasbourg, opened in December 2000 at a cost of £8 billion. It is circular, several tiers high and has a section of the upper part missing because it is fashioned on Rome's Coliseum. This same Roman arena, where many thousands were slaughtered in the blood sports of Rome's heyday, inspired the famous painting of The Tower of Babel by Pieter Brueghel. This gives further insight about the ancient rebellious spirits that are still at work in our day. The proposed treaty omits the mention of God, as the various beliefs of the leaders generally accept an "all roads lead to God" doctrine. Tragically, this excludes the one true way, through the new birth in Christ. Just like the first Tower of Babel, man is building a modern one to make a name for himself, glorifying and magnifying his own efforts without God's help. This independence is, of course, happening in all the nations of the world, but the significant point about the revival of the Roman Empire is that it is specifically prophesied in the Bible. The original Tower or Ziggurat of Babel is mentioned in Genesis:

> *"They said to each other, 'Come, let's make bricks and bake them thoroughly.' They used brick instead of stone, and bitumen for mortar. Then they said, 'Come, let us build ourselves a city, with a tower that reaches to the heavens, so that we may make a name for ourselves.'"*
>
> (Genesis 11:3–4)

Today, many of Europe's leaders, including many MEPS, see a vital role for the Roman Catholic Church in the Superstate. Although the Roman Church has greatly diminished, Pope John Paul II believed it was his literal calling from God to preside over the crucial formative years of the EU and witness a restoration of the Holy Roman Empire under his spiritual oversight and direction, which is still continuing. He said in 1975:

"Can it not be said that it is faith, the Christian faith, the Catholic faith that made Europe?"

In Poland, in 1979, he declared,

"Europe, despite its present and long-lasting divisions of regimes, ideologies and economic systems, cannot cease to seek its fundamental unity and must turn to Christianity. Economic and political reasons cannot do it. We must go deeper."

In 1982 he said,

"I, Bishop of Rome and Shepherd of the Universal Church, utter to you, Europe of the ages, a cry full of love. Find yourself again. Be yourself. Discover your origins; revive your roots."

He referred, of course, to a return to the unbiblical Roman Catholic doctrines and not to the Bible-based Reformers.

The Vatican consecrated Europe to Mary in 1309. The shrine of "Our Lady of Europa" in Gibraltar was renovated several years ago using a £200,000 grant from the EU, with the Vatican statement:

"It is the prayer of His Holiness that the shrine will be an ever more effective centre of unification, a place where, under the patronage of Mary, the human family will be drawn ever more closely into a fraternity and peaceful co-existence."

It was also openly reported by the Vatican that the Pope spent much of his time praying to Mary to accomplish this vision, and regularly received instruction from her. In May 2005 the current Pope Benedict XVI was consecrated to Our Lady (The Virgin Mary) who had appeared to three children in Fatima, Portugal, in 1917. An incident exposing the deceptive manifestations of Mary to the biblically aware, was experienced by an evangelist I know.

He came across a shrine to an apparition of her near his outreach
venue in Europe. In his afternoon prayertime the Lord showed
him to pray against this shrine. He was confronted in his
bedroom by the face of "Mary" asking him why he was speaking
against her, imploring him to leave her alone and saying that she
was doing no harm to the people. He could feel a manipulative,
drawing power trying to seduce him to accept her words and
become tolerant of her hold over the area. He spoke firmly
and said, "You are not Mary but the false queen of heaven", and
commanded the spirit to leave in the name of Jesus. Remarkably,
the face was suddenly removed, as if a mask had been peeled
off, to reveal a grotesque beast that roared at him and then
disappeared! There was a tremendous sense of break-through in
the spiritual realm and that night nearly everyone at his meeting,
about 200 people, gave their lives to Christ with many healed and
delivered from evil spirits. Indeed, Satan can appear as an angel of
light (2 Corinthians 11:14).

The EU seeks political control, and Roman Catholicism,
headed by the Pope, considers itself spiritual overseer of the
Christian world, and seeks spiritual control with its home base in
Western Europe. Catholicism has been, and still is, inextricably
involved in Europe's politics. For instance, when the European
Union was expanded to fifteen nations, the EU's own newspaper,
*The European*, ran an article responding to those who had
expected the flag's design of twelve stars to change to fifteen,
one star for each country, similar to the flag of the United States
of America. It was officially confirmed that it would remain
twelve gold stars on a blue background, as this has been
replicated from the stained glass window in Strasbourg's Roman
Catholic Cathedral and has nothing to do with the number
of countries in the EU. The Catholic orientated bureaucrats of
Brussels headed the article "12 Forever." Revelation 12, quoted
below, inspired the window painting where the woman in the
vision is adorned with twelve stars around her head. Roman
Catholicism believes that she represents Mother Mary.

*"A great and wondrous sign appeared in heaven; a woman clothed with the sun, with the moon under her feet and a crown of twelve stars on her head. She was pregnant and cried out in pain as she was about to give birth. Then another sign appeared in heaven: an enormous red dragon with seven heads and ten horns and seven crowns on his heads. His tail swept a third of the stars* [angels] *out of sky and flung them to the earth. The dragon stood in front of the woman who was about to give birth, so that he* [Herod] *might devour her child* [Jesus] *the moment it was born. [5]She gave birth to a son, a male child, who will rule the nations with an iron sceptre. And her child* [neuter] *was snatched up to God and to his throne. [6]The woman fled into the desert to a place prepared for her by God, where she might be taken care of for 1,260 days* [the last three and a half years]*."* (Revelation 12:1–6)

Firstly, Mary did indeed give birth to the Christ Child, verse 5, "a male child", but on investigation we find the woman does not refer solely to Mary as an individual, but to the nation of Israel. The first clue to the correct interpretation is found in Genesis. Joseph, as a young man, received a vision of the sun, moon and eleven stars bowing down to him (Genesis 37:9–10). The stars here represent the other eleven sons (twelve sons in total) of Israel. The same imagery is deliberate in the passage in Revelation, where the sun with which "the woman was clothed", depicts Jacob, whose name God changed to Israel, the father of all the tribes; the moon under her feet represents Rachel, his wife. Secondly, we see from verse 6 that this woman remains on earth until the end of the age, living through the last three and a half years of the Great Tribulation, protected by a great eagle. So, she could not represent Mary alone. Thirdly, one must note that the word "child" at the end of verse 5 "*her **child** was snatched up*" is neuter and not masculine, as at the beginning of verse 5. This then either refers to Jesus returning to heaven in His resurrection body, which does not have the male reproduction organs (Jesus said there is no marriage in the resurrection [Luke 20:35]) or to the born-again Church reigning with Jesus (Ephesians 2:6). And finally, God again associates the existence of Israel with the sun, moon and stars when He says that if they cease, so will Israel (Jeremiah 31:35–36). Notice another example of a 2,000-year gap between verses 5 and 6.

Continuing with the same passage:

> *"And there was war in heaven. Michael and his angels fought against the dragon, and the dragon and his angels fought back. But he was not strong enough, and they lost their place in heaven. The great dragon was hurled down – that ancient serpent called the devil, or Satan, who leads the whole world astray. He was hurled to the earth, and his angels with him. Then I heard a loud voice in heaven say:*
>
> > *'Now have come the salvation and the power and*
> > > *the kingdom of our God,*
> > *and the authority of his Christ.*
> > *For the accuser of our brothers,*
> > > *who accuses them before our God day and night,*
> > > *has been hurled down.*
> > *They overcame him*
> > > *by the blood of the Lamb*
> > > *and by the word of their testimony;*
> > *they did not love their lives so much*
> > > *as to shrink from death.*
> > *Therefore rejoice, you heavens*
> > > *and you who dwell in them!*
> > *But woe to the earth and the sea,*
> > > *because the devil has gone down to you!*
> > *He is filled with fury,*
> > > *because he knows that his time is short.'*
>
> *When the dragon saw that he had been hurled to the earth, he pursued the woman who had given birth to the male child. The woman was given the two wings of a great eagle, so that she might fly to the place prepared for her in the desert, where she would be taken care of for a time,*

*times and half a time* [the last three and a half years], *out of the serpent's reach. Then from his mouth the serpent spewed water like a river, to overtake the woman and sweep her away with the torrent. But the earth helped the woman by opening its mouth and swallowing the river that the dragon had spewed out of his mouth. Then the dragon was enraged at the woman and went off to make war against the rest of her offspring – those who obey God's commandments and hold to the testimony of Jesus."* (Revelation 12:7–17)

Ephesians 2:2 states that Satan is currently *"the ruler of the kingdom of the air"* – the first heaven, which is the atmosphere around the earth containing the clouds. The second heaven is the sun, moon and stars, the universe. It is not clear when he was cast out of the third heaven, the spiritual heaven where Jesus is, and relegated to the first heaven. We know Jesus, through the cross, disarmed Satan and the demons but we read in the above verses that he is going to be cast even further down from the air to the earth at the time of the Antichrist's reign of terror, when the woman (Israel) is still on earth. Satan was able to offer Jesus the kingdoms of the earth (Luke 4:6), because man has authority here and has given it to Satan through sin and ignorance but that did not mean Satan was cast down to earth at that time Jesus was in the wilderness. He will be cast even further down at the return of Jesus when he will be imprisoned in the Abyss and eventually cast into the eternal lake of fire! So, Satan's prospects are not good!

Some believe the eagle's wings represent the USA emblem and her protection of Israel. We have certainly seen this to date, as she has championed Israel's cause since Britain reneged on her mandate to protect and establish a Jewish homeland in Israel. The blessing of God has moved from Britain with the loss of her empire etc. The USA has certainly been blessed through her Christian values and support of Israel but her move from the Bible and efforts to set up a Palestinian State in Israel will change America's standing before God, and the eagle might then just represent the Holy Spirit during the last years. But whichever way, the Jews are protected from total destruction as the **"earth helped the woman"**. The rest of the woman's offspring are believers in Christ with an increasing number being Jews.

Since God gave His wonderful promises to Abraham and his descendants, we have seen over the centuries various floods of hatred from the dragon towards the Jews. The major attacks came from Pharaoh when he slaughtered the Israelite male babies to try and kill Moses and instigated slave labour in Egypt, from the Babylonians in their capture and burning of Jerusalem, Herod killing all the male children under the age of two after the birth of Jesus, the second destruction of Jerusalem by the Romans in AD 70, the Muslims capturing Jerusalem followed by the Catholic Crusaders in taking it back, the Turks capturing Jerusalem, the Nazis in Europe slaughtering six million Jews and lastly the Muslims around the world continuing Satan's absolute hatred for them.

The apologies from the late John Paul II for the slaughter of thousands of Protestants in Europe and Jews in the Holy Land, before, during and after the Reformation, are extremely welcome. Just as the prophets in the Old Testament were killed for preaching the truth, so many great men of God such as Cranmer, Foxe etc. gave their lives for the gospel. However, the Pope's confessions may be designed to create acceptability from the average worldly individual, who does not understand what the Scriptures teach or the deadly game that Satan is playing. If the Roman Church repents, together with the sections of the Protestant Church who hold teachings directly at odds with the Bible, then that would be truly wonderful, and of God.

Although Roman Catholicism's belief system includes the truth that Jesus is God's divine Son and Lord, it puts its own non-biblical ideas above the teachings of Jesus. In effect, it sets itself higher than Him, so actually denies Jesus' lordship. Rather than studying at a college where the Bible is the benchmark, the priests train at Catholic Seminary to learn the teachings of Rome, many of which, on biblical investigation, are actually anti-Christian.

The apostle John also wrote concerning the "Mother of Prostitutes":

*"This title was written on her forehead:*

MYSTERY

BABYLON THE GREAT

THE MOTHER OF PROSTITUTES

AND OF THE ABOMINATIONS

OF THE EARTH.

*I saw that the woman was drunk with the blood of the saints, the blood of those who bore testimony to Jesus."* (Revelation 17:5–6)

The Catholic Church fits the description of this woman exactly. She has the blood of many hundreds of thousands of true Christians on her hands and has created anti-Christian doctrine. Although she tries to give the appearance of godliness and Christianity to natural eyes, she actually keeps a believer subject to religious spirits. Pope John Paul II was very actively pursuing the ecumenical joining of major world religions with the intention of being their overseer or "mother". Every non-biblical religion is a spiritual prostitute as far as God is concerned, and the Catholic Church has been making efforts to mother them. The late Pope prayed with the Dalai Lama, Buddhists, and Hindus, and even received the red dot on his forehead from a Hindu priestess! What spiritual blindness! Rome is moving in the direction of fulfilling the role of the "Mother of Prostitutes". The following scriptures say the prostitute will preside over all the peoples of the world:

*"Come, I will show you the punishment of the great prostitute, who sits on the many waters. With her the kings of the earth committed adultery and the inhabitants of the earth were intoxicated with the wine of her adulteries."* (Revelation 17:1–2)

*"The waters you saw, where the prostitute sits, are peoples, multitudes, nations and languages."*                           (Revelation 17:15)

*"The woman* [the spiritual prostitute] *you saw is the great city that rules over the kings of the earth."*                           (Revelation 17:18)

The "waters" not only refer to the peoples of the original Roman Empire, which accounted for all the major populated areas at that time, but to all the countries that have since developed throughout the whole earth. The Catholic religion has many churches around the world and is in a unique position to oversee every nation. The New Age movement is praying for a one-world religion. The World Council of Churches will also be involved, one of whose pronouncements is, "the theory of the atonement is not required!" There is also a growing interfaith movement under the umbrella "The sons of Abraham". This consists firstly of liberal Muslims who, amongst other teachings, modify Muhammad's clear writings on *Jihad* to mean war solely against social wrongs and not against all other religions. Secondly, there are nominal Christians who omit the requirement of the "new birth", and the thirdly there are liberal Jews who modify their religion to have no other God beside Jehovah to blend in with the other two. These three faiths are being altered to work in harmony with each other and, along with many others, will gain more influence as the spiritual vacuum of godless materialism grows and is shown to be totally void of fulfilment. These so-called Abrahamic faiths are the basis of Tony Blair's Faith Foundation which seeks to, in his words, "awaken the world's conscience to the failure in tackling poverty, illiteracy and poor health in the developing world". He delivered his first major speech on religion, as reported by *The Times*, at the Roman Catholic Westminster Cathedral in April this year. The Foundation desires to also embrace the other main line religions of Hinduism, Sikhism and Buddhism. It is tragically a case of the blind leading the blind. Satan is very busy today preparing the world to accept the Antichrist and it is obvious that the Roman Catholic Church would love to head up an alliance between the various religions, so she can ride the political Beast.

Some have thought that the prostitute represents the apostate Jewish religious system. This interpretation falls down as the Jews haven't exactly been riding the Roman Empire. Just the reverse. The latter has been killing and suppressing the Jews. Granted, the Jews did have Jesus put to death, but the early Church did not see the Scarlet Woman as pharisaic Judaism but as the spirits which ruled Rome and her Empire. As mentioned earlier, Martin Luther and the other Reformers clearly saw that the Roman Catholic faith had been developed by the same spirits governing Rome and was indeed the Great Harlot.

The Vatican has been in favour of Jerusalem becoming an international city. This resolution was made by the United Nations in the 1947 Partition Plan but has never been implemented. When in power Shimon Peres suggested to Arafat that Jerusalem should become a kind of "second Vatican City", administered by two mayors, one Jewish and the other Palestinian, acting under the authority of Rome.

Watching the catastrophic mass murder of nearly 3,000 office workers in the World Trade Centre reminded me of the scene painted in Revelation 18, describing the fall of Babylon:

> *"When the kings of the earth who committed adultery with her and shared her luxury see the smoke of her burning, they will weep and mourn over her. Terrified at her torment, they stand far off and cry:*
>
> *'Woe! Woe! O great city,*
> *O Babylon, city of power!*
> *In one hour your doom has come!'"* (Revelation 18:9–10)

9/11 was a microcosm of the events in Revelation 18, which will happen in both the revived Roman Empire and the whole earth at the end of this age. I believe it is a warning that we cannot serve both God and mammon. The Twin Towers surely represent mammon and all the temptations that money and power bring. These events shook the entire developed world, causing a major change in our thinking. We are accepting more state intervention with identity cards for security, and as the world moves towards this, people will welcome with open arms someone who promises peace, even with the loss of individual freedom. Although there were ID cards in Europe during the Second World War, today it is happening on a far larger scale with all computer systems gradually being linked throughout the world. We are relentlessly approaching the situation described in Revelation 13 where ID marks in or on the body will be accepted, only to be misused by the False Prophet and the Beast.

As America, Britain and other Protestant countries move further away from their biblical heritage and into sin, they are opening themselves up to more and more satanic attack. If they, and the rest of the world, do not repent and if the Church does not pray, we will sadly see more atrocities. God does not want these tragic things to happen, but as man rebels against Him, man allows Satan a greater foothold in his life and the whole situation goes further downhill.

It is encouraging to know that true scriptural Christianity flourished and grew dramatically under the Roman Empire. It was not until the Church became assimilated into the state religious system that the rot set in. Therefore, all will not be lost if we become further enmeshed in the European Superstate and the single currency. However, the true Church must fervently resist what is in its control, namely any amalgamation with the doctrine of Roman Catholicism, whilst not disassociating itself from those Catholics who have a real faith in Jesus. They need our support to evangelise those in their churches and bring them to new birth in Christ.

We Britons should of course be friends with Europe, trade fully with her and cooperate in areas of common interest. However, this need not lead to Great Britain losing more of her sovereignty and coming under further political and, more importantly, spiritual control. There are very good economic arguments for coming out of the EU while maintaining full trading agreements like Norway and Switzerland. Who wants to be in the fast track to put on a political straitjacket? For instance, if Britain came out she would regain 75% of the fishing waters lost to other EU members. These have been so over-fished that even the 25% we retain is now on a tight quota. It could once again be a thriving industry for Britain. There are many convincing arguments for negotiating a legal way out of the various treaties we have naively signed, but because there is a spiritual blanket cast over the whole enterprise, it is difficult for most to see what is really happening, let alone find a way out.

These are some of the reasons why we should remove ourselves from this developing union and the religious control that will no doubt emerge. We must ask the Lord to show us what to do. At some stage, the whole world will follow the Antichrist, so ultimately the options will be somewhat limited – but not with God!

> *"The whole world was astonished and followed the beast."*
>
> (Revelation 13:3)

The EU is gaining ascendancy, not because of God, but because of other spiritual forces. It is therefore important for the true Church in every nation to be aware of these things and join together in prayer, because every person throughout the earth will be affected. I quote a further passage, which highlights this point:

> *"He* [the second beast, the false prophet] *had two horns like a lamb, but he spoke like a dragon. He exercised all the authority of the first beast* [the Antichrist] *on his behalf, and made the earth and its inhabitants worship the first beast, whose fatal wound had been healed. And he performed great and miraculous signs, even causing fire to come down from heaven to earth in full view of men. Because of the signs he was*

*given power to do on behalf of the first beast, he deceived the inhabitants*
*of the earth. He ordered them to set up an image in honour of the beast*
*who was wounded by the sword and yet lived. He was given power to*
*give breath [a deceiving spirit] to the image of the first beast, so that it*
*could speak and cause all who refused to worship the image to be killed.*
*He also forced everyone, small and great, rich and poor, free and slave, to*
*receive a mark on his right hand or on his forehead, so that no-one could*
*buy or sell unless he had the mark, which is the name of the [first] beast*
*or the number of his name. This calls for wisdom. If anyone has insight,*
*let him calculate the number of the beast, for it is man's number. His*
*number is 666."*                          (Revelation 13:11–18)

The fatal wound being healed seems to refer to the Antichrist
receiving a seemingly fatal wound from which he recovers.

From these scriptures, we see that the mark of the Beast will be
applied worldwide. Not understanding the true gospel, which
leads to the new birth in Christ, Rome could easily accommodate
a conglomeration of beliefs in order to enjoy the powerful
position of overall spiritual leader. Roman Catholicism has
quite happily cohabited with other religions in various parts of
the world, parading idols of Mary through the streets along with
other local gods. The previous Pope convened meetings
with leaders of the major religions in an attempt to provide the
world with so-called spiritual and moral guidance. The Catholic
good works ethic will come to the fore in strength, to blind many
as to what is happening spiritually.

Let us not be beguiled by the more open and seemingly relaxed
attitudes on certain issues by the leaders in the Vatican, from
where all the wrong doctrines have emerged and are perpetuated.
Any changes introduced so far do not fundamentally change
anything but are designed to make the Catholic Church function
better and bring the Protestant Church back under Rome's
oversight, rather than move the Catholic Church nearer to the
teachings of Christ. Their core doctrines remain sacrosanct rather
than being tested against the Bible.

There is no other religious group that so precisely fits the description of the Woman riding the Beast, and who is seated on seven hills. Catholicism has indeed ridden the political and military powers of Rome for over 1,000 years and fits every possible aspect mentioned in Scripture.

We will have to wait and see how all this works out in detail, but the Bible says that just before the return of Jesus there will be a strong combination of a false Church and a repressive state, particularly against Jews and born-again Christians.

And lastly, it is interesting that God sums up mankind as three "women". The born-again Church as the Bride of Christ, Israel as the woman adorned with twelve stars and false religion as the woman astride the seven-headed beast.

# CHAPTER 15

# Baked Clay and the End-time Scenario

I have dealt with the western part of the original Roman Empire but what has transpired in the eastern half? Emperor Constantine accepted Christianity in AD 330 and chose the Greek city port of Byzantium on the Bosphorus as its capital, renaming it Constantinople after himself. He finished building the Church of the Holy Sepulchre in Jerusalem in AD 335. The western part of the Empire disintegrated about AD 476 under various Germanic armies whereas the eastern half continued and flourished, peaking under the Christian Emperor Justinian between AD 527–565. He was able to regain some of the lost south-western territories such as Italy, North Africa and Spain.

A power vacuum occurred in Israel after the Roman Empire withdrew from the country before the seventh century began, of which Islam took full advantage. Muhammad introduced Islam to the world in AD 610 but twelve years later was chased out of Mecca together with a small band of converts. His following grew in Medina where he started to introduce violent ways of imposing his beliefs on the people, particularly the Jews – the *Jihad* was born. He returned to Mecca with an army and subdued the area, expanding his new religion from there. He died in AD 632 but Islam spread quickly throughout the Middle East, enforced by the scimitar. Caliph Abu Bakr succeeded Muhammad, capturing and occupying Jerusalem with little opposition eight years after the latter's death.

In AD 1009 the Muslims destroyed the Church of the Holy Sepulchre but the Byzantine emperor rebuilt it in 1027. However, the Turkish Muslims captured Jerusalem in AD 1070 and stopped Catholic pilgrims travelling to the city. In AD 1095 Pope Urban II responded by calling Christians to free Jerusalem from Muslim control and launched the first Crusade in AD 1096. After three years they occupied Jerusalem and held the city for over 100 years. Unfortunately, most of them were no more godly than the Muslims and Jews they slaughtered. Just as the Muslims had conquered by the sword, so did these spiritually unenlightened Roman Catholic knights. It was during this time of occupation, on the site of King Solomon's Temple, that Freemasons, Knights Templars and other confused sects were spawned. Saladin recaptured Jerusalem for the Muslims in AD 1187 but the sixth Crusade in AD 1228 temporarily reversed this. However, it fell back into Muslim hands in AD 1244 and so it remained, until liberated from Muslim Turkish rule in 1917 by the British and Allied Armies.

Could this religion, which is also political, be the clay in the feet of the statue in Daniel chapter 2? I believe the Lord has shown me that it is. Understanding that the figure refers to the political empires that have ruled Israel provides further clarification on what Scripture has to say today. Some theologians have said that the clay represents democracy being introduced into the western part of the Roman Empire and weakening it. It could be argued that it has removed the power of the Roman style dictatorship, but democracy has actually strengthened the West by bringing flexibility and development, not the brittleness and weakness of baked clay. However, baked clay is a very apt description of Islam, which is the only new political power of significance introduced into the original territories of the Roman Empire since the time of Christ. Its inflexibility and incompatibility are well described by this material.

The non-European part of the original Roman Empire completely encircles the remainder of the Mediterranean and comprises Turkey, Syria, Lebanon, Israel, northern Saudi Arabia, Egypt, Libya, Tunisia, Algeria and Morocco – all now firmly Islamic, except for Israel. However, as far as the world is concerned, half or all of Israel's territory remains under dispute, depending on who you listen to.

Others have sensed this Muslim factor in the seventh head of Revelation 17 but have overlooked some scriptures and consequently misinterpreted it to be the Turkish Empire rather than the Roman one. This head is stated to last only a "short time" (Revelation 17:10), whereas the Turkish Empire ruled for some 600 years. As previously explained, Daniel 2 depicts the whole Roman Empire as two legs made of iron (East and West) continuing right down into two feet and ten toes. This shows that the empire will be present until the ten end-time kingdoms are briefly established just prior to Jesus' return, also referred to by the ten horns of Daniel 7:7. I have shown in previous chapters that during the time of the feet, the spirits behind the empire tried unsuccessfully to re-impose their control through various European tyrants. We have also seen from *"he who confirms the covenant"* (Daniel 9:27) that the Antichrist is to be from the Roman Empire.

In the eastern part of the Roman Empire, Islam has dominated for over 1,300 years since Muhammad. As we know, the Islamic spirits have designs on the whole world and on Israel in particular. This political religion has significantly permeated Europe and other parts of the globe, just as the baked clay in the iron depicts, but it will not bring unity within the EU nor any other country. Indeed Islam is incapable of harmonising with anything. Iran, Afghanistan, the separation of Pakistan from India and Hizbullah in Lebanon are some examples, as is the Palestinian situation with Israel, of course.

> *"Just as you saw the iron mixed with baked clay, so the people* [of the revived Roman Empire] *will be a mixture and will not remain united, any more than iron mixes with clay."*　　　　　　(Daniel 2:43)

Islam is obliged to coexist in a host nation until it has the opportunity to take power by force. Then it will seek to exclude all other religions and ideologies, only allowing unbelievers to live if they agree to be second-class citizens. I quote from the Quran, which consists of numerous revelations called Surahs, given to Muhammad by Allah:

> "But if they repent [*turn to Islam*] and establish the Prayer and pay the Zakat [*tax levied on those who do not believe*], let them go their way." (Surah 9:5)

> "Fight them until persecution is no more, and religion is all for Allah. But if they cease, then assuredly Allah is Seer of what they do." (Surah 8:39)

Muhammad introduced the new religion of Islam in AD 610, being deceived into thinking he was the long-promised prophet spoken of by Moses some 2,000 years before:

> "*I* [God] *will raise up for them* [the Israelites] *a prophet like you* [Moses] *from among their brothers* [fellow Israelites] . . . *If anyone does not listen to my words that the prophet speaks in my name, I myself will call him to account.*" (Deuteronomy 18:18–19)

Because of his confused and scant knowledge of the Bible, Muhammad did not understand that Jesus, who had come over 500 years before, was indeed the great prophet. The spirit speaking to Muhammad demonstrated it was not from God, because it did not confess Jesus as Lord. It said that God had chosen Muhammad to correct the lies written by Jews in the Old Testament and Christians in the New Testament. The spirit basically said that anything in the Bible that conflicted with what it taught Muhammad should be treated as error. However, the Old and New Testament scriptures were not tampered with and are the infallible Word of God inspired by the Holy Spirit. They clearly state that the great prophet would be from the Jews, which disqualified Muhammad! Jesus also fulfilled hundreds of Old Testament prophecies regarding the promised Messiah, such as being born in Bethlehem and being a descendant of King David through the royal line to Joseph (Matthew 1:1–17; Luke 3:23–38). God attested to Him by countless miracles, signs and wonders. No one taught like this Man, and Peter declared Him to be *"the Christ, the Son of the living God"*, which Jesus acknowledged as the truth.

The Quran, however, is a collection of revelations from a spirit, totally at odds with both Jesus and the God of the Old Testament. Although Islam says it recognises Jesus as a prophet, it actually ignores what He taught. Far from loving your enemies as Jesus taught, the Muslims are instructed by Muhammad to hate and kill them if they do not accept his revelations. The Bible declares that God is love and longs to be with people, whereas the Quran reveals Allah as a remote deity who decrees death and subjugation in this life to those who refuse him! Jesus didn't just say that what He taught was the way and the truth but that He Himself is the Way, the Truth and the Life and that no man can come to the Father but by Him. This is because He is the Word become flesh (made a man) and only He dealt with our sins through the cross. Jesus was crucified for His claim of being the Son of God, but Islam denies this. Islam is the opposite of Christianity.

Also, Muhammad's total ignorance that the essential requirement of the perfect Holy God is that every sin needs to be punished and not just forgiven means that Muslims do not see the necessity of Jesus' sacrificial death as prophesied in Isaiah 53. Because of this, Muslims are quite unconcerned when the Quran teaches that Judas was secretly and deceitfully swapped with Jesus, to die in His place.

> "And because of their [*the Jews*] saying, 'We slew the Messiah, Jesus son of Mary, Allah's messenger.' They slew him not, nor crucified him, but it appeared so to them, and those who disagree concerning it are in doubt thereof, they having no knowledge

thereof except pursuit of a conjecture, they slew him not for certain." (Surah 4:157)

The footnote to this verse in the Quran says – "it was Judas Iscariot, who was said to betray Jesus, who was arrested and crucified instead of the prophet Jesus".

It is extremely important to understand that Muhammad never spoke of *Jihad* during his first years in Mecca, and it is these verses from the Quran, which are quoted by moderate Muslims today, giving the impression that Islam is a religion of peace:

*"There is no compulsion in religion. True guidance is distinct from error."* (Surah 2:256)

In Medina Allah introduced *Jihad* to Muhammad, which imposed the faith with military force. The choices were now, either to believe, not accept and be a second-class citizen paying taxes or die! Most of the pagans were not prepared for the latter two and so they accepted Allah, but Jews and the few Christians who lived there did not submit and suffered accordingly.

The first to experience the *Jihad* were a large community of Jews living near Medina who refused to accept Muhammad's teaching – at least 600 men were forced to dig their own communal grave in which they were slaughtered. Their women and children were sold as slaves.

Here are some of the more aggressive verses from the Quran, written after his arrival in Medina, overruling the peaceful approach shown in Mecca.

"Fight against those from among the people of the book [*Bible-Jews and Christians*] who do not believe in Allah." (Surah:9:29)

"O you who believe [*Islam*]! Take not the Jews and Christians for friends. They are friends to each other. He among you who takes them for friends is of them." (Surah 5:51)

"For it is not for a prophet to have captives until he has made slaughter in the land."                          (Surah 8:67)

"O you who believe! Fight [*in Jihad*] the disbelievers who are near to you, and let them find harshness in you; and know that Allah is with the righteous."                          (Surah 10:123)

"When the forbidden months are past [*the four months, in which the citizens of Mecca were given to repent on Muhammad's return from Medina, before he slaughtered those who rejected his teaching*], then fight them and slay the pagans wherever you find them, and seize them, beleaguer them, and lie in wait for them everywhere. But if they repent [*turn to Islam*] and establish the Prayer and pay the Zakat [*tax levied on those,who do not believe*], let them go their way."
                          (Surah 9:5)

Muhammad was challenged on why he had changed from being peaceful to violent and the various other contradictions that he subsequently taught. The spirit gave him these answers:

"If we abrogate [*cancel*] any verse or cause it to be forgotten, we replace it by a better or similar one. Do you not know that Allah has power over all things?"                          (Surah 2:106)

"When we exchange a revelation in place of another revelation – and Allah knows best what he reveals – they say – 'You are an impostor.' Indeed, most of them have no knowledge."
                          (Surah 16:101)

Hardly the hallmark of the Creator who is all-knowing and sees the end from the beginning. But these two quotes show us that the contradictions found in the Quran are to be dealt with by understanding that the later revelations received by Muhammad overrule the earlier ones. *Jihad*, therefore, supersedes the more moderate earlier passages and cancels the previous peaceful approach. The zealots who obey Muhammad's latter writings are consequently the true wholehearted followers of Islam – they are the fundamentalists. They correctly describe the moderates as liberals in how they handle the Quran. The moderates say the Zakat tax of Surah 9:5 only really means giving alms to the poor, and they also change the meaning of *Jihad* to "being a fight against injustice", which is falsifying the message.

Surah 9:5, quoted above, was used by Mahmoud Ahmadinejad, President of Iran, in his letter to George Bush, delivered in 2006, inviting him and the nation to repent and turn to Islam. It offered peace if the Americans converted, otherwise they would either be obliged to pay a subjugation tax or become legitimate targets to be killed. Because neither Mr Bush nor the American people have turned to Islam, Muhammad's teaching requires that he and the rest of America be destroyed. (Most do not like paying taxes to their own government let alone to a group of fundamental Muslims!)

With regard to a Muslim who turns from his faith, the spirit instructed Muhammad as follows:

> "Whosoever on that day turns his back to them [*Muslims*], unless manoeuvring [*moving from a difficult situation to a place where you are able to fight*] for battle or intending to join a company [*regrouping*], he truly has incurred wrath from Allah, and his habitation will be hell, a hapless journey's end."          (Surah 8:16)

> "Those who reject Islam must be killed. If they turn back [*away from Islam*], take them and kill them where ever you find them, and choose no friend or helper from among them." (Surah 4:89)

Therefore, every Muslim is duty bound on pain of death to continue in the teaching of Muhammad. He is to enter *Jihad* against the non-believer and follow the example Muhammad gave in spreading Islam by force wherever it is not accepted. The liberal Muslim also tries to interpret *Jihad* to mean that a Muslim can only attack if he is being attacked, but this flies in the face of Muhammad's actions and teachings. Therefore, despite the protestations of the moderates, al Qaeda is one of the many groups displaying Quranic Islam.

It is instructive to look at some of Muhammad's background to discover the root of Islam. His father died before he was born, followed by his mother's death when only six years of age. He was placed in the care of his paternal uncle, Abu Talib, the acknowledged leader and guardian of some 360 idols around Mecca. Their tribe, the Quraysh, controlled most of the Arab holy places, the most important being the Ka'aba, meaning "the Cube". This building was the residence of the highest of their gods named Hubal, who very significantly required his devotees to process around the cubic stone building several times in homage to him. A statue of this moon god stood in a prominent position in the building with 360 other lesser gods surrounding it.

The Cube has been renovated over the centuries, but is essentially the same one that Muslims are required to pray towards five times a day. They must visit Mecca once in their lifetime and walk around the Ka'aba seven times. According to the Quran, this is the centre-piece of Muslim worship. The encircling of the building is a continuation of the same instruction given by the spirit to Arabs long before Muhammad was even born. The spirit who spoke to Muhammad told him to destroy all the other buildings and idols, including the statue of Hubal, but not the Ka'aba.

Various stones were also spared including the famous "Black Stone", which is still seen today in the eastern wall of the Cube. It is said to have fallen from heaven and given to Abraham by the angel Gabriel. Arabs worshipped this stone long before Muhammad's birth, as they believed it had the power to absorb all sins when kissed. This veneration and kissing of the stone is still required today when processing around the building.

Muhammad is said to have cleansed the Cube from the previous spirit but God, under the Old Covenant, always said that every idol and shrine should be utterly destroyed by fire, not just ritually cleansed.

As this Cube is the focus of Islam, and is still known as the house of Allah, their name for God, it can only be concluded that it is the continued residence of the same spirit who was previously worshipped there but has now assumed Creator status. Today, the building is draped in a black curtain and is the centrepiece of the large white mosque in Mecca. The moon on the Islamic flag is an indicator that Allah and Hubal are the same spirit.

It is reported that Muhammad was terrified by his first encounters with the spirit, as he thought he was being possessed by a demon. He also had what some describe as "falling spells" whilst receiving some of the revelations. The spirit declared itself to be the angel Gabriel, the one who brought the Black Stone to Abraham. Judging from these points, it was probably Hubal himself from the original Ka'aba that spoke to him. Hubal, being the dominant spirit, formed a new principality with the other gods whose idols were destroyed, introducing what has become known as Islam. This new religion expanded further as other spirits around the world joined the bandwagon. It teaches outlandish things such as Jesus being a true Muslim, along with Adam, Abraham, David and all the other Bible characters.

The Quraysh tribe claim descendency from Ishmael and believe Muhammad is justified in saying he is the long promised prophet of which Moses spoke, despite Moses saying the prophet was to be from the Jews. The deceiving spirit said that God established His covenant with Abraham through Ishmael because he was the elder son, and that the Jews have secretly altered the Bible to say the inheritance is through the younger son, Isaac. There is no truth in these statements. Firstly, Hagar was only Abraham's maidservant, not his wife, and so Sarah's son took precedence. Secondly, Ishmael was cast out of the land and married an Egyptian woman, not a Jewess. Thirdly, Abraham took a second wife Keturah (Genesis 25:1), whose sons would also have superseded Ishmael, and fourthly, Jesus agreed with everything in the Old Testament. He said nothing could be changed in Scripture, which repeatedly states that the inheritance was only to be through the descendants of Jacob, renamed Israel. His apostles also confirmed the Scriptures' inerrancy. And finally, the Holy Spirit witnesses today to the correctness and truths in the Bible.

The notes in the Quran, next to Surah 4:159, say the prophet Jesus will return with the Holy Quran in His hand to convert Jews, Christians and all other faiths to Islam and then rule the world. So, Islam is not just another religion but one hundred percent anti God. Its teaching seeks to nullify everything that Jesus taught, His work on the cross and, of course, to deny the truth of His divinity.

Research into the reliability of the Quran itself has unearthed major inconsistencies. Arthur Jeffrey, a noted European archaeologist, has discovered other Surahs written by Muhammad that were not included in the original canonisation by the second Caliph Umar. Jeffrey found differences between these and the Quran we have today. He also found from the Hadith (a collection of sayings that Muhammad is reported to have said, which have as much weight as the Quran itself) that Umar destroyed some Surahs because there were further contradictions in them, and yet each Surah is said to be exactly what Allah had revealed to Muhammad! He concluded that, "There is little doubt that the text canonised by Umar was only one among several types of text in existence at that time." Other fragments found in the Yemen in 1972 reveal more textural variations and additions. Professor Andrew Rippon at Calgary University is continuing investigations. (*Source*: "Is the Quran the Word of God? – www.zactrust.org)

The Quran records Muhammad being miraculously transported from the mosque in Mecca to the Farthest Mosque, after which he ascended into heaven and then returned to Mecca.

> "Glory be to Him [*Allah*] who carried his servant by night from the Sacred Mosque [*Al-Haram Mosque in Mecca*] to the Farthest Mosque." (Sura 17:1)

An article from an Egyptian Ministry of Culture publication featured a Muslim questioning the whereabouts of the Farthest Mosque referred to in this passage. He discovered that from their earliest traditions and literature, the As'ad ibn Zura mosque in Medina, the second most holy site, was originally spoken of as the Farthest Mosque!

He said this tradition changed at some point to say that the Farthest Mosque was the one on the south side of the Temple Mount in Jerusalem. The Muslim army, led by the second Caliph Umar, did not take Jerusalem until AD 638, six years after Muhammad's death in AD 632. There were no Muslims in Israel before this conquest and consequently there was no mosque on the Temple Mount for Muhammad to fly to. The first Muslim shrine, a wooden structure built by Umar's son over the exposed rock on Solomon's Temple foundations, was not erected until fifty-three years after his father captured Jerusalem. It was a further twenty-three years later that Umar's grandson built a Mosque on the south side of the Temple Mount – eighty-two years after Muhammad's death! Some significant time later this became known as the al Aqsa (the Farthest) Mosque. The assumption, therefore, that the Farthest Mosque is in Jerusalem rather than Medina is seriously brought into question and looks to be incorrect.

After the 1967 war the head of the Israeli army, Moshe Dayan, could have taken the Temple Mount back in its entirety, but being a secular Jew, he allowed the Muslim keepers of the site, the Waqf, to retain supervision. In the last few years Muslims have built a further mosque within the body of the Temple Mount.

As we see in the media, Jerusalem remains uppermost in Muslims' thinking. There is a monumental fight going on in the spiritual realm of which the world, and alas much of the Church, is unaware. Muslims have successfully duped the world into thinking that the injustices the Palestinians have suffered are caused by the Israelis, whereas it is mostly brought about by themselves. God said, *"Whoever curses you* [Jews] *I will curse."* The

Palestinians could be living in prosperity and peace with the Jews as envisaged by the Muslim leaders who fought with the allied armies to free the lands from Turkish rule rather than living under a curse.

Understanding Islam and the issues in the previous chapters give us a clearer picture of the end-time scenario. In chapter 9 we saw that Antiochus IV was a type of Antichrist, but Hitler is a modern day example of how he will come to power. After the First World War there was mass unemployment. He promised Germany utopia, full employment and realisation of true German supremacy under his rule. Once in power, he eliminated all opposition and proceeded to develop his evil agenda, consulting the stars and even thinking he was doing God's will. A situation of global crisis will enable the end-time Antichrist to rise in the same way, mesmerise the people and be welcomed to take control. The world situation will increasingly centre on the problem of Israel.

Anti-Semitism in the Middle East is as bad as that incited by Hitler in Germany but somehow the Jews will rebuild the Temple and recommence animal sacrifice. They will reason that their problems can only be overcome if they obey the whole Law.

I showed in chapter 9 that Daniel 11:36 speaks of the Antichrist but it is worth looking at some very significant additional points in this passage regarding him and the ten end-time kings:

> "[36] *The king [the Antichrist] will do as he pleases. He will exalt and magnify himself above every god and will say unheard of things against the God of gods. He will be successful until the time of wrath is completed, for what has been determined must take place.* [37] *He will show no regard for the gods of his fathers or for the one desired by women, nor will he regard any god, but will exalt himself above them all.* [38] *Instead of them, he will honour a god of fortresses; a god unknown to his fathers he will honour with gold and silver, with precious stones and costly gifts.* [39] *He will attack the mightiest fortresses with the help of a foreign god [Satan] and will greatly honour those who acknowledge him.* **He will make them rulers over many people and will distribute the land**

*at a price.* <sup>40</sup>*At the time of the end the king of the South* [Egypt and that
area] *will engage him in battle, and the king of the North* [Assyria and
that area] *will storm out against him with chariots and cavalry and a
great fleet of ships. He will invade many countries and sweep through
them like a flood.* <sup>41</sup>*He will also invade the Beautiful Land* [Israel].
*Many countries will fall, but Edom, Moab and the leaders of Ammon will
be delivered from his hand.* <sup>42</sup>*He will extend his power over many
countries; Egypt will not escape.* <sup>43</sup>*He will gain control of the treasures of
gold and silver and all the riches of Egypt, with the Libyans and Nubians*
[Northern Sudan] *in submission.* <sup>44</sup>*But reports from the east and the
north will alarm him, and he will set out in a great rage to destroy and
annihilate many.* <sup>45</sup>*He will pitch his royal tents between the seas at the
beautiful holy mountain* [Jerusalem]. *Yet he will come to his end, and
no-one will help him."*          (Daniel 11:36–45, emphasis added)

Firstly, the Antichrist is recognised as a ruler who will lead an
army which Daniel 9:27 indicates is from the revived Roman
Empire. Daniel also points to him reinstating Temple sacrifice.
After confirming something like the Old Covenant for three and a
half years he will renounce it, try to change the Law and set
himself up above the Creator. Daniel 11:39 reveals that many will
give their allegiance to the Antichrist and he will make some of
them rulers of his empire. These are the ten end-time kings, not
elected by the people but enthroned by dictatorial decree.

*"The ten horns you saw are ten kings who have not yet received a
kingdom, but who for one hour will receive authority as kings along with
the beast. They have one purpose and will give their power and authority
to the beast. They will make war against the Lamb, but the Lamb will
overcome them because he is Lord of lords and King of kings – and with
him will be his called, chosen and faithful followers."*

(Revelation 17:12–14)

Three of the ten rulers fall foul of the Antichrist, who overthrows
them.

*"It had ten horns. While I was thinking about the horns, there before me was another horn, a little one, which came up among them; and three of the first horns were uprooted before it. This horn had eyes like the eyes of a man and a mouth that spoke boastfully."*

(Daniel 7:7–8)

Daniel 11:40, quoted above, states that the kings of the South (Egypt and surrounding areas) and the North (Syria and surrounding areas) attack him, confirming that the Antichrist's campaigns are regional not global.

Currently the situation with the Muslim nations in the eastern part of the revived Roman Empire sees Turkey actively trying to join the EU. Colonel Gaddafi in Libya, has softened his attitude towards the West out of convenience, and the EU has signed a "Cooperation" agreement with him. He deeply fears the likes of al-Qaeda deposing his political Islamic state. Other secular led Islamic countries such as Syria, Egypt, Algeria and Morocco may move further towards Europe for the same reasons.

The statue of Daniel 2, representing the nations that rule over Israel, shows us that the Roman Empire will rule over Israel up to the return of Jesus, when the Rock smashes the feet. This must mean that we will see Israel join the European Union.

Daniel 11:41 says that the Antichrist will invade the Beautiful Land – Israel. The scenario could be that because the fundamental Muslims become so powerful around Israel, seeking to destroy her, that the EU led by the Antichrist steps in to deal with the militants – a modern-day Crusade. The fundamental Muslims from the north and the south attack him. He will turn south, subdue Egypt and that area (Daniel 11:43) but reports from the north (Syrian area) and east (Iran and other Muslim countries from that direction) will alarm him (Daniel 11:44). So, these last years will be very traumatic to say the least. This EU leader will take matters into his own hands and seek to rule from Jerusalem, seeing himself as the Messiah. But we know that this will be the final act as Jesus upstages him and casts him and the False Prophet into the lake of fire. Jesus then takes His rightful place on the throne in Jerusalem (Daniel 11:45). Praise God!

Jesus warned that many would come claiming to be the Christ but not to be deceived by them. The Jews who reject Jesus are still expecting another Messiah. President Mahmoud Ahmadinejad of Iran says that he is the herald of the twelfth Imam who has given him instructions to destroy the state of Israel and kill all Jews who do not convert to Islam. This is primarily a Shia expectation but Sunnis may accept him too. They believe this Imam is due to appear any day now to take up the final Caliphate and rule from Jerusalem. The prophet Jesus is also supposed to appear from Damascus to assist him in bringing the world to Islam, with all dissenters being beheaded. There are some similarities between the Muslim version of end-time events and the Bible. Muslims were obviously informed of some of the Bible scriptures and Allah has put an Islamic twist to them. With the various antichrists operating against the true Church, and both utilising beheading, the words spoken by Jesus are brought into focus:

> *"You will be handed over to be persecuted and put to death, and you will be hated by all nations because of me. At that time many will turn away from the faith and will betray and hate each other, and many false prophets will appear and deceive many people."*     (Matthew 24:9–11)

> *"And I saw the souls of those who had been beheaded because of their testimony for Jesus and because of the word of God. They had not worshipped the beast or his image and had not received his mark on their foreheads or their hands."*     (Revelation 20:4)

But when the real Jesus returns every eye will see Him in an instant and every knee will bow, even those on the other side of the earth. There will be no confusion, as the Holy Spirit will reveal to every survivor of the Tribulation in the same instant, believer and unbeliever alike, that the true King of kings has returned to rule the world from Jerusalem. Jesus said:

> *"For as lightning that comes from the east is visible even in the west, so*
> *will be the coming of the Son of Man."*                    (Matthew 24:27)

One issue I haven't touched upon are the scriptures on Gog and
Magog. Ezekiel 36 deals with the restoration of the Israelites to
the mountains of Israel. In chapter 37 he prophesies to the dry
bones in the valley, which describe the Israelites without Christ.
The bones come together and as Ezekiel continues to speak,
breath comes into them and they stand up – a vast army,
representing the nation being born again and becoming part of
the body of Christ. In chapter 38 Gog (the King) and Magog (the
land and people of Gog), who live in the far north, come with
many nations against Israel. A close study of the countries listed
indicate that the countries to the far north to be the regions
around Turkey and the other countries surrounding Israel to be
the Muslim ones – an Islamic army. However, this army will
die on the mountains of Israel as burning sulphur and other
horrible things rain down on them and their bodies are given to
carrion birds and animals to eat. This seems to be speaking of
Armageddon but there is a problem. Ezekiel 38:1 says Israel
would be unwalled, peaceful and unsuspecting, which is certainly
not the situation in Israel at the moment! Revelation 20:7–10 also
speaks of Gog and Magog rising up against Israel, but this is after
the 1,000-year reign of Christ. This very last rebellion is also put
down with fire from heaven. So, it is not clear whether the events
of Ezekiel 38 and 39 occur before, after the millennium or both. If
we see the current fences and walls removed by the Antichrist
and a period of peace ensue, albeit a false one, then Ezekiel is
referring to events just prior to Jesus' return. Otherwise, they will
be later. Paul warns of this false peace:

> *"You know very well that the day of the Lord will come like a thief*
> *in the night. While people are saying, 'Peace and safety', destruction*
> *will come on them suddenly, as labour pains."*

> (1 Thessalonians 5:2–3)

There is a further prophecy that shows God will eventually release the peoples to the north and south of Israel from the bondage of Islam. At some stage, they will come to Christ and join Israel in bowing the knee to Jesus before His return:

> *"In that day there will be a highway from Egypt to Assyria. The Assyrians will go to Egypt and the Egyptians to Assyria. The Egyptians and Assyrians will worship together. In that day Israel will be the third, along with Egypt and Assyria, a blessing on the earth. The LORD Almighty will bless them, saying, 'Blessed be Egypt my people, Assyria my handiwork, and Israel my inheritance.'"*

(Isaiah 19:23–25)

Throughout this study I have tried to piece together the jigsaw puzzle of Jewish history. Watching world events develop is rather like watching a film having read small parts of the end of the book (the Bible) on which it is based.

# Conclusion:
# How Can We Respond to All This?

I trust this study has helped open up your hearts and minds to the *"times of the Gentiles"* and how their completion affects the whole world. Please prayerfully consider all I have written and reject what the Spirit and Scripture do not witness to. My aim is not to unravel these issues for the sake of intellectual argument, but to reveal more clearly how God views Israel, Europe and the Middle East in the run up to the return of Jesus. May we be like Daniel, who petitioned God and fasted as he discovered from Scripture where he was in God's timing – in his case, at the end of the seventy years exile. He wrote:

> *"In the first year of Darius [king of the Medes and Persians], I, Daniel, understood from the Scriptures, according to the word of the LORD given to Jeremiah the prophet, that the desolation of Jerusalem would last seventy years. So I turned to the Lord God and pleaded with him in prayer and petition, in fasting, and in sackcloth and ashes."*
>
> (Daniel 9:2–3)

Daniel identified with Israel's sin. He became fully involved spiritually, mentally and emotionally with the Lord in prayer for the exile to end. Reading further into Daniel we find that God gave him more revelation because of his earnest response to the written Word of God. Likewise, as we humble ourselves, pray and understand the Scriptures, the Lord will give us more revelation about what He requires of us. Many Christians have a burden for a nation other than their own and I am aware God puts Israel specifically on the hearts of certain Christians but I believe that as the whole Church becomes aware of just how important she is in God's plans, every believer will pray for her. The Psalmist instructs us to:

> *"Pray for the peace of Jerusalem:*
>    *'May those who love you be secure.*
> *May there be peace within your walls*
>    *and security within your citadels.' "*     (Psalm 122:6–7)

This is not just for the city but for our security and for the whole earth. Jerusalem with her rightful King is the only means of world peace but because of Satan's activity against her and man's rebellion against God, the world experiences the very opposite.

Isaiah gives an overall insight into God's heart for her:

> *"For Zion's sake I will not keep silent,*
>    *for Jerusalem's sake I will not remain quiet,*
> *till her righteousness shines out like the dawn,*
>    *her salvation like a blazing torch.*
> *The nations will see your righteousness,*
>    *and all kings your glory;*
> *you will be called by a new name*
>    *that the mouth of the* LORD *will bestow.*
> *You will be a crown of splendour in the* LORD*'s hand,*
>    *a royal diadem in the hand of your God.*
> *No longer will they call you Deserted,*
>    *or name your land Desolate.*
> *But you will be called Hephzibah* [my delight is in her],
>    *and your land Beulah* [married];
> *for the* LORD *will take delight in you,*
>    *and your land will be married.*
> *As a young man marries a maiden,*
>    *so will your sons marry you;*

*as a bridegroom rejoices over his bride,*
    *so will your God rejoice over you.*

*I have posted watchmen on your walls, O Jerusalem;*
    *they will never be silent day or night.*
*You, who call on the LORD,*
    *give yourselves no rest,*
*and give him no rest till he establishes Jerusalem*
    *and makes her the praise of the earth.*

*The LORD has sworn by his right hand*
    *and by his mighty arm:*
*'Never again will I give your grain*
    *as food for your enemies,*
*and never again will foreigners drink the new wine*
    *for which you have toiled;*
*but those who harvest it will eat it*
    *and praise the LORD,*
*and those who gather the grapes will drink it*
    *in the courts of my sanctuary.' "*                    (Isaiah 62:1–9)

Isaiah expresses the Lord's heart that the land will be married to the people of Israel. So far we have seen the desert bloom in certain areas and her economy develop in a totally miraculous way despite the wars, trade embargoes etc. Even the ardent atheistic Jew sees Jerusalem as central to his heart but when it comes to dying for it, most are happy to see the mountains of Israel become a Palestinian State for the sake of peace. The orthodox Old Testament Jews are much more committed to the land but not the State of Israel. They say only the Messiah can set it up properly and they are right but God is working through the situation to bring about His declared will. The Messianic Jews need to understand the issues clearly outlined in this book, that the whole land is theirs and Jesus is their King. It need not be handed over to Gentiles because God will defend her fully if they believe His Word and stand on it. However, if they hand over land He cannot defend them. Who knows how the current negotiations this year will bring about the situation that God has revealed by His foreknowledge will happen. The Messianic Jews are key in prayer for the continued restoration of the land, and the rest of the Body of Christ must stand with them and intercede to see them possess the whole land, turn to Jesus as a nation, and then see the Kingdom come on earth as it is in heaven.

The Lord started to bring about His ancient promises through the first Jewish converts, as recorded in the New Testament. However, because most of the nation rejected Jesus, they were scattered around the world and have continued without a king to this day, with the consequent delay in seeing the glory that God has promised Jerusalem. Because the aftereffects of the *"times of the Gentiles"* have not been fully removed, many of her enemies are still eating her grain and drinking her wine in the West Bank. Isaiah 62:9 can only be speaking of natural food rather than spiritual, as non-believers cannot drink or eat God's spiritual provision. Jesus spoke of this natural wine at the last supper when He saw that He would drink the wine produced in Israel with His disciples during His millennium reign on earth:

> *"I tell you, I will not drink of this fruit of the vine from now on until that day when I drink it anew with you in my Father's kingdom."*
>
> (Matthew 26:29)

Jesus also said to the Jews during His last week in Jerusalem:

> *"For I tell you* [the Jews], *you will not see me again until you say, 'Blessed is he* [the Son of King David, the Messiah King Jesus] *who comes in the name of the Lord.'"*        (Matthew 23:39; see also Psalm 118:26)

Many recognised Jesus as the Messiah as He walked their dusty roads, many only saw a prophet, but the majority, particularly leaders, tragically could only see a false prophet and Messiah. He was actually their King but He used their rejection of Him to die for their sin and that of the whole world – what mercy and grace!

God dealt with the nation accordingly and withdrew the spiritual kingdom from all those who rejected Jesus. It is vital to see that although He removed the Kingdom of God from them because of their unbelief, the land remained theirs because of His promise to Abraham. But Jesus said to the Jewish nation that He would revisit them when they acknowledged Him as their Messiah.

The world has its "Road Map" to bring peace to Jerusalem but it will soon lead to the beginning of the last seven years of Tribulation and to its only conclusion – Armageddon, death and eternal damnation for multitudes! Mercifully, God also has a plan which will bring many Jews, Muslims and other Gentiles together in true peace – it's the only Way that will work and it is called "the one new man in Christ":

> "For he himself is our peace, who has made the two one and has destroyed the barrier, the dividing wall of hostility, by abolishing in his flesh the law with its commandments and regulations. His purpose was to create in Christ one new man out of the two, thus making peace, and in this one body to reconcile both of them to God through the cross, by which he put to death their hostility."          (Ephesians 2:14–16)

A wonderful expression of this today is the House of Victory Community on Mount Carmel where Jews, Muslims, Druze, atheists, drug addicts etc. have come to Christ and are sharing their lives with each other in love.

The Kingdom of God has so far been experienced in the spiritual realm, "hidden in Christ", with the attendant spiritual gifts such as physical healings etc., but the Lord's words to his apostles, just before ascending, promised that one day the Kingdom would be physically restored to the Jews with Jesus enthroned as their King.

> "They asked him, 'Lord, at this time are you going to restore the kingdom to Israel?' He said to them: 'It is not for you to know the times or dates [literally, "seasons"] the Father has set by his own authority.'"
>
> (Acts 1:6–7)

Jesus taught His disciples to pray for the Kingdom when He gave them the model prayer:

> *"Your kingdom come.*
> *your will be done*
>     *on earth as it is in heaven."*          (Matthew 6:10)

This prayer does not just refer to the spiritual kingdom, which is entered through the new birth in Christ, but to the establishment of the physical kingdom at the return of Jesus. It was at His resurrection that Jesus was made King of kings, so He will not only return to reign as King of the Jews, but will also rule over every nation! All the many outstanding promises to Israel will be fulfilled during His 1,000-years rule in Israel such as:

> *"He will judge between the nations*
>     *and will settle disputes for many peoples.*
> *They will beat their swords into ploughshares*
>     *and their spears into pruning hooks.*
> *Nation will not take up sword against nation,*
>     *nor will they train for war any more."*          (Isaiah 2:4)

> *"I will bring health and healing to it; I will heal my people and will let them enjoy abundant peace and security. I will bring Judah and Israel back from captivity and will rebuild them as they were before. I will cleanse them from all the sin they have committed against me. Then this city will bring me renown, joy, praise and honour before all nations on earth that hear of all the good things I do for it; and they will be in awe and will tremble at the abundant prosperity and peace I provide for it."*
>          (Jeremiah 33:6–9)

The angel Gabriel said to Daniel that the end-time prophecies were sealed until the last years. We have now entered this period and, as promised, God is opening up His Word to the Church on these issues. Paul taught the Thessalonian Church that it would go through the Tribulation and see the return of Jesus:

> *"Now, brothers, about times and dates we do not need to write to you, for you know very well that the day of the Lord will come like a thief in the night. While people are saying, 'Peace and safety', destruction will come on them suddenly, as labour pains on a pregnant woman, and they will not escape. **But you, brothers, are not in darkness so that this day should surprise you like a thief.** You are all sons of the light and sons of the day. We do not belong to the night or to the darkness. So then, let us not be like others, who are asleep, but let us be alert and self-controlled. For those who sleep, sleep at night, and those who get drunk, get drunk at night. But since we belong to the day, let us be self-controlled, putting on faith and love as a breastplate, and the hope of salvation as a helmet. For God did not appoint us to suffer wrath but to receive salvation through our Lord Jesus Christ. He died for us so that, whether we are awake or asleep, we may live together with him. Therefore encourage one another and build each other up, just as in fact you are doing."*
>
> (1 Thessalonians 5:1–11, emphasis added)

Paul is saying here that, because we are sons of the light and can understand God's timing, Jesus' return will not take us by surprise. Although Christians will not suffer at God's hands during the Tribulation, they will suffer from those who are opposed to Him. But God will bring in a righteous judgment at the end:

> *". . . Rejoice, saints and apostles and prophets!*
> *God has judged her* [Babylon] *for the way she treated you . . .*
> *In her was found the blood of the prophets and of the saints*
>     *and of all who have been killed on earth."*      (Revelation 18:20, 24)

So, if you are not already praying for Israel, I urge you to do so. Join or start a prayer group and share the points made in this book with as many as possible. We need to seek the presence of God and touch His love for ourselves and for others, in order to release His grace in our lives because faith works by love. With prayer, praise and thanksgiving, we need to spread the good news of the Kingdom to all our contacts, both Jew and Gentile.

Peter's pleading with the Jews to repent is still as relevant as it ever was:

> *"God fulfilled what he had foretold through all the prophets, saying that his Christ would suffer. Repent, then, and turn to God, so that your sins may be wiped out, that times of refreshing may come from the Lord, and that he may send the Christ, who has been appointed for you – even Jesus. He must remain in heaven until the time comes for God to restore everything, as he promised long ago through the holy prophets."*
>
> (Acts 3:18–21)

Praise God, we Gentiles who believe are included in God's redemption for the Jews, to reign on earth with Jesus.

> *" 'Shout and be glad, O daughter of Zion. For I am coming, and I will live among you,' declares the* LORD. *'Many nations will be joined with the* LORD *in that day and will become my people. I will live among you and you will know that the* LORD *Almighty has sent me to you. The* LORD *will inherit Judah as his portion in the holy land and will again choose Jerusalem. Be still before the* LORD, *all mankind, because he has roused himself from his holy dwelling.' "*        (Zechariah 2:10-13)

To achieve this, God is requiring us to trust and obey and then He will act:

> *"If my people would but listen to me,*
> *    if Israel would follow my ways,*
> *how quickly would I subdue their enemies*
> *    and turn my hand against their foes!*
> *Those who hate the* LORD *would cringe before him,*
> *    and their punishment would last for ever.*

> *But you would be fed with the finest of wheat;*
>     *with honey from the rock I would satisfy you."*     (Psalm 81:13–16)

When the nation of Israel listens to God and comes to Christ, we will see God swiftly intervene to comprehensively save both her and the rest of the Church and then bring in the Kingdom. To achieve this, He will have to shake everything to reveal that which is unshakeable, namely His Kingdom and those in it.

May I leave you with a sobering vision one of our prayer for Israel partners received in January this year. The events today are very, very serious indeed and need prayer and understanding of the Scriptures. We were interceding for Israel and the surrounding countries regarding the big push to divide the land and establish a Palestinian State. America has cajoled several Arab countries to be party to the Road Map, even though most of them do not recognise the right of Israel to exist. The intercessor saw President George Bush standing before God, who had His arm pointing towards him in the form of a very large sword of judgment because the President was acting in direct contradiction to His preordained will. The land is not to be divided by anyone because it has been given to the Jews in the covenant God made with Abraham. Mr Tony Blair was standing behind President Bush and is directly implicated in the rebellion to His word (Joel 3:1–2).

Let us all stand together in unity, watch, pray and obey what God shows each one of us to do. Amen and amen.

# ESSAYS ON AFRICAN WRITING

**2** Contemporary
Literature

Edited by Abdulrazak Gurnah

Heinemann

Heinemann Educational Publishers
A Division of Heinemann Publishers (Oxford) Ltd
Halley Court, Jordan Hill, Oxford OX2 8EJ

Heinemann: A Division of Reed Publishing (USA) Inc.
361 Hanover Street, Portsmouth, NH 03801-3912, USA

Heinemann Educational Books (Nigeria) Ltd
PMB 5205, Ibadan
Heinemann Educational Boleswa
PO Box 10103, Village Post Office, Gaborone, Botswana

FLORENCE   PRAGUE   PARIS   MADRID
ATHENS   CHICAGO   MELBOURNE   JOHANNESBURG
AUCKLAND   SINGAPORE   TOKYO   SAO PAULO

Introduction and selection © Abdulrazak Gurnah 1995

Essays © individual contributors 1995

First published by Heinemann Educational Publishers in 1995

British Library Cataloguing in Publication Data
A catalogue record for this book is available from the British Library.

ISBN 0435 917633

Phototypeset by
Wilmaset Ltd, Birkenhead, Wirral
Printed and bound in Great Britain
by Clay Ltd., Bungay, Suffolk

95 96 97 98 10 9 8 7 6 5 4 3 2 1

# Contents

# Introduction

The focus of this second volume of essays on African writing has been on reading the work which followed that of the first 'generation' of post-independence African writers, whose writing was the subject of the first volume.[1] Referring to writers like Dennis Brutus, Wole Soyinka, Chinua Achebe, Ngũgĩ wa Thiong'o and Nuruddin Farah as a 'generation' is not to suggest that they constitute a group, or share characteristic backgrounds or occupy corresponding positions with regard to writing, politics or whatever, though no doubt many generalisations are possible. It is rather to refer to the fact that these were voices which established themselves in the period immediately following de-colonisation, and in their differing ways captured something of the optimism and the apprehensions of the times. Now with hindsight we can see that it was the optimism which was overplayed, and that the apprehensions were understated. Though Soyinka presented *A Dance of the Forests* (1960) as a cautious celebration of Nigeria's independence – 'a sobering look at history'[2] – its underlying emphasis was the future's possibilities. Thirty-five years later, Soyinka has been chased out of his country in fear of his life, and it is the frantic brutalities of *Opera Wonyosi* (1977) that seem as if they might have been a better prediction. Nuruddin Farah has spent the last thirty years living in exile from Somalia, banned and harrassed by rapacious 'authorities' who have now turned Somalia into a nightmarish shooting gallery. And of course Ngũgĩ has been living in exile since his release from detention in Kenya in 1989.

Farah, Ngũgĩ and Soyinka are still writing, and their work has moved on and changed directions, so talk of 'generation' is not an attempt to fix them in a particular writing mode, but a way of suggesting a contrastive organising principle for what this collection means by 'contemporary'.

One of the more striking absences of that earlier period were the voices of women. To some extent the predominance of writers who were men is reflected in the presentation of patriachal structures as unproblematic. It is also evident in certain thematic preoccupations: the ambiguous effects of education on 'cultural identity', corruption, women's sexuality. Of course women writers treat these themes as well, but it is the differential treatment which is the significant dimension. For the narrator of Assia Djebar's *L'amour: la fantasia*[3] (1985) learning to speak French at school not only exposes her to the narrative of her inferiority as a colonised Algerian, but to fears for her sexual 'purity' as a woman. She is oppressed both by a discourse of imperialism and by a native patriarchal construction of women's subjecthood. In this latter sense, a woman is required to be the passive signifier of cultural integrity, and 'education' can only seduce her into wrongdoing and cultural treachery. In Tsitsi Dangarembga's *Nervous Conditions* (1988), in order to get school at all, Tambudzai has to fight her whole family, for they can see no point in wasting such a scarce commodity on a mere girl, as well as fight an unjust, racist and colonial education system.

The treatment of 'corruption' is also interestingly differentiated. In the early novels of Achebe, Soyinka, Ngũgĩ and many others, 'corruption' is what men did (usually at work in an office) to swell their bellies. As C. L. Innes' essay in this collection demonstrates, Aidoo's reading of the effects of 'corruption' on social life has ramifications on the figuring of women and their roles. In these senses, writing by women such as Assia Djebar, Ama Ata Aidoo and Tsitsi Dangarembga has a dimension of challenge to oppressive realities as well as to earlier writing.

Assia Djebar and Tahar Ben Jelloun are both from North Africa – Algeria and Morocco respectively – and both write in French. In their distinctive ways, their work addresses issues which are central to their cultures, and do so using brilliantly inventive narrative forms. The essays on these two writers are included in this volume to bring them more prominently to the attention of readers of African writing. Their work deserves to be better known and the fact that it isn't reflects the implicit sub-heading for 'African literature' as writing from south of the Sahara, though their relative neglect is also just as much to do with the ambivalent cultural affiliations of North African societies.

Three other essays in this collection also offer studies of individual authors: Ben Okri, Moyez Vassanji and Dambudzo Marechera. Marechera has enjoyed or suffered long under the reputation of the wild man of African writing. Recent criticism, in particular the work of Flora Veit-Wild, has focused more on his writing which, aside from *The House of Hunger* (1978), has tended to be neglected, rather than on the man and his outrageous antics.[4] His passionate defence of the writer's freedom to choose his methods and his subject does not seem so daring now that critics of African writing have stopped speaking with such high-handed assurance about African aesthetics, identity and so on. The breadth of subject that his writing embraced is greater than the narrow reading of Marechera as the angst-ridden pseudo-Modernist, high on drink, egotism and pot. Something of this range of subject, but employing quite different methods, is evident in Ben Okri's writing. Despite the tremendous achievement of *The Famished Road* (1991), Okri's Booker Prize-winning novel, his work has not yet received extended critical attention. Okri's writing has changed dramatically over his five novels and two collections of stories. While some critics have read his work as magical realism, and therefore affiliated to a kind of cosmopolitan *avant garde*, others have read it as both rooted in and profoundly influenced by writers such as Amos Tutuola and Fagunwa. Another contemporary novelist with a new perspective on an African subject is Moyez Vassanji, Tanzanian-born and now living in Toronto. He takes as his subject an Indian community in Dar es Salaam. His first novel had offered a historical account of the community, and his third its emigration to Canada. Issues of identity are central to his work, and intimately connected to reflections on location in its construction.

Finally, there are two essays on Nigerian and Malawian poetry. They study the work of important contemporary poets from these two countries, and offer a critical overview of the uses of poetry in the contexts they study. It is evident from the discussions in the fine essays in this collection just how much harder it is now for African writing and its criticism to escape the realities of social decline and political oppression by speculating, however cautiously, about an optimistic future. Femi Osofisan's description of Nigeria as 'a raft commanded by cannibal louts'[5] has a frightening clarity which finds echoes in contemporary African writing.

## Notes

1. *Essays on African Writing 1: A re-evaluation*, ed. Abdulrazak Gurnah, Oxford: Heinemann, 1993.
2. 'Soyinka in Zimbabwe: A Question and Answer Session', ed. James Gibbs, *The Literary Half-Yearly*, 28, No 2, July 1987, p. 68.
3. *L'amour, la fantasia* has been translated by Dorothy Blair as *Fantasia, an Algerian Cavalcade*, London and New York: Quartet Books, 1985.
4. See for example Flora Veit-Wild, *Dambudzo Marechera: A Source Book on his Life and Work*, London: Hans Zell Publishers, 1992.
5. *Wole Soyinka: An Appraisal*, ed. Adewale Maja-Pearce, Oxford: Heinemann, 1994, p. 45.

# Conspicuous Consumption:
# Corruption and the Body Politic in the Writing of
# Ayi Kwei Armah and Ama Ata Aidoo

## C. L. INNES

At the close of *A Man of the People*, Chinua Achebe's novel depicting the rise and fall of a corrupt Nigerian politician, the narrator, Odili, declares:

> For I do honestly believe that in the fat-dripping, gummy, eat-and-let-eat regime just ended – a regime which inspired the common saying that a man could only be sure of what he had put away safely in his gut or, in language evermore suited to the times: 'you chop, me self I chop, palaver finish'; a regime in which you saw a fellow cursed in the morning for stealing a blind man's stick and later in the evening saw him again mounting the altar of the new shrine in the presence of all the people to whisper into the ear of the chief celebrant – in such a regime, I say, you died a good death if your life had inspired someone to come forward and shoot your murderer in the chest – without asking to be paid.[1]

This passage encapsulates themes and metaphors that are common to a number of novels emanating from West Africa in the late 1960s and early 1970s. In many of these novels, a preoccupation with political corruption and consumer capitalism is mediated through images of the consumption of food, eating, bodily decay, and defecation. To these images are linked metaphors of pollution, which may be imaged as natural or cultural or linguistic, 'a language evermore suited to the times'. As in Odili's flight of rhetoric, the association between political and cultural corruption or pollution is assumed and so powerfully interwoven as to pass easily unquestioned by the reader. Frequently disgust at political corruption is also linked to a disgust for the body and its processes. (An earlier and fairly lighthearted example can be found in Sagoe's satiric philosophy of 'Voidancy' read at length to his patient underlings in Wole Soyinka's *The Interpreters*.[2]) It is this intertwining of metaphors and attitudes I wish to try and untangle in this essay, so that we can begin to follow the political and psychological implications inherent in that collapsing of different meanings of consumption and corruption – as moral and political temptation or wrongdoing, as natural decay, and as pollution. Although other writers will be mentioned in

1

passing, my focus will be on the responses of two contemporaneous Ghanaian writers, Ayi Kwei Armah and Ama Ata Aidoo, to the later years of Nkrumah's regime and to Nkrumah's political manifestos. The 1960s African novel with the most intense concentration and intermingling of such images is surely Ayi Kwei Armah's *The Beautyful Ones Are Not Yet Born*,[3] first published two years after *A Man of the People*. In the first chapter of this novel, the reader and the nameless protagonist alike are unceasingly assaulted with the smells, sights, and feel of physical decay and corruption. The bus conductor breathes in happily 'the rotten stench' of an illicitly withheld cedi note; the protagonist sleeps in a pool of drool trickling from his own mouth; he passes filthy litter bins piled high with rubbish and oozing with waste. The chapter ends with the Man's disgusted recoil from the feel of the wooden banisters in his place of work, the Railway and Harbours Administration Block: 'The touch of the banister on the balls of his fingertips had something uncomfortably organic about it. . . . The sight was like that of a very long piece of diseased skin.' Although parts of the following passage have been cited and discussed by many critics before, including Chinua Achebe and Ama Ata Aidoo, I quote these two paragraphs in full below, because they manifest so potently several features of Armah's writing in this novel:

> The wood underneath would win and win till the end of time. Of that there was no doubt possible, only the pain of hope perennially doomed to disappointment. It was so clear. Of course it was in the nature of the wood to rot with age. The polish, it was supposed, would catch the rot. But of course in the end it was the rot which imprisoned everything in its effortless embrace. It did not really have to fight, being was enough. In the natural course of things it would always take the newness of the different kinds of polish and the vaunted cleansing power of the chemicals in them, and it would convert all to victorious filth, awaiting yet more polish again and again and again. And the wood was not alone.
>
> Apart from the wood itself there were, of course, people themselves, just so many hands and fingers bringing help to the wood in its course toward putrefaction. Left-hand fingers in their careless journey from a hasty anus sliding all the way up the banister as their owners made the return trip from the lavatory downstairs to the offices above. Right-hand fingers still dripping with the after-piss and the stale sweat from fat crotches. The callused palms of messengers after they had blown their clogged noses reaching for a convenient place to leave the well-rubbed moisture. Afternoon hands not entirely licked clean of palm soup and

remnants of *kenkey*. The wood would always win. (*The Beautyful Ones*, pp. 14–15).

The preoccupation with decay and corruption, reiterated persistently through the novel, is imaged as a natural and inevitable process intrinsic to the wood, but which is hastened by external, human corruption, or by the addition of human waste matter and decay. There is, as in *A Man of the People*, but here even more intensely and rebarbatively, the mounting disgust and piling-up of images of bodily repulsiveness. But while Odili's disgust turns to celebrating, however naively and romantically, a moment of 'pure' heroism and human intervention, the Man's imagination turns in the second paragraph to an increasingly excremental, repelled and repellant vision of human interaction. What is also striking and typical of Armah's style in this, his first novel, is the seemingly incongruous jump from a meditation on a not very clean wooden banister to abstract and absolute philosophical conclusions, to 'only the pain of hope perennially doomed to disappointment'. So much hope and despair invested in one wooden banister! It is the accumulation of images in the sentences following this which overwhelms the reader, and perhaps the meditator, and prevents either from stopping and questioning the equivalence, and indeed the logic, between the natural image and the philosophical assertion. Armah's critics have not escaped this difficulty in mediating between the concrete and the visionary, and on the whole have wavered between ascribing Armah's attitudes to those of a man overwhelmed by existential excrementalism or the more Platonic vision of the Teacher, who has removed himself from the squalor and the struggle.[4] Robert Fraser responded to such critics by arguing that the novel depicts accurately and forcefully the situation of the typical working-class Ghanaian, 'not like Sartre's characters . . . a free agent [but] in common with all the other characters . . . an expression of his society'.[5] More recently, detailed explorations of Armah's debts to Akan myth and to the work of Fanon have modified and questioned these earlier reactions and read the novel in dialectical terms. Derek Wright persuasively argues that the novel counterpoints two kinds of time, cyclical time related to communal values and ritual, and linear, chronological time, tied to Western concepts of individual progress.[6] But 'traditional' African time has been robbed of meaning, and has become mere repetition in neo-colonial Ghana. Wright perceptively describes the differing experiences of time for the poor and the wealthy:

There is a bitter inverse proportion between the small precious time which the leaders have at their disposal to rush through vast amounts of leisure consumption, and the heavily redundant hours over which the office clerks have to stretch out their tiny amounts of unproductive work. The two categories of experience are mutually determinative. The rich who cram their time with frivolities and novelties are seen to create a vacuum of time for the poor to live and work in, since the government's corrupt neglect of production and services leads to stopped trains, uncollected refuse and bureaucratic boredom in jobs without work. Time 'consumed' by the big men thus generates a residue of time as 'waste' for poor men, time spent inactive in enforced boredom. (*Ayi Kwei Armah's Africa*, pp. 90–1)

All that is produced in the Railway office is time, timesheets, overtime slips, graphic time recording cancellations and stoppages. At the end of the novel, the two kinds of time collapse into one another, as Koomson runs out of time, plunges through a parodic version of expulsion which is both excrement and rebirth, and the Man returns to begin the whole weary repetition of work and family demand again, his mind '*consumed* with thoughts of everything he was going back to – Oyo, the eyes of the children after six o'clock, the office and every day, and above all the never-ending knowledge that' this aching emptiness would be all that the remainder of his own life could offer him' (*The Beautyful Ones*, p. 215 [my italics]).

For Neil Lazarus the novel should be read as a dialectic between the real and the visionary, and he would have Armah's readers give far more weight to the hope invested in the Man's heroic resistance to corruption.[7] Both Wright and Lazarus also emphasise the influence of Fanon, especially of *The Wretched of the Earth* and the chapter 'The Pitfalls of National Consciousness', on Armah's portrayal of Ghana's elite, the new leaders who merely ape the colonisers, and thus betray the masses.[8]

But the novel is not so much a testament to 'the fatal legacy of Western time values for modern Africa when they become the exclusive possession of a privileged minority' (Wright, *Ayi Kwei Armah's Africa*, p. 92), as to the fatal legacy of Western capitalism and consumerism, which distorts time and communal values marked by seasonal and cyclical ritual. In the modern Ghana portrayed by Armah, nothing is produced; there is only consumption and waste. In his first two novels, the emphasis on European and American imports, such as Toyotas, whisky, beer, and refrigerators, or the representation of Estella Koomson as a woman who despises all things African, can be read not only as a satire on the mimicry by black men of white men, as in Achebe's *A Man of the People* or Soyinka's early play *The Lion and the Jewel*; it can also be read as part of an economic analysis. Thus, on the one hand, Armah's novel takes from Fanon the argument that dependency is the psychopathology of colonialism and neo-colonialism. The novel draws as well on a Marxist analysis of capitalism which might have found favour with Nkrumah in the first stages of his regime before it adopted the romantic versions of 'African Socialism' which Armah condemned in an essay written at about the same time he was working on his first novel. Armah's essay, 'African Socialism: Utopian or Scientific', published in 1967, offers a scornful critique of what he terms the 'myth' of African Socialism, or communalism, promulgated by Senghor, Nkrumah, and Nyerere, not least for the contradictions implicit in their elevation of the pomp and grandeur of past African kings and kingdoms simultaneously with their insistence on essentialist African spirituality which values the welfare of the community above individual wealth and fulfilment.[9] Armah quotes from Nkrumah's 1964 manifesto, *Consciencism*, which argues that pre-colonial African societies represented an original and pure form of socialism, where 'if one seeks the social political ancestor of Socialism one must go to Communalism. Socialism stands to Communalism as Capitalism stands to Slavery.'[10] The myth of an Edenic Africa, Armah argues, allows African leaders to pretend that the mere dispersal of colonialism will allow Eden to be restored. Romantic African Socialism thus bypasses the necessary 'purgatorial stages', the class struggle which according to 'Scientific Socialism' must precede the establishment of an egalitarian order. Armah comments further:

> It is important to note that Socialism is here conceived of as a projection into the present and the future of certain *moral* qualities that are supposed to have been characteristic of pre-colonial Africa. As to the location and time and space of this virtuous old Africa, the available formulae are vague and at times unhistorical tales of kings dressed in scintillating robes, possessing countless slaves and spending gold with grand *insouciance*. These fables defeat the purpose of African Socialism, for though they might warm the cockles of spectacle hungry bourgeois nationalist hearts, they leave any informed socialist quite unimpressed. Conspicuous waste of resources in conditions of scarcity is not one of the tenets of Socialism. ('African Socialism', p. 24)

Armah concludes his essay by directing his readers to the study of Frantz Fanon's analysis of the 'mystification' practised by African leaders. The particular emphasis in Armah's first two novels on consumption and waste as a continuing metaphor for the impact of consumer capitalism on Ghanaian society and its values may also be linked to another aspect of Fanon's writing, the chapter on 'Colonial War and Mental Disorders' in *The Wretched of the Earth*. In several of the cases, the symptoms of mental distress include eating disorders, difficulty eating or swallowing, accompanied often by distaste for all physical contact. Fanon links the 'mental anorexia' in these cases to the denial of humanity and the sense of prevailing injustice experienced under the rule of the colonisers. Of one Algerian prisoner sent to his hospital for treatment, Fanon writes:

> What we saw in front of us was a thoughtful, depressed man, suffering from a loss of appetite, who kept to his bed. He avoided political discussion and showed a marked lack of interest in everything to do with the national struggle. He avoided listening to any news which had a bearing on the war of liberation. (*The Wretched of the Earth*, p. 256; but see also pp. 274, 276, 282)

Although Armah is writing about the period after independence, his portrayal of Teacher might well be summarised in Fanon's description of this Algerian's symptoms. The similarity between these two cases might lead us to be wary of the supposition that Teacher speaks on behalf of Armah. Rather, his withdrawal may be seen as a pathological response, not to colonial, but to neo-colonial Ghana, and Armah may be read as leading us to conclude that the effects are similar. A more pronounced but comparable response to the discovery that the 'revolution' promised by African leaders such as Nkrumah had been betrayed and corrupted is delineated in Armah's third novel, *Why Are We So Blest?*, when Solo describes his reaction to the discovery that the Angolan independence leaders are contributing to the inequality their rhetoric denounces:

> The initiation was a quick death of the hopeful spirit. For days my body shook with the realization. Refusing to renew itself, rejecting sustenance, it threw out life already stored in it. All my apertures ran with fluid, living and dead, escaping a body unwilling to hold them; blood, urine, vomit, tears, diarrhea, pus.[11]

Teacher's response is less extreme than Solo's and less self-destructive than Kofi Billy's suicide, or Manaan's madness, or Rama Krishnan's refusal of food, but it derives from the same 'nervous condition' and provides no solution to the problem.[12] Indeed, as Rama Krishna's death from consumption and fasting reveals, it may only hasten the process of corruption.

Nevertheless, denial of food can bring momentary relief, as it does for Armah's protagonist in *The Beautyful Ones*:

> The sourness that had been gathering in his mouth went imperceptibly away until quite suddenly all he was aware of was the exceedingly sharp clarity of vision and the clean taste that comes with the successful defiance of hunger. . . . Nothing oppressed him as he walked along now, and even the slight giddiness accompanying the clarity of his starved vision was buried way beneath the unaccustomed happy lightness. (p. 26)

For perhaps an hour or two, the refusal of food allows release from cycle of desire, consumption, waste. The 'clarity of his starved vision' also highlights for the Man the symbolism of the clear water which escapes momentarily from the banked-up dirt, to appreciate briefly the 'purity and peace' of that 'clearness before the inevitable muddying', and to contrast it with the 'ambiguous disturbing tumult within awakened by the gleam'. Now he is emptied of desire, and the thought of food brings 'a picture of its eating and its spewing out, of its beginning and endings, so that no desire arose asking to be controlled' (p. 28). This moment of vision and relief presages and encapsulates the longer moment of escape and relief which ends the book, the expulsion of Koomson, the long cleansing swim in the sea, before the Man's slow return to the demands of 'the loved ones' and the new regime with its old corruption.

The recurring analogy between eating, temptation, desire and corruption, of necessity implies the inevitability of corruption, since man must eat, food must be digested, and finally evacuated. Nowhere is there pleasure in eating: food can never be an end in itself, but is always a mere necessity for the poor, and a sign of status for the wealthy. It is a world, as Teacher declares, where there are 'No saviours. Only the hungry and the fed. Deceivers all' (p. 106). Bribery and eating are frequently equated, as is wealth and food. Thus, as in Ngũgĩ's *Devil on the Cross*, the corrupt and the wealthy are not merely well-fed, but grotesquely fat and flabby.[13] Armah's description of Koomson's double chin, his chubbiness, his inability to fit comfortably in the chair provided by the man, his flabby hands, all connect him to the nation's rulers before and after colonisation. As Armah comments: 'And yet these were the socialists of Africa, fat, perfumed, soft with the ancestral softness of chiefs who have sold their people and are celestially happy with the fruits of the trade' (pp. 153–4). The sentence might well be read as a direct rebuttal of Nkrumah's celebration of an original and essential socialist Africa, innocent of class division. The 'fruits' mentioned here recall an earlier point in the novel associating celestial happiness with the collaboration between black and white men in depriving Africans of 'fruits' which rightfully belong to them, when the Man remembers the incident of the stolen mangoes from the white man's garden (pp. 78–80). Here the mangoes become a forbidden fruit in a paradisal enclosure. The boys steal the fruits, but before they can eat them are forced to run and, in an image which foreshadows Koomson's escape at the end of the novel, squeeze through a tiny hole at the bottom of the wall, and run away from the paradisal white garden, which, however, encloses not European apple trees, but African mangoes and almonds.

The analogy here with the biblical story of the Garden of Eden and the expulsion of man for eating the forbidden fruit, reminds us how widespread and fundamental is this association of eating with desire for greater power and knowledge, the desire to be godlike. It also reminds us of the widespread association between such temptations and the role of women as temptresses. Throughout the novel, Oyo is portrayed as a kind of Eve, urging the Man to eat of the forbidden fruit, and so become godlike. Certainly the Man believes that she provides the main source or pressure of temptation to sin, to lose his purity, and Teacher endorses this reiterated view of the dangerous seduction of 'the loved ones':

> But you know that the loved ones are dead even when they walk around the earth like the living, and you know that all they want is that you throw away the thing in your mind that makes you think you are still alive, and their embrace will be a welcome unto death. (pp. 64–5)

Here, 'the loved ones' have become like those so named in Evelyn Waugh's novel, the living dead; they are vampire figures, who will suck the life and goodness from those who fall into their embrace.[14] Oyo envies and would like to emulate Estella Koomson, who is also scathingly satirised as more desperate to disassociate herself from all things African than her husband, able to consume only Western drinks, and shrinking from the contamination of poverty in the man's house.

In West Africa, the figure of Mammy Water provides an indigenous myth of the dangerously seductive female. She features in Achebe's story, 'Uncle Ben's Choice', recurs in many of Soyinka's plays and in his novels, perhaps most potently as Simi in *The Interpreters*, and, as both Sarah Chetin and Derek Wright have demonstrated, her myth plays a significant role in Armah's first two novels and in his fellow Ghanaian Kofi Awoonor's novel, *This Earth, My Brother*. . .[15] Like the mermaid in Western mythologies, the role of Mammy Water is an ambiguous one. In 'Uncle Ben's Choice', she offers the seductions of wealth in return for renunciation of family attachments, and Uncle Ben feels his choice of 'loved ones' has been a wise one. In *The Beautyful Ones*, however, Teacher seems to have rejected Manaan (as Wright points out, her association with the sea and her promise of unworldly knowledge and power through wine and 'wee' marks her as a Mammy Water figure), and in so doing has rejected wealth and family as well.

For Armah and Awoonor, the Mammy Water figure seems to signify not merely the dangers of seduction and false knowledge, but also an Africa which has been despoiled and calls for redemption. This is how Awoonor speaks of Dede and Adisa, respectively the cousin and mistress of his protagonist Amamu:

> Adisa is a warm womanly woman, the essence of womanhood, the essence of Africa in a way: or one aspect of Africa. Adisa is like Africa, like the little girl who is raped and dies before she has even been initiated into the puberty rites. All that lives on is her tiny mite of woman's wisdom. And so we see her again as the mermaid, the woman of the sea. . . . I was trying to incorporate the imagery of that myth into another symbol of Africa. Somewhere she does exist as the final repository of wisdom. . . . She knows what I must do, what Amamu must do, what we all must do. And I must go with her in order to acquire this knowledge and survive the truncation of the soul that society imposes. Unless we follow this path to wisdom, the Dance of Death will continue, onward and onward.[16]

Armah's novel, like Awoonor's, also includes in contrast to the seductive Dede/Adisa/Manaan figure, a demanding and dangerous Oyo figure. Amamu's wife, like Oyo and Estella Koomson, seeks all the consumer goods and accoutrements of the West. Her Anglo-African name, Alice Johnson, contrasts with Adisa's wholly African one. She is associated not with the sea, fields of butterflies and almond trees, but with the airport (where she is first introduced). Her teeth, unlike the gapped teeth of Adisa and Dede, are 'pure and artificial, products of one of those little factories in Europe that specialise in articles that could be stuck into any receptacle on the human body' (*This Earth, My Brother . . .*, p. 124). Oyo's deviation from African naturalness is figured in the Caesarian scar which inhibits the man's rare moment of desire for her. But whether 'vampire' or 'mermaid', cold and demanding or 'warm, womanly woman', each figure is in some sense a cause of Africa's corruption – Dede and Manaan by their very vulnerability, their innocent eagerness to offer themselves to others, and ultimately the prostitution of their bodies; Oyo and Alice by their failure to recognise the worth of the protagonist who can be their true redeemer, and their prostitution of 'African values' for European ones.

Like Armah's Man, Awoonor's protagonist escapes from the artificial and empty 'gleam' promised by upper-middle-class suburbia and chatter to the sea. His escape also involves a journey through the 'dungheap' of the city to save another human being, through the shanty towns huddled around two huge latrines and circumvented by gutters which carry the city's filth. But while Armah's protagonist returns, reluctantly, to 'the loved ones', Amamu escapes into madness and his vision of the woman of the sea, as Manaan also sinks into madness.

Although Ama Ata Aidoo's two plays offer a different perspective on the roles of African men and women in contributing to the desertion of traditional African values and contemporary corruption, there are correspondences with Armah's portrayal of Ghana during Nkrumah's regime. Her first play, *Dilemma of a Ghost*, interestingly foreshadows Armah's second novel in its dramatisation of the search of an African-American woman for wholeness in Africa with her been-to lover.[17] Eulalie's demand for refrigerators and coca–cola, her refusal to have children, her alienation from African foods and family expectations are all traits which make her comparable to Oyo, Estella, Efua (Baako's mother in Armah's second novel, *Fragments*[18]), and Alice. But the play ends with her recognising and being recognised by her mother-in-law, and her movement towards African communal values while Kofi, her been-to husband, remains alienated. Aidoo's second play reviews the role of women in urging Westernisation, however. Written in the final years of Nkrumah's increasingly disreputable reign, and completed the year before Armah's first novel was published (although not performed until 1969), Ama Ata Aidoo's *Anowa* also takes up the theme of corruption and heroic resistance by refusal. Like Armah, Aidoo links the inroads of capitalism and a consumer-oriented society to Africa's internal history of slavery and class division. Like Awoonor's Amamu and Armah's Baako (in *Fragments*) her protagonist disintegrates into madness at the end. But unlike the central figures in those two novels, her protagonist is a woman and, as the title signifies, she is a heroine in her own right, not as a symbol of 'the essence of womanhood, the essence of Africa' who awaits a male redeemer. In Aidoo's second play, it is not Anowa but her husband who presses for consumer goods, and who seeks to turn Anowa herself into an ornament, a status symbol.

It is possible to see *Anowa* as a rewriting of two dominant versions of African history proposed by two fathers, Chinua Achebe as literary father and Kwame Nkrumah as political father. Aidoo has expressed her admiration for Achebe, and indeed declares that he inspired her to write.[19] *Anowa*, like Aidoo's earlier play, is characterised by its use of an Africanised English idiom reminiscent of Achebe's, drawing on proverb, folk tale, and the imagery of rural village life. Like *Things Fall Apart* it is set first in a rural village untouched by the impact of European mores and customs, and ends with the figurative presence of Queen Victoria and the suicide of the hero whose shame is linked to loss of manhood. Denied poetry and music, Nwoye rebels against his conservative father, leaves his community, and seeks fulfilment in Christianity; denied a career as priestess or dancer, Anowa rebels against her conservative mother, leaves her community and seeks fulfilment in what is often claimed to be another European ideal, romance. But whereas the main sources of corruption of traditional African values in Achebe's *Things Fall Apart* and *Arrow of God* are religious, Aidoo emphasises economic causes, and links them to the fate of the marginalised characters in Achebe's works, women and slaves.

In her foregrounding of the issue of slavery and its acceptance by Ghanaians for the creation of their own wealth in the nineteenth century, Aidoo's rebuttal of Nkrumah's portrayal of traditional African society is even more emphatic than Armah's. Her play rejects the idealisation of traditional Africa as devoid of class divisions, and at the same time brings to the fore the issue of gender divisions. Its plot also parallels Nkrumah's rise and fall, reiterating the charismatic appeal of its male protagonist, Kofi Ako, who appears at first in working clothes and seems to promise Anowa a life of comradeship and shared productivity, but ends in sterile and ostentatious display, having as Anowa declares, 'exhausted [his] masculinity acquiring slaves and wealth' (p. 61).

*Anowa* takes as one of its main themes the link between the objectification of women and economic structures which demand slave labour or a division between producers and consumers. In becoming a mere consumer, Kofi Ako becomes sterile; he 'eats up' his own manhood, and is incapable of producing children. As in Armah's Railway Administration Block, work also becomes meaningless; everything is for show, and the ultimate dramatisation of waste labour is surely the slave children fanning Kofi Ako's empty chair. The slave children, who call Kofi and Anowa 'Father' and 'Mother', represent the distortion of meaningful family ties in a society which no longer provides models of productive activity. No longer permitted to participate in the work of trading, Anowa drifts aimlessly around the opulent house. Like Armah's protagonists she becomes an object of scorn and contempt because of her refusal to deny her convictions. Her insistence on remaining true to her own vision that slavery is wrong and that men and women must live by the fruits of their own labour involves also her refusal to be merely a status symbol, the elegantly adorned wife of a rich man. Thus for Anowa, what she is and what she wears are inextricably connected, and she refuses to change her apparel from the old cloth she wore as co-labourer and partner to Kofi. In contrast, Kofi's changing apparel, from work clothes to leisure clothes to opulent gold cloth and jewellery, represents not only his loss of authenticity but his 'feminisation'. In turning himself into a mere status symbol, Kofi becomes a 'woman'. As Anowa blurts out, 'My husband is a woman now . . . he is a corpse. He is dead wood. But less than dead wood because at least, that sometimes grows mushrooms' (p. 62). But in betraying himself, Kofi has also betrayed Anowa, who despite the energy and vision which allowed her to 'make something' of Kofi, can find no significant role of her own except implicitly as one who speaks truths and reveals what is hidden. Anowa and Baako, the protagonist of Armah's second novel, both seek to demystify, to remind the community of Africa's true past, involving slavery, and its present betrayal of the vision of a just and egalitarian society which was promised with independence. Both are cast out as a result, and branded as madman and witch.

Aidoo's plays eschew the squalor and exrementalism which dominate the early novels of Armah and Awoonor, although like Soyinka's Sagoe she notes, in her story 'For Whom Things Do Not Change', that in newly independent Africa it is not skin colour but the lavatory which most clearly marks class distinctions. Ama Ata Aidoo's very favourable review of *The Beautyful Ones Are Not Yet Born*, particularly endorsing its unrelenting castigation of Nkrumah and contemporary Ghana, indicates that she shared Armah's assessment of the condition of Ghana, and it is interesting to note that Armah's second novel is dedicated to Ama Ata.[20] Both authors end their second major work ambiguously. Aidoo's stage directions state that for the producer 'the choice is open' whether to end the play with Anowa's final exit, or with the epilogue in which the Old Man and Old Woman explicitly tell the audience that Anowa has also committed suicide (*Anowa*, p. 3). It is not clear from the final pages of *Fragments* whether Baako will be 'healed' in the psychiatric hospital under Juana's care, whether he will sink into permanent 'madness', or whether he will be forced to take the drugs which curtail his vision. The later works of Armah and Aidoo diverge, however. Armah's African protagonists in *Why Are We So Blest?* (1972) find only disillusionment and death when they return to Africa from the West, while *Two Thousand Seasons* seems in many ways to endorse the very analysis Armah had condemned so forcefully in his essay on 'African Socialism'. Although here, and in his later novel *The Healers* (1978) he is consistent in his contempt of the ostentation, show and inequality of African royalty, he also seems to promulgate Nkrumah's 'myth' of an essential African communalism to be found in 'the way' and among 'the Healers,' an African communalism which can only come into being when all foreign influences have been dispersed.

In the decade after Nkrumah's fall, Armah's writing moves towards myth and historical romance, where good and evil are clearly distinguished, the corrupt are bloated and ugly while the good are lithe, beautiful and good at games. Aidoo's writing after *Anowa*, on the other hand, is set firmly in the present, and discards any suggestion of the allegorical. Whereas Anowa, like Armah's protagonists, is able at great cost to maintain her integrity, her separateness, Aidoo's men and women in her stories and later novels find the borders between good and evil much more blurred. The well-intentioned teacher of the title story in *No Sweetness Here* fails to come to terms with her own responsibility for the well-being of her pupils and is unable to offer comfort to the mother of one who is bitten by a snake.[21] The disapproving and concerned older sister in 'Two Sisters' benefits from the gifts brought by a corrupt politician for the sister who is his mistress. *Our Sister Killjoy* fragments the narrative voice to dissipate the illusion of a unified self grounded in a sure sense of moral certainty.[22] Such fragmentation is also linked to the ways in which different languages and audiences may influence self-images and relations to others. Sissie's overhearing of herself named 'das Schwartze Madchen' in Germany forces her for the first time to become aware not only of herself but others in terms of skin colour (pp. 39–40). Her visit to Europe also makes her aware of her body as consuming and consumable, and the long section titled 'Plums' which recounts this visit is replete with imagery of food, eating and desire. Sissie's first encounter with fresh plums also occurs in Europe and is redolent of her changing awareness of self as seen in the mirror of European eyes:

> So she had good reason to feel fascinated by the character of Marija's plums. They were of a size, sheen and succulence she had not encountered anywhere else in those foreign lands. . . . What she was not aware of, though, was that those Bavarian plums owed their glory in her eyes and on her tongue not only to that beautiful and black Bavarian soil, but also to other qualities that she herself possessed at that material time:
>
> > Youthfulness
> > Peace of mind
> > Feeling free:
> > Knowing you are a rare article,
> > Being
> > Loved.
>
> So she sat, Our Sister, her tongue caressing the plump berries with skin-colour almost like her own, while Marija told her how she had selected them specially for her, off the single tree in the garden. (*Our Sister Killjoy*, pp. 39–40)

Like the mangoes and the 'celestial fruits' fenced off in the European gardens recalled in Armah's novel, the plums 'selected specially for her, off the single tree in the garden', may tempt and seduce the innocent African protagonist. Marija attempts to seduce Sissie, and the desire to be admired and loved by this quite appealing young German woman is indeed enticing. Nor are the plums deceptive in their appearance, as were the mangoes which in the end tasted green and sour. For Sissie and her compatriots, the attraction of Europe and the United States has much to do with the abundance of good foods they offer for the appreciative consumer, and the resulting sense of well-being. Here Sissie *is* what she consumes, 'her tongue caressing the plump berries with skin-colour almost like her own'. The 'almost' is significant, however. Marija offers Sissie a flattering and lovable self-image, but Sissie realises that she herself is in danger of being consumed, and rejects Marija's advances. However, in her refusal of Marija there is also complexity and blurring of motives. As Caroline Rooney points out, Sissie

> ultimately cannot allow herself to be seduced: she will not respond to the demand for love that the working husband, the wage slave, fails to supply. In refusing to take the German husband's place, she redupli-

cates it in not meeting Marija's, the wife's demand, as Sissie realises. She realises that she comes to occupy the place of ungiving white male, empowered by the vulnerability of another person.[23]

And for a moment Sissie also feels the pleasure of that power. What I particularly want to draw attention to in this episode is the blurring of roles; the distinctions between male and female, black and white, self and other, consumer and consumed, moral and immoral, are repeatedly constructed and deconstructed. The heroine's selves are multiple; there is no single authentic self to whom she can remain true by refusing the impositions of others. Whereas in Armah's fiction and in Aidoo's drama, language is transparent and categories remain distinct, in Aidoo's later fiction, the sense of a problematic identity is linked to the sense of language as a confused and blurring medium which obscures political and personal relationships: 'Since so far I have only been able to use a language that enslaved me, and therefore, the messengers of my mind always come shackled' (*Our Sister Killjoy*, p. 112). Paradoxically, however, the realisation of the lack of clear boundaries, the urgent internal debate and self-questioning as well as the external debate which constitutes the novel, leads not to despair and withdrawal, or the stoical endurance of endlessly reiterated cycles of consumption and waste, but a positive re-identification with the African continent and return to rejoice in its sensual qualities: 'Besides she was back in Africa. And that felt like fresh honey on the tongue: a mixture of complete sweetness and smoky roughage. Below was home with its unavoidable warmth and even after these thousands of years, its uncertainties' (p. 133).

Almost two decades after the publication of Aidoo's and Armah's earliest works, another African country with a Socialist programme has produced two writers whose visions and imagery bear comparison with those of Armah and Aidoo, and both of whom have to some extent drawn on Fanon. Dambudzo Marechera's *House of Hunger* and *Black Sunlight* plunge the reader into squalor and disorder far more surreal than the world portrayed by Armah, but equally repellent and full of disgust for the body, especially the female body. Tsitsi Dangarembga's *Nervous Conditions* has two young female protagonists who resist mental and material corruption by refusing. Images of eating, digesting and excretion recur throughout the novel. Tambudzai, the narrator, tells how her brother hated riding on the bus because 'the women smelt of unhealthy reproductive odours, the children were inclined to relieve their upset bowels on the floor, and the men gave off strong aromas of productive labour.'[24] Like Aidoo's Kofi, Tambudzai's brother resists 'productive labour', including work on the farm, and aspires to the status of privileged and educated male, marked by having others work for him and carry his bags. As did the Ghanaian writers of an earlier generation, Marechera and Dangarembga express the effects of colonialism and neo-colonialism in terms of an assault on the body, a condition which is internalised, and becomes indistinguishable from the daily cycle of consumption, digestion and evacuation. Like so many of Armah's and Aidoo's protagonists, the majority succumb to temptation; they take of the fruit and eat, in their desire to emulate the powerful and the wealthy. But a few defy the temptation, by violent rejection – oral, anal and sexual, as in Marechera's fiction, or by refusal to allow the food to become part of the system, as in the case of Nyasha, Tambudzai's cousin, who consumes and then secretly vomits up her food, or refuses to eat. In all cases, there seems to be a choice only between welcoming insidious destruction by others and self-destruction by refusal, through anorexia or madness. Only Aidoo's later fiction envisions the possibility of a less harmful process of consumption, of welcoming and becoming part of an Africa which feels 'like fresh honey on the tongue.' But the optimism of this ending, with its invocation of natural foods and rejection of European consumer goods, is qualified by its abandonment of hope for those African men who, in Sissie's narrative, have so succumbed to its seductions that they can no longer detach themselves from the West and have been consumed by it.

*Notes*

1. Chinua Achebe, *A Man of the People*, London: Heinemann, 1966, p. 167.

2. Wole Soyinka, *The Interpreters*, London: André Deustch, 1965; published in Heinemann African Writers Series in 1970.

3. Ayi Kwei Armah, *The Beautyful Ones Are Not Yet Born*, Boston: Houghton Mifflin, 1968; published in Heinemann African Writers Series in 1969. Further references will be to the Heinemann edition and will be included in the text.

4. See, for example, 'Africa and Her Writers', *Morning Yet On Creation Day*, London: Heinemann, 1975, pp. 19–29.

5. Robert Fraser, *The Novels of Ayi Kwei Armah*, London: Heinemann, 1980, pp. 15–29.

6. Derek Wright, *Ayi Kwei Armah's Africa*, London: Hans Zell, 1989, pp. 90–1.

7. Neil Lazarus, *Resistance in Postcolonial African Fiction*, New Haven: Yale University Press, 1990, pp. 46–79.

8. Frantz Fanon, *The Wretched of the Earth*, trans. Constance Farrington, London: Macgibbon & Kee, 1965; New York: Grove Press, 1968; first published in French in 1961. Page references will be to the Grove Press edition.
9. Ayi Kwei Armah, 'African Socialism: Utopian or Scientific', *Présence Africaine*, No. 64, 1967), pp. 6–30.
10. Kwame Nkrumah, *Consciencism*, London: Heinemann, 1964, p. 20.
11. Ayi Kwei Armah, *Why Are We So Blest?*, London: Heinemann, 1974, p. 114.
12. 'Nervous conditions' borrows Sartre's description of 'native': 'The status of "native" is a nervous condition introduced and maintained by the settler among colonized people *with their consent*', 'Introduction', *The Wretched of the Earth*, p. 20. The phrase is taken as the title of her first novel by Tsitsi Dangarembga, London: The Women's Press, 1988.
13. Ngũgĩ wa Thiong'o, *Devil on the Cross*, London: Heinemann, 1982; first published in Gikuyu 1980.
14. Evelyn Waugh, *The Loved One*, London: Chapman & Hall, 1948.
15. See Sara Chetin, 'Armah's Women', *Kunapipi*, Vol. 6 No. 3 (1984), pp. 47–56. Kofi Awoonor, *This Earth, My Brother . . .*, New York: Doubleday Anchor, 1972. In a seminar discussion at the University of Nice in 1993, Professor Jacqueline Bardolph commented that certain features of Mammy Water as she is depicted in African art and folk legend may derive from the figureheads on European ships, including slave ships, which visited West Africa.
16. Interview with John Goldblatt, *Transition*, No. 41 (1972), p. 44. Regarding his poetry and his first novel, Kofi Awoonor has commented: 'My concern is not . . . to provide a picture of a particular society at a particular time, but rather to provide through a series of selected images, the idea of a continuous process of corruptibility which the human society without strength and vision can be locked in'. Personal letter to Richard Priebe, quoted R. Priebe, *Myth, Realism and the West African Writer*, Trenton, NJ: Africa World Press, 1988, p. 65.
17. Ama Ata Aidoo, *Dilemma of a Ghost* and *Anowa*, London: Longman, 1987. *Dilemma of a Ghost* was first published in 1965, while *Anowa* was first published in 1970.
18. Ayi Kwei Armah, *Fragments*, Boston: Houghton Mifflin, 1969; London: Heinemann, 1970.
19. See Maxine McGregor, Interview with Aidoo in *African Writers Talking*, ed. Duerden and Piertese, London: Heinemann, 1972, pp. 19–27, in which Aidoo discusses *Anowa*.
20. In 'No Saviours', *African Writers on African Writing*, ed. G. D. Killam, London: Heinemann, 1973, pp. 14–18. See also Aidoo's review of Oginga Odinga's *Not Yet Uhuru* in the same 1967 issue of *Présence Africaine* as Armah's essay on African Socialism. Reading Odinga's book, she concludes, 'any non-East African would come to understand why in certain quarters [Kenyatta] is the most hated African politician next to Kwame Nkrumah', *Présence Africaine*, No. 64, p. 181).
21. Ama Ata Aidoo, *No Sweetness Here*, London: Longman, 1970.

22. Ama Ata Aidoo, *Our Sister Killjoy*, London: Longman, 1981. Page references will be to this edition and will be included in the text.

23. C. L. Innes and Caroline Rooney, 'African Writing and Gender', in *Writing and Africa*, ed. Paul Hyland and M. H. Msiska. To be published by Longman, 1995.

24. Tsitsi Dangarembga, *Nervous Conditions*, London: The Women's Press, 1988, p. 1.

# Strategies of Transgression in the Writings of Assia Djebar

BELINDA JACK

Towards the end of his novel *Harrouda*, Tahar Ben Jelloun cites Roland Barthes: 'To speak is to seek to exercise power', but for North African *women* to speak, Tahar Ben Jelloun's text continues, is to assume a power which is not theirs. They therefore commit a transgression: 'It was necessary to say words in (to) a society which doesn't want to listen to them, which denies their existence when it's a woman who has dared to take them up.' But what is spoken may be illusory: 'because it is enunciated in the language of the Other. But what is most important is not what my mother says, but that she should have spoken. Speech itself is already the assuming of a position in a society which denies it to women.'[1] For Assia Djebar, a North African *woman* writer, language is part of a complex set of relationships between corporeal confinement and freedom, encountered in multiple guises:

> A l'âge où le corps aurait dû se voiler, grâce à l'école française, je peux davantage circuler [. . .]
> —Elle ne se voile donc pas encore, ta fille? interroge telle ou telle matrone [. . .] qui questionne ma mère, lors d'une des noces de l'été. Je dois avoir treize, quatorze ans peut-être.
> —Elle lit! répond avec raideur ma mère.
> Dans ce silence de gêne installée, le monde entier s'engouffre. Et mon propre silence.
> 'Elle lit', c'est-à-dire, en langue arabe, 'elle étudie'. Maintenant je me dis que ce verbe 'lire' ne fut pas par hasard l'ordre lancé par l'archange Gabriel, dans la grotte, pour la révélation coranique. . . 'Elle lit', autant dire que l'écriture à lire, y compris celle des mécréants, est toujours source de révélation: de la mobilité du corps dans mon cas, et donc de ma future liberté.

> At the age when I should be veiled already, I can still move about freely thanks to the French school [. . .]
> 'Doesn't your daughter wear a veil yet?' asks one or other of the matrons, gazing questioningly at my mother with suspicious kohl-rimmed eyes, on the occasion of one of the summer weddings. I must be thirteen, or possibly fourteen.

'She reads!' my mother replies stiffly. Everyone is swallowed up in the embarrassed silence that ensues. And in my own silence. 'She reads', that is to say in Arabic, 'she studies'. I think now that this command 'to read' was not just included in the Quranic revelation made by the Angel Gabriel in the cave . . . 'She reads' is tantamount to saying that writing to be read, including that of the unbelievers, is always a source of revelation: in my case of the mobility of my body, and so of my future freedom.[2]

Reading and writing as subjects recur within Djebar's texts and it is the density of the poetics associated with these which in part explains why Djebar's texts have assumed privileged status as touchstones within the growing corpus of Francophone texts written by North African women. Furthermore reading and writing generate an ever-proliferating web of associated figures, most obviously: the exposed body, forbidden sexual, and often violent, encounters, and illegitimacy of various kinds.

Djebar also lucidly articulates the specificities of the North African woman writer's position:

All the early attempts, for women of/in the Arab world, to seek both to come out and 'come out in the òther language' risked a double expulsion: experienced both by the writing [. . .], on the one hand, and the speaking body, on the other. To write in the foreign language becomes almost making love outside the ancestral faith: the taboo, in Islam, spares men, in this regard, even gives them greater credence.[3]

The 'expulsion' which is the response to Arab women's 'transgression' can be read as an explanation for the response of North African critics to Assia Djebar's first novel, La Soif (1957). Influenced by French critics' characteristically ethnocentric gesture – their appropriation of Djebar as a new Françoise Sagan – Algerian critics denounced her. How could a writer explore sexuality and feminine desire during a bloody colonial war? Danielle Marx-Scouras argues: 'La Soif takes on a new meaning today. The absence of any reference to the revolution implicitly refutes the claims of Algerian militants that national liberation would inevitably result in the liberation of Algerian women.'[4]

The transgressive strategies deployed and developed in Djebar's later works are explicit and more complex. The short texts of Femmes d'Alger dans leur appartement (1980), and particularly her novel, L'Amour, la fantasia (1985), (later texts include Ombre Sultane (1987) and more recently, Les soeurs de Médine (1991)), are subversive in terms of form and genre in ways which her early texts are not.[5] Certain crucial antitheses are proposed, and later questioned, as are unstable and shifting relationships between these pairs. These antitheses are associated with space (open and closed), the female body (veiled and naked), associated with language in the French sense of *langue* ['tongue'] (French and Arabic), and language in the sense of *langage* ['linguistic system'] (written and oral).

*Femmes d'Alger dans leur appartement* counters the multiple appropriating gestures of Eugène Delacroix's famous, and perhaps emblematic painting of the same name, by appropriating its title and starting afresh. Delacroix (1798–1863), one of the influential artists associated with Orientalist painting, participated in the Western representation and appropriation of the 'Orient' explored in Edward Said's pioneering work of the same name.[6] Djebar 're-paints' Delacroix's canvas in the following way:

> 'Femmes d'Alger dans leur appartement': trois femmes dont deux sont assises devant un narguilé [. . .] Tout le sens du tableau se joue dans le rapport qu'entretiennent celles-ci avec leur corps, ainsi qu'avec le lieu de leur enfermement. Prisonnières résignées d'un lieu clos qui s'éclaire d'une sorte de lumière de rêve venue de nulle part – lumière de serre ou d'aquarium –, le génie de Delacroix nous les rend à la fois présentes et lointaines, énigmatiques au plus haut point. (*Femmes d'Alger dans leur appartement*, p. 170)

> 'Women of Algiers in their Apartment': three women, two of whom are seated in front of a hookah [. . .] The whole meaning of the painting is played out in the relationship these three have with their bodies, as well as with the place of their enclosure. Resigned prisoners in a closed place that is lit by a kind of dreamlike light coming from nowhere – a hothouse light or that of an aquarium – Delacroix's genius makes them both near and distant to us at the same time, enigmatic to the highest degree. (*Women of Algiers in their Apartment*, pp. 135–6)

This describes the first version, painted in 1834. In 1849 Delacroix painted a second canvas. Djebar writes:

> Femmes en attente toujours. Moins sultanes soudain que prisonnières. N'entretenant avec nous, spectateurs, aucun rapport. Ne s'abandonnant ni ne se refusant au regard. Etrangères mais présentes terriblement dans cette atmosphère raréfiée de la claustration. (*Femmes d'Alger*, p. 171)

> Women always (still) waiting. Suddenly less sultanas than prisoners. They have no relationship with us, the spectators. They neither abandon nor refuse themselves to our gaze. Foreign but terribly present in this rarefied atmosphere of confinement. (*Women of Algiers*, pp. 136–7)

It was shortly after the French conquest that Delacroix was granted permission to see the cloistered women. His *regard volé* [stolen glance] resulted in the paintings. His 'Femmes d'Alger', however, are not the only ones:

> Alors que débutait à peine la guerre de libération en Algérie, Picasso va vivre, de décembre 1954 à février 1955, quotidiennement dans le monde de 'Femmes d'Alger' de Delacroix. Il s'y confronte et bâtit autour des trois femmes, et avec elles, un univers complètement transformé: quinze toiles et deux lithographies portant le même titre. (*Femmes d'Alger*, p. 186)

As the war of liberation in Algeria was just barely getting started, Picasso, from December 1954 to February 1955, goes to live (will live) every day in the world of Delacroix's 'Women of Algiers'. There he comes face to face with himself and erects around the three women, and with them, a completely transformed universe: fifteen canvases and two lithographs carrying the same title. (*Women of Algiers*, p. 149)

It is for the liberation of women represented by Picasso's paintings and lithographs that Djebar writes:

> Je ne vois que dans les bribes de murmures anciens comment chercher à restituer la conversation entre femmes, celle-là même que Delacroix gelait sur le tableau. Je n'espère que dans la porte ouverte en plein soleil, celle que Picasso ensuite a imposée, une libération concrète et quotidienne des femmes. (*Femmes d'Alger*, p. 189)

Only in the fragments of ancient murmuring do I see how we must look for a restoration of the conversation between women, the very one that Delacroix froze in his painting. Only in the door open to the full sun, the one Picasso later imposed, do I hope for a concrete and daily liberation of women. (*Women of Algiers*, p. 151)

*L'Amour, la fantasia* (1985) dramatises the contradictions and paradoxes inherent in Djebar's project to 'restore women's conversation'. Here it is the oppositions of reading and writing, and the written and oral, that are dramatised. The novel is divided into a number of sections: three 'parts' each divided into smaller sections, followed by five 'movements' of three parts each and a finale composed of four parts. The first two 'parts' constitute more than half the novel. Two types of discourse are interwoven, one autobiographical, the other historical. In the first part it is French accounts, written by men, of the conquest of Algeria which are considered, and these alternate with autobiographical vignettes. In the second part it is oral accounts from interviews with women who participated in the Algerian war of independence, interspersed with autobiographical accounts, that constitute the text. *Ecriture* ('writing', associated with French) and *kalaam* (the 'word' in Arabic) are juxtaposed.

Djebar's reading of the French texts is described as 'spéléologie' (p. 91), which alludes both to hidden depths and to the caves in which large numbers of Algerians were suffocated during the wars of conquest. 'Voix' ('Voices') describes the accounts of Algerian women who survived the war. Various strategies are used to convey a sense of the women's oral discourse. They are transcribed and translated into French, but a French which is rendered unfamiliar in various ways. These texts are not written in *the* French language but *a* French language. One of the most effective subversions of French is a function of literal translation from the Arabic. Cherifa, whose account is transcribed and translated, says, for example, 'La France est venue et elle nous a brûlés' ['France came and burnt us out']. *Françia*, in dialectal Arabic, means both France and the French and this reveals a conceptual difference in terms of the ideas of nations and their people. Simultaneously, the nature of the French of the nineteenth-century military accounts, the density of figurative language, for example, emerges more clearly by contrast. The most striking, when compared with the direct and uncomplicated language of the women's accounts – the absence of adjectives and adverbs and the simplicity of the syntax and sentence structures – is a letter written by a French Captain (Montagnac) to his uncle:

> Ce petit combat offrait un coup d'oeil charmant. Ces nuées de cavaliers légers commes des oiseaux, se croisent, voltigent sur tous les points, ces hourras, ces coups de fusil dominés, de temps à autre, par la voix majestueuse du canon, tout cela présentait un panorama délicieux et une scène enivrante. (*L'Amour, la fantasia*, p. 67)

> This little fray offered a charming spectacle. Clouds of horsemen, light as birds, criss-crossing, flitting in every direction, and from time to time the majestic voice of the cannon rising above the shouts of triumph and the rifle-shots – all this combined to present a delightful panorama and an exhilarating scene. (*Fantasia, an Algerian Cavalcade*, p. 54)

Djebar *has* spoken for silenced Algerian women. Her texts function as re–viewings and re-readings of male, colonial constructions (in painting and writing). What is problematic is the meaning of the texts'

heterogeneity. The form of *L'Amour, la fantasia* underlines the impossibility of homogeneity. *Ecriture*, the written word associated with French
and French written discourse, and *kalaam* the spoken (Arabic) word
associated with the oral tradition remain distinct and separate.[7] The
fragments which make up the novel abide by the conventions of a
number of genres: historical document of the nineteenth century,
commentary on historical material, Arabic women's oral accounts,
transcribed and translated into the (post-) colonial language, and
autobiographical pieces. The diversity is suggestive of the irreconcil-
able. Yet the heterogeneous parts find their point of convergence in the
writing subject: Assia Djebar, an Algerian woman writing in the (post-)
colonial language. The psychological corollories are ambiguous:

> On me dit exilée. La différence est plus lourde: je suis expulsée de là-
> bas pour entendre et ramener à mes parents les traces de la liberté . . . Je
> crois faire le lien, je ne fais que patouiller, dans un marécage qui
> s'éclaire à peine. (*L'Amour*, p. 244)

> They call me an exile. It is more than that: I have been banished from my
> homeland to listen and bring back some traces of liberty to the women of
> my family . . . I imagine I constitute the link, but I am only floundering
> in a murky bog. (*Fantasia*, p. 218)

Multiple formulations of the difficulty have been voiced. Fanon put it
memorably in the following way: 'To speak is also to employ a certain
syntax, to posses the morphology of this or that language, but it is above
all to assume a culture, to bear the weight of a civilisation.'[8] Memmi's
account has been equally influential:

> current social life . . . the entire bureaucracy . . . uses the colonizer's
> language . . . mak(ing) the colonized feel like a foreigner in his own
> country. Possession of the two languages is . . . participation in two
> psychic and cultural realms. Here the two worlds symbolized and
> conveyed by the two tongues are in conflict; they are those of the
> colonizer and the colonized.[9]

The colonial language is inseparable from the Colonial Symbolic
Order: that is inseparable from the series of interrelated signs, roles and
rituals which regulate colonial societies. In learning the colonial
language – in order better to function within that society – the colonised
child internalises the Colonial Symbolic Order through language. The
more the colonised child submits to the linguistic rules of colonial
society, the more those rules are inscribed in the unconscious. In

relation to the patriarchal dimension of the Symbolic Order, Luce Irigaray argues similarly with regard to the patriarchal order: 'we shall continue to write the same old [his]story if we continue to speak the same old language.'[10] Bilingualism may, however, bring the Symbolic (Colonial) Order to light, throw it into relief. In an early section of *L'Amour, la fantasia*, entitled 'Mon Père écrit à ma mère', Djebar exposes this possibility:

> Ma mère, commes toutes les femmes de sa ville, ne désignait jamais mon père autrement que par le pronom personnel arabe correspondant à 'lui'. [. . .]
> Après quelques années de mariage, ma mère apprit progressivement le français. (*L'Amour*, pp. 46–7)

> Whenever my mother spoke of my father, she, in common with all the women in her town, simply used the personal pronoun in Arabic corresponding to 'him'.
> [. . .]
> After she had been married for a few years, my mother gradually learnt a little French. (*Fantasia*, p. 35)

What follows is an account of the relationship between her mother's acquisition of French and her parents' marriage:

> Des années passèrent. Au fur et à mesure que le discours maternel évoluait, l'évidence m'apparaissait à moi, fillette de dix ou douze ans déjà: mes parents, devant le peuple des femmes, formaient un couple [. . .]! (*L'Amour*, p. 47)

> Years went by. As my mother's ability to speak French improved, while I was still a child of no more than twelve, I came to realise an irrefutable fact: namely that, in the face of all these womenfolk, my parents formed a couple. (*Fantasia*, p. 36)

Djebar's own position, however, is different. Seeking to subvert patriarchal colonial history, and to act as a spokeswoman for Arab women, she finds herself, simultaneously, and to a greater degree than her mother, alienated from the oral Arabic world of her women compatriots. Koranic Arabic is described as autogeneous: 'I remember how much this Quranic learning, as it is progressively acquired, is linked to the body' (*Fantasia*, p 183).[11]

Djebar's experience of French contrasts markedly with her experience of Arabic; no 'naturalness' is suggested about the relationship between the body, the signifier and the signified as is the case in the earlier description of learning the Koran. The 'foreign' language is distant:

> J'écris et je parle français au-dehors: mes mots ne se chargent pas de réalité charnelle. J'apprends des noms d'oiseau que je n'ai jamais vus, des noms d'arbres que je mettrai dix ans ou davantage à identifier ensuite, des glossaires de fleurs et de plantes que je ne humerai jamais avant de voyager au nord de la Méditerranée. (*L'Amour*, p. 208)

> I write and speak French outside: the words convey no flesh-and-blood reality. I learn the names of birds I've never seen, trees I shall take ten years or more to identify, lists of flowers and plants that I shall never smell until I travel north of the Mediterranean. (*Fantasia*, p. 185)

Or again:

> Le français m'est langue marâtre. Quelle est ma langue mère disparue, qui m'a abandonnée sur le trottoir et s'est enfuie? [. . .] Après plus d'un siècle d'occupation française – qui finit, il y a peu, par un écharnement – , un territoire de langue subsiste entre deux peuples, entre deux mémoires; la langue française, corps et voix, s'installe en moi comme un orgueilleux préside, tandis que la langue maternelle, toute en oralité, en hardes dépenaillées, résiste et attaque, entre deux essoufflements. Le rythme du 'rebato' en moi s'éperonnant, je suis à la fois l'assiégé étranger et l'autochtone partant à la mort par bravade, illusoire effervescence du dire et de l'écrit. (*L'Amour*, pp. 240–1)

> French is my 'stepmother' tongue. Which is my long-lost mother-tongue, that left me standing and disappeared? [. . .] After more than a century of French occupation – which ended not long ago in such butchery – a similar no-man's land still exists between the French and the indigenous languages, between two national memories: the French tongue has established a proud *presidio* within me, while the mother-tongue, all oral tradition, all rags and tatters, resists and attacks between two breathing spaces. . . . I am alternately the beseiged foreigner and the native swaggering off to die, so there is seemingly endless strife between the spoken and written word. (*Fantasia*, pp. 214–15)

In a brief article, '*L'Amour, la fantasia*: une grammatologie maghrébine', Denise Brahimi stresses the 'tragedy' of *L'Amour, la fantasia*. Although Djebar seeks to 'ramener à (ses) parents les traces de la liberté' ['bring back some traces of liberty to the women of my family'] Brahimi argues:

It would be fallacious to see in these too rare examples some kind of optimistic denouement to which the work as a whole, on the contrary, gives lie. Superimposed onto the image of the hand stretched out by the little girl to her father is that of another image of a hand, the anonymous Algerian woman's severed hand which Fromentin saw in Laghouat in 1853. The historical tragedy at the heart of *L'Amour, la fantasia* would have it that the two images are inseparable.[12]

Yet the encoding of alienation and heterogeneity in language and literature can be read as a deconstructive act. It constitutes a critique of the dominant, totalising structures of the Symbolic Colonial Order. Thus it celebrates Otherness. Lacan and Derrida emphasise the difficulty of challenging the Symbolic Order when the only words available to do so are words that have been issued by that order. However, Djebar's polyphonic *fantasias* (all her texts from *Femmes d'Alger* onwards could be thus entitled), suggest the *failure* of (post-) colonialism's totalising strategy. The many 'voices' of Djebar's texts remain distinct (hence 'polyphonic'); the idea of improvisation (fundamental to the *fantasia*), suggests both *kalaam* and the ability to metamorphose while retaining an essential identity. What the French assimilationists sought was a fixed cultural 'whole' (symbolic of 'union'). Jean de Castellane, for example, delivering the opening speech at the 1931 Exposition Coloniale in Paris, emphasises 'solidarity' ('oneness') and 'integrity' ('wholeness'):

> In a spirit of patriotic solidarity and brotherly union, the peoples will come to Paris to look at, appreciate and love in the laughing atmosphere of this verdant woodland, the faithful image of the whole of France, the France of the five corners of the globe.[13]

Djebar's 'polyphonic' texts deny the 'wholeness' so fundamental to cultural assimilation.

François Lionnet has argued that '*metissage* is the fertile ground of our heterogeneous and heteronomous identities as postcolonial subjects.'[14] *Dialogisme* or *polylogisme* (the linguistic equivalents of *metissage*), were until recently seen as 'congenital abnormalities' (to extend Todorov's term). In an essay in a collection concerning bilingualism, Todorov argued:

> In the not so distant past, everything which could be said to come close to what we now call dialogism, was perceived as a defect. It would be pointless to refer here to Gobineau's invectives against mixed races, or those of Barrès against uprooted peoples. I will cite, more as a curiosity,

this more recent sentence of Malraux's which relies, furthermore, on another authority: 'Colonel Lawrence said from experience that any man who truly belonged to two cultures . . . lost his soul.' If I don't dwell on these kinds of assertion, it is not because they no longer exist, nor because the positions from which they issue are not powerful ones; but because I share no common territory with them, to the point where I can't even engage with them in dialogue. [. . .] Today these attitudes seem to me to belong, historically, to the past; they are consonant with the great patriotic moment of bourgeois states, which has certainly not passed, but whose end can nevertheless be glimpsed, if only on the ideological level. Who, today, would not rather claim to be representative of the dialogic, of the plurality of cultures, of tolerance for the voices of others?[15]

Djebar's tactics expose the inadequacies (if not epistemological emptiness) of simple binary oppositions: black/white, man/woman, self/ other. The plurality and 'strangeness' of the self is exposed, explored and encoded. Julia Kristeva's essay *Etrangers à nous-mêmes* is explicitly concerned with this:

At a time when France is becoming the melting-pot of the Mediterranean, a question is asked, and one which is the touchstone for the ethics of the twenty-first century: how can we live with others, without rejecting them and without absorbing them, unless we recognise that we are 'strangers to ourselves'.[16]

To explore the self in writing, as a North African woman, is a subversive act. But a considerable number of women in and from the Maghreb are now writing, encoding their experience in language and literature. As their experience is alien to the (post-) colonial language/Symbolic Order, their attempts to write their experience will necessarily disturb that language/Symbolic Order. One of the earliest autobiographical texts by a North African woman is Fadhma Aith Mansour Amrouche's, 'Une femme kabyle (1882–1967)'. Describing her definitive move to France in 1959, she writes, 'I gave myself over entirely to them [my children], having always lived under the guidance and protection of my husband who only saw through my eyes.'[17] Here a number of associated binary oppositions are subverted: one who sees as opposed to one who is seen, active/passive, powerful/impotent, self/other, male/female. How mistaken Gabriel Camps is when he paraphrases the subversive poetics of Amrouche's text, returning them to the cliché of the Symbolic Order: 'How better to define the eminent role of the Kabyle woman, perpetual inferior according to tradition but true mistress in her own home.'[18] Amrouche's language demands a reconsideration of the relationship between seeing and being seen, and the relationship between these and power. In French (as in English), to see is not only to perceive with the eyes, but to understand, to comprehend; and to understand is to have power over the object of understanding. In Arabic, however, to see (*ra'a*) means simply to perceive with the eyes; its meaning is entirely to do with the visual. This raises a kind of epistemological difference.

For a long time, within Western cultural forms (and to a large extent within Arabic cultural forms), men had a monopoly on the representation of North African women. Delacroix painted what he saw, and that representation, along with other comparable representations, was the 'truth' about North African woman. Djebar's *Femmes d'Alger* invites (re-)consideration of Delacroix's *regard volé* and the validity of the representation which resulted. Does the viewer of the painting *see* with the painter's eyes or can we *look* and see something different and more complex? Djebar's texts, like all powerful post-colonial productions, reveal the stupidity of the colonial assumption that knowlege of other cultures could be surreptitiously stolen, like the glance stolen by Delacroix. As Christopher Miller has pointed out: 'Knowledge – particularly Western knowledge of Africa, far from being simply *lux et veritas*, can most often be revealed as a corrosive project of appropriation.'[19]

## Notes

1. My translations from *Harrouda* (Paris, 1973): 'Parler, c'est exercer une volonté de pouvoir' (p. 183); 'Il fallait *dire* la parole dans (à) une société qui *ne veut pas* l'entendre, *nie* son existence quand il s'agit d'une femme qui ose la prendre' (p. 184); 'Cette prise de la parole est peut-être illusoire puisqu'elle s'énonce dans le langage de l'Autre. Mais le plus important [. . .] n'est pas *ce* que ma mère dit, mais qu'elle ait *parlé*. La parole est déjà une prise de position dans une société qui la refuse à la femme' (p. 184).

2. Assia Djebar, *L'amour, la fantasia* Paris: J-C Latte's, 1985, pp. 202–3. Translated into English by Dorothy Blair as *Fantasia, an Algerian Cavalcade*, London and New York: Quartet Books, 1985, pp. 179–80. Page references will be to these editions and will be included in the text.

3. 'Du français comme butin', *La Quinzaine Littéraire*, No. 436 (16–31 March 1985), p. 25: 'Toutes les premières tentatives, pour les femmes du monde arabe, de vouloir à la fois sortir au dehors et "sortir en la langue différente" étaient risque d'une double expulsion: que subissait d'une part l'écriture [. . .] et d'autre part, le corps parlant. Ecrire en la langue étrangère

devient presque faire amour hors la foi ancestrale: le tabou, en Islam, épargne, en ce cas, les mâles, bien plus, les valorise.'

4. Danielle Marx-Scouras, 'Muffled Screams/Stifled Voices', in *Post/Colonial Conditions: Exiles. Migrations. and Nomadisms, Yale French Studies*, Vol. 1, No. 82 (1993) p. 174.

5. *Femmes d'Alger dans leur appartment*, Paris: des femmes, 1980, 3rd edn 1983, trans. Marjolijn de Jager as *Women of Algiers in their Apartment*, Charlottesville: University of Virginia Press, 1992. Further page references will be to the 1983 edition and to the 1992 translation. *Ombre Sultane*, Paris: J-C Latte's, 1987, trans. D. S. Blair as *Sister to Scheherazade*, London: Quartet Books, 1988; *Les soeurs de Médine*, Paris: Editions Albin Michel, 1991, trans. D. S. Blair as *Far From Madina: Daughters of Ishmael*, London: Quartet Books, 1994.

6. Edward Saïd, *Orientalism* (1978): for a recent discussion of Orientalism, see 'Orientalism after "Orientalism" ', *L'Esprit Créateur*, Vol. 34, No. 2, Summer 1994.

7. *Kalaam* is also important in Tahar Ben Jelloun's writing. It is *kalaam* which gives the subject access to the ancestral past, thus offering the speaking subject a new and more complete, if also more complex, sense of individual identity.

8. Frantz Fanon, *Black Skin White Masks*, trans. Charles Lam Markman, New York: Grove Press, 1967. First published in French as *Peau noire, masques blancs*, Paris: Seuil, 1952. This reference is to the Paladin edition (1970), p. 13.

9. Albert Memmi, *The Colonizer and the Colonized*, pp. 106–7; quoted by H. Adlai Murdoch in an interesting recent article, 'Rewriting Writing: Identity, Exile and Renewal in Assia Djebar's *L'Amour, la fantasia*', *Post/Colonial Conditions: Exiles. Migrations. and Nomadisms, Yale French Studies*, Vol. 2, No. 83 (1993), pp. 71–92 (p. 88).

10. D. Marx-Scouras (1993) p. 182.

11. 'Je me souviens combien ce savoir coranique, dans la progression de son acquisition, se liait au corps' (*L'Amour*, p. 201). See in relation to this Eric Cheyfitz's extrapolation of Barthes' essay 'L'ancienne rhétorique': 'The division between the proper and the figurative can govern the division between foreign languages, with the national language becoming the proper language, and the foreign, figurative.' *The Poetics of Imperialism: Translation and Colonization from The Tempest to Tarzan*, New York: Oxford University Press, 1991, p. 36.

12. Denise Brahimi, '*L'Amour, la fantasia*: une grammatologie maghrébine', *Itinéraires et contacts de culture*, Vol. 2, Paris, 1990, p. 123: 'Il serait fallacieux de voir dans ces trop rares exemples une sorte de dénouement optimiste, que l'ensemble du livre, au contraire, dément. A l'image de la main tendue par la fillette vers son père qui la conduit à sa "leçon d'écriture", se superpose une autre image de main, une main coupée d'algérienne anonyme que Fromentin a vue à Laghouat en 1853. La tragédie historique qui est au coeur de *L'Amour, la fantasia* veut que les deux images soient inséparables.'

13. Jean de Castellane, opening address for the Exposition Coloniale, 1931: 'Dans une pensée de solidarité patriotique et d'union fraternelle, les peuples

viendront à Paris examiner, apprécier et aimer dans le riant décor de ce bois verdoyant, l'image véritable de la France intégrale, la France de cinq parties du monde.' My translation.

14. *Autobiographical Voices: Race, Gender, Self-Portraiture*, Ithaca, NY: Cornell University Press, 1989, p. 8; quoted by Murdoch (*Rewriting Writing*), p. 87.

15. Tzvetan Todorov, 'Bilinguisme, dialogisme et schizophrénie', *Du bilinguisme*, ed. Abdelkebir Khatibi, Paris, 1985, pp. 12–13. My translation.

16. *Etrangers à nous-mêmes*, Paris, 1988, back cover: 'A l'heure où la France devient le *melting pot* de la Méditerranée, une question se pose, qui est la pierre de touche de la morale pour le XXIe siècle: comment vivre avec les autres, sans les rejeter et sans les absorber, si nous ne nous reconnaissons pas "étrangers à nous-mêmes" '?

17. Quoted by Gabriel Camps, *L'Afrique du Nord au feminin*, Paris, 1992, p. 296: 'Je m'en remis entièrement à eux [mes enfants], ayant toujours vécu sous la tutelle et la protection de mon mari qui ne voyait que par mes yeux.'

18. My translation: 'Comment définir plus clairement le rôle éminent de la femme kabyle, éternelle mineure d'après la tradition mais véritable maîtresse chez elle?' (Camps, *L'Afrique du Nord au feminin*, p. 296).

19. Christopher Miller, 'Theories of Africans: The Question of Literary Anthropology', *"Race". Writing and Difference*, ed. H. L. Gates Jr., Chicago and London, 1986, pp. 281–300 (p. 284).

# Tahar Ben Jelloun's Post-Modern Folly? The Writer through the Looking-Glass

## LUCY STONE MCNEECE

Since receiving the Prix Goncourt in 1987, the Moroccan writer Tahar Ben Jelloun has become an internationally known author and possibly the dominant figure in Maghreb literature. A member of the prolific literary culture of Morocco which emerged following independence from France, Ben Jelloun has attained a uniquely large readership among European and American audiences, a distinction which has accorded him controversial celebrity. After completing a degree in Social Psychiatry in France, Ben Jelloun turned to poetry and then to the novel. He collaborated on the radical Moroccan review, *Souffles* (1966–71) from 1968 to 1970, and has regularly contributed articles to *Le Monde* and other newspapers on issues ranging from literature to the fate of Maghreb immigrants abroad.

Ben Jelloun has been praised by critics in the West for his sophisticated style but condemned by many Moroccans for betraying his culture. Like many post-colonial authors writing in French – or other languages of Empire – Ben Jelloun naturally invites criticism from those who conceive of national and cultural identity in linguistic terms. Yet he has also sparked debate because he seems to ignore the 'serious' political and social issues plaguing his culture, content to play seductively with his readers on both sides of the Mediterranean. Tahar Ben Jelloun is no stranger to ambiguity and contradiction. A master of paradox and illusion, he is a magician in the realm of narrative akin to what Méliès was in early French cinema. His mercurial writing involves the use of elaborate word-play and the manipulation of modern literary conceits which seem to take precedence over any cultural 'message'. Ben Jelloun seems to be using language and narrative form as a mode of experimentation that has no objective other than to delight in its own artful energy.

Why, then, does this writer generate such passionate commentary? One reason may lie in his historical moment: the post-independence writers of Morocco, Algeria and Tunisia found themselves often at odds with their own people who were seeking to redefine their national identity. The generation of writers who came of age in the 1960s longed to break away from the predominantly ethnographic narratives produced during the French occupation as part of their effort to eliminate the vestiges of colonialism. For these writers, much existing Moroccan literature written in French was 'reactive' and tied to a colonial mentality which perpetuated stereotypical images of the Maghreb. To contest the legacy of the French protectorate in Morocco, several young writers joined Abdellatif Laâbi in founding *Souffles*, a literary review with a strong political and ideological orientation that radically altered the development of Moroccan literature. Despite its relatively short existence, *Souffles* caused a fundamental break with tradition in Maghreb literature as a whole.

Although the preceding generation of Moroccan authors writing in French generally tended to celebrate Moroccan folkloric traditions, it also included the controversial figure of Driss Chraïbi, whose virulently parodic *Le Passé simple* (1954) became a subject of passionate debate. Chraïbi's first novel stirred violent reactions because it criticised Moroccan patriarchal society at a time when most Moroccans wanted to present a positive image of their newly decolonised nation to the world. Chraïbi was denounced and harassed until he issued a public apology for his 'treason', but the issues that had been raised concerning the role of literature with respect to political and social realities remained unresolved. The writers of *Souffles* eventually redeemed Chraïbi's reputation in a series of articles demonstrating that his insights had been prophetic and revolutionary. The debate sparked by *Le Passé simple* became symptomatic of a schism about the relation of ideology to literature and the appropriate path to cultural decolonisation.

The writers of *Souffles* denounced what they saw as 'false independence', and called for a radical revision of the forms as well as the subjects of literary representation. Attacking the complacency of Morocco's neo-colonial bourgeois élite, these writers produced explosive and lyrical texts which decimated the academic literary heritage that had been taught under French occupation. Some, such as Mohammed Khaïr-Eddine, known as the 'guerrilla' poet, drew inspiration from the early poetry of Aimé Césaire and the Surrealists. They all wrote without respect for traditional boundaries of genre, using intensely physical imagery and drawing upon popular culture for opaque symbols to translate states of heightened passion, hallucination and fantasy. The writings of Mostafa Nissaboury, Abdelkebir Khatibi, Abraham Serfaty, and Abdellatif Laâbi, as well as that of others like Ben Jelloun who joined them, inevitably raised the question of writing in French, and the review became bilingual in 1968. This complex question has continued to animate heated debate on both sides of the

Mediterranean, centering on whether it is possible – or effective – to dismantle structures of power from within the languages of imperialism or whether writing in those languages necessarily conditions the terms of the argument and thus precludes the possibility of real dissent. The debate raises the complex question of how one defines 'difference'.

The original *Souffles* was outlawed in 1971–2 and its founder, Laâbi, was imprisoned for almost ten years. His disciples took refuge in a review, *Intégral*, which devoted itself solely to literature and the visual arts. The writers of *Souffles*, most of whom continue to publish in French, hoped to revolutionise the role of Moroccan literature in the expression of a post-colonial consciousness. The immediate goals of the review were to divest literary production of its mimetic relation to European models on the one hand, and, on the other, to transcend the 'exotic' or 'folkloric' vision of Moroccan culture. They hoped to avoid the trap of polarising themselves into an 'anti-Western' identity, and sought to re-examine their own history and complex cultural heritage for inspiration free of both religious and nationalist orthodoxies. Their attention to elements of popular Berber culture allowed them to forge a violent poetic idiom that revitalised their use of French and also provided a powerful antidote to Islamic dogma and the often stultifying weight of tradition.

The early affiliation of Tahar Ben Jelloun with *Souffles* suggests that his use of literary artifice was not purely esthetic. But it may be that the category of 'esthetic' itself needs to be redefined in relation to different cultural contexts. Ben Jelloun appears to invoke European traditions and cultural conventions intentionally, although he is not using them in a conventional manner. But how are we to understand his use of Western references and techniques? In addition to Arabic poets and thinkers, there are references to Greek myth and philosophy, to Shakespeare, Dante, Nietzsche, Eliot, Calvino, Borgès, Barthes, Beckett and many other contemporaries. The high level of intertextuality present in Ben Jelloun's work is often cited as a symptom of his 'postmodernity'. The metanarrative dimension of his writing and his use of such devices as shifting registers, polyphony and elaborate mirroring effects, appear to mimic the literary symptoms of Western society's contemporary cultural crisis involving the collapse of absolute structures and the daily confrontation with radically different traditions.

The question of the relation of the post-modern to the post-colonial is, of course, highly complex. It is so not only because the condition we loosely term 'post-modern' in the West is so varied in its manifestations and so difficult to define, but because its effects are experienced and therefore judged differently by different classes and cultural groups. For example, the supposedly liberating effects upon certain groups of the principle of indeterminacy and the break-up of totalising myths are often undermined by the indiscriminate commodification of their cultural productions. The ideal of pluralism itself has become banalised by token policies that mask neglect and intolerance with apparently benign indifference. The very rhetoric of difference tends to supplant any sustained attempt to articulate specific dissonances within an increasingly monotonous hymn to 'multiculturalism'.[1]

With respect to Tahar Ben Jelloun, we must look first to the literary effects and the question of 'textuality' that have been identified with post-modern culture. The indeterminacy of the sign, sometimes referred to as the 'slipping of the signifier', is the most visible symptom of a systematic revision of the nature and role of language that reached its apogee in France in the 1960s and 1970s. The consequences were paradoxical: on the one hand, it became clear that language as a vehicle of culture structures individual thought and expression, and on the other hand, the severing of meaning from a stable ground of authority also implied that it was open to manipulation. The implications that Barthes explored for literary interpretation – whereby a large portion of agency to assign meaning was passed to the reader – became part of a generalised dismantling of established cultural authority. The emergence of language as a metaphor for other cultural processes directed attention to the common dynamics that governed many apparently distinct domains and opened the way for the subordination of historically determined value to various particular present realities. According to some, such realities became increasingly determined by invisible transnational economic forces that continue to prevent the interaction of genuinely diverse histories and cultures.

For the avant-garde of the 'centre', the loss of governing myths and the unhinging of language from meaning and permanence have constituted a divisive ontological and epistemological rift. The much-discussed 'crisis of the Subject' in contemporary Western culture appears to place writers and individuals before what may be finally a specious, or, at least, limited, choice: to lament as tragic the collapse of humanistic ideals or to create an alternative, artificial 'universe' where writer and reader can express their Promethean yearnings through linguistic play. In some countries of the West, one has tended to assume that the latter can only represent an abandonment of reality and history. In the case of Tahar Ben Jelloun, we must look differently at the symptoms of what some are quick to label the 'disease'. Instead of trying simply to imitate Western conventions, Ben Jelloun may be using 'postmodern' techniques as a means of transcoding his own cultural crisis and possibly as a way of demonstrating that one's relation to one's own language and representation is often invisible.

Ironically, the generalisation of the language metaphor in postmodern culture suggests analogies with some aspects of the function of language for traditional, less industrialised cultures. Metaphor, allegory and parable performed essential social functions in communities where the various spheres of human activity were more closely connected than they have become in highly populated urban societies. They worked as agents of understanding by translating particular experiences into poetic figures which could be transmitted orally and shared across time. Their 'hidden' truths, or enigmas, encoded collective wisdom and served as repertoire of knowledge whose very decoding provoked mental processes that led to meaningful action. Ben Jelloun's texts can be seen to operate in a similar manner, as imaginative projects designed to effect transformations of consciousness.

We may also observe that Ben Jelloun's conception and practice of fiction-as-enigma places him within the tradition of experimental authors writing 'from the margins' such as Jose Luis Borgès (whom he cites extensively) for whom the function of literature was never to reproduce or to describe empirical reality, but to reflect on our relation to representations of myriad realities.

The inspiration for Ben Jelloun's literary strategies and use of language has complex roots in his own Arabo-Berber traditions. These include the tradition of the public storyteller, popular Berber legends, the doctrine of Islam and the tradition of Sufism, but also calligraphy and the highly stylised decorative arts. Rather than being strategies of obfuscation or purely esthetic gymnastics, Ben Jelloun's mysteries are designed to alter his readers' epistemological ground and to challenge their ways of ordering experience. It should not surprise us that our appraisal of Ben Jelloun's writing depends on aspects of our cultural difference, upon cultural habits of reading and the place of writers and writing within different cultures. Western readers associate certain narrative strategies with various cultural moments and the ideology that shaped them. Self-reflexivity, formal play and oneiric fantasy might remind these readers of the late nineteenth century's hermetic symbolists, while an aggressive shattering of syntax and the dismantling of traditional forms might well suggest the later, more provocative, work of the Surrealists.[2] Other experimental techniques might recall the obsessive 'chaos' of the New Novel or the critical/literary texts that emerged during and after the period of structuralism in France. The status accorded the signifier by the practitioners of deconstruction, the importance of cultural codes for semiotics, the replacing of the 'body in language' for psychoanalysis and the emphasis on chaos and fragmentation in 'post-modern culture', all provide tempting models for reading some of the surprising literary production of 'post-colonial' writers. Yet, for the very reason that the effects of some post-colonial writing appear to mirror post-structuralist techniques, we must be attentive to the different contexts of their production. The tendency to view Ben Jelloun's writing as 'post-modern' is, in part, a way for non-Maghreb readers to appropriate his work that spares them the challenge of recontextualising it within its own traditions.

If we try to read Ben Jelloun's texts with an eye on his Arabo-Berber culture, we may find that its stylistic features are also connected to another repertory of meanings and have a different cultural resonance than those we are tempted to impose upon them. The Maghreb, and Morocco in particular, retains several layers of tradition and belief that have remained active despite successive periods of colonisation. The effects of such syncretism include magico-religious Berber elements mingled with varying degrees of Islamic doctrine as well as strong traces of Spanish, Ottoman and Arab influence. Morocco's history has also been shaped by her diverse linguistic culture.[3] Most importantly, perhaps, French colonisation brought Christianity, science and later technology (often more fantastic than myth) and the culture of the (reproducible) image to a people who lived in a world of oral parables and sacred writing.

Tahar Ben Jelloun is highly conscious of the implications of writing in a 'foreign' language. He believes, however, that the displacement of writing in French allows him the critical space to view his culture both differently and 'differentially', to identify those elements impossible to translate that tend to be effaced and elided by others seeking sameness in the guise of the exotic. He states, 'J'écris pour dire la différence.' ('I write to express difference.')[4] The author's use of the verbs 'écrire' ('to write') and 'dire' ('to say' or 'tell') in this context raises the question of translating or 'rewriting' other traditions and explicitly includes the world of popular oral culture indispensable to Moroccan cultural 'identity'. In many of his works, Ben Jelloun openly seeks to reinvest words with the collective power they once had through the person of the public storyteller, 'le conteur public'. The public storyteller is above all a translator who shapes communal history into parables and allegories

that act to crystallise into consciousness a circumstantial reality that
would otherwise remain anecdotal and gratuitous. He forms experience
into narrative and linguistic patterns which themselves embody principles that govern the listener's relation to others and to the cosmos.
In reading Ben Jelloun's texts, therefore, one must focus upon
narrative forms as the carriers of information rather than on the diegesis
or evenemential sequences as such. Accordingly, the bizarre characters
who govern the action of Ben Jelloun's novels, such as the prostitute,
the madman, the androgyne, the transvestite or the criminal, are not to
be understood as 'aberrant' social types but as metanarrative figures.
They are not psycho-social entities, but allegories of epistemological
problems adressed by the form of the text. We may find, surprisingly,
that instead of constituting an 'escape' from reality, Ben Jelloun's
writing seeks to refocus his readers' relation to a history that has been
dramatically blind to a host of realities. In his writing, the problem of
cultural identity is also a question of language: not merely language as
native or foreign, but language as a mode of expression that is also a
mode of knowing, in which the individual and the community affirm
themselves as agents – subjects – in their own destiny. His often
fantastic, always ambiguous, characters are metaphors which translate
the individual's relation to culture and to history, and demonstrate how
language, as a vehicle of culture, structures one's reality and defines
one's possibilities. Consciousness of the dynamics of language in
culture can perhaps give people a measure of freedom. Ben Jelloun
makes his fantastic tales an apprenticeship for his readers in the
understanding of a world made foreign by rapid change so that they may
participate in the shaping of it.
    His 'hybrid' use of linguistic conventions encourages his readers to
explore other dimensions of experience (dream, myth, fantasy) that
transport them away from familiar routines and habits of thought and
feeling so that they may perceive analogies and relations that are
normally invisible. In these altered states, fixed boundaries between
worlds such as those of myth and history, fact and fiction, slip away to
allow for unexpected associations and configurations of meaning. For
readers of industrialised societies, such a blurring of boundaries may be
experienced as amusement or purely imaginary play. For members of
more traditional societies, however, in which such boundaries were
traditionally fluid and categories of experience were not ordered
according to a true/false paradigm, it permits the application of
traditional modes of thought to contemporary problems. Occasionally
Ben Jelloun exploits the cultural prejudices that have accrued to such

states of mind with modernisation, using the supposed 'innocence' of dream and fantasy to entice his readers towards brutally realistic insights.

*Moha le fou Moha le Sage* [*Moha the fool Moha the wise*] (1973), Ben Jelloun's first novel, quickly became an exemplary text about post-colonial Moroccan society deformed by lust for power and economic gain. The narrator is a nomadic poet who lives in cemeteries and sleeps in a tree. He exists outside of social and economic structures, and serves as a witness to the corruption of Moroccan society following independence from France. He shamelessly crosses all types of boundaries, listening to the muffled voices of the poor and the outcast to whom he lends his own voice like a ventriloquist. Stylistically, his story rewrites narrative and linguistic conventions, proceeding like a series of dream-sequences in which the reader is never sure 'who is speaking'. Moha's speech moves between poetry and a range of other discourses and voices. Like a phantom, Moha slips across continents and moves between past and present, surviving even his own death. The reader is dissuaded from regarding Moha as either simply a 'fool' or a victim of society; in fact, Moha revises the connotations of words and images often used as tools of oppression, endowing them with positive resonance. Moha is a derelict, a liar, a loiterer, a 'crazy'. He 'prostitutes' himself by lending his voice to anyone who wants it. He violates all kinds of rules, including rules of social decorum and the laws of empirical reality. Yet his antic imagination and selflessness generate a sense of ludic joy that is none the less deeply tied to reality and to history. Ben Jelloun places the reader in the position of the flawed king in Shakespeare. Moha becomes our wise fool, telling us in coded language truths we fear to confront. He invokes the encroaching forest which signalled the king's defeat in *Macbeth*, but expands the metaphor to embrace our generalised blindness and fear of the unknown. In *Moha*, the forest connects Morocco to the North American Indians who live according to sacred values and understand their 'place' in a larger scheme. Moha's errant, elusive character, his plural identity, serves as a concrete model for negotiating difference through imaginative displacement.

Ben Jelloun directly addresses his readers through the very form of the narrative: the sequences are often scenes within scenes which displace the emphasis from questions of fact or truth to the level of value, meaning or interpretation. As readers we oscillate between subjective and objective identifications, often within the space of a few moments. Our vertigo is the physical symptom of our ontological distress. Moha's narrative begins enigmatically, addressing a young boy being tortured in the personal 'tu' ('you') form:

> Ton corps. Deposé sur une table froide. Attaché. Immobile. Ouvert par des mains gantées. Des doigts métalliques ont fait des trous dans ta poitrine. Le sang est la rosée de l'innocence.... Les questions tombaient et tournaient comme l'epée dans l'oeil. Au bord de la nuit, une larme.[5]

> Your body. Laid on a cold table. Tied. Immobile. Opened by gloved hands. Metallic fingers have made holes in your breast. Blood is the dew of innocence.... Questions fall and turn like a sword in the eye. At the edge of night, a tear.

The atomistic syntax in the passage transmits effectively the clinical dispassion of a developing technocracy determined to eradicate even apparently benign opposition. Anonymous, the boy is none the less intimately depicted for the reader, who feels at moments as if he or she were witnessing his or her own torture. Typically, Ben Jelloun plays on the ambiguity of the familiar personal pronoun, 'tu', which connotes intimacy among equals, but which also was used frequently by colonials to patronise their indigenous subjects.

Thrown into a scene without an establishing view of the context, exposed to an unknown youth lacking bodily integrity, the reader finds himself subjected to an experience analogous to that of victims of arbitrary authority. Gradually, other personal pronouns are introduced, shifting erratically to suggest both a crisis of identity and the impossibility of assigning responsibility for the events. Only much later in the text does it occur to us that the adolescent undergoing torture may have been Moha himself. Ben Jelloun systematically displaces the story's interlocking frames to demonstrate how arbitrary are the various ways of looking at reality, and how, as readers and as subjects, people automatically accord themselves a privileged position with regard to events. From the very opening of the text, Ben Jelloun creates shifting illusions of depth which threaten to neutralise one another. This experience is analogous to the use of 'trompe-l'oeil' ('eye-deception') in the plastic arts, where the viewer projects a structure of three dimensions where only two are present. Ben Jelloun similarly obliges his readers to confront their need for a world of psychological depth and coherence that supports humanistic values.

The shifting narrative frames in *Moha* have their counterpart in the interlocking planes found in the geometric designs of Arabo-Berber decoration. There, each figure in the pattern is linked to another in such a way that the side of one figure may also be seen as a different plane in another. This 'differential' configuration gives readers a concrete sense of the precariousness of ontological placement and its dependence on the structure that happens to be in focus.

Instead of addressing cultural difference as a topic of intellectual reflection, Ben Jelloun plunges the reader into the direct apprehension of insecurity by providing competing knowledge. As in some of Borges' stories, the reader hovers between opposing modes of experience. Ben Jelloun demonstrates the relativity of meanings frequently assumed to be absolute, revealing how 'placement' conditions the structure of one's reality.[6] Moha, like most of Ben Jelloun's protagonists, is a traveller, always 'out of place', a transgressor of boundaries. Yet, as we have noted, the apparent 'ambiguity' of many of Ben Jelloun's characters is less a symptom of psychological complexity than it is a sign of their narrative function: to destabilise the structures that normally confirm one's sense of continuity and coherence, placing the reader suddenly within the text.

In *L'Enfant de Sable* (1985) (translated as *The Sand Child* and published in English in 1987), Ben Jelloun makes the tale itself the basis for a hermeneutical quest that becomes a kind of 'reader's progress'. Ostensibly it is the shocking story of a girl born to a father of seven daughters who decides to raise the eighth girl as his only son. The child, Ahmed, embodies the principle of uncertainty or ambiguity typical of many of Ben Jelloun's characters, functioning as a complex and paradoxical figure of difference which also becomes a metaphor for writing. The enormous success of the novel derives in part from the way Ben Jelloun plays with his readers, whom he addresses directly through a series of narrators. The text is seeded with words and images that must be read metanarratively rather than as elements of the diegesis. In a sense, the novel is a 'reading lesson' in which Ben Jelloun progressively alters our habits of interpreting literary language as he shifts our position with respect to the narrative. Ben Jelloun is often accused of writing to please European readers, offering them an exotic and distorted vision of Moroccan culture. It is quite possible that he is speaking simultaneously in several codes to readers on both sides of the Mediterranean about their common misperceptions.

*L'Enfant de Sable* opens with the chapter entitled 'Homme' ['Man'], a noun that alludes not only to the patriarchal society of the Maghreb, but also to the edifice of universalising humanistic thought that has dominated the intellectual history of Europe. The fate of this tradition may be reflected in the opening lines which give us a description of an ageing, scarred and ravaged face that none the less is never revealed as an individual. Our first lesson entails a mistrust of appearances, or rather, a mode of deciphering appearances for elements of truth. The initially genderless creature described above shrinks from light which might expose its tortured soul. Images of physical suffering – 'blessure' ['wound'], 'chair' ['flesh'], 'nu' ['naked'] – are used to convey psychic vulnerability that paradoxically coexists with a sense of superiority. This enigmatic presence, apparently hovering on the brink of death but intensely conscious, inaugurates our relation to the novel-as-enigma. Ben Jelloun introduces early a principle that conditions many of his texts: a surfeit of sensory detail combined with a paucity of cognitive information. Similar to the dominance of music over sense or that of idiom over meaning that often occurs in poetry, Ben Jelloun offers us descriptions rich in evocative detail that none the less leave us searching for 'the point'.

A similar disproportion between material signifier and signified characterises the visual ornament that decorates the spaces of Maghreb life. A characteristic example would be the arabesque, used to create stylised patterns within patterns whose undulating forms proliferate endlessly, or the mirroring designs of geometrical patterns in which figures disappear into one another. For non-Maghreb viewers, such non-representational decoration captivates the senses while leaving the mind desiring definition and closure. Often stunning in colour and elaborate in the delicate complexity of their designs, these prolific patterns adorn both the intimate objects of daily life and the architecture of public space. The absence of anthropocentric representation in visual design has its counterpart in Ben Jelloun's novels in the elaborate deferral of closure by the deployment of a plethora of 'clues' that none the less do not lead to resolution the way they normally do, especially in tales of suspense. Non-Maghreb readers, used to searching for psychological or dramatic logic, sometimes 'foreclose' by assigning a specific definition to a given element instead of allowing the full play of associations to resonate. Ben Jelloun invites the reader to project his supposedly 'enlightened' myths about 'otherness' and the 'Orient' upon the text, revealing them to be tautological, ultimately familiar fantasies that protect the reader's existing frame of reference, producing the illusion of security.[7] He also demonstrates how those exotic fantasies are connected to structures of thought that reduce and trivialise real differences.

The opening chapter of *The Sand Child* is full of descriptions of physical and psychological decay. The 'malady' is perhaps simply that of age, but it involves a painful heightening of the senses which filter nothing out. The ageing creature, ostensibly a man, has become a recluse in a high, isolated room, where he keeps a huge journal of secrets and is supposedly beginning a novel. We might read this as a cynical portrait of the romantic poet in his ivory tower; but what is the implication of the combination of extreme vulnerability and arrogance? The man reigns over a household and family who follow his bidding from a distance, avoiding contact with him. Possibly a caricature of the ailing Patriarch, the hunched and limping figure awaits death in the throes of melancholy. His death is to be exceptional, sublime, as was his life. Finally he senses the arrival of death within his room, concrete, palpable, like a spider. He expires while writing in his journal, in which he is determined to chronicle his own death: 'dire qu'il avait cessé d'exister' ['to say that he had ceased to exist'].[8]

This figure emerges as a monstrous parody of the European or the Maghreb Subject, whose refined sensibility and supposedly heroic posture clings to power even in death. The allegory of empire is evident, but it may refer equally to the tyranny of Islamic law administered by the Father. Here, as in *Moha*, the problem of frames is foregrounded. Rhetorically, we are caught in a structure like that of Chinese boxes where we cannot distinguish event from narration or the narrator from his tale. Thematically, we are also focused upon the writer and writing as metaphor. Is not the writer a person with heightened powers whose secret ambition is to create himself and his world *ex nihilo*? After opening his tale with a horrifying vision of death, the storyteller stops, then recounts his experience of reading the journal himself. On the forty-first day after the death, he opened the journal. Suddenly, another world emerges:

> J'ai été inondé par le parfum du paradis, un parfum tellement fort que j'ai failli suffoquer. J'ai lu la première phrase et je n'ai rien compris. J'ai lu le deuxième paragraphe et je n'ai rien compris. J'ai lu toute la première page et ju fus illuminé. . . . Ce livre, mes amis, ne peut circuler ni se donner. Il ne peut être lu par des esprits innocents . . . Soyez patients; creusez avec moi le tunnel de la question et sachez attendre, non pas mes phrases – elles sont creuses – mais le chant qui montera lentement de la mer et viendra vous initier sur le chemin du livre à l'écoute du temps et de ce qu'il brise. Sachez aussi que le livre a sept portes percées dans une muraille large d'au moins deux mètres. . . . En vérité les clés, vous les possédez mais vous ne le savez pas. (p. 13)

I was overwhelmed by perfume. I read the first sentence and understood nothing. I read the second paragraph and understood nothing. I read the whole of the first page and was illuminated. . . . This book, my friends, can be neither borrowed nor loaned. It cannot be read by innocent minds. . . . Be patient. Dig with me the tunnel of questioning and learn to wait not for my sentences – for they are empty – but for the song that will slowly rise from the sea and guide you on the road of the book. Know, too, that the book has seven gates pierced in a wall at least two yards thick. . . . In truth, you possess the keys yourselves, but you do not know it. (p. 6)

This passage contains the seeds of several dominant themes whose development structures the novel. The repetition concerning reading–comprehension focuses on the importance of analysis of large figures rather than detail, and on the necessity of moving from a psychological to an allegorical level of meaning. The language of mysticism, including the references to illumination and the initiation into a Secret, is significant as a paradigm for the reading quest. The differentiation between the narrator's sentences ('phrases creuses' ['empty sentences']) and 'the song' ('chant') again asks the reader to focus on the formal properties of language and of narrative rather than upon content or message. Finally, the image of the city's walls perforated by doors to which we unknowingly hold the keys makes explicit the question of frames and boundaries through an architectural metaphor that connects psychic with social space and emphasises placement as a structuring principle of meaning.

The image of the traditional city becomes a complex trope for the narrative itself: 'Amis du Bien, Sachez que nous sommes réunis par le secret du verbe dans une rue circulaire' (L'Enfant de Sable, p. 15) ['Friends of the Good, know that we have met through the secrecy of the Word in a circular street (The Sand Child, p. 7)]. The old city, with its intricate passageways, functions as a mystery-text, inscribed with the traces of a collective memory. The image of the Labyrinth is the first of many allusions to Borgès' Ficciones, whose tales share with Ben Jelloun's both metanarrative figures and elaborate conundrums. In a later chapter entitled 'Le Troubadour aveugle' ['The Blind Troubador'], Borgès enters the fiction himself as one of the storytellers. Ben Jelloun exploits Borgès' gift for uncovering meanings affecting our present lives by searching the apparently oblique traces of etymological reference as it interacts with memory and historical contingency. He also shares Borgès' belief in the 'truth of dreams', in the modes of knowing that occur when the conscious mind is open to suggestion.

In the tale of Ahmed in the chapter 'La Porte du jeudi' ['The Thursday gate'], itself a market-day characterised by modes of exchange and the circulation of goods, the narrator summons a range of suggestive images that have resonance in a variety of cultural traditions. He describes Ahmed's story as a long vigil: 'lorsque nous arriverons à l'aube, nous serons délivrés, nous aurons vieilli d'une nuit, longue et pesante, un demi-siècle et quelques feuilles blanches éparpillées dans la cour en marbre blanc de notre maison de souvenirs' (*L'Enfant de Sable*, p. 15) ['when we reach dawn, we shall be delivered. We shall have aged by a night, a long, heavy night, a half-century, and a few white pages scattered in the white marble courtyard of our house of memories' (p. 7)]. Further on, the narrator invokes the symbolism of the desert, a parchment of forgotten traces of other voyagers, other tales:

> Car cette histoire est aussi un désert. Il va falloir marcher pieds nus sur le sable brûlant, marcher et se taire, croire à l'oasis qui se dessine à l'horizon et qui ne cesse d'avancer vers le ciel, marcher et ne pas retourner pour ne pas être emporter par le vertige (*L'Enfant de Sable*, p. 15)

> For this story is also a desert. You will have to walk barefoot on the hot sand, walk and keep silent, believing in the oasis that shimmers on the horizon and never ceases to move toward the sky, walk and not turn around, lest you be taken with vertigo (*The Sand Child*, p. 7)

Allusions to the experience of a long 'night of the soul' and to solitude in the desert evoke in different ways both Christian and Islamic traditions, while the final caution about turning around recalls the fate of Lot's wife in the Old Testament and possibly the Greek myth of Orpheus emerging from the Underworld. These traditions refer to diverse systems of reference that cannot easily be entertained simultaneously. To imagine inhabiting another cultural sphere, one must leave home, move away from familiar categories and suspend belief, float or 'free-fall'. Ben Jelloun's text constantly pushes the reader towards the precipice. The reader is tempted to grasp at false equivalences and to ignore elements that resist 'translation'.

Ben Jelloun's recurring images of the medina and the desert are two related but separate spaces that govern the Moroccan imagination in ways which appear to reflect but in fact differ from their function in other cultures. The medina is, among other things, a symbol for the Moroccan social structure, an elaborate web of interconnections that must be known to be negotiated. It is equally an image of the Moroccan

Imaginary, in that it suggests the intricate interweaving of memories and experience that bind the individual to his collective history. Distinct from the hierarchised grid of the modern European cities built in the Maghreb during French occupation, the medina remains a space in which a network of sensory signals (smells, movements, textures, sounds, graphic images) articulate a deep layer of common knowledge that is often impervious to the foreigner.

The desert, on the other hand, stands as an image of the ascetic life of the spirit, but not necessarily that of Jews or Christians. The desert is hardly exotic for the Moroccans; it is a quotidian image with a varied topography. It may suggest a physical or spiritual journey, and often takes the form of an ascetic adventure like that codified in the doctrine of Sufism. As the private, more spontaneous, face of Islam, Sufism became the means of converting most of the resilient Berber tribes. Frequently repressed, Sufism has become a renewed source of inspiration for writers of Ben Jelloun's generation. Its mystic quest involves a series of stages of progressive renunciation of selfhood that none the less is accompanied by great sensual delight. We may understand narratives like *The Sand Child* as adventures that, in certain respects, follow an analogous model. The reader is encouraged to renounce a privileged place as perceiving subject, and with it a desire for both sentimental identification and cognitive possession in his or her progress through the novel. Each stage presents itself as a test or challenge to the reader's intelligence, which is ultimately 'disappointed' because the text fails to offer the confirming 'substance' which will mirror the reader's desire. As in the case of Oedipus' relation to the Sphinx's riddle, the reader discovers that what first appeared to be a mystery inherent in the objects of narration is actually his or her own.

Images and symbols have a different status and a different function within different cultural codes. For Moroccans and other Maghreb peoples, an image is not primarily iconic, but a mosaic of signs, a text, somewhat analogous to Medieval or Renaissance painting in the West, in which the things depicted – humans, animals, landscape, architecture – were not mimetic renderings but elements in a highly coded discourse expressing culturally specific meanings. Travelling between cultural systems of reference is not merely a voyage between different geographical regions and between different ideals and practices; it is also inevitably a passage between different conceptions of representation and different types of signification. Instead of exploiting similarities between cultures, Ben Jelloun explores the intermediate, transitional space between the known and the unknown to help readers become aware of what it means to confront difference, to look again at what they think they know.

As a governing symbol, the desert circulates, appearing metonymically in the title of Ben Jelloun's novel. The expanse of the desert conjures up a space of writing which is a palimpsest of traces that resembles Maghreb history. Writing as a poetics of the trace implies a conception of reading unlike that of the Western model, which is governed by dramatic logic and psychology. Ben Jelloun asks his readers to open their minds to unfamiliar sounds and echoes, to allow themselves to be inhabited by 'other voices'. For some readers, the desert sand is the shifting and elusive medium of the narrative itself slipping through their fingers.

The intersection of differing cultural registers in *The Sand Child* operates as a pattern of deferral and displacement that moves away from identity even as it evokes resemblances. In an early issue of *Souffles*, Abdellatif Laâbi declared that the relation of these writers to the French language was always 'une coexistence non-pacifique' ['an unpeaceful coexistence'].[9] The same principle applies to the language of cultural reference. Ben Jelloun's text obliges the reader to shuttle constantly between seemingly recognisable words and images and, in so doing, to discover more completely the infinite specificity – difference – of each. In a sense, all the images and references in the novel are guiding the reader in the apprenticeship of a transformative process which is simultaneously reading and writing. The weaving and interweaving of echoes and traces of other texts is the writer's discovery as much as it is his creation. The reader, by reading other traces (the traces of Others), learns to attend to those already inscribed in his own Imaginary. Ben Jelloun's hybrid narrative is an initiation out of a false sense of individual autonomy and creativity, a refusal of an idealist notion of the self.

In *The Sand Child*, the story of the ageing writer of the opening chapter is also that of Ahmed, the eighth child. Ahmed's childhood is a violent initiation into difference by sexual displacement and social transgression. He endures an imposed, premature separation from a world of presumed harmony and meaningfulness that sets him irrevocably apart from both men and women. Ahmed's education provides an entry into the world of appearances ('le paraître'), where he becomes scandalous for reasons other than his double identity or his violation of social law. The scandal surrounding Ahmed comes from his apparent lack of attachment to any code. Because his existence is based upon illusion, everything is inverted for him. He is swept up by the material dimension of language as if it were purely arbitrary, unconditioned by any structure of cultural reference. His visits to the Mosque and to the language of the Koran reflect this terrible freedom:

> Je m'amusais. La lecture collective du Coran me donnait le vertige. Je faussais compagnie à la collectivité et psalmodiais n'importe quoi. Je trouvais un grand plaisir à déjouer cette ferveur. Je maltraitais le texte sacré. . . . Ce fut là que j'appris à être un rêveur. Cette fois-ci je regardais les plafonds sculptés. Les phrases y étaient calligraphiées. Elles ne me tombaient pas sur la figure. C'était moi qui montais les rejoindre. J'escaladais la colonne, aidé par le chant coranique. Les versets me propulsaient assez rapidement vers le haut. Je m'installais dans le lustre et observais le mouvement des lettres arabes gravées dans le plâtre, puis dans le bois. . . . Je m'accrochais au Alif et me laissais tirer par le Noun qui me déposait dans les bras du BA. (*L'Enfant de Sable*, p. 38)

> I enjoyed it all. The collective reading of the Koran made me feel dizzy. I lost my place and intoned anything that came into my head. I got great pleasure out of undermining all that fervor, mistreating the sacred text. . . . It was there that I learned to be a dreamer. I examined the carved ceilings, the sentences written on them. These did not fall on my face; I rose to join them, scaling the column with the help of the Koranic chant. The verses lifted me fairly quickly to the top. I settled in the chandelier and observed the movement of the arabic letters engraved in the plaster and wood. I clung to the *alif* and let myself be pulled by the *nun*, which laid me in the arms of the *ba*. (*The Sand Child*, p. 26)

Ahmed relates to language as an opaque and purely arbitrary system, much the way anyone first experiences a foreign language. His vision of the Arabic letters is similar to the language of a rhebus or that of dreams, in which words and letters can have the same objective empirical substance as real objects. Displaced in his bodily identification, Ahmed is like a 'wild child' whose experiences resist organisation into structures of permanent meaning because they have no physical 'placement'. He is a creature of artifice who could become a 'monster'. Ben Jelloun makes Ahmed a metaphor of the alienating effects of society and conservative religion in his culture, but allows us also to imagine him as an exaggerated metaphor of deranged genius inhabiting a twighlight zone – a parody of the writer himself.

Ahmed's adolescence brings with it a deracinated will and consciousness which challenge the rules that have governed his existence. He participates actively in the deceit. He becomes authoritarian, cynical, demanding. He wants to marry. He says: 'N'est-ce pas le temps du mensonge, de la mystification? Suis-je un être ou une image, un corps ou une autorité, une pierre dans un jardin fané ou un arbre rigide? Dis-moi, qui suis-je?' (*L'Enfant de Sable*, p. 50). ['Isn't it a time of lies and mystification? Am I a human being or an image? A stone in a faded garden or a stout tree? Tell me, what am I?' (*The Sand Child*, p. 34).] The dialogue concerning individual identity cannot be read merely psychologically. It introduces the reader to the possibility that anyone could be any or all of the above, depending on the context and the particular mode of discourse. Rather than merely an allusion to the animation of the objective world, Ahmed's query is a window upon a world in which the truths of reality and imagination interact as equals rather than competing for authority.

The shadow that falls between Ahmed's biological self and his cultural self has opened a space that is sometimes experienced as a terrible freedom, at others, a suffocating prison: 'Elle m'ouvre des portes et j'aime cela, même s'il m'enferme ensuite dans un cage de vitres' (*L'Enfant de Sable*, p. 50). ['It opens doors for me, and I like that, even if it then locks me in a glass cage' (*The Sand Child*, p. 34)]. Ben Jelloun's threatened protagonist inverts subject and object by turning his sense of helplessness and failure into 'virtue', demanding to live it to the logical extreme. Ahmed determines to incarnate his social *persona* with a vengeance by marrying Fatima, an intelligent but physically handicapped woman. Ahmed's behaviour suggests pleasure in trans-gression. His wilful folly indicts the hypocrisy of his own family, but also their complicity with the oppressive social code that attempts to keep women confined to silence and servitude. Instead of attempting to change his world, Ahmed becomes a model that demonstrates the logical absurdity of its cultural practices. As a grotesque caricature of his father and his culture, Ahmed appears to 'imitate' modernist 'anti-heroes' who rebelled against the hegemony of high culture in the West. Yet we are worlds away. Ben Jelloun invokes the culture of high modernism to illustrate how easily revolt is appropriated by the dominant class, and his allusions to canonical modernist authors suggest that the writer is exposed to this danger.

This comparison of the character of Ahmed to a modernist 'anti-hero' exposes the artificiality of conceptions of historical periodisation. It points to the way Ben Jelloun's use of literary and cultural reference pivots back upon itself to suggest different interpretations of seemingly familiar phenomena. As a character in a narrative, Ahmed transcends most modernist narratives because of his elaborate metanarrative function. Ahmed is only at moments 'a character struggling with issues of identity'. He or she is above all a metafictional device for interrogating the connection between novelistic and other artistic conventions and cultural ideology, and for exploring other ways of imagining difference. Our narrator intervenes to declare that the character of Ahmed is somehow getting away from us, taking on a life of its own. Returning to Ahmed's journal, he transcribes the effects of a sudden self-consciousness that throws everything into question:

> Dans les bras endoloris de mon corps, je me tiens, je descends au plus profond comme pour m'évader. . . . Je suis enfermé dans une image. . . . Je tombe. . . . J'essaie de ne pas mourir. J'ai au moins toute la vie pour répondre à une question: Qui suis-je? Et qui est l'autre? Une bourrasque du matin? Une feuille tremblante?. . . Une fenêtre sur une précipice? Un jardin de l'autre côté de la nuit? Une vieille pièce de monnaie? (*L'Enfant de Sable*, p. 55)

> In the aching arms of my body I hold myself; I descend to the depths as if to escape myself. I am shut up in an image, and the tall waves pursue me. . . . I fall. . . . I am trying not to die. I have at least the whole of my life to answer a question: Who am I? And who is the other? A gust of wind at dawn? A motionless landscape? A trembling leaf? . . . A window upon a precipice? A garden on the other side of night? An old coin? (*The Sand Child*, p. 38)

Ahmed's mercurial nature makes it possible for him to take virtually any form. Self-condemned to solitude, Ahmed imagines scenes and writes poems to control his fears. He enjoys a terrifying freedom that places him above good and evil. He says, 'je vis des deux côtés du miroir' (p. 57). ['I saw from both sides of the mirror' (p. 40).]

Ahmed challenges the reader's identifications by refusing interiority and investing in the image that has been created for him. He begins to explore the limits of his imposed destiny: 'Unique passager de l'absolu, je m'accroche à ma peau extérieure dans cette forêt épaisse du mensonge' (p. 69). ['A lonely passenger from the absolute, I cling to my outer skin in this forest of lies' (p. 49).] Yet one tends to forget that the figure of Ahmed is, in every sense, the product of the narrators Ben Jelloun offers us, each denouncing the reliability of the preceding one. In the present instance, it is Fatima's brother who takes the stage, claiming he alone has access to a darker truth: 'Cet homme vous cache la vérité. Il a peur de tout vous dire. Cette histoire, c'est moi qui la lui ai racontée. Elle est terrible. Je ne l'ai pas inventée. Je l'ai vécue' (p. 67). ['That man is hiding the truth from you. He is afraid to tell you everything. It was I who told him this story. It is a terrible story. I did not invent it. I lived through it' (p. 47).] The case of the disappearing narrator articulates the complex problem of reference in setting up a pattern akin to C. S. Pierce's notion of 'regressive semiosis'. The reader is caught up in a relay that he can never arrest because Ben Jelloun has not made the Secret an index of the narrator's knowledge, but of the narrator's function.

Ahmed's father dies, propelling the young man into a long and painful metamorphosis. Ahmed retreats into solitude and begins to explore his physical being. His only contact with the outside are letters he exchanges with an anonymous admirer. Ahmed begins an inverted voyage ('le jour inversé dans une nuit sans étoiles' ['the day inverted in a night of stars']), seeking to return to the state of coincidence with his body that he has never known. He writes to his unknown friend:

> Croyez-vous que vos émotions sauront me réapprendre à vivre? C'est-à-dire à respirer sans penser que je respire, à marcher sans penser que je marche, à poser ma main sur une autre peau sans réfléchir, et à rire pour rien comme l'enfance émue par un simple rayon de lumière? (*L'Enfant de Sable*, p. 99)

> Do you think your emotions will be capable of teaching me to live once more? To breathe without thinking I'm breathing, to walk without thinking I'm walking, to put my hands on someone else's skin without hesitation, and to laugh at nothing in particular, like a child moved by a sunbeam? (*The Sand Child*, p. 73)

Will our hero be capable of emerging from the shadow-world of masks and illusions? Ahmed's discovery of his impossible ontological contract coincides with a heightened consciousness of the importance of writing which, in turn, corresponds paradoxically with a loss of 'faith' in the organic value of words, a shift that clears the way for creativity. The narrator describes a language of artifice that none the less has real power:

> Fragmentaire mais non dépourvu de sens, l'événement s'impose à ma conscience de tous les côtés. Le manuscrit que je voulais vous lire tombe en morceaux à chaque fois que je tente de l'ouvrir et de le délivrer des mots, lesquels empoisonnent tant et tant d'oiseaux, d'insectes et d'images. Fragmentaire, il me possède, m'obsède et me ramène à vous

qui avez la patience d'attendre. Le livre est ainsi: une maison où chaque
fenêtre est un quartier, chaque porte une ville, chaque page est une rue;
c'est une maison d'apparence, un décor de théâtre où on fait la lune avec
un drap bleu tendu entre deux fenêtres et une ampoule allumée.
(*L'Enfant de Sable*, p. 108)

Fragmentary, but not without meaning, the event is stamped on my
consciousness. The manuscript I wanted to read to you falls to pieces
whenever I try to open it and free its words, which poison so many birds,
insects, and images. Fragmentary, it possesses me, obsesses me, and
brings me back to you, you who have the patience to wait. The book is
like a house in which each window is a district, each door a town, each
page a street; it is only a sham house, a theatrical set in which the moon
and sky are represented by a lightbulb and a blue sheet held between two
windows. (*The Sand Child*, p. 80)

The metamorphosis described above evokes poetically a conception of
art and writing which has often incurred the criticism of being 'false' or
'irrelevant' by those who feel that social and political issues must be
addressed explicitly, in 'plain language'. Here again we must remind
ourselves of the value-system that sustains the perception of such
things: artifice has a negative connotation in some cultures because it is
inscribed in a binary logic that privileges explicitness over the oblique
and the indirect. In the Maghreb, artifice is admired as the highest
tribute to a God which transcends representation. Unlike the ideals of
mimesis or empiricism which make direct visual apprehension the
primary vehicle of knowledge and truth, the arts of the Maghreb
emphasise abstract stylisation and the elaboration of forms as the
vehicles of a reality that resists anthropomorphic figuration.

Following the description of a book as a house that is in turn the stage
of writing described above, the narrator, much like a stage-manager,
characterises the birth of writing as 'l'heure de l'écriture' ['the writing
hour'], a solemn but also violent hour in which the structure of the
house and its contents are shaken to their foundations by the 'fab-
rication des mots' ['the making of words'].

For Ahmed, the revelation of the arbitrariness of signs ironically
seems to signal the death of the simulacrum and the birth of an
'authentic' self:

Aujourd'hui, je cherche à me délivrer. De quoi, au juste? . . . De cette
relation avec l'autre en moi, celui qui m'écrit et me donne l'étrange
impression d'être encore de ce monde? . . . En fait je ne vais pas

changer mais simplement revenir à moi, juste avant que le destin qu'on m'avait fabriqué ne commence à se dérouler et ne m'emporte dans un courant. (*L'Enfant de Sable*, p. 111)

Today I am trying to deliver myself. From what, exactly? . . . From that relationship with the other in myself, he who writes to me and gives me the strange impression of being in this world? . . . I am not actually going to change, but will simply return to myself – just before the destiny that was laid down for me begins to unroll and carries me off on its current. (*The Sand Child*, p. 83)

Ahmed emerges from his prison and sets out to discover both himself and his feminine body. He encounters a wild woman who lifts his Djellaba and sucks on his breast, giving him the first sensations of sexual pleasure. He comes upon a country circus, where he meets Malika, a woman with a beard who encourages him to replace another dancer who dresses as a woman. Ahmed learns the gestures and the movements of a woman as a transvestite learning impersonation. He becomes Zahra, 'princess of love'. Our hero's dream-life suddenly becomes active. Zahra is soon the star of the circus and enjoys her first period of happiness.

Ahmed/Zahra has a series of bizarre adventures in which he is never quite able to differentiate between dream or fantasy and reality. In fact these categories elide to dissolve almost all basis for the distinction. Narrators die, the journal is burned, members of the crowd suddenly offer their versions of the story which is perforated by blanks, ellipses, digressions and sudden shifts of direction. Then a blind troubador enters the scene and declares: 'Le Secret est sacré, mais il n'en est pas moins un peu ridicule' (p. 171) ['The Secret is sacred, but still ludicrous' (p. 133)]. Poised between the tragic and comic modes, this man immediately establishes himself as a masked figure of ambiguity who inhabits several worlds. He states unequivocally that he has spent his life falsifying other people's stories and inventing memories, depending on his interlocutors. He speaks in riddles, recounting a tale of a magician who dreamed a strange dream of being able to walk upon fire. At the end the magician recognised that he was not dreaming, and realised that he was the subject of someone else's dream. The troubador announces that he has come as a messenger. He tells of having met a strange woman who had a voice like a 'castrato'. Being blind, he could not see this person, but he claims that the encounter reminded him of a tale from *The Thousand and One Nights* in which a servant saves her master by answering the most difficult questions imaginable in the presence of the Sultan. The anonymous collection of tales known as *The Thousand and One Nights* serves as an infinite repertory of 'profane' literature in the Maghreb. The allusion to this collection of stories explodes the question of authorship and the authority of origins, and throws us back upon our desire to 'possess' the elusive history of Ahmed as well as upon our obsession with literal authenticity. As we discover, truth is always coded, in many 'languages,' taking many unexpected forms.

The blind storyteller further problematises the relation of story to frame by saying that he suddenly believed himself to be inside a book:

> Situation étrange! On aurait dit que j'étais dans un livre, un de ces personnages pittoresques qui apparaissent au milieu d'un récit pour inquiéter le lecteur; j'étais peut-être un livre parmi les milliers serrés dans cette bibliothèque où je venais naguère travailler. Et puis un livre, du moins tel que je le conçois, est un labyrinthe fait à dessein pour confondre les hommes, avec l'intention de les perdre et de les ramener aux dimensions étroites de leurs ambitions. (*L'Enfant de Sable*, p. 178)

> What an odd situation! I felt as if I were in a book, one of those picturesque characters who appear in the middle of a story to throw the reader off the scent; perhaps I was one book among the thousands pressed together in that library where I had long ago come to work. Besides, a book – at least that's how I see it – is a labyrinth created on purpose to confuse men, with the intention of ruining them and bringing them back to the narrow limits of their ambitions. (*The Sand Child*, p. 138)

The comparison between book and labyrinth reminds us that the act of reading – like that of writing, perhaps – is an unending and circuitous journey that leads 'nowhere', but is rather an exercise in deciphering traces, in decoding mysteries. The maze emphasises the circularity of history and the reversibility of time, permitting readers to encounter many travellers. But the comparison also suggests that reading is a descent into the recesses of the psyche where one may discover, like the troubador, that one is always not only a reader but a character in other narratives, other histories, in other places and times. Forcing his readers to balance precariously between subjective and objective modes, Ben Jelloun invites them to contemplate analogies that connect the visible to the invisible world, insisting on the latter's very real effects.

Finally the blind man begins to speak of his love for a 'princesse échappée d'un songe' ['a princess escaped from a reverie'] who had given him a fifty centimes piece. He recounts the relation of two different coins (the Zahir and the Battène) embodying the two dimensions of the protagonist's identity (male and female) but which also articulate opposing symbolic references of 'apparent-visible' and 'interior-hidden'. The choice of coins allows us to understand these seemingly inherent attributes as a function of point of view, as differential, rather than absolute, characteristics analogous to the values of signs.

The mind of the blind man, undistracted by visual phenomena, is freer than others to circulate between categories of experience, in a more literary but ultimately similar manner to Moha. But most importantly, he is a reader and writer of signs, an artisan of parables and symbols. He transmits a kind of 'meta-enigma' involving the two coins, seven keys to the gates of the city, a large clock without hands, an erotic design on a prayer-rug and an account of a dream, all of which generate in the reader an ambiguous and fetishistic energy which seeks certainty while simultaneously longing to be transported beyond the world of measurable data. The text probes 'active' and 'passive' orientations in readers who seek the unknown and yet long for the familiar, in order to demonstrate the reader's deep ambivalence to the changing reality before him or her. Like a two-sided coin, the ambiguous identity of Ahmed/Zahra begins to function like a kind of double-sided signifier, circulating through times and spaces (as through stories) from which it accumulates trace upon trace. Readers project upon the mystery of Ahmed/Zahra their own doubts and longings. Ben Jelloun has employed a sexual metaphor to speak about our relation to language and culture that expands our notion of the constructions of 'male' and 'female' to challenge the entire range of culturally conditioned attitudes that govern our contacts with Others. Yet Ben Jelloun infuses the question of gender and sexuality with another, less familiar resonance. In the Sufi tradition, according to the scholar Ibn Arabi, the disciple yearning for union with God is encouraged to 'make himself female', to let go of his 'phallic' self and to project himself imaginatively into the female psyche, in order to be open to the wisdom and friendship of women and to prepare for the revelation of the Absolute.[10] The separation of gender from sexuality figured by the character of Ahmed is therefore also a parodic inversion of a 'divine' displacement. The ideal of identity predicated on a dream of primal, seamless unity, a fantasy shared by both 'nativists' in the Maghreb and 'purists' in the West, is perhaps the truly 'primitive' and regressive model. The entire

story of Ahmed/Zahra is a parable of the dislocation that engenders a
different, hybrid, and creative self.

One of the last images of Ahmed occurs in the opulent gardens of the
Alhambra in Granada, Spain, where the narrator hears the sound of a
young voice pronouncing the first letters of the Arabic alphabet:

> 'Aleph . . . Bà . . . ta . . . Jim . . . Hâ . . . dal . . .' C'était une voix de
> femme dans un corps d'homme . . . Est-ce un être humain, un ange du
> malheur, un fantôme, un oiseau condamné à mourir seul, était-ce un
> homme ou une femme? (*L'Enfant de Sable*, p. 196)

He is not sure whether he has truly experienced or merely dreamed the
event, but it matters little. Throughout the novel, dream and fantasy
sequences have had the same if not greater dramatic and logical weight
than 'waking' scenes. Our ability to decipher the world is at least as
dependent upon dreams and reflections as it is upon direct observation.
Just as in reading Ben Jelloun's narrative, our understanding is
governed by perceptions coloured by our expectations and our desire.
In *The Sand Child*, Ben Jelloun has systematically intruded upon our
automatic responses, opening up a space between sensory phenomena
and cognitive inference that supports the elaboration of a range of
normally invisible connotations that often belie 'common sense'.

At the end of the novel, Ahmed/Zahra's journal is revealed to be a
pile of empty pages, or rather pages with only the faintest trace of
writing. The last scene involves a man in a blue turban who speaks of
the presence of death among them like a living being who resembles the
figure of Ahmed/Zahra. This final narrator describes how he has been
'inhabited' by a secret that took possession of him, saying that its evil
curse has scarred him deeply. He describes going mad, seeing
characters from his stories surge before him, preventing him from
retreating into a 'safe' world in which reality and fantasy remain clearly
delineated. He finally disappears, having issued a warning about the
burden of secret knowledge and leaves behind him another, different,
manuscript purported to be the famous 'journal d'Ahmed'.

The reader is left alone in the now deserted public square to ponder
the paradoxical intersection of storytellers and characters and to sift
through the tissue of dream and memory that has mobilised the text.
The enigma of Ahmed/Zahra recedes, haunting the reader like a riddle
he knows too well but cannot find the exact words to explain. Indeed,
the mystery of Ahmed/Zahra is far less about sexual or even social
politics than it is about our inability to understand – to imagine – and to
tolerate our own and others' enigmatic difference. The writer, however,

seeks out this condition of 'travesty', displacement and incongruity that has so bewildered us in the reading of the novel, because it opens a space in which the structures of culture and language may be suspended long enough to explore the other face of the reality we call familiar. Passing beyond the barriers of common sense and convention, the writer ventures into a vertiginous region where his loyalties appear clouded, but that is only one of many deceptive appearances. To accuse the writer of treason is to confuse epistemology with politics. It is a way of avoiding the 'perilous but fertile' passage through the mirror, across the no-man's land of intercultural ambiguity, that could lead to the discovery of our different selves.

## Notes

1. See Homi Bhabha's essay, 'The Postcolonial and the Postmodern', in *The Location of Culture*, London and New York: Routledge, 1994, pp. 171–97.

2. Several readers have observed the connections between the work of this generation of authors and Surrealism, emphasising the collapse of the boundaries of genre and the use of literature as an arm of cultural revolution.

3. For an account of Morocco's linguistic and cultural diversity and its ideological implications, see Abdelkebir Khatibi, *Maghreb pluriel*, Paris: Denoel, 1983.

4. 'L'Ecriture et la différence', *Le Monde*, an interview with Tahar Ben Jelloun published in *Le Monde*, 27 March 1988.

5. The French edition of *Moha le fou* was published in Paris by Editions du Seuil, 1978 in the 'Points' series. Page references will be to this edition and will be included in the text. The English translations are mine.

6. In *El Sur*, Borgès' narrator enters a hospital and while under anesthesia dreams he is a sacrificial victim in a pre-Columbian ceremony.

7. For a series of articles on the evolution of the idea of the Orient and orientalism, see *L'Esprit createur*, Vol. 34, No. 2, Summer 1994.

8. *L'Enfant de Sable*, Paris: Edition du Seuil ('Points'), 1985: *The Sand Child*, translated by Alan Sheridan, New York: Ballantine, 1990. Page references will be to these editions and will be incorporated in the text.

9. *Souffles*, No. 18, 1967, p. 24.

10. See Abdewahab Meddeb's article, 'Epiphanie et jouissance', in *Intersignes*, No. 6–7, Spring 1993.

# Daring the Beast: Contemporary Nigerian Poetry

## STEWART BROWN

Arguably the defining characteristic of Nigerian poetry in English has been its confrontational attitude to authority: from the poets of the high colonial period like Dennis Osadebay who used their verse to oppose the deculturing practices of imperialism, most famously in his poem 'Africa's Plea':

> Don't preserve my customs
> As some fine curios
> To suit some white historian's tastes[1]

through the labyrinth of Christopher Okigbo's mythologising to that strand of his work, in 'Path of Thunder', where – in no uncertain terms – he declares his opposition to a power-élite which is set on the destruction of the new Nigeria's potential for national fulfilment:

> parliament has gone on leave
> the members are now on bail
> parliament is now on sale
> the voters are lying in wait[2]

and through to Achebe's and Soyinka's responses to the civil calamity of the Biafran war in direct and pointed verse, and to J. P. Clarke's commentaries on the state of the nation in the 1970s. But it is among the generation of poets who began publishing in the 1970s and 1980s that the notion of the poet as being duty-bound to confront the political events of the times, or more particularly the antics of the country's rulers, has become axiomatic. Of course across the continent writers have argued over the extent to which they should become, in Nadine Gordimer's phrase, 'more than writers',[3] and the arguments about *commitment* and *responsibility* are well rehearsed, not to say well worn, but in Nigeria – as with much else – the issues are felt and expressed in extreme terms. Several poets have incurred the wrath of the politicians or soldiers in power, victimised in one way or another for their outspoken criticism, although it is still hard to believe that Nigeria's presidents and generals spend much time reading poetry.

In 'The Emperor and the Poet', a lucid and passionate introductory essay to his book-length poem *A Song from Exile* (1992), the much-lauded young Nigerian poet and artist Olu Oguibe – compared by Chinua Achebe to the young Christopher Okigbo – describes the circumstances of his 'exile' from Nigeria and the strength of his feeling about the state of the country. He lists intellectuals, artists and writers who, like himself, have been effectively forced out. He is full of praise for those few, including Niyi Osundare and Tanure Ojaide, who stayed and risked speaking out, 'daring the beast' as he puts it. His poem *A Song from Exile* is a lyrical account in eight parts exploring feelings of anger, shame and despair at being away from the society which both abuses and yet feeds his creative spirit. Outside Nigeria, Oguibe's poetic persona feels his

> tongue is blunt
> The songster has journeyed
> Without his voice.[4]

Oguibe acknowledges both anguish and a sense of guilt over his exile status, aware of the relative comfort of his situation as a doctoral student in London, considering himself, in one mood, 'A coward fled home and the battlefront'. He is unable to accept that there can be any 'peace away from home' and is tortured by a conscience that:

> makes my bed with a quilt of thorns
> Ah, conscience that leashes a man to his past
> Conscience that stakes a man in the open courtyard
> and pelts him with rain
> (*A Song from Exile*, p. 13)

*A Song from Exile* is a moving expression of the author's dilemma and distress. If it reads as rather gauche and heart-on-sleeve in places that is to some extent proof of the authenticity of its sentiments. But what does such a poem do, beyond establishing Oguibe's sense of his own commitment to Nigeria and the pain of his exile? And why have so many Nigerian poets persisted in pitching their writing against successive regimes in this way? It can seem, after a while, like nothing more than a self-aggrandising *style*, a relatively safe way of asserting one's radicalism. In 'The Emperor and the Poet', Oguibe addresses the issue himself:

> It is arguable to what extent the artist can influence or turn the course of history, and we in Nigeria have had so long a history of battles between the artist and the state that we have even greater reason to be doubtful

> . . . we are simply saying what we see, for it is seeing and not saying, our
> people say, that kills the elder. It is hearing and not heeding that will kill
> the child. That, for us, is the fate of the Emperor and the poet. (*A Song
> from Exile*, p. 7)

That recourse to the oral tradition and its proverbial lore as validation
for the poet's literary practice is another familiar assertion about
contemporary Nigerian poetry in English, that there is a filial relationship between that body of writing and the oral traditions of the region.
Quite how the influence of the one tradition is expressed in the other is
not always clear. Oguibe, though, is calling up the notion of the oral
poet as the literal spokesman for the common people in the courts of the
powerful. In some West African traditions poets were indeed 'licensed'
to air grievances or criticisms of the rulers in praise-song or at
communal gatherings when those being criticised were obliged to hear
and to react. Perhaps, as Odia Ofeimun has suggested, by their
responses to the poets' critiques the generals have just been acting out
their part in the cultural transition![5]

Certainly in claiming that traditional duty to speak out and in
challenging the politicians' contempt for the 'alter-native'[6] poetic
licence so openly, Oguibe joins a throng of contemporary Nigerian
poets[7] who have often seemed more concerned with that public role,
and with the political content and effects of their poems, than they have
been with the techniques of their craft. Their engagement with this role
has perhaps resulted in neglect of the wider implications of writing a
hybrid 'English poetry', or of ways in which that borrowed role might be
more effectively underpinned by an adaptation of the oral poets'
techniques.

One defence against that charge has been the urgency of their
situation. For Tanure Ojaide, confronting the desolation of Nigeria's
civil society by successive corrupt governments is a sacred duty, and
words, given appropriate poetic shape by the very pressure of the
circumstances, are the only weapon available to him. As he writes in
'Before Our God':

> Neither bullets nor other savageries can arrest words
> that have already been aired –
> paper is witness to the lone mind.
>
> . . .
>
> These words file out on the dirt road
> to stop nerve-wrecking waves of despots;
> they are the charms worn before battle[8]

That poem answers the question of 'why write at all' and in terms of Oguibe's presentation of the necessary opposition between the Emperor and the poet in Nigeria, Ojaide's poem 'What poets do our leaders read' is unequivocal in its condemnation of poets who take a less critical, less forthright stand than his own. They are, he says:

> Perjurers of the Word,
> drummers of bloated drums,
> carriers of offensive sacrifice;
> fanners of vanities.[9]

Over six collections now Tanure Ojaide has practised what he preaches, using his poetry to expose the perceived evils in his society and imply the necessity of a different morality. His poetry is much admired and has won prestigious Nigerian and international prizes. His work has been compared with that of David Diop, Pablo Neruda and Mayakovsky, and certainly he shares their socialist commitment and values. In plain-spoken, interventionist poems like 'When soldiers are diplomats', 'The levelling rule' and 'Song for my Land', he chronicles the destitution and despoilation of Nigeria in recent times:

> More and more the land mocks my heart.
> Where are the evergreens of my palm;
> why is the sun of salvation eclipsed
> by coups and intolerable riots?
>
> Wherever I pass, mockery of the land;
> naked trees flaunt sterile bodies at me
> ('Song for My Land', *The Fate of Vultures*, p. 41)

There are other, gentler, strands in Ojaide's poetry – he has written some fine love poems for example – but for the most part his poems are blunt 'messages from the front', sacrificing imagistic complexity or formal musicality for a rhetorical outrage that overwhelms the 'poetry' – insofar as we equate poetry with subtlety, ambiguity and linguistic cunning.

That is a charge which might be levelled at the work of many of Nigeria's contemporary poets, particularly when their work is read *en masse*. While there can be no doubting these poets' sincerity or the depth of their anguish, the unending self-righteousness of the narrative voice, the artless predictability of the sentiments and the clichéd language of 'protest' undermine, at least for this reader, the force of so many of these poems, *as poems*. But that 'at least' is, of course, an immense qualification. Where, in cultural and ideological as well as in geographical terms, is such a response coming from?

Nigerian poets and critics – not noted for their reticence or the gentleness of their own critical judgements – have been loud in their assertion of the particularity of African and especially Nigerian circumstances which have aesthetic and cultural as well as economic and social aspects. Indeed another explanation of the younger Nigerian poets' obsession with social and political commentary – advanced most eloquently by Funso Aiyejima[10] – is that it stems precisely from their production by and continuing reaction to that most cataclysmic event in recent Nigerian history, the Biafran war. This is the generation of writers who 'saw' as children or young men (they are almost entirely men) both the horror and the passion that went into that war and understood most vividly what it cost their peers who were caught up in and killed by it. Their collective vision of a better society is, Aiyejima argues, as much a consequence of that historical experience, that memory, as it is a reaction to the reality of the corrupt and ineffectual governments that their country has since endured. So that 'alter-native' aesthetic, informed both by that sense of an historical duty and notions of poetic function in some way derived from the oral tradition, seems largely to foreground content over form, to value accessibility above linguistic or imagistic subtlety and to prefer 'statement' to 'song'.

And yet the poet who was effectively the founder of that 'alter-native' tradition, Odia Ofeimun, whose poems are as uncompromising as Ojaide's, as outraged as Oguibe's, is very much concerned with both form and the power of wit and startling imagery as poetry's most effective agents. Ofeimun is set apart from many of his contemporaries too in the grounded experience that underlies his political vision. He was not always part of the society's educated élite. For several years after leaving school he worked at a variety of manual and petty clerical jobs, including three years as a factory labourer with the West African Thread Company in Apapa. Then after studying political science at university and a spell spent teaching and working as a civil servant he was Chief Awolowo's private secretary for several years. That broad working experience clearly shapes the moral agenda that drives all his poetry.

Paradoxically the withdrawal of the original 1980 edition of *The Poet Lied* by Longman when J. P. Clarke decided that the title poem pointed a finger too uncomfortably at him and threatened to sue for libel – that 'scandal' ensured that Odia Ofeimun's name would be well remembered even though few people, even in Nigeria, had had the opportunity to read much of his work. 'It put my name on the literary map in a way that I find intimidating,' Ofeimun has remarked.[11] Several poems were well known of course, from journal and anthology publications, and his reputation as a powerful 'performer' of his own work was well established from his days at the University of Ibadan. That original edition of *The Poet Lied* was a very slim volume indeed and it was clear that the selection of poems included there represented a very thin trawl of Ofeimun's work up to that point. His second collection, *A Handle for the Flutist* came out in Nigeria in 1986 to wide critical acclaim – if to some political discomfort – and quickly sold out. In 1989 a new, much expanded edition of *The Poet Lied* appeared in Nigeria (Update Communications Ltd, Lagos). It was effectively a provisional Collected Poems, including all that was in the Longman collection plus many of the poems of that period which were edited out of that volume, all the poems in *A Handle for the Flutist*, and, significantly, a long interview with Onwuchekwu Jemie, which explores many of the philosophical and political ideas that underpin his poetry.

The interview provides a very useful context for a reading of the poems, establishing that the heart of the book is indeed the poet's consideration of the events and ramifications of the Civil War, or rather, as Aiyejima suggests, what that dreadful experience meant for the artists of the society in terms of their understanding of the roles and functions of art. Ofeimun's ambition in 'The Poet Lied' was to establish – by parodying its opposite – a moral position for the 'committed' poet of the post-war Nigeria into which he spoke. So the lying poet asked only:

> to be left alone
> with his blank sheet on his lap
> in some dug-out damp corner
> with a view of the streets and the battle fields
> watching the throngs of calloused lives,
> the many many lives stung by living.
> He would put them in his fables
> sandwich them between his lions and eagles,
> between his elephants and crocodiles.
> ('The Poet Lied', *The Poet Lied*, pp. 40–1)

Ofeimun weaves echoes, half-quotations and some well-known literary positions into the ironic fabric of his poem, and for those who felt themselves thus identified it must have been a painful experience. But as Ofeimun makes clear in the interview, that was not the main intention of the piece. It was rather to construct a manifesto for himself and his generation of writers against which their own integrity might be measured.

Clearly Ofeimun takes the business of writing seriously, this is no therapeutic, leisure-time activity. His ambition is to make a poetry that is both committed and crafted, relevant and resonant. He cites Salvatore Quasimodo, Rilke and Martin Carter among his formative influences and his work does read – in a way that much contemporary Nigerian poetry in English pointedly doesn't – as if it, too, acknowledged a notion of 'poetry' that transcends regional and even cultural boundaries. You feel that the language, not just the writer, is under pressure:

> She whose tongue could coil
> a rig of pythons to break oaks
> She whose fire could raze
> palaces to dust in rainstorms
> She whose hands could wield pestles
> to make miscreants footloose with dread
> She was always the first
> to call the doves to witness
>
> ('Our Wild Christian', *The Poet Lied*, p. 87)

Robert Fraser in his book *West African Poetry* characterises Ofeimun as 'a manic harlequin' in the courts of post-independence Nigeria's corrupt leaders.[12] Fraser reads the poems in the 1980 edition of *The Poet Lied* as seething against 'the pure absurdity of injustice it [the poetry] knows itself powerless to redress' (p. 307). But Ofeimun sees himself rather as a literary 'guerrilla' and certainly in the later poems he clearly feels that such poetry *can* make things happen in societies where the written word is still regarded with some suspicion[13] – and so is attended to – and where the formalised spoken word has long been one of the accoutrements of power. As he puts it in 'A Handle for the Flutist', a poem rich in literary allusions and yet located very precisely in contemporary Nigeria:

> the worshipped word is enough
> to expiate crimes and to lay honour
> upon whom the pleaded grace of song has fallen.
>
> (*The Poet Lied*, p. 118)

Indeed he argues in that poem that it is the very fear the generals – 'the executives' – have of poetry's loaded words, more potent than the loaded guns of more familiar kinds of guerrillas, that has lent poets such authority as they have in Nigeria. Echoing that image of the oral poet able to make 'gods crumble to their knees/questioned by simple images', Ofeimun declares with characteristic irony, and with an awareness of the paradox in what he, the scourge of the tyrant, is saying:

> so let us praise those who will track down
> folksongs with police dogs
> They will not live with poets
> in the Peoples' Republic
> ('A Handle for the Flutist', *The Poet Lied*, p. 119)

If Ofeimun is the voice of the harlequin, the goad, the wit puncturing the pomposities of Nigeria's rulers with his ironic barbs and bells, then Niyi Osundare is the high priest of the 'alter-native' vision. Perhaps it is significant that, like Ofeimun, he is not from a traditional élite background – 'farmer born peasant bred' he asserts in an early poem. He is the one poet whose lyrical and critical intelligence seems to offer both an alternative politics and a notion of poetics which suggests a real way forward for Nigerian – indeed African – poetry in English. Osundare's work is at once aware of both the cultural traditions that feed its roots and of the potential for a unique flowering in the fertile hybridities of an 'African English'. Much of his poetry addresses issues of global significance although his poetry speaks directly into the topical debates of modern Nigeria. There is a gravitas and weight about Osundare's poetry that, while the reader is aware of the characteristic quality of anger that is so prized in this 'alter-native' tradition, makes his arguments seem the more considered, the more measured. And indeed they are measured, for the other quality of Osundare's poetry, which might seem at odds with the notion of gravitas and weight, is its musicality, its lightness of touch. One never feels that Osundare is preaching, nor that – as reader – one is being harangued, yet the effect of much of his poetry is both to teach and to inspire a critical rage against the global inanities that are the targets of much of his own wit and anger.

These general comments are true of Osundare's work as a whole, from his first collection, *Songs of the Marketplace* (1983), through to his most recent book, *Midlife* (1993),[14] but I would like to look at the two volumes that to me best exemplify, on the one hand, the philosophical and political ideas that underpin his work, and on the other, the techniques and cultural resources that so distinctively shape his poetry.

*The Eye of the Earth* (1986), his third collection, is as much a celebration of the natural world and the peasant traditions of his Ikere people, as it is a critique of the geo-political and economic forces which he feels threaten the earth's very existence. Osundare's commitment is not exclusively to one race or to one nation but rather to an ecological vision of an ideal harmony between Man and Nature. But despite the urgent passion of his concerns, Osundare seems always conscious of the priorities of his craft. *The Eye of the Earth* is by turns lyrical and declamatory, carefully structured and yet rich in bold, original imagery. The sequence is broken into three movements. It begins autobiograph-ically by delving into Osundare's childhood memory of peasant life in Ikere, and then, by contrasting that seemingly idyllic past with the present circumstances of his people and their land he draws out the political criticisms that are the heart of his concern.

The sequence opens with 'Forest Echoes', an extended praise-song to the Nigerian forest, drawing vivid portraits of its trees and creatures. The poet's intention here is more than just to celebrate the landscape of his childhood: it is to demonstrate the balance in nature, the reliance of each element on the others in maintaining the ecological harmony. So the Iroko, the ironwood tree that defies the 'sweating sawyer' and 'champion machet' is king of the forest, but even he will fall eventually to the 'block-headed termites' and the 'scalpel-toothed' squirrel, that 'adzeman of the forest'.

The poem goes on then to consider the land itself, and the balance Osundare's ancestors understood between harvesting its mineral and vegetable wealth and paying due respect to the earth mother as the provider of such riches. He contrasts that traditional honouring with the cynical and short-sighted way today's entrepreneurs exploit the earth's gifts. Addressing Olusunta, one of the gold-bearing rocks sacred to his Ikere people, he asks, 'how dig the gold/without breaking the rock?'[15] Of course the rock is not just the mountain itself, it is the community, the whole social system that has developed around it. For the poet recognises as perhaps only a modern Nigerian could, how easily sudden wealth, if not carefully managed, can turn from a blessing into a curse.

In 'Rainsongs', the second movement of the sequence, the poet celebrates the gift of rain as nature's 'arbiter between plenty and famine, life and death'. The seven poems in this movement focus on different aspects of the experience of the rainy season. First comes a prayer for rain, 'Let Earth's Pain be Soothed' but soon enough, looking at the lush transformation of the countryside after the first rains, the poet can ask 'Who says that drought was here?'

'Homecall', the final movement of the sequence, brings Osundare's political argument into focus. The decline of his people from that balanced lifestyle he remembers as the world of his childhood is used as a metaphor for the experience of the whole nation, indeed of the whole Third World. The life of the child who was 'Farmer born and peasant bred' was rich in spiritual experience that helped sustain his community, in material as well as religious terms. But the culture was not strong enough, the poem argues, to resist 'alien' ideas and values, unadapted to local circumstances, that began in school and ultimately produced a national culture of materialism, envy and corruption which resulted in a whole people being reduced to dependence on imported food for its very subsistence:

> Farmer-born peasant-bred
> classroom-bled
> I have thrown open my kitchen doors
> and asked hunger to take a seat,
> my stomach a howling dump
> for Carolina rice
> (*The Eye of The Earth*, p. 44)

That decline inspires Osundare's rage, not only in *The Eye of the Earth* but throughout his work, and in essence, is the source of Osundare's political vision. As I've described it Osundare may seem something of a romantic, a reactionary figure even, lamenting the passing of a golden age. Rather his poetic and political vision spring from a profound awareness of African history and the debilitating effects of the long-term contact with Europe which has disrupted the mechanisms of 'balance' he sees in the experience of his own people. What, in human terms, most disrupted that balance was the Atlantic slave trade, and Osundare's bleak, passionate but restrained poem 'Goree', responding to a visit he made to the notorious Senegalese slaving station in 1989, establishes the force of his historical imagination. Elsewhere in his work, and in common with the other poets of the 'alter-native' tradition, he is not averse to pointing out the injustices of 'traditional' as well as contemporary governments. So he is no reactionary. And while the notion of a 'balance', in nature and in political structure, that sustains the community, may be idealistic, as one critic has remarked,[16] it does represent an *imaginable* alternative to both the brutalising crude capitalism of post-independence Nigerian governments and the crude ideological socialism of the intellectual 'opposition'. Osundare's alternative political vision, as it is enmeshed and expressed in his poetry, is both pragmatic and practical, informed by an essentially optimistic view of humanity's ability to change and a belief in the fundamental instinct of mankind to both respect and nurture the earth and its resources.

That pragmatic optimism is evident, too, in *Waiting Laughters*, which won the 1991 NOMA award for poetry. It is this collection – and Osundare's books usually seem to have been conceived as extended poems – which seems to me to best represent Osundare's notion of poetic craft and his relationship to the oral tradition. Subtitled 'a long song in many voices', it is broken into six sections, each of them announced by a different musical setting. For example the opening, 'Some laughters are very significant', has the instruction *flute and/or clarinet; medley of voices*. As a mere reader one has to try and 'hear' the poem in that performance context in order to get a sense of how effective the words *off* the page might be. As straight text, sections of the poem occasionally seem over-ornamented, particularly in the first section where there is an almost baroque quality to the language, *every* noun encrusted with adjectives, *every* line an image. But it is clear Osundare knows what he's doing, and knows what effect he is striving for. A note to the poem explains that the sequence:

> is about waiting in different and often contrasting circumstances, and the behaviour of time in the waiting process. But more than anything else, it is a poetic response to the gloom and despair which seems to have gripped contemporary African society.[17]

The opening section of the poem establishes various 'levels' of waiting; from the political:

> Every tadpole is a frog-in-waiting
> in the wasted waters of my greed en-tided land

through the elemental:

> Oh teach us the patience of the Rain
> Which eats the rock in toothless silence

to the cosmic:

> Waiting
>           on the stairs of the moon
>           creaking up and down
>           the milkyways of fastidious comets
>                     (*Waiting Laughters*, p. 25)

In such contexts, the poet seems to imply, there *is* time to indulge in the playfulness of a language rich in puns, alliteration and the mannered laughter of literary wit. In section two of the poem, 'The freedom of any

society varies proportionately with the volume of its laughter', the social
and historical context of African, particularly Nigerian, history is drawn,
and issues like those he explores in *The Eye of the Earth* are considered.
So is the fundamental question, for a poet, of language:

> The tongue is parrot
> Of another forest
>
>               . . .
>
> A white white tongue
> In a black black mouth
>
>               . . .
>
> And the tongue hangs out its blade
> blunted
> by the labyrinthine syntax of ghostly histories
>
>               . . .
>
> History's stammerer
> when will your memory master
> the vowels of your father's name?
>                         (*Waiting Laughters*, p. 40)

It is in his brilliant use of that 'borrowed tongue' – as he calls it
elsewhere – breaking and remaking English, capitalising on the tension
set up by that confrontation of language and culture, that Osundare
answers, for his generation, the question of 'authenticity'-in-English
that dogged the previous generation of African writers. Osundare is
doing for African poetry what Derek Walcott did for Caribbean poetry,
claiming and maiming the language for his own ends. No English poet
*could* use the English language in the way Osundare does. He uses it to
confront the same outrage and distress that Oguibe and Ojaide lament,
but with an understanding of the power of wit, of mockery, of laughter,
to both discomfort its targets and revitalise its users.

Aderimi Bamikule has usefully pointed to the close relationship
between Osundare's techniques and the devices of the Yoruba oral
tradition – from the more or less literal 'translation' of certain poems of
occasion[18] to the more subtle adaptation of forms and functions and, as
with *Waiting Laughters*, the incorporation of music into the fabric of the
poem's 'event'. The notion of the poet 'speaking for' a community is as
important to Osundare as to the other poets of the 'alter-native'
tradition, but this need not be the overt assertion of that right and duty
that Oguibe and Ojaide claim, but can be expressed rather in that
nuanced adaptation of the oral poets' devices which signal his awareness of the responsibility that accompanies those forms. This is

apparent in the ways he has used both aspects of the praise-song tradition to genuinely praise the person or even object that is its subject, as in 'Sowing':

> When a long-awaited shower
> has softened the pilgrimage of the dibble,
> corn-grains sing their way to germinal roots
>
> of lying ridges. Seedlings dream truant tendrils
> in the moistening bed of unpunctual heaps;
> the tuber is one patience away,
>
> climbing through stalks
> through pinna-leaved groves
> through vines which twine the moons
> > like wayward pythons
> > > *(Waiting Laughters*, p. 88)

or to be bitterly ironic in debunking its subject's hypocrisies:

> Waiting,
> > like the corpulent clergy
> > > for his tithes
>
> like the white-wigged judge
> > for his turkey
>
> like the hard-faced don
> > for his chair
>
> like the policeman
> > for his bribe
>
> waiting
> > *(Waiting Laughters*, p. 48)

Neither of those examples takes praise-song forms as a literal template for the English-language poem, but the effect, within the sequence as a whole, is to recall that dual function of praise-song in Osundare's tradition, and the risks that the praise singer who was more than just a sycophant always took.

Similarly his use of proverbs – and by all accounts his poems are rich in echoes of Yoruba proverbs – is a subtle adaptation rather than a simplistic translation. Even for the reader without knowledge of Yoruba proverbs, much of Osundare's work bears the cast of proverbial utterance. Indeed some of the more obvious echoes are from proverbs that exist in English:

> The plough has no share in
> the malady of running swords
> (*Waiting Laughters*, p. 53)

And in a sense it doesn't matter about such origins. Osundare's sources, his technique, like his language, are hybrid, and his poetry is inevitably *about* crossing boundaries. 'Peasant born and farmer bred' but, in Walcott's words 'with a sound colonial education', Osundare's genius is in welding his several inheritances into a unique and appropriate voice for his times. That quality is evident at the conclusion of *Waiting Laughters* where Osundare uses the 'traditional' techniques of poetry, traditional across boundaries of culture and race: unusual imagery, a rhythmic surge, a concise, considered use of a language crafted to produce more of a sense of threat to the status quo than any number of ranting, breast-beating statements of the kind he satirises in the opening couplets of this quotation:

> Our laughter these several seasons is the simper-
> Ing sadness of the ox which adores its yoke,
>
> The toothless guffaw of empty thunders
> In epochs of unnatural drought
>
> The season calls for the lyric of other laughters
>
>> New chicks breaking the fragile tyranny
>> of hallowed shells
>>
>> A million fists, up,
>> In the glaring face of complacent skies
>>
>> A machet waiting, waiting
>> In the whetting shadows of stubborn shrubs
>>
>> A boil, time-tempered,
>> About to burst.
>> (*Waiting Laughters*, pp. 96–7)

Unlike some of his more outspoken contemporaries, Osundare 'dares the beast' not only at the level of rhetoric but also in terms of ideas. If the generals would object to his poetry they must first *read* it; they cannot skim the surface for the obviously offensive word but must explore the metaphor, understand the irony, consider the ambiguities, discover its measured 'beauty'. Beauty and the Beast! Now that would be, in Oguibe's words, for a poet to 'turn the course of history'.

## Notes

1. Donatus Nwoga, *West African Verse*, London: Longman, 1967, p. 17.
2. Christopher Okigbo, *Labyrinths*, London: Heinemann, 1971, p. 68.
3. Nadine Gordimer, 'The Essential Gesture: Writers and Responsibility', in *Granta*, No. 15, 1989, pp. 137–51.
4. Olu Oguibe, *A Song from Exile*, Bayreuth: Boomerang Press, 1990, p. 9.
5. See the discussion of Ofeimun's poem 'A Handle for the Flutist' later in this essay.
6. 'Alter-native' tradition – the term seems to have derived from Femi Osofison's *Guardian* essay 'The Alternative Tradition: A Survey of Nigerian Literature', but is used by Funso Aiyejina in its broken form in his essay 'Recent Nigerian Poetry in English: an Alter-Native Tradition' (see note 10 below) to draw attention to the *alter*ation of the consciousness in the work of the younger generation of Nigerian poets who are self consciously *native* – with all the ramifications of that term – in their language, their cultural orientation and their concerns. It has become a reviewers' and critics' shorthand for the writers of that generation.
7. See, for example, the work of Femi Fatoba, Funso Aiyejina, Fred Agdeyegbe, Silas Obadiah, Emerwo Biakolo, Femi Osofisan, Eman Shehu . . . ; and see the Association of Nigerian Authors' anthology, edited by Harry Geruba, *Voices from the Fringe*, Lagos: Malthouse Press, 1990.
8. Tanure Ojaide, *The Blood of Peace*, London: Heinemann, 1991, p. 28.
9. Tanure Ojaide, *The Fate of Vultures*, Lagos: Malthouse Press, 1990, p. 9.
10. Funso Aiyejina, 'Recent Nigerian Poetry in English: an Alter-Native Tradition' in *Perspectives on Nigerian Literature: 1700 to the present*, ed. Yemi Ogunbiyi, Vol. 1, Lagos: Guardian Books (Nigeria), 1988.
11. Onwuchekwa Jemie, 'A Conversation with Odia Ofeimun', in *The Poet Lied*, Lagos: Update Communications Ltd., 1989, pp. 148–76.
12. Robert Fraser, *West African Poetry*, Cambridge: Cambridge University Press, 1986.
13. Onwuchekwa Jemie, 'A Conversation with Odia Ofeimun'.
14. For a full bibliography of Osundare's work – and a useful bibliographical essay – see Don Burness' essay on Osundare in the forthcoming edition of *The Dictionary of Literary Biography*. See also Biodun Jeyifo's essay 'Niyi Osundare' in volume two of Yemi Ogunbiyi's *Perspectives on Nigerian Literature*, pp. 314–20.
15. Niyi Osundare, *The Eye of the Earth*, Lagos: Heinemann, 1986, p. 14.
16. Aderemi Bamikunle, 'Niyi Osundare's Poetry and the Yoruba Oral Artistic Tradition', in *African Literature Today*, No. 18, 1988, pp. 49–61.
17. Unattributed jacket note to *Waiting Laughters*, Lagos: Malthouse Press, 1990.
18. Aderemi Bamikunle, 'Niyi Osundare's Poetry and the Yoruba Oral Artistic Tradition', pp. 52–3.

# Geopoetics: Subterraneanity and Subversion in Malawian Poetry

## MPALIVE-HANGSON MSISKA

In his essay in the *Bloomsbury Guide to English Literature*, Jonathan Sawday describes Renaissance poetry as a poetry of secrecy and concealment.[1] Largely as a result of the political and cultural circumstances under which they worked, Renaissance poets developed an elaborate language of circumvention. Notwithstanding historical and cultural differences between the two traditions, Sawday could have been describing Malawian poetry written during the regime of President Banda, which similarly constitutes itself as a poetics of ideological concealment.[2] All the three poets whose work I discuss in this essay – Jack Mapanje, Frank Chipasula, and Steve Chimombo – fashioned distinct ways of defamiliarising the dominant political discourse in Malawi.

Chimombo's poetry is characterised by the practice of geological subterraneanity, a conception of poetic political agency as a constant movement between the terrestrial world of dominant political discourse and the multiple locations provided by the labyrinthine space of pre-colonial myth. He uses the myths of the subterranean serpent, Napolo, and that of the Christ-like figure of Mbona for a repertoire of counter-discursive devices. Napolo is supposed to reside under Zomba mountain which overlooks the colonial capital and now the University town. When the serpent is unhappy it causes climatic and geological change, as happened between 1945 and 1946 when a cyclone devastated Zomba Town and claimed a number of lives, including that of a colonial district commissioner.[3]

In his anthology, *Napolo* (1987), Chimombo's adaptation of the Napolo narrative allows him to inhabit subversively an otherwise dangerous political time and space. Like the serpentine Mbona, the poet's agency is lodged in the subterranean temporality of myth, beneath the time of the modern nation, from where an alternative subjectivity and language are forged. The specific subversive allegorisation of political conflict in Chimombo's poetry is reminiscent of past figuration of conflicts between rulers and subjects in Southern Malawi, in which the lion represents the aristocracy and the python, commoners.[4] Given that President Banda was known as the 'Lion of

Malawi', the poet's choice of a countervailing serpentine agency shrewdly foregrounds the oppositional space which the regime's metaphorical self-representation has elided in order to erect itself as the sole subject of discourse.

Myth also offers a key metaphorical term for the new dispensation, since Napolo is also the name for the repressive Malawian political regime. The representation of the regime as a profane assault on ancestral peace in the title poem serves to undermine its claim to be the custodian of tradition, as the regime is placed in the same paradigmatic category as the evil characters of mythology:

> Mlauli's tomb roared. . .
> Mbona was checked in mid-leap,
> Chilembwe turned over and went back to
> sleep (p. 1)

The mention of Mbona alludes to the mythic hero's flight from his bloodthirsty pursuers whose capacity to destroy goodness is reproduced in the character of the dictatorship, just as John Chilembwe's name underlines the similarity between the colonial and the present government's undemocratic practices.[5] By linking his own critique of the regime to Mbona and Chilembwe, Chimombo invests it with the legitimacy of an ancient autochthonous anti-authoritarian practice.[6] However, as the elegiac tone of the poem suggests, it is the absence of such transformative agency in the present that the poet bemoans, for Napolo is left to destroy the land unchecked.

As Napolo moves across the country, from the Southern to the Northern region, he simulates the negative unity of the surface: 'Mulanje, Zomba, and Nyika fled their places,/ whispered and hid their faces' (p. 1). Napolo's erasure of cultural difference is analogous to the indiscriminate violence of the regime, a form of negative unity which Gayatri Spivak, in a different context, describes as 'a unity of exploitation and domination'.[7] By revealing the existence of a destructive subterranean space underneath the nation space, the poet contests the view engendered by the state that there are certain zones of safety within the social formation which the 'good' subject can inhabit without fear of persecution. In fact, all subjects have equal chance of being deemed bad.[8]

The advent of Napolo forces the persona to revisit the founding moment of sociality. In the poem 'Path', when he tries to consult the oracle at Kaphirintiwa, the cradle of mankind, he finds only 'the desolation of the shrines' which 'portends retribution and revision'

(p. 2). In 'Messengers', the hero's quest for an explanation of the Napolo phenomenon is transposed into a universal search for the meaning of human destiny similar to that enacted at the beginning of history. The poem presents a well-known Malawian creation myth in which man sent lizard, chameleon and madman to God to find out whether or not man would be immortal. God sent each animal with a different message: chameleon, who had been sent first, was told that man would live forever; lizard, that man would suffer death, and the madman was given some incomprehensible message. Since lizard was the fastest of all, he arrived first, announcing that man will not be immortal. When slow chameleon arrived with the good news, the negative message had already been received and God refused to change his mind, as he had promised that only the message mankind received first would be valid. As in the beginning of creation, the present does not offer any reliable explanation for the existence of human suffering, since the meaning of Napolo depends as much on the limitations of interpretation and location as on the content of the message.

In 'Message' the Banda regime is presented as the sentence of death promised by God. As the persona looks back at the Napolonic era from the future, he recounts what it was like to live under the dictatorship of Napolo:

> Was it a decade after Napolo
> I met you, friend?
> No matter.
> We lived to tell the story around the fire
> in whispers and behind locked doors (p. 4)

The Napolonic era is characterised by fear, but fear engenders alternative ways of articulation, as is evident by the transfer of the site of political conversation from the public domain to the privacy of the hearth, the place from which tradition was transmitted orally to the young generation. However, the fact that the poet has chosen to narrate the poem from a time when the Napolonic era has passed counters the regime's official myths of permanence articulated, for example, in the designation of Banda as 'Life President'. Nevertheless, the transience of the regime does not mean that the effects of the Napolonic era will be absent in the constitution of future subjectivity.

Temporal hybridity is displaced into cultural hybridity in 'Aftermath', as Napolo's powers of self-transformation are examined closely:

> The snarl of brakes strangled the sepulchral
> voice,

> boots crushed the gravel,
> and muzzles of machine guns
> confronted the dawn.
> Napolo was here to stay (p. 5)

Chillingly, the poem alludes to the regime's brutal treatment of its opponents. In the second section of the anthology, 'Napolo's metamorphosis', we are told that:

> Bark cloth was no longer considered
> appropriate . . .
> Field green replaced bark cloth (p. 6)

Cultural hybridity becomes the agency of death and cultural deracination. In the 'Sons of Napolo', the opposition between Western and African culture is used to satirise Banda's personal efforts at cultural hybridity:

> We danced the Ingoma
> in worsted wool and crimplene,
> shoes strapped to our jiggered soles.
> The shields we carried
> were emblazoned with a motto
> written in a foreign tongue
>
> We danced Nyau steps
> to the rhythm of rock 'n' roll:
> sycophants to the frenzied music
> of our adopted forefathers (p. 9)

Clearly, something needs to be done about the regime of Napolo and his offspring. The poem 'Napologia' considers possible ways of destroying Napolo. In the poem, narrative point of view is allotted to two speakers, an adult and an adolescent. Whereas the adult counsels caution, the adolescent thinks the best way is to challenge Napolo directly. The exchange is in the form of proverbial discourse, with each speaker countering the opposing view with a proverb. The language highlights the need for discursive concealment of subversive agency if it is to escape surveillance. This form of concealment is reminiscent of the use of secret society ideolects in the anti-colonial struggles of Central and Southern Malawi.[9] Furthermore, by problematising the status of traditional African epistemology, through positing proverbial textuality as necessarily contradictory, Chimombo undermines, once again, that aspect of the regime's legitimacy that is dependent on simplifying the textual complexity of history and oral tradition.

In contrast to the deadly hybrid identity of the sons of Napolo, in the third section of the anthology, 'Napolo: In the Beginning', the persona recuperates abandoned traditional rituals of prayer for a spiritual regeneration of the nation:

> Ambuye.
> Pepa.
> Aumasoka.
> Pepa.
> Ajumizimu.
> Pepa.
>
> For seven nights
> Your sons have not known their wives.
>
> Pepa.
>
> For seven nights
> your daughters have not seen the moon.
>
> Pepa . . . (pp. 10–11)

In 'Beggar Woman' the persona takes on the mantle of defender of the common person as he describes the extent of the beggar's plight:

> Napolo found me in the streets.
> I sought sanctuary in the shops,
> the offices, the church, the school,
> but they had all put up the sign:
> 'Trespassers Will be Persecuted' (p. 17)

Furthermore, her body, on which are inscribed numerous highways used by lice, is a microcosm of Napolo's invasion of the body politic. Yet, this despised figure offers one of the few instances in the anthology of explicit emancipatory agency:

> In the aftermath of Napolo,
> I emerge from the chaosis
> and march down rainbathed pavements
> singing on the fingernails of the rainbow (p. 18)

The beggar has engaged Napolo in battle and survived. Nevertheless, the poet counsels caution, presenting the beggar's method as admirable, but also hazardous.

In 'Four Ways of Dying', four animals – crab, chameleon, mole, and Kalilombe – provide different ways of concealing and enacting subversive agency. Crab's strategy is to be cautious and to conceal its intentions:

> Avoid
>> direct action on public matters
>> confrontation,
>> commitment;
>
> Meander
>> to confuse direction or purpose,
>>> meaning,
>>> sense;
>
> Squat
>> to balance the issues,
>> weigh,
>> consider (p. 21)

As for Chameleon, one must simulate the colours of the enemy in order to undermine him:

> I'll match my colours with yours,
> snake my tongue out to your fears,
> bear my teeth to puncture your hopes,
> tread warily past your nightmares,
> curl my tail round your sanctuaries,
> clasp my pincer legs on your veins,
> to listen to your heart beat (p. 22)

In contrast to the manoeuvres of Crab and Chameleon, Mole's way is to burrow 'intricate passages and halls', to 'tunnel utopias and underground Edens' and 'substitute surface with subterranean vision'. While Mole's idea of martyrdom undermines the foundation of the dictatorship, it does not guarantee the survival of the agent of change.

It is Kalilombe, chameleon in English, who provides the ultimate blood sacrifice through regenerative death:

> I grit my teeth, grab the slippery surface
> and hoist myself up the nation's trunk.
> On the topmost branch I have momentary
> possession of eternity whirling in the
> chaosis;
> with the deathsong floating from my lips,

> I fling myself down on Kaphirintiwa rock
> as multivarious forms of art and life
> issue out from the convulsions
> of the ruptured womb;
> and die (p. 23)

The difference between chameleon's and Kalilombe's ways of agency is that the former relies on identification and self-preservation without the certainty of profound change, whereas the latter effects a strategic counter-identification which circumvents history by linking itself to an autochthonous moment beyond that of the modern nation, the moment of Kaphirintiwa. This difference privileges authentic rather than hybrid subjectivity as a source of redemptive agency.

Like Kalilombe, the persona goes to the mountain top in 'Derailment: A Delirium', to survey the Napolonic effects on the nation. The journey is undertaken under spirit possession which in the persona's case takes the form of hepatitis. However, unlike Kalilombe's, the persona's journey does not lead to an act of public heroism, but to domestic bliss. The hesitation between commitment and withdrawal is further elaborated in 'Three Songs', 'Of Promises and Prophecy' and 'The Suppliants'. In the last poem of the anthology, 'Chingwe's Hole Revisited', it is Napolo's return that is prophesied:

> And when my grandmother, that perpetual
> watcher,
> (Napolo is going to return, son.)
> hears Napolo's scales detonating the boulders
> on his way back to the womb of the nation,
> whose startled limbs will hurtle
> into the chaosis that was Chingwe's Hole?
> What will petrify Napolo in his hole forever? (p. 55)

Thus, after considering a number of ways of counteracting Napolo, the anthology concludes by presenting Napolo as essentially indestructible. Chimombo's complex narrative poem employs the device of geological subterraneanity to produce a space of critique under a dictatorship, but, as in Mole's case, part of the message is submerged under the weight of myth.

If Chimombo's poetry inhabits the formal geological recesses of myth and folklore, the poetry of Jack Mapanje occupies the discourse of everyday language.[10] Representing agency as a chameleon indicates a mode of counter-identification in which subversive agency positions itself within everyday language in order to produce what Mapanje describes in his introduction to the anthology as an alternative voice:

> The verse in this volume spans some ten turbulent years in which I have been attempting to find a voice or voices as a way of preserving some sanity. Obviously where personal voices are too easily muffled, this is a difficult task; one is tempted like the chameleon, who failed to deliver Chiuta's message of life, to bask in one's brilliant camouflage. But the exercise has been, if nothing else, therapeutic; and that's no mean word in our circumstances![11]

In a situation where speech is subject to surveillance, it is writing that affords the poet enunciative possibility, endowing him with expressive autonomy and rescuing his subjectivity from being merely a function of the regime's ideological State apparatus.

The opposition between animate and inanimate provides one of the principal means by which Mapanje implements discursive subterraneanity. This is illustrated in the opening poem, 'Kabula Curio-Shop', which turns a broken artefact into a symbol of the regime's impermanence and its leader's mortality:

> A broken symbol thrown careless
> in the nook of a curio-shop: a lioness
> broken legs, broken neck, broken udder? (p. 3)

The use of the device is further evident in 'The Songs of Chickens' (p. 4), an allegorisation of the political situation in Malawi through the idea of the keeper turned poacher:

> Master, you talked with bows,
> Arrows and catapults once
> Your hands steaming with hawk blood
> To protect your chicken . . .
>
> Why do you talk with knives now,
> Your hands teaming with eggshells
> And hot blood from your own chicken?
> Is it to impress your visitors? (p. 4)

Here, the everyday Malawian practice of slaughtering chicken for guests becomes a metaphor for the leadership's betrayal of the ideals of the anti-colonial struggle.

Imprisonment is represented as analogous to the laboratory practice of preserving animal specimens. The poem, 'Waiting for the Electronic Forceps (For Felix)' (p. 51), does not immediately strike one as a political statement, yet it is a lament to Felix Mnthali, Mapanje's colleague detained in 1976. The poem is addressed to a Michael who prayed for the butterfly: that the 'Lord might still grant her/ a distant sense of humour with the Sun/ or the bright colours of her wings.' Before his arrest, Mnthali had written a poem, 'Prayer for a Butterfly' in which a pilgrim in search of a miracle and a vanished millennium discovers 'a butterfly conversing with the sun'.[12] The allusion to Mnthali's poem serves as a device for recuperating a silenced identity.

Moreover, 'Waiting for the Electronic Forceps' achieves further referential complexity when examined in the context of the preceding experimental poem, 'For a Friend Taken, 1976' (p. 50), in which the title is followed by a blank space and then the following lines:

> Even robots flick amber first
> And you can whizz down the bloody
> Road before the red if you like! (p. 50)

The title of the poem tantalisingly promises an account of the detention of a friend; however, the blank space frustrates that expectation, reproducing the silence expected by the regime following such incidents. Nevertheless, enforced silence is circumvented by deferring the narration of the story about the detention of the poet's friend to the poem 'Waiting for the Electronic Forceps', which conceals its political meaning by presenting itself as a poem about an innocuous butterfly.

History forms another site of discursive subterraneanity in Mapanje's anthology as exemplified by the poem 'A Marching Litany to our Martyrs (3rd March, 1971)' (pp. 5–6). The president's account of the history of decolonisation in Malawi portrayed the regime as the final culmination of all previous anti-colonial struggles, including the Chilembwe uprising. In Mapanje's poem, the persona starts off by identifying himself with the official line, insisting that Martyrs' Day should be taken seriously by everyone and employing the regime's favourite term of abuse, 'stooge', for local collaborators of the colonial government and criticising the trivialisation of Martyrs' Day by post-colonial imitators of Western culture:

> Have we really about swung to these
> Frantic maxi-skirts slit to thighs

> Opening to whispers and caresses of
> Midnight breezes and coins? (p. 5)

All this would be acceptable to a regime obsessed with banning mini-skirts and dresses with slits; but, as the following lines demonstrate, the poem is an attack on the government:

> In the name of our growing bellies,
> Batons, buggers and bastards rife,
> Let us revel in parades, lowering the emblem
> Of the precious bones long laid asleep.

> Amen! (p. 6)

Thus the marching litany to the martyrs turns out to be a satire in praise of political folly and greed. In 'Before Chilembwe Tree' (pp. 18–19), the poet condemns the wholesale preoccupation with the past, particularly the persona's view that the past is the only source of models of political leadership. As far as Mapanje is concerned, this is a disabling use of history and one which is as unhelpful as the nationalist's appropriations of the past.

In a series of four poems based on Malawian creation myths, Mapanje, like Chimombo, conceals his critique of the Malawian regime in myth. However, unlike Chimombo's style which employs an elaborate geological structure, Mapanje's approach to myth is colloquial and critical. The second poem of the series, 'The First Fire' uses myth to argue that the regime exhibits the same abuse of powers of creativity shown in man's destructive invention of fire at Kaphirintiwa. In the third poem, 'Man on Chiuta's Ascension', God's hasty ascent to heaven on spider's thread is perceived not so much in terms of the traditional moral, the illustration of man's irresponsibility, but rather as evidence of God's selfish withdrawal to his 'Ivory Tower', and as a demonstration of the fact that those in power always withdraw when they are most needed. In 'So God Became a Chameleon' the leadership's abdication of responsibility is represented as a function of abnormality:

> A muezzin
> with gelded
> tongue
> slunk in
> celibacy

> A politician
> empiric

> muffing
> easy balls
> fearing fear (p. 10)

The metamorphosis of God into the earthly chameleon or politician, which is accompanied by the loss of reproductive power, is indicative of the general sterility that attends the fall from the great heights of redemptive nationalist ideals to the unholy plane of unethical and defensive politics.

In the poem, 'If Chiuta were Man', Mapanje points towards the final reconciliation of mankind, god and animal life through the agency of human love:

> Woman, hold my shoulders
> we'll drift and drift until
> we reach the promised Nsinja
> Forest and river of life . . .
>
> Meanwhile hold on woman
> Let's glide and glide
> On our pioneer project:
> Hope is our only hope (p. 7)

In its insistence on hope, the poem transcends its immediate religious and mythical context, articulating a secular vision of the future as the present is endowed with the power to change the structure of political relations bequeathed by both myth and history. In the section, 'Re-entering Chingwe's Hole', the poet employs geological subterraneanity, but not as a means of recuperating the structures of traditional narratives as in Chimombo's poetry, but rather in order to interrogate the essentialist investment of places and events with mythical value. The hole is demythologised and revealed as simply a prison and grave in which pre-colonial and post-colonial tyrants have dumped bodies of opponents. In 'Visiting Zomba Plateau', finding little of mythical significance in the hole, the persona asks:

> Where is the spirit that touched the hearts
> Lightly – chameleon colours of home?
> Where is your creation myth? Have I come
> To witness the carving and jingling only of
> Your bloated images and piddling mirrors? (p. 42)

In the poem, 'Re-entering the Shrines of Zomba', it is suggested that the reason 'the Gods have deserted/these noble shrines', is not solely a function of the poet's interrogative reading practice, but also of the advent of a secular religion characterised by 'tax-collectors ominously wink[ing] at each other/weighing the genuineness of your travellers cheques' (p. 43).

Mapanje's reinterpretation of oral tradition is also evident in the poem 'The Tussle' where the speaker warns:

> And so Son
> next time you're
> on sand playing animal
> play not hyena carried
> away by lion rather
> the lion,
> if forced
> carry him away
> make the hyena that
> killed the lion,
> when he grumbles
> tell him it's only
> a game – animal game
> you are men and
> he'll lead the next
> chick-stealing
> pig-blood-tapping
> party anyway.
> You've seen the latest
> tussle! (p. 11)

Thus, an ordinary children's game has been invested with political significance, highlighting the extent to which the differential attribution of power in folklore and political discourse are mediated by the uncritical acceptance of the values proffered by dominant ideology. Mapanje suggests that effective counter-identification is only possible when one inverts the hierarchical terms of dominant or received discourse and inserts one's own subversive identity in the very space from which it is excluded.

Yet another way in which dominant discourse is undermined is through representing the self as being more authentic than the leadership, as in the poem 'New Platform Dances' (pp. 12–13), whose title plays on the ambiguity of the word 'platform' which refers to the once-fashionable platform-soled shoes as well as to Banda's penchant for dancing with women during public meetings. The persona, like Banda, enjoys dancing with women and brandishing his flywhisk, but his style is rooted in tradition rather than the synthetic culture of Banda's performances. The persona views the new platform dance with sadness:

> Now, when I see my daughters writhe
> Under cheating abstract
> Voices of slack drums, ululate
> To babble-idea-men-masks
> Without amulets or anklets,
> Why don't I stand up
> To show them how we danced
> Chopa, how IT was born?
> Why do I sit still
> Why does my speech choke
> Like I have not danced
> Before? Haven't I
> Danced the bigger dance?
> Haven't I? (p. 13)

In poems such as 'Messages' and 'When this Carnival Finally Closes', the poet nostalgically looks back to the past to highlight the harrowing effects of the present moment on the citizens of the country, but, more importantly, in order to expose the present as a manifestation of cultural deviancy.

In the section, 'Sketches from London', Mapanje employs external location as a vantage-point from which to examine the Malawian political situation. 'Drinking the water from its Source' rehearses the disenchantment of the post-colonial élite with the centre's failure to conform to its valorized and sanitized representation in colonial and some post-colonial accounts. However, the poet uses this familiar theme of African writing to question the terms by which the regime legitimises itself as the continuation of the civilising mission of the centre. For Mapanje, London is a symbol of death rather than of civilisation.

This deployment of external location also enables the poet's use of other forms of writing as narrative devices. In 'From *Florrie Abraham Witness*, December, 1972', a letter from home describing the persecution of members of the Jehovah's Witnesses, invests the poet's portrayal of life under the dictatorship with the authority of an eye-witness's account. Equally important, the letter enables the poet to disguise the political function of his writing. The outside also provides comparative experiences which are used to comment on the politics of Malawi. In 'Steve Biko is Dead', the persona ponders the manner in which Biko's death will be reported by the media. However when he says: 'why or for how long/ Steve Bikos will waste/ we'll not bother to ask' (p. 65), it becomes clear that Biko is a generalised category of persecution and martyrdom equally applicable to the waste of human life in Malawi. The location of the Malawian experience in a broader international context is also discernible in 'On being asked to Write a Poem, 1979', a poem about the Year of the Child which talks about 'Skeletal Kampuchea children staring, cold/ Stubborn Irish children throwing grenades' and argues that:

> The year of the child must make no difference then
> Where tadpoles are never allowed to grow into frogs! (p. 74).

Thus the external angle provides the poet with an important location for discursive subterraneanity, in addition to the strategic positioning of counter-hegemonic agency in the discourses which constitute dominant ideology in Malawi. Although it would be wrong to reduce the complexity of the anthology to a narrow political reading, it clearly bears the stamp of the historical moment of its production.

The first two sections of *Chattering Wagtails of Mikuyu*, 'Another Fool's Day Homes In' and 'Out of Bounds', which were written before Mapanje's arrest, predominantly deploy the same strategies of concealment at work in *Of Chameleons and Gods*.[13] However, the last two sections, 'Chattering Wagtails' and 'The Release and Other Curious Sights', written in York, after Mapanje's release from detention, evidently are less concerned with political concealment than with preserving the distinctiveness of poetic practice from being undermined by the affective immediacy of the experience of incarceration as well as the new-found freedom of expression provided by exile and the changing political situation in Malawi.

In the section, 'Another Fool's Day Homes In', the poet returns from abroad to a life dominated by utter despondency and spiritual sterility. In the poem, 'Another Fool's Day touches down: shush', fool's day is used to present the irrationality and monotony of the national anniversaries which have now lost their original significance:

> Another Fool's Day touches down, another homecoming . . .
> Shush. Bunting! some anniversary; they'll be preoccupied;
> Only a wife, children and a friend, probably waiting (p. 5)

In 'Kadango Village, Even Milimbo Lagoon Is Dry, Fools', deprivation is shown to be inscribed in the landscape as well as the human body:

> In the cracking heat of October, our village market.
> A queue of skeletal hands reaching out for the last
> Cowlac tin of loose grain, falters against hope . . . (p. 6)

Furthermore, the traditional means of political narration now come under censorship:

> Those fishermen who dreamt up better weather
> Once, no longer cast their nets here, and their
>
> Delightful bawdy songs to bait the droughts are
> Cloaked in the choking fumes of dawn, banned. But
> Our fat-necked custodians despatch another tale (p. 6)

Thus, the poet's record of the times recuperates the suppressed social and political role of the artist.[14]

There are some irrepressively loud voices such as the market vendor's in 'The Haggling Old Woman at Balaka':

> The old woman at Balaka never stops
> She haggles over every new event: . . .
>
> you girls today are cocked up,
> You sell chicken eggs for cokes and fantas
> To suckle your babies, then you ask me
> Why your babies are rickets and ribs? (p. 9)

The old woman's criticism of the effect of modernisation on the health of the children is a cover for criticism of government policies:

> And from now on I will keep my crop to
> Myself – you have no shame building your
> Brick houses on old women's dying energies
> Under the lie of national development!
> No, I've sung too many tattered praises,
> Spare me these spotted desires, children . . . (p. 9)

Once again, discursive subterraneanity is implemented through the device of apparent identification with the terms of dominant ideology.

The device of embedding subversive textuality in other, perhaps innocuous texts, is employed in 'No, Creon, there's No Virtue in Howling' (p. 12), which is a reference to Sophocles' *Antigone*, one of the many classical texts not banned by the regime because of the President's reverence for classics. Mapanje's ingenuity lies in exploiting the regime's élitist ideology for a revelation of its ruthlessness:

> How can you hope to repair Haemon, your
> Own blood, our only hope for the throne,
> By reproaching his body mangled by your
> Decree and put to rest without the requiem
> Of our master drums? What tangential sentries
> Advise you to bemoan the dead by scoffing
> Them publicly thus? Those accidents your
> Flunkies master-stroked, those tortures &
> Exiles fashioned, and the blood you loved
> To hear, did we need more lies? (p. 12)

Analogously, Haemon functions as the name for those that have suffered death or exile at the hands of the regime. However, the Creons of this world abhor being told the truth. 'On Banning of Chameleon and Gods (June, 1985)', in the section, 'Out of Bounds', argues that the banning of the poet's first anthology elides the fact that it only describes what is common knowledge:

> How do you enjoy squinting only
> At lines without bothering to ask what even
> Swallows perched on the barbed wires of your
> Central Prisons already know? . . .
> No, for children's sake, unchain these truths;
> Release the verse you've locked in our hearts! (p. 35)

The banning of the collection is also symbolic of the suppression of the creative energies of the nation.

In 1987, Mapanje was detained and spent four years at Mikuyu Prison near Zomba. The third section of the collection, 'Chattering Wagtails', is an account of his prison experience. In some ways subterraneanity here is achieved by the location of the poet in the dreaded 'Chingwe's Hole'. External and faraway experiences form an important frame through which prison life is mediated, as, for example, in the poem 'The Strip-Tease at Mikuyu Prison, 25 September, 1987' which compares the detainee's enforced removal of clothes with a striptease in London:

> It was not like the striptease at Birds' Nest
> On London Street Paddington in the seventies, with

> Each piece undone underscored by the thump of
> Your pint of London Bitter . . . (p. 43)

The lightheartedness of the London experience is in sharp contrast to the 'strip-tease' of the Malawian prison, which is characterised by methodical psychological torture:

> First, the ceremony of handcuff
>
> Disposal, with the warder's glib remarks about how
> Modern handcuffs really dug in when you tried to
>
> Fidget; then the instructions: take off your glasses,
> Your sweater, your shirt. Shove these with your
>
> Jacket into their shroud-white bag or your handbag (p. 43)

In the poem 'Chattering Wagtails' the poet employs a secondary narrative agent to reveal the hidden stories embedded in prison architecture:

> When the Secretary General of the Party
> First conceived the New Building it was
> On behalf of the people, to liberate
> Them from the despot they'd nominated
> For life and who had extorted their
> Traditional naivety to his craze. And
> When the Chief of Special Branch chose
> Himself head of detentions and detainees,
> The two conspired to cure the monster's
> Tics permanently here (p. 48)

While providing the means of distantiation, the secondary narrator enables the use of prison as a strategic place from which to uncover the suppressed history of the regime's own internal problems.

There are other narratives that the persona retrieves. In 'Scrubbing the Furious Walls of Mikuyu', he discovers inscriptions left on the wall by previous occupants of his cell:

> But here, scratches, insolent scratches!
> I have marvelled at the rock paintings
> of Mphunzi Hills once but these grooves
> and notches on the walls of Mikuyu Prison,
> how furious, what barbarous squiggles!
> How long did this anger languish without

> charge without trial without visit here and
> what justice committed? This is the moment
> we dreaded; when we'd all descend into
> the pit, alone; without a wife or a child
> without mother; without paper or pencil
> without a story . . . (p. 53)

The reference to pre-historic rock paintings makes the poet's document a record of the almost primal signs of resistance, articulations of the numerous helpless and unknown subterranean voices. The poet's determination that such voices should continue to speak is expressed most strongly in the following lines:

> We have liquidated too many
> brave names out of the nation's memory;
> I will not rub out another nor inscribe
> my own, more ignoble, to consummate this
> moment of truth I have always feared! (pp. 53–4)

Biblical narratives provide another resource for mediating prison experience. 'The Famished Stubborn Ravens of Mikuyu' contrasts biblical ravens with Banda's:

> These could not be Noah's ravens, these crows
> of Mikuyu Prison groaning on our roof-tops (p. 55)

Unlike Noah's ravens, those of Mikuyu prison are agents of torture:

> These can only be from the heathen stock of
> famished crows and carrion vultures sent here
> to peck at our insomnia and agony-blood-eyes (p. 55)

The comparison reveals the gap between the purported religious foundations of the new nation and the regime's political practice. In addition to biblical mythology, other forms of writing are used for strategic distantiation. In 'To the Unknown Dutch Post-card Sender (1988)', a postcard the persona receives and which provides momentary hope also foregrounds the limits of the plenitude of the immediate outside from which the persona has been excluded by the regime:

> You send me those Dutch tourist colours
> . . . You proffer Dutch bell-shaped houses beside
> Fruit trees, a family strolling along
> The avenue; this concrete church with
> Arches and Corinthian columns probably

> Beat the bombs . . .
> and I present
> You these malaria infested and graffiti
> Bespattered walls, without doctors, priests
> and twelve months of barred visits from
> Wife, daughters, son, relatives, friends! (p. 57)

The contrast between northern plenitude and southern poverty accentuates the degree of deprivation suffered by the detainee as the Malawian prison is presented as deprivation within deprivation.

It is the loss of writing's authenticity that, for the poet, signifies the degree to which the regime has dispensed with the common standards of honesty. In the poem 'Mikuyu Prison Visit of Head of Detainees', the regime is presented as given to forgery:

> He returned here in October 'for security
> Reasons' to get me to sign my Detention
> Order; 'Sign here, beside His Excellency
>
> Life President's own signature' (so visibly
> Photocopied from the Malawi Congress Party
> Card of 1960, perhaps for security reasons!) (p. 59)

Thus archives of prison life and government conduct are less a function of truthful representation than the constant rewriting by petty officials over whom even the government itself does not have much control, which reveals a serious defect at the centre of the regime's exercise of power. This is further evident in the poem, 'The Trip of Chief Commissioner of Prisons, (1990)' (p. 64), which depicts a prison official whose power is such that he grows marijuana on the prison farms and uses prison food for his family and prison favourites. Thus the president's preoccupation with political dissent is accompanied by blindness to the regime's own corruption.

Taken together, Mapanje's prison poems enact a geological critique of the system, undermining it from below, but as a whole, the collection shows Mapanje's attempt to mediate the immediate and traumatic experiences through a number of devices of estrangement.

Most of Frank Chipasula's verse was written in exile. It is thus less constrained in its criticism of the Malawian regime than the poetry produced inside the country. Nevertheless, like Mapanje's poetry written after his release from detention, Chipasula's shows a poet struggling to prevent his poetry becoming a mere documentary register of political oppression. In this regard, exile functions as another site from which the inside monolithic discourse is undermined, constituting itself as paradigmatically substitutable with the inside. Indeed, the devices of representation in exile poetry, in many ways, resemble those of the poetry written inside.

In Chipasula's anthology, *O Earth, Wait For Me*, Malawi is refigured as a lover, transferring the public to the private in order to highlight the sense of personal loss, but above all, as a way of concretising the abstract idea of belonging.[15] The poem, 'A Love Poem for My Country', depicts Malawi as an object both of desire and loathing:

> Here, week after week, the walls dissolve and are slim
> The mist is clearing and we see you naked like
> A body that is straining to find itself, but cannot
> And our hearts thumping with pulses of desire or fear,
> And our dreams are charred chapters of your history (p. 7)

In 'A Painful Love', the persona re-inscribes himself in the story of the nation, bringing to the fore the degree to which the fear of being forgotten or written out of the national story haunts the exiled subject:

> I am the one who went to gather
> handfuls of song on the mountain paths,
> songs that dangle on branches and grass
> like early morning pearly dew.
>
> Because the night cannot close his eyes
> insomnia has taken my dreams abroad (p. 7)

Exile becomes another name for a contained subjectivity, but in the dialectic of political subterraneanity, loss is recuperated as a site of another, if not different style of critique:

> Remember the heaviness of these years
> drenched in blood in the nightly witch-
> hunts,
> exiles trudging wearily the world's
> highways.
> Malawi, look at the cracked face in the
> ruins (p. 8)

The outside enables a more explicit critique of the inside. In 'When they took him away' (pp. 44–5), a third-person point of view is employed to narrate an incident of detention without sentimentality or sloganising:

> They did not give him time
> to kiss his children or stroke
> his wife before leaving.
> My brother did not weep.
>
> They bundled him roughly
> into the black Maria, chained,
> guarded, drove him to the grill.
> My brother did not weep (pp. 44–5)

A similar technique is used in the 'The Tea Picker', in which the poet registers the plight of farm workers:

> Your shoulders like overloaded sacks
> sag, droop and sink into your chest swelling
> into a grain of tuberculosis slowly ripening
> until your stale blood gives a deep tint
> to the choicest grade tea for the London
> Market.
> You wade through the soft tufts of the
> carpet
> Of undulating seawaves of the tea plants
> plucking tender buds violently by their
> slender necks . . . (p. 49)

The critique of the local regime focuses on its neo-colonial relations of production which mostly work to the advantage of international capital and the local comprador class:

> The high pitched wail in your sweet song
> swells
> the round belly of Tennet, his sons bloom as
> you wither (p. 49)

Thus, the external point of view enables the placing of the local authoritarian discourse in the broader international capitalist relations.

External subterraneanity also enables a more productive universalisation of the local. In a number of poems in the anthology, Chipasula, like Mapanje, connects the struggle to free Malawi with other international struggles against oppression. In the 'Beauty of Anger', commenting on South Africa, the poet asks:

> Tell me the colour of oppression,
> You who boldly went down the mine
> And, with pick and shovel, scooped out
> The metal ore later melted and moulded
> Into the shackles you strain from . . .
> I will be with the crowd watching you
> As you brandish and whip yourself, black,
> Through your fellow men for our colour too
>
> Harbours despots. Dispossessed now, you may
> Call to arms comrades in the dust, but
> Let your words stand up for the truth (pp. 51–2)

The discourse of Pan-Africanism serves not simply as a celebration of a romantic racial or geographical identity, but as a moment of sharing the limitations of essentialism as a basis for organising resistance to oppression, for the persona has learnt that sameness does not guarantee the erasure of other forms of difference.

There is also evidence of a geological rereading of history, as a way of revealing the contingent status of dominant political discourse, which, by recovering a moment anterior to the present-day political formation, presents externally located agency as a vehicle for counter-knowledge. In 'Warrior', the current regime in Malawi is portrayed as a reincarnation of the colonial order:

> Imitation warrior
> in synthetic monkey skins
>
> over a three piece suit,
> Inevitable overcoat, stick,
>
> homburg hat, dark glassed
> and false toothed smiles,
>
> begging his masters for a new name,
> a flag and a new anthem (p. 35)

According to Chipasula, one needs to understand the history of the modern African state in order to know, as Achebe says in a different context, 'where the rain started to beat us'. As Chipasula puts it in 'Going Back Patiently':

> And here we are back
> to the point we started from
> trying to point the path we took

> finding only traces and trails of ash
> on burned down tarmac highways
> showing that we too contributed
> to our own destruction
> letting it go on
> as if it never mattered (p. 25)

Exterior agency enacts a geological remapping of the nation's story, by going back to the origin beyond the historical origin and 'scanning the footprints of our memory', but also by retracing the history of resistance in the country:

> We must ask and ask and ask
> about the hidden road that Chilembwe took,
> sitting at crossroads in dilemma (p. 25)

The return to the past is not motivated by the desire to recover a finished text, but a movement of an enabling agency, which is in sharp contrast with the instrumentalist use of history of the regime. It is the representation of exile as a site of a more explicit interrogation of the inside that is being elaborated here.

It is not only the narrative of anti-colonial resistance that is retrieved, but also the concrete instances of colonial oppressive relations, mediated through the experience of the interpellated subjectivity of the Second World War veterans in 'Returning Soldiers' who:

> have returned from killing
> strangers without knowing why
> and they sing of their victory.
>
> The Union Jack flutters indifferently
> above their heads saluting a faraway king
> to whom they sing the songs of praise (p. 33)

The veterans' anger is deployed by the nationalists against colonialism, but nothing changes fundamentally between subjects and authority in the new dispensation. Nevertheless, for the poet, the anger that dislodged the colonialists cannot be obliterated, as it is still simmering beneath the yoke of oppression as he proclaims: 'these exhausted soldiers will always return' (p. 33). The poet erases the division between the colonial and post-colonial eras as the history of the nation is depicted as a continuation of oppressive social and political relations.

Exile, like home, mediates its critique through other texts in order to augment the authority of personal experience and dissolve the boundary between inside and outside. In 'Because the Wind Remembers' the poet recalls a film representation of a folk tale about a man who kills his brother in a foreign country because he fears that the brother will put him to shame when they get home because he is the wealthier of the two. Thus, reminiscences of home provide a way of articulating the fear of betrayal among exiles.

Sometimes it is artefacts which provide the means of imagining home. In 'A Man Searching for the Truth', dedicated to the Malawian artist Berlings Kaunda, the poet celebrates the sculptor's quest for meaning:

> Your hands know the shape
> Of truth, follow feeling through the
> intricacies
> of the deep curves in our wood, stone or
> mind,
> Each layer baring a new wise world, spring-
> filled
> With the primal song sung, the original
> force found (p. 70)

The act of investing creative practice with epistemological agency relates equally to the poetic practice itself which assumes the role of an interrogative discourse in a context where discursive clarity is interdicted. In short, Frank Chipasula's *O Earth, Wait For Me* exemplifies how exile, as a form of political subterraneanity, transforms the opposition between inside and outside, on which totalitarian regimes base their imaginary stability, into a strategic position, from which the inside can be undermined. Moreover, the outside is the place from which the fictional narratives of inside can be stripped completely, as other temporalities of the story of the nation are retrieved.

Clearly, Malawian poetry demonstrates the ability of poets to inhabit both the inside and outside of an oppressive political formation, through an aesthetic of concealment in which agency reformulates its identity and relocates itself to circumvent censorship. However, the political situation which shaped the character of the poetry has been replaced by a more democratic regime which so far has shown an exceptional capacity for tolerance of criticism. This poses a great challenge for Malawian poets. The example of Steve Chimombo's recent long poem shows the pitfalls of an aesthetic that has not adapted itself adequately to changed political circumstances. Chimombo's *A Referendum of the Forest Creatures* (1993), written during the transition from a one-party state to multi-party democracy, employs the same methods of representation as his earlier anthologies.[16] For instance, the competition for power between the various political parties is represented in terms of the animal world. However, the use of allegory here does not defamiliarise reality convincingly enough for our perception of the political situation being described to be enriched. This is evident in the opening section where the subject of the whole poem is sketched out:

> The Kalilombe's tongue used to sing
> In impenetrable verbal thickets
> At the height of universal woe or doom;
> At the brink of disaster or edge of
> catastrophe;
> Or the advent of another Napolo.
> But now, the tongue circumcised, sings
> Wearing webs of moonlight
> Garlanded by soft stardust
> and loops of translucent rain drops
> of the referendum of the forest creatures (p. 1)

Though the metaphorical density of myth and folklore is still there, it no longer has the multiple referentiality of the geological agency of the *Napolo* collection. As the poem develops, its subtitles begin to read like newspaper headlines: 'The Forest Republic', 'Lament of Prisons', 'Lament of the Roads', 'A referendum is announced', 'A State Banquet' and 'A Crop Inspection Tour'. The formulaic structure of the poem is shorn of the complexity of the structural organisation of *Napolo* whose dialectical and cyclic movement enacts the intricate web of political positioning.

The Russian Formalist, Victor Shklovsky, once said that 'habituation devours works of art, clothes, furniture, one's wife (perhaps even one's husband).'[17] Notwithstanding the mechanistic view of literary development underpinning Shklovsky's statement, the example of recent Malawian poetry suggests that Malawian poets need to be wary of quarrying the same ground with the same implements if they are to preserve the stylistic inventions of the past.

### Notes

1. Jonathan Sawday, 'Reading Renaissance Poetry', *The Bloomsbury Guide to English Literature*, London: Bloomsbury, 1989, pp. 201–4.
2. For a detailed discussion of the subversive function of orature, see Leroy

Vail and Landeg White, *Power and the Praise Poem: Southern African Voices in History*, London: James Currey, 1991, pp. 278–318.

3. Steve Chimombo, *Napolo Poems*, Manchichi, 1987, pp. iiv-ix.

4. See J. Matthew Schoffeleers, *River of Blood: The Genesis of a Martyr Cult in Southern Malawi, c. A.D. 1600*, Madison, Wis.: The University of Wisconsin Press, 1992, p. 47.

5. Mbona was a famous Malawian rainmaker during the seventeenth century. He was accused of withholding rains by interfering with the rainmaking powers of a senior rainmaker. The King ordered that he should be killed, but it was not easy, for Mbona would magically turn himself into a tree, an animal or mist. In the end, he told them that they should take a blade of grass and chop off his head with it, if they wanted to kill him. After his death, he turned into a serpent, like Napolo. For a good and complex account of the Mbona myth, see Schoffeleers, *River of Blood*.

6. Rev. John Chilembwe, an American-trained theologian, in 1915 mobilised farm workers and members of his church, The Providence Industrial Mission, against the colonial government in Nyasaland (Malawi). He was captured and shot, but his name inspired subsequent generations of nationalists. The Banda regime saw itself as the successor to Chilembwe and other early nationalists. However, opponents of the regime regarded it as having abandoned the ideals of selflessness and patriotism which Chilembwe represented. For a detailed account of the Chilembwe uprising, see George Shepperson and T. Price, *Independent African*, Edinburgh: Edinburgh University Press, 1958.

7. Gayatri Chakravorty Spivak, 'Woman in Difference: Mahasweta Devi's *Douloti the Bountiful*', in Andrew Parker et al. (eds), *Nationalisms and Sexualities*, London: Routledge, 1992, p. 99.

8. According to Michel Pecheux, a good subject is one whose subjectivity accords with that of an interpellating sovereign and the bad subject is one who counter-identifies with dominant ideology. Michel Pecheux, *Language, Semantics and Ideology*, London: Macmillan, 1982.

9. See I. and J. Linden, *Catholics, Peasants and Chewa Resistance in Nyasaland*, London: Heinemann, 1974.

10. Jack Mapanje, *Of Chameleons and Gods*, London: Heinemann, 1981. Page references will be to this edition and will be included in the text.

11. See the following works: Angela Smith, *East African Writing in English*, London: Macmillan, 1989, pp. 102–9; Adrian Roscoe and Mpalive-Hangson Msiska, *The Quiet Chameleon: Modern Poetry from Central Africa*, London: Hans Zell, 1992, pp. 44–6; Vail and White, *Power and the Praise Poem*; Landeg White, 'Chattering Wagtails: Jack Mapanje interviewed by Landeg White', *Kunapipi*, No. 19 (Summer, 1994), pp. 54–7.

12. See Felix Mnthali, *When Sunset Comes to Sapitwa*, London: Longman, 1982, pp. 82–4.

13. Jack Mapanje, *Chattering Wagtails of Mikuyu Prison*, Oxford: Heinemann, 1993. Further page references will be to this edition and will be included in the text.

14. See Vail and White, *Power and the Praise Poem*, for further discussion of this issue.
15. Frank Chipasula, *O Earth, Wait For Me*, Bloomfontein: Ravan Press, 1984.
16. Steve Chimombo, *A Referendum of Forest Creatures*, Zomba: Wasi Publications, 1993.
17. See Lee T. Lemon, *Russian Formalist Criticism: Four Essays*, Lincoln: Nebraska, 1965, p. 12.

# 'The mid-point of the scream': The Writing of Dambudzo Marechera

## ABDULRAZAK GURNAH

We are not at the beginning, we are not at the end – we are at the mid-point of the scream. . . . That, for me, is the unifying factor of contemporary literature.[1]

In his remarkable story 'House of Hunger', Dambudzo Marechera constructs a complex and critical social metaphor around concrete space.[2] The 'house' image is the most striking example of this method, sustained in the story in eloquent and nuanced variety. In the most direct way, it represents the squalid and dilapidated African township in segregated Rhodesia, what Marechera refers to elsewhere as a 'seething cesspit'.[3] But the house images also represent other things: the fragmented community living in the township, the oppressing family, and the frenzy of the individual mind. The future's emptiness is figured as 'life stretched out like a series of hunger-scoured hovels' (p. 3), while the empty house near the end of the story, a scene of loneliness and utter futility, is 'a picture of my skull' (p. 77). The dereliction of public spaces – toilets, bars – demonstrates the physical deprivation as well as the profound decline of the community. From the opening of the story, these images describe disorientation and distance, for both the narrator as well as everyone he knows. 'House of Hunger' is both the outside world and the inner condition, body hunger as well as 'soul-hunger', until in the end 'one steadily became' the same inside as the 'gut-rot' outside (p. 13). Thus the mind's entrapment is also figured in the 'house' image – rooms run off other rooms like an inescapable warren – while the image of the 'warren' simultaneously describes the mind's inadequacy against 'the painful reality of concrete history'.[4] But the mind is trapped by more than the foulness of the world and its consequences. Its desire for release from the 'concrete history' of racist and colonial Rhodesia can only be fulfilled through Mission education and the ambiguous seductions of European learning – ambiguous because for the colonised such learning, with its narratives of European righteousness and triumph, can never be innocent.

*The House of Hunger*, in both the title story and the seven other shorter pieces (only one other, 'The Writer's Grain', gets into double figures), describes the complex yearnings and pains of the township boy who goes to Mission school, to University in Rhodesia and Oxford, and has ambitions to write. This sequence is very like Marechera's own history, and it is difficult to fault Veit-Wild's bald summary, at least in so far as it refers to *The House of Hunger*: 'The roots of Dambudzo Marechera the writer lie in the overcrowded township where he spent his youth and childhood.'[5] Also, Marechera's own account of his work and his method stresses its autobiographical emphasis, as we shall see later.

Marechera was born in Vengere, the African township of Rusape in eastern Rhodesia. He was the third of nine children, who together with their parents lived in a two-roomed house belonging to the council. His father worked as an assistant to a truck driver, and later as a mortuary attendant. His mother worked as a nanny to a white family in Rusape. At the age of 13, Marechera became a boarder at St Augustine's, a prestigious Mission school for Africans. He was to stay there for six crucial years, recording academic triumphs and reading widely in European literatures. During this period, his family's circumstances entered a catastrophic decline. His father was knocked down and killed at night by a hit-and-run driver. Later his mother lost her job as a nanny (because she asked for a pay-rise), was evicted from her house and had no choice but to move with her children to the shanty-area of the township called Tangwena. They built a shanty-house for themselves and shared the filth of their surroundings with other destitutes. The mother took to drink and became a prostitute. On the one hand, St Augustine's was a sanctuary of order and self-fulfilment, on the other Tangwena was a place of poverty and humiliation – a house of hunger. Despite all this, Mrs Marechera was able to keep her son (and all her other children) at school, and Marechera graduated brilliantly, winning a scholarship to the University of Rhodesia where he went to read English. It was there that he started drinking, an aspect of his life which would grow to mythic proportions in years to come. Just over a year later, amid student disturbances that followed episodes of petty harrasment and talk of creating a 'blacks-only university' in the whites-only parliament – because black students made the place filthy – Marechera was one of fourteen students who were expelled from the University. With the help of his tutors, he was offered a place at New College, Oxford in England. He was there from October 1974 until he was expelled again in March 1976, disorderly, drunk and unable to do his academic work. It was during this period after Oxford, living on friends and hand-outs, a period of distress and some despair, that he began to write 'House of Hunger'.

In many ways 'House of Hunger' is a characteristically *modernist* text.

The narrative begins in the middle of an action – the narrator leaving – abruptly breaking into an arbitrary universe. After this the narrative pays no further attention to chronology. The narration moves backwards and then forwards in what is predominantly a monologue, hard-bitten and cynical, but also with a note of confession and truth-telling. The narrator is unnamed: unheroic and victimised. His narration is fragmentary and irreverent, at times privileging idiom over meaning and suggesting both the alienation of the narrator and the disorderly reality which the text can only engage with in metaphors of chaos and violence. Existence is a 'seething cesspit' where brutalised people act out their betrayal and anguish.

Yet despite its familiar metaphors of alienation, the text is anchored in precise social and historical space: Rhodesia under Ian Smith's government. The paradox is that the writing deliberately aspires for this historical specificity while aligning itself with conceptions of 'literature' that take such particularity to be pernicious. This affiliation is evident in a remark that Marechera made in the lecture 'The African Writer's Experience of European Literature' referred to above:

> From early on in my life I have viewed literature as a unique universe that has no internal divisions. I do not pigeon-hole it by race or language or nation. It is an ideal cosmos co-existing with this crude one. (p. 362)

To a great extent, this is a response to the criticism that Marechera's writing is 'alien' to Africa, a criticism he had both anticipated in 'Thought-tracks in the Snow' and to which he later responded in a number of ways in both *Black Sunlight* and *The Black Insider*.[6] Juliet Okonkwo, for example, had cautiously praised *The House of Hunger* for its 'energy' and its capacity to see the unexpected 'relatedness' of phenomena, but found Marechera's gift 'wasted' because of its 'nihilism'. 'All this is alien to Africa,' she wrote in 1981:

> Marechera has in these stories grafted a decadent avant-garde European attitude and style to experiences that emanate from Africa and Africans. . . . Africa, in which years of expectation are beginning to flower into full promise, cannot afford the luxury of such distorted and self-destructive 'sophistication' from her writers. But then, when Marechera's persona left the shores of Angola for Britain, he knew deep inside him that he 'had said goodbye to Africa, forever'.[7]

Okonkwo's voice suggests that she speaks from a consensual position which gives her assessment authority. Marechera's stories are done cynically and demonstrate the writer's self-treachery – and both are irrelevant to Africa's needs, as we all know. It is a familiar argument, including the device of making the offending writer treacherous to a collectivity as well as to him/herself. Along similar lines, Musaemura Zimunya, who was later to aid Marechera in a number of ways, said of *The House of Hunger*: 'the vision is preponderantly private and indulgent. . . . The artist . . . succumbs to the European temptation in a most slatternly exhibition.'[8] In his lucid and well-contextualised essay 'New Writing from Zimbabwe', Mbulelo V. Mzamane made a case against the reading of *The House of Hunger* as 'nihilistic', and argued instead that Marechera was the spokesman for the disenchantment of a generation. In this respect, the essay sees the narrator's profound alienation from his environment and the consequent crushing of the spirit, and therefore the focus on violence and defeat, as an expression of political disillusion with Smith and Muzorewa – not self-hate but outrage. But Mzamane also has a little lecture for Marechera:

> In this respect it can be said that his literary analogies owe very little to the African tradition, and rob his work of a Zimbabwean authenticity. Indeed there is a sense in which Marechera could try to write within the 'African tradition' – and that does not necessarily imply churning out conformist or imitational work – instead of scoffing at such suggestions as the Nigerian student makes in 'Thought-tracks in the Snow'.[9]

It is to criticism like this that Marechera is responding with his refusal of an instrumental account of 'literature'. As he declared defiantly in the lecture referred to above: 'The writer has no duty, no responsibility, other than to his art' (p. 366). There are obvious echoes in this, as in the earlier remark on literature as a 'unique universe', of the European high-modernist position which saw engagement with writing at any level – producing as well as consuming it – as a vocation, requiring application and discipline, but also requiring a sensibility which refuses the petty for the ideal. The roots of this élitism lie in a rejection of the pulp-individualism of poetic discourse of the late nineteenth century in Europe, as much as in the social transformations that brought with them challenges to bourgeois culture. The writers of high modernism claimed allegiance not to 'race or language or nation' but to an idea of a cultural tradition which went back in a direct line to 'classical Greece', to a moment of essential European origin. This is not the place to pursue this aspect of modernism, nor is it the intention of this discussion to suggest that modernism was an unfragmented set of positions. It is to locate Marechera's description of 'literature', and his disavowal of its particularity, in a historical context. The claim that 'literature' is 'a unique universe', in other words, is implicated in ways of looking at the world and seeing there hierarchies which privilege the 'race . . . language . . . nation' of Europe over its irrational, inarticulate Other. Marechera's text is well aware of this, as is evident in 'Thought-tracks in the Snow', as well as in the story 'Black Skin What Mask', and the theme figures prominently in 'House of Hunger' itself in its treatment of Mission education. The alignment with the 'ideal cosmos' aspiration for literature is primarily a refusal of the cultural-nationalist argument that has dominated African cultural discourse for most of this century. The insistence of that argument on identity loyalty for writing finds an echo in the liberation rhetoric for women which is mocked in 'House of Hunger' as a capacity 'to shout LIBERATION, POLYGAMY without feeling that something is unhinged' (p. 44), and in both cases the demand for obedience is a means to dominate and direct. This mistrust of authoritarian direction finds more intense expression later in the anarchic rebellion in *Black Sunlight* and in the endless war in *The Black Insider*, but it is also evident in *The House of Hunger*.[10] In some respects Marechera's is a modernist argument disengaged from its cultural context, focusing selectively on the mystique of the writer creating in poverty and freedom, for example, and unable to resist its ironic and transgressive postures. His writing, though, also has the scepticism about hegemonic narratives which is so characteristic of modernism. As he says of himself in the lecture 'The African Writer's Experience of European Literature':

> I have been an outsider in my own biography, in my country's history, in the world's terrifying possibilities. It is, therefore, quite natural for me to respond with the pleasure of familiar horror to that section of European literature which reflects this. (p. 364)

In this sense, Marechera's writing is both an account of alienation and a celebration of alienated writing.

All his writing, from *The House of Hunger* to *The Black Insider*, contests the possibility of community. Marechera sometimes cited 'the Beat Generation' writers as an influence on his work: writers like Kerouac, Ginsberg and Burroughs. He also cited several dozen others from different countries and a variety of centuries, but he admired 'the Beats' for their valorisation of individualism and confrontation, and for their vision of a tormenting and indifferent world. It seems completely plausible that Marechera should say that Ginsberg's opening lines to his poem 'Howl' 'were echoing in my ears' during the writing of 'House of Hunger'.[11] As with 'the Beats', his text figures communal life as nightmare and individual fate as a kind of self-liberating frenzy. But as we have seen, especially in the case of *The House of Hunger*, Marechera's writing has a historical specificity which takes it beyond alienated outrage. The joyless and fragmented township in which the 'brutalised humanity' of black Rhodesia live, had come about via 'capitalists, imperialists . . . And the bloody whites' (p. 9) – arising out of the need to have a pool of labour nearby, and a desire to keep it segregated and out of sight of the whites. The Africans in the township came from everywhere, as Marechera describes, 'from every place you could think of in the country . . . from Malawi . . . from Zambia and so on; so there was no common culture at home. The only common thing among all of us was work'[12] – as well as poverty, squalor and violence with its consequences of endemic disorder and 'gut-rot'.

This absence of 'common culture,' of community, is powerfully figured in the representation of 'family'. In many African fictional texts, among them dominant voices over the last few decades, the father figure appears as the unifying authority. In Chinua Achebe's *Things Fall Apart* (1958), for example, Okonkwo's neurosis stems from the failure of his father to act in the 'manly' way demanded by the customs of his people, and Okonkwo's own actions are governed largely by a desire to occupy fatherhood with appropriate dignity. In all four novels the patriarchal figure represents the unified centre. In *No Longer At Ease* (1960), the Umuofia Progressive Union acts as a gathering of village men keeping everyone up to the mark, which is only the patriarchal hierarchy in metaphor. In *Arrow of God* (1964), Ezeulu performs this function in an even more direct manner, imagining himself the spiritual father of Umuaro and also able to make life and death decisions for his wives and children. Even Chief Nanga in *A Man of the People* (1966) is the patriarchal figure gone wrong, and hence in some way reflects the degeneracy in the community. This is not to say that Achebe's use of the patriarchal figure is not complex. Okonkwo's obsession with manliness also makes him inflexible and intolerant. Obi's father's Christian zeal cannot overcome more deeply grounded horror of the slave curse which would befall his family were Obi to marry the young woman he wishes to. Ezeulu's wounded pride drives him to punish Umuaro in order to avenge himself and his god. But the criticism of these patriarchal figures is largely the degree to which they have failed to act with the appropriate sense of restraint and responsibility. Their failures trigger the profound social events which are the real subject of Achebe's fictions, and their dramas and their sons' dramas have a significance which their wives and daughters, twittering away in the background, do not even aspire to share.

In Ngũgĩ wa Thiong'o's writing, the patriarch progressively becomes the towering figure of authority.[13] Soyinka's *Death and the King's Horseman* (1975) poses the dilemma of how the 'whole' ways of the people are to survive through the actions of a father and his son. Elesin Oba, the King's Horseman, fails to commit suicide at the last minute because the pleasures of life were too sweet to give up, and his son Olunde performs the act of sacrifice in his place. Olunde is a student in England, nurtured to a Western education by the District Officer and his wife, and therefore by committing suicide demonstrates his greater allegiance to his culture and its viability. For it is supremely the act of violence on the self which affirms the continuing authority of the Yoruba cultural and historical perspective that is figured as under threat. Elesin Oba's failure to follow his King joyfully into the spirit-world had endangered the whole Yoruba cosmos because it cast doubt on the inviolability of its observances. Even if the act of allegiance required is as patently mindless as the suicide of a son for the failure of a father, the renunciation is necessary to affirm the integrity of the culture. Above all, the playing out of the drama confirms once again that it is fathers and their sons whose actions are capable of bringing about such transformations. And if we take 'history' to be a narrative of the community's view of itself, that narrative cannot but be dependent on an idea of an essential unity. Not only does the patriarchal figure come to suggest this unity, but it is here also that the idea of 'community' is located.

In Marechera's story, the patriarchal figure is 'de-centred', and the home and the family represent chaos and oppression. The father of the story's narrator is a long-distance truck driver. He is promiscuous and an alcoholic with a savage streak of violence against his own sons. The mother too is a heavy drinker, and takes other men to her bed in front of her children. The elder brother Peter is vicious and violent, boiling with rage against everything and made even more manic by recent imprisonment. He beat 'his woman', Immaculate, until she was 'just a red stain', because that was how men behaved with women. They beat them, possessed them, and knew themselves to be more than worthless. So, on this occasion, Peter beats Immaculate as 'a show' for his younger brother, to demonstrate his manhood to him. The narrator has slept with her, and maliciously speculates that her child is fathered by him rather than his brother. Rather than being a metaphor for social unity (even in its oppressions), here the family is figured as bizarre and sadistic, and every relationship and role reveals the individual's capacity for despair. And Immaculate provoked Peter even more because she somehow in this nightmare 'clung rebelliously to her own unique spirit' (p. 4).

The biography of Peter describes the frenzy that has become endemic within the community, feeding on the violence which simultaneously destroys their lives. While Peter is beating Immaculate, her baby is crying in the darkness in the other room. The neighbours are torturing a cat (to death eventually), and its wails mingle with the baby's screams. At the same time, because Immaculate desires and responds to kindness, the narrator 'loathes' her (p. 7). Immaculate, so named by a father who is an over-zealous Christian but also a fraud, is ambivalently figured. She is one of the few images of tenderness in the story. She is both an image of inspiration – 'I could still glimpse the pulses of her raw courage in her wide animal-like eyes. They were eyes that stung you to tears' (p. 4) – and also an image of loathing because of the duplicity of the promise she offers – 'It was not possible that a being like her could have been conceived in the grim squalor of our history. She made me want to dream, made me believe in visions, in hope. But the rock and grit of the earth denied this' (p. 12). So the image of Immaculate, one eye puffed from the blows, another completely closed, also describes a mindless optimism, a habit of hoping which she sustains despite her cruel misuse: 'And the holy bitch still dreamed, still hoped, still saw visions' (p. 17). In another story in the same collection, 'Burning in the Rain,' the description of Margaret recalls Immaculate: 'Once more he wondered how and by what alchemy she had been conceived out of such squalor' (p. 84). Both are images of impossible beauty and delicacy in the ugly township, a special quality which the environment mocked before turning the women into 'stains'.

Early in 'House of Hunger' the narrator describes his first sexual experience. He goes to a prostitute and catches VD: 'The experience left me marked by an irreverent disgust for women which has never left me' (p. 3). Mbulelo V. Mzamane sees this as an act of 'depravity' which in itself is a reflection of 'their ailing society' ('New Writing from Zimbabwe', p. 207), sex and violence offering brutal short-lived ecstacy for the men and women in the township. Marechera himself is much more direct on the way women are figured in his story. They were 'the ultimate victims of racism in this country' 'because at that time black men were used to being the slaves of the whites and the only slaves they had were their women'.[14] It is for this championing of women, and the sympathy the narrator feels for the special burden of young black women in a racist culture,[15] that Mzamane grants him 'strong feminist views' (p. 207). This conception of sexuality as a metaphor for exploitation and dominance is no more brutally portrayed than in the wife-beating incident which ends with the man publicly raping the wife, expressing his disdainful authority over her with this display (p. 50).

But there is another dimension to this 'irreverent disgust'. In the same interview in which he had spoken of women as 'slaves' ('And I make no apology for the way I have depicted that'), Marechera described his disgust at the discovery that he had caught VD after his first encounter with a prostitute, which was also his first sexual act with a woman – precisely the incident which appears in the story. He continued:

> that left me very much with a certain disgust about sex, about women. I can never really divorce the feeling that the very desire, the lust, the passion for a woman, will make me come out of this more and more diseased. (p. 17)

In 'House of Hunger' sex is an act of rage and frenzy, no more clearly achieved than in the description of the coupling with the skin-lightened dancer who takes the narrator home one despairing night. The narrative powerfully fuses images of alienation, violent containment and sex:

> That night all the lights I had known flashed through my mind. . . . The skin-lightened dancer – she was burning, burning the madness out of me. The room had taken over my mind. My hunger had become the room. There was a thick darkness where I was going. It was a prison. It was the womb. It was blood clinging closely like a swamp in the grass-matted lowlands of my life. (p. 25)

And this way of seeing sex as violence and degradation is evident in both the narrator's 'irreverent disgust' and the manner in which it is metonymically represented as 'a stain'. (In another story in the collection, 'The Writer's Grain', the narrator's double summarises brutally: 'every woman is a stain on a sheet' p. 107.) It is also evident in the way the common form of woman in the township is the prostitute: Nestar, the beautiful coloured girl ('half and half') who ends up fulfilling the fantasies of white men; Julia, who is 'transformed' into 'a beerhall doll'; the narrator's mother who 'brings men home' and services them while her son, made calm with threats of violence, lies wide-awake on the floor beside the bed. Sooner or later every woman ends up being a whore.

In contrast to the way other women are portrayed in the story, Immaculate is idealised. Despite the beatings and her dumb sexual needs, the narrator invests her with a reverence that is only matched by the description of Patricia. Of the latter, the narrator says: 'There was a tiny burning in her eyes; a fierce tenderness I had never seen before' (p. 71). The idealisation of Immaculate, and of Patricia and Margaret, lies specifically in their impossible delicay, their unalikeness to other women. Immaculate has a stubborn quality of tenderness which makes her resist brutalisation against the odds: 'And the holy bitch still dreamed, still hoped, still saw visions' (p. 17). Patricia, the 'club-footed' white liberal woman, already marginalised in an authoritarian and racist culture, and further marginalised by her affair with the narrator, finally retreats into solipsism before achieving a kind of muted self-expression. And Margaret's gentleness in 'Burning in the Rain' only brings out 'the ape' in the narrator during their first sexual union, when the act is figured as humiliation accompanied by monstrous feelings of guilt and rage. The 'ape in the mirror' who surfaces here is the narrator's submerged self, ugly and brutish, but an inescapable companion to the life of the mind, more substantial than Margaret's resigned acceptance and more real than 'the huge emptiness' of the narrator's own particular experience. The mute tenderness of these women, their capacity for vision, is none the less aligned with the brutish environment it is contrasted with. In the end, these women will fall victim to brutality, because their self-fulfilment is only possible through sensuality.

For the narrator, the secret life of the mind is more real than himself, as is suggested by the topos of the physical being as empty or absent. In 'The Writer's Grain' the self exists as a separate consciousness, one which coldly observes the other, floundering, guilt-ridden, ugly 'self'. By this doubling, the narrator is figured as divided and alienated into habitual scepticism. The 'circles and squares' which the narrator writes, and which are transformed into grains that are a concrete symbol of the narrator-as-writer, turn out on analysis to contain 'nothing'. Yet paradoxically, this 'nothing' is everything. The writer's mind, in other words, cannot be given a substantial representation in such a way, for its existence is above all 'an act of desperate faith' (p. 101). The writer becomes one, in the first place, by 'faith' and vocation. It is this act which releases the imagination, that 'ever watchful devil' 'which makes us frantic and anxious and . . . empties us in our very fulfilling' (p. 103). This image of writing as a process unavoidably incomplete and futile, and yet vital and inescapable, recalls T. S Eliot's lines in 'East Coker'[16] as much as Marechera's own words which form the epigraph to this chapter:

> We are not at the beginning, we are not at the end – we are at the mid-point of the scream. . . . That, for me, is the unifying factor of contemporary literature.

With such statements Marechera aligns himself with the modernist enterprise in literature. His narrator in 'The Writer's Grain' echoes this faith in writing by describing it as the 'only secretest part of me that was somehow significant' (p. 106). The life of the mind is valorised as the narrator's only means of keeping at bay the ugly and mocking phantom other – the 'real' world. But the 'real' world with all its brutishness is also the writer's subject, so the act of affirmation is also one of self-wounding, one of confronting guilt and ugliness.

The beatings in 'House of Hunger' are only the most concrete form of coercion and exploitation which is endemic to existence, and the chaos in this small social sphere indicates larger confusions and failures as it repeats itself across every other situation. If 'family' is this bizarre torment, 'community' is only more anonymously savage. In this context, that is to say Rhodesia, a late-twentieth-century African territory still ruled by Europeans at the time Marechera was writing the story, 'community' also implies and requires a narrative of pre-colonial plenitude. But 'community' is contested here, as is the possibility of a narrative which would describe its historical integrity, would rebut the atomised communities of the imperialist narrative. The desire for a unified narrative, which is a yearning for lost wholeness in historical and cultural experience, is also a desire for order. It imposes and expresses an imperative which is simultaneously self-defining and self-validating. A number of African texts, of course, set out to do just this by offering resistance to the self-justifying accounts of the European incursion into 'primitive' Africa, and these texts have taken many narrative forms. Ngũgĩ uses Gikuyu creation myths as both an authentic expression of the African self and as a claim to ownership of the land. Achebe describes a complex and ordered community, and does so in direct challenge to European narratives that had seen Africa as a place of darkness and unknowable strangeness. Soyinka has announced himself engaged in a project of 'self-retrieval', and this is clear in his valorisation of Yoruba myth and culture. As will have been clear already, it is precisely this self-definition and self-validation which Marechera's story challenges. In 'House of Hunger', the narrator is unable to offer resistance to the imperialist narrative by valorising history. His refrain of 'where are the bloody heroes' articulates this inability. The period of rupture for Rhodesia (or what became Rhodesia) were the events which led to the invasion by the Pioneer Column from South Africa in 1890, after Rudd, the agent for Cecil Rhodes, had tricked the Ndebele King Lobengula into signing a document giving away land he did not even have a right to. The document provided the justification for invasion, war and conquest, as both the King's people and the Mashona were bent into submission with Maxim guns. This is the 'black hero' the narrator comes up with in his mocking monologue on 'history' addressed at Julia, who, in any case, is inattentive with lust:

> Poor chap. I don't like to blame him though, for making us all like this. Of course he was rather silly. . . . Deserved what he got. Like a baboon poking his hand into a gourd-trap.
>
> . . .
>
> The one thing that bugs me about the man is that he even loved white men. That he killed my people like cattle, the way Germans killed Jews. And he loved white men. Even trusted them. And then he wanted to know if Queen Victoria really existed. Wives and all that. What I mean is: is this all there is to our history? There is a stinking deceit at the heart of it. Petty intrigues. White hoboes. Bloody missionaries singing Onward Christian Soldiers. Where are the bloody heroes? (p. 43).

Elsewhere in the story this view of history is expressed in another version of 'gut-rot' which suggests a larger paradigm of colonial rupture – not just white domination but a proliferation of consequences: 'We were whores; eaten to the core by the syphilis of the white man's coming' (p. 75). The 'white' diatribes are not simply a matter of blaming Europeans for the 'gut-rot' of the times, but of seeing the 'soul-hunger' colonial oppression created in the colonised. In other words, it is not just colonialism in the sense of injustice and denial of rights which is the issue, but the transformation of the colonised. In a passage of crushing despair, one of the narrator's friends, Philip, desc..bes their condition in this way:

> There is nothing to make one particularly glad one is a human being and not a horse, or a lion, or a jackal, or come to think of it a snake. Snakes. There's just dirt and shit and urine and blood and smashed brains. There's dust and fleas and bloody whites and roaches and dogs trained to bite black people in the arse. There's venereal disease and beer and

lunacy and just causes. There's technology to drop on your head wherever you stop to take a leak. There's white shit in our leaders and white shit in our dreams and white shit in our history and white shit on our hands in anything we build or pray for. Even if that was okay there's still sell-outs and informers and stuck-up students and get-rich-fast bastards and live-now-think-later punks who are just as bad. (pp. 58–9)

The narrator's response to this is a post-modern one: that we can only see things in fragments and yet futilely desire the large design. 'Only rarely do we see the imminence of wholes' (p. 60). Against Philips's despair and the narrator's attempt at disengagement, is set a third position, that of Stephen, avidly and militantly African: 'he was always petitioning for African history to be taught' (p. 64). But Stephen is also 'mean, a bully; a typical African bully'. His arguments are authoritarian and the account he favours of what it is to be African desires to dispense with complexity in favour of a homogenising narrative of the unified African self. His special victim at school is a boy called Edmund, who is quiet, reads Russian writing avidly and is kept at school by the money his mother is able to earn as a prostitute. It is interesting how elements of Marechera's own story have been displaced to Edmund's, the boy tormented by Stephen's aggressive African nationalism. Eventually Stephen provokes Edmund into a fight then beats him insensible. Later Edmund runs off to join the guerrillas, and his picture appears in the newspaper as a captured guerrilla, the only survivor amid twenty-two corpses. Both in the fight with Stephen and in the newspaper photograph, Edmund is the pathetic image of Zimbabwean heroism, 'doggedly' living out his 'tortured dreams in the face of humiliation' (p. 61).

Beatings, oppression, poverty, and apparently limitless self-contempt. Is this anything more, to quote from Marechera's story, than 'black despair lit up by suicidal vision'? Is the resignation to beatings also a desire for them, an expression of profound guilt? For the calamitous and contingent nature of this existence is not to do with moral alienation but brutal indifference to individual suffering. Despite the narrator's agony, 'the sun still climbed as swiftly as ever and darkness fell upon the land as quickly as in the years that had gone' (p. 4). Both here and in the other stories ('The Writer's Grain', for example), existence is figured as malign chaos in the natural world. This is brilliantly evident in the description of the storm which climaxes the narrator's nervous breakdown:

That rain, it drummed the drum until the drum burst, stitching the mind with thongs of lightning. It was like a madman talking incessantly; whispering rapidly into the ear of the sky. It was like a man who, suddenly bereaved, breaks down and hurls himself at the wall. It was a great river plunging over a falls and roaring the cerebral rage that can only be broken by the rocks below. The rain, it broke down the workers' compound; it felled the huts with its brute knuckleduster. It knocked down the mud walls and brought the flimsy roofs crushing down upon the unlucky occupants. All over the compound men women and children fought for their homes that night, building, rebuilding, groaning against its blows until once again the walls of that malice came crushing down. And still the skies dribbled compulsively upon the earth. That rain: it chattered its sharp little teeth; it foamed at the mouth against everything. . . . Something diseased had been unleashed among us' (p. 32).

The unrestrained power of the rain here figures a mindless universe, and its boiling malice suggests that existence is a malady. But the voices and the shadowy figures that had preceded this explosion of malice had beeen taunting and accusing, mocking the narrator for the division and alienation he represents as a result of his 'Mission' education. When he says 'I knew then what was in store for me' (p. 33), he refers to the discontent which is a consequence of this experience of alienation and self-knowledge.

In Peter's summary, the narrator is 'like this' because of 'education'. We see an example of the divisions that 'education' brings about in the scene in which the narrator as a boy returns joyfully home 'on heat with life', and talks to his mother in English, unaware that he is doing so. His mother takes his behaviour to be mockery and slaps him. Later, the father beats him violently, knocking his front teeth out and 'looking down at me as though I was a cockroach in a delicatessen' (p. 14). The scene is significant in a number of ways. Not only does it reveal the deeply internalised confusions in the boy's mind, but it demonstrates just how brutally and casually oppressive is the family space, and just how capriciously authoritarian the patriarchal figure is in this environment. In another sense, 'education' is seen as divisive because it diminishes the authority of the unified community. In both Ngũgĩ's and Achebe's fiction, exposure to European 'education' is shown to have, at best, problematic consequences. Despite their problematic nature, though, these outcomes suggest a dynamic potential. Ngũgĩ's *Weep Not, Child* (1964) was the first fiction by an African which Marechera read, and he did so with great excitement. The story of the African boy who through his talents and labour gets into Siriana High School must have had its own echoes for Marechera. In 'House of Hunger', though, we see without amelioration the stark polarity 'education' brings about. An example of this is the 'Shona–English' argument that is figured as taking place in the narrator's mind, and which we later understand to be the beginning of breakdown:

> I began to ramble, incoherently, in a disconnected manner. I was being severed from my own voice. I would listen to it as to a still, small voice coming from the huge distances of the mind. It was like this: English is my second language, Shona my first. When I talked it was in the form of an interminable argument, one side of which was always expressed in English and the other side always in Shona. At the same time I would be aware of myself as something indistinct but separate from both cultures. I felt gagged by this absurd contest between Shona and English. (p. 30)

The passage addresses the divided self in terms of language, to the point where the narrator is struck violently dumb by confusion. We can see an elaboration of this in the shockingly frank reply Marechera made to the question 'Did you ever think of writing in Shona?':

> Shona was part of the ghetto daemon I was trying to escape. Shona had been placed within the context of a degraded, mind-wrenching experience from which apparently the only escape was into the English language and education. The English language was automatically connected with the plush and seeming splendour of the white side of town. As far as expressing the creative turmoil in my head was concerned, I took to the English language as a duck takes to water. I was therefore a keen accomplice and student in my own mental colonisation.[17]

It is precisely for this sense of self-treachery, his affiliation with the values of his Mission education, that the narrator describes himself as a 'little Judas'. As Anthony O'Brien effectively argues in his paper 'Against the Democracy Police', education is figured in this story as another 'house of hunger', the source of an implacable 'gut-rot'. And Marechera's later inability to finish work, his evasion of closure, is both an aspect of his modernist narrative practice, but also demonstrates the failure of language to express 'the house of hunger in its manifold brutalities'.[18]

Running through 'House of Hunger' are references to an old man. He dies on page 9, is smashed to pieces on page 45 ('The old man died beneath the wheels of the twentieth century. There was nothing left but stains'), and finally makes an appearance on page 82. The old man's enigmatic appearances in the narrative describe the condition of Africa overtaken by the changes that have befallen her. When he re-appears at the end of the story, it is to express the enduring qualities of survival:

> He simply wandered into the House one day out of the rain, dragging himself on his knobby walking stick. And he stayed. His face was like a mesh of copper wire; his wrists, strings of muscle; and his broken body looked so brittle and insubstantial that a strong wind or an expletive would probably have blown him right back into the rain. His broken teeth, tobacco-stained, were those of an ancient horse which even the boiler of glue would reject. But his deep-set eyes, the colour of fire reflected in water, were as full of stories as his tongue was quick to tell them. He would sun himself in the happy company of the local chorus of flies and choke on some secret chuckle. He would take out his tobacco pouch and slowly roll a cigarette, using strips of the *Herald*. What he loved best was for me to listen attentively while he told stories that were oblique, rambling and fragmentary. His transparent, cunning look, his eager chuckle, his wheezing cough, and something of the earth, gravel-like, in his voice – these gave body to the fragments of things which he casually threw in my direction. (p. 79)

The old man's stories have the same fragmentary allusiveness of Marechera's narrative. In his lecture 'The African Writer's Experience of the European Novel', Marechera refers to Mikhail Bakhtin's idea of the 'carnivalesque' with predictable enthusiasm (p. 363), and his account of what it is very much recalls the figure of the old man and Marechera's method in this as well as his other writing. And it is the old man who is given the task of closing the narrative. He does so with a gesture of real complexity, returning a package of photographs and notes on the narrator, collected by Harry, a former school-friend who had become a police spy. The old man returns another narrative to him, in other words, one which figures his story on the outside. That story, by its inclusion here, is contained within the narrator's narrative, and diminishes within this much larger account. Making the old man into a kind of visionary storyteller not unlike the narrator, whose stories expand into inarticulacy because of the sheer scope of their subject, expresses a desire for closure, to some extent. In this respect, the narrative form has the last word again, but the status the old man is given as both survivor and storyteller also locates in him the qualities which endure despite every oppression.

As well as in its narrative method, and its unique study of colonised consciousness, Marechera's writing is distinguished by a savage and sarcastic humour. If the fragmentation of narrative implies a failure of language to deliver the narrator's alienated experiences, there is a sense in which the self-ironising humour signifies a kind of disengagement from the failure. Marechera's own frenzied neglect of his 'surroundings' – 'I made a careful decision that I no longer want to see my surroundings in any clear way at all'[19] – can be seen not as the privileging of the life of the mind to which the narrators of his writing had aspired, but as the unavailing resistance of 'the little Judas' who had written with undiminished stubbornness of the colonised consciousness he himself was so representative of.

## Notes

1. Dambudzo Marechera said this in a lecture entitled 'The African Writer's Experience of European Literature' delivered in Harare, Zimbabwe on 15 October, 1986. It was first published in *Zambezia: The Journal of the University of Zimbabwe*, 14, 2 (1987), pp. 99–105, and is reproduced in Flora Veit-Wild, *Dambudzo Marechera: A Source Book on his Life and Work*, London: Hans Zell Publishers, 1992, p. 363.

2. Dambudzo Marechera, *The House of Hunger* (London: Heinemann, 1978).

3. In answer to a question about 'influences' Marechera says: 'The seething cesspit in which I grew, in which all these I am talking about went about making something of their lives. These are the ones who influenced me'. 'Dambudzo Marechera Interviews Himself', in Veit-Wild, *Dambudzo Marechera*, p. 1.

4. Marechera, 'The African Writer's Experience of European Literature', in Veit-Wild, *Dambudzo Marechera*, p. 362.

5. 'The "House of Hunger": Family and Childhood', Veit-Wild, *Dambudzo Marechera*, (1992), p. 49.

6. In 'Thought-tracks in the Snow', *The House of Hunger*, the narrator reports a conversation with a Nigerian student in Oxford: 'He had, he said, read my stories and found them quite indigestible. Why did I not write in my own language? he asked. Was I perhaps one of those Africans who despised their own roots? Shouldn't I be writing within our great tradition of oral literature rather than turning out pseudo-Kafka-Dostoyevsky stories?' (pp. 142–3). And in *Black Sunlight* (London: Heinemann, 1980) the narrator answers his vociferous critics with these words: ' "I am astonished at the audience's ignorance. I did not expect such a low cultural level among you. Those who do not understand my work are simply illiterate. One must learn" ' (p. 110). See also the portrayal of the embattled and misunderstood poet Owen towards the end of *The Black Insider* (London: Lawrence & Wishart, 1992), first published in Harare, 1990.

7. Juliet Okonkwo, 'A Review of *The House of Hunger*', in *Okike*, June 1981, pp. 87–91. The quotation is from the closing paragraph.

8. Musaemura Zimunya, *Those Years of Drought and Hunger: The Birth of African Fiction in English in Zimbabwe*, Gweru: Mambo, 1982, p. 126.

9. Mbulelo V. Mzamane, 'New Writing from Zimbabwe: Dambudzo Marechera's *The House of Hunger*', *African Literature Today* 13 (1983): Recent Trends in the Novel, pp. 201–25.

10. Warthog's advice to the narrator in the second part of 'The Writer's Grain' is an example of this radical non-conformity:

> insist upon your right to go off at a tangent. Your right to put the spanner into the works. Your right to refuse to be labelled. . . . To insist on your right to confound all who insist on regimenting human impulses according to theories. . . . Insist upon your right to insist on the importance, the great importance, of whim. (p. 122)

Also, in an interview with Alle Lansu, which took place in 1986, Marechera said: 'Literature is now seen as another instrument of official policy and therefore the writer should not practise art for art's sake or write like Franz Kafka or like James Joyce or explore the subconscious of our new society. All that is for European bourgeois literature. . . . When culture is emphasised in such nationalistic ways, that can lead to fascism.' ' "Slow brain death can only be cured by a literary shock treatment" : Dambudzo Marechera interviewed by Alle Lansu', Veit-Wild, *Dambudzo Marechera*, p. 39.

11. 'The African Writer's Experience of European Literature', in Veit-Wild, *Dambudzo Marechera*, p. 368. And here are the opening lines of 'Howl':

> I saw the best minds of my generation destroyed by madness,
>     starving hysterical naked,
> dragging themselves through the negro streets at dawn looking for
>     an angry fix

Allen Ginsberg, *Howl and Other Poems*, San Francisco: City Light Books, 1959, p. 9.

12. ' "Slow brain death can only be cured by a literary shock treatment": Dambudzo Marechera interviewed by Alle Lansu', Veit-Wild, *Dambudzo Marechera*, p. 7.

13. I discussed this aspect of Ngũgĩ's writing in my essay 'Transformative Strategies in the Fiction of Ngũgĩ wa Thiong'o' in *Essays on African Writing*, Oxford: Heinemann, 1993, pp. 142–58.

14. ' "Slow brain death can only be cured by a literary shock treatment": Dambudzo Marechera interviewed by Alle Lansu', Veit-Wild, *Dambudzo Marechera*, p. 13.

15. See the section which opens the narrator's reflections on Nestar: 'But the young woman's life is not at all an easy one. . . . She is bombarded daily by a TV network that assumes that black women are not only ugly but also they do not exist unless they take in laundry, scrub lavatories, polish staircases, and drudge around in a nanny's uniform' (p. 50).

16.                              and every attempt
              Is a wholly new start, and a different kind of failure
              Because one has only learnt to get the better of words
              For the thing one no longer has to say, or the way in which
              One is no longer disposed to say it. And so each venture
              Is a new beginning, a raid on the inarticulate
              With shabby equipment always deteriorating
              In the general mess of the imprecision of feeling

T. S. Eliot, 'East Coker' Section V, *Collected Poems*, London: Faber, 1974, pp. 202–3.
17. 'Dambudzo Marechera Interviews Himself', Veit-Wild, *Dambudzo Marechera*, p. 4.
18. Anthony O'Brien, 'Against the Democracy Police', a paper delivered at the History Workshop, University of Witwatersrand, July 1994.
19. ' "Slow brain death can only be cured by a literary shock treatment": Dambudzo Marechera interviewed by Alle Lansu', Veit-Wild, *Dambudzo Marechera*, p. 34.

# Re-Possessions: Inheritance and Independence in Chenjerai Hove's *Bones* and Tsitsi Dangarembga's *Nervous Conditions*

## CAROLINE ROONEY

I am prompted, somewhat reluctantly, to enter a 'note on the contributor' here, namely: I/Rooney was born in Zimbabwe, and grew up there during the 'liberation war years' of the 1960s and 1970s, as did Hove and Dangarembga.[1] In approaching *Bones*,[2] my position, that of a white woman with a concern for an African mother, may, in some ways, approximate to that of an educated African son, who from a certain distance can maintain a close concern for non-élite African women. This remains too specific and too generalised. It is necessary to re-propose, or propose in more accessible terms, the intersections between personal, private, public and national histories. Are the traumas of colonialism unique, vicarious, shared? Consider, for instance, these two responses by Marie Cardinale and Hélène Cixous, respectively, to the experience of colonialism in Algeria:

> It seems that the Thing took root in me permanently when I understood that we were to assassinate Algeria. For Algeria was my real mother, I carried her inside me the way a child carries the blood of his parents in his veins.[3]

> I learned everything from this first spectacle: I saw how the white (French), superior, plutocratic, civilised world founded its power on the repression of populations who suddenly became 'invisible' like proletariats, immigrant workers, minorities who are not the right 'color'. Women.[4]

A voice in *Bones* comments: 'There is no end to the types of madness, especially after this war which has eaten into the lives of everybody' (p. 79). The man who speaks in the above citation goes on: 'If I were the police I would arrest them all.' And as he says this a crowd of listeners move away, 'pointing at his head and indicating circles in the air' (p. 80). It can be mad to say all is madness; mad to police madness. Or, when is madness a fiction?[5]

Is *Bones* a story? Does it possess or is it possessed by one? In certain respects that I will deal with later, it is a story without a story. In other respects, its several stories tell one story whose transmission is the mission of the text. Hove's story, his story, is about a woman, her story. It is about a woman called Marita who is killed in the city when she is trying to trace her freedom-fighter son's whereabouts, about a dead woman who lives on in the minds of others. *Bones*, in effect, says: 'Remember her, remember this, remember me.' This is what some Zimbabwean 'mothers of the revolution',[6] or liberation war, have to say:

> When my son did not return home I thought, if my son has left with the guerrillas, this is not so bad. . . . But we have never seen my son again. . . . We waited and hoped to see him but . . . nothing (p. 24)

> We said, surely the *vakomana* will not forget us, after we have done so much for them. . . . Now some of those freedom fighters are in high places . . . and yet those freedom fighters have forgotten us (p. 151)

> What makes it worse is that our leaders do not even acknowledge the death of our children. . . . The least they could have done is tell those parents whose children died in the war that they are sorry (p. 258)

> After independence . . . we who had children who died, never got a word of appreciation . . . no one has told me that they appreciate us, the parents of those children (p. 268)

The above statements are taken from a collection of interviews with Zimbabwean women, mothers, mainly from the peasantry, who give grassroots accounts of their experiences of the war of independence.[7] These statements, and further similar statements, indicate that *Bones* is close to the concerns of many non-literate or semi-literate, non-élite Zimbabwean women of a certain generation. That is, it addresses the sufferings of mothers who have lost their sons, women who have been forgotten, and it engages with the need for consolation, mourning and remembrance, and for the paying of respects. Hove's text appeared in print two years before the interviews collected in *Mothers of the Revolution* and yet it is doubtful that it reached the constituency of women that it seeks to give representation to. Hove takes this up in the prologue to his subsequent novel *Shadows*: 'This is their story. . . . One day they will read it . . . They will never read it. The world of written words is hidden away from them.'[8] Hove's writing performs a paradoxical transition from the oral story to the written, in which the former is to be preserved, forever, at the same time that it is to be unavoidably surpassed or outlasted as it enters the domain of the literate and literature.

However close *Bones* might seem to the unrecorded histories of mothers of the revolution, it is necessary to consider the text in terms of a story of writing. It may be proposed that in order to write home, the first step is to leave home, even if this means leaving your own flesh and blood, in order that you may start to remember, re-call, re-present. And, it is when you are not there ('fort,'[9] gone), that you feel the pull of an invisible thread of guilt or desire. What *Bones* writes of – most summarily, departure of the son, abandonment of the mother – would seem to be structural conditions of writing, or what occasions the departure of writing. My point, at this stage, is that *Bones* writes the makings of its writing. As such, it signals its self-composition, which is to suggest it signs itself as literature. It is important to note this, since I am about to set up interactions between it and other discourses in which questions of borderlines and authorisation will both disappear and reappear.

Marita, the Unknown Woman, Janifa, the three main female personae of *Bones*, might all be said to be Antigone figures. The significance of this is not that they resemble each other, but that each character is compelled to repeat a defiant demand and sacrificial destiny, or is compelled to take up an unintentionally self-destructive role in an on-going drama. Defying patriarchal laws and representatives of the state, they persist in their unanswered demands or appeals, to the point of death or incarceration. What possesses these women? What makes them do it? This is what other characters, especially the male characters, in the story cannot understand. The three main women figures in the story are regarded as social pariahs, associated with what is dangerous or taboo. Marita and Janifa are treated as witches, or contaminated women, in their inability or refusal to conceive children and in their advoidance or rejection of the desires and demands of men. That is, from a certain perspective, they are posited as turning their backs on the social imperatives of sex and reproduction: they will not be the custodians of eros. It would seem that there is something more pressing for them and it would seem, in ways to be considered later, that this is an obligation to act as custodians of 'thanatos'.[10]

Marita is almost tortured to death by security forces seeking information concerning her terrorist son. She is then beaten to death by 'men in uniform' when relentlessly searching for her son after Independence. The Unknown Woman who berates her 'sell-out' husband for causing the death of a group of freedom fighters is accused by him of being a lover of corpses. When Marita dies and the Unknown Woman tries to reclaim the corpse for proper burial, she is perceived as a corpse who wants to sleep with corpses, and she is also brutalised to death. Janifa is obsessed with the dead Marita, restlessly compelled to trace her destiny, and she is raped for her non-conformity. Conventional society sees these women as courting death: either in terms of 'asking for it' through their stubborn refusal to yield, for their persistence in their own desires, or in terms of being lovers of the departed, necrophiliacs. From the point of view of conventional society, traditional or modern, these abnormal women dare to refuse to guarantee the future of society or the future society. As far as the new state of Zimbabwe is concerned, these women are not going to be mothers or midwives of the nation – but instead they are going to threaten it with decomposition, degeneration, or terrifying regression to a deathly pre-history.

If *Bones* is set up against this societal opinion of the women as perversely wilful transgressors, it may be precisely in order to propose that this condemnation be reversed and suspended. That is, we may well ask what possesses the bearers and executors of the law to treat such women so mercilessly. Is it, perhaps, the legitimate state (or state of legitimacy), as opposed to the women, that ought to be judged criminally perverse and inflexible? What begins to emerge is a certain dilemma. The women could be said to be victims, killed for no good reason other than for being too 'inquesting', asking too many questions about the dead. Or, they could be said to be symptoms of what the state cannot tolerate within or admit to itself. For example, and it is only an example since we are considering the inadmissable or unspeakable here, it may be the senselessness of killing that cannot be admitted. An 'inquesting woman' would then be the persistent marker of a traumatic question that cannot be posed or answered. Then again, it could be argued that these troublesome women do represent a real danger to the state, a threat to its self-sustainability.

What I am driving at is something of an 'Antigone effect' that can only be roughly glossed here. Most briefly, Antigone inflexibly insists on a proper burial for her criminal or non-heroic brother. Creon, the representative and enforcer of the laws of the state, inflexibly refuses. What ensues is a deadlock between two necessities, one on the side of the law, and the other without any legal representation as such. The deadlock in *Bones* is not some simple opposition. There is a law of the father and the state or father-state, a law of man in two senses. Firstly, it is a law which de-sacrilises a law of the spirits (the old gods), and, secondly, it is a law, in the analysis attributed to Marita, based on the will-to-power of the self-aggrandising, self-universalising of the masculine libido: 'Did your mother not say that your grandfather died fighting a war started by a man called Hikila[11] who wanted to rule the whole earth? . . . That is what men are like. They look at their things erect in front of them and think they are kings. They do not know that it is just desire shooting out of them, nothing else' (p. 28). Marita continues: 'So child, you do what you can with the weaknesses of men, but do not let them play around with your body . . . do not let people waste it like any rubbish' (p. 28). If the women repeat the inflexibility of the law, they force it to show itself as ugly brute force, enact itself as terror. The women in Hove's novel do not contend that there should have been no war of liberation, no 'terrorism'. Rather, it is a question of a law which will not acknowledge that it 'is a law that originates in a violation of a law'.[12] In this respect, it could be said that the non-admission of an inaugural injustice is the law's enabling transcendence, what enables it to judge between the just and unjust.

Normally, it would be the women who would rightfully conduct proper rites for burial, this rite of homecoming and mourning. However, in a war in which it cannot be known or remembered precisely who died and where, this rite cannot be performed: the unhoused dead must be bestially left, anomymous and forgotten.[13] The protest of an Antigone is that the irreplaceable singularity of the dead person is to be recognised, as well as that the laws of the living do not apply to the dead who deserve, according to death's customs, equal respect regardless of whether they are heroes or criminals – or war-fodder – in the eyes of the state. In *Bones*, Marita in particular stands for 'love for each and all in death'. While she is dying for her son, longing for and giving her life to her son's homecoming (dead or alive), she also recognises an equality in death. When she is asked why she did not denounce her racist white employer to the guerrillas, she answers: 'Child, what do you think his mother will say when she hears that another woman sent her son to his death?' (p. 63). In daily life she sees that this white man, Manyepo (the name means 'lies'), is an enemy whom she stands up to and defies, but in death, he would be a child just like her child. This 'love or respect for each and all in death' is not a law as such, but a demand, an unanswerable appeal. It is the beyond of the law, its limit. Meanwhile, the law posits a Marita as the absolute limit to what it can endure or have patience with.

Lacan, in his by no means disinterested reading of *Antigones*[14] [*sic*], aligns Antigone with the death drive. He says: 'She incarnates that desire' (p. 282), a pure and simple desire for death. While Lacan addresses Antigone's inflexibility in terms of the question of an ethics of psychoanalysis, certain political questions remain unaddressed. As far as a Marita is concerned, another character in a different text to be sure, would it not be problematic to say that she is simply and supremely death-driven, over and above her being put to death by men in uniforms? While Antigone does commit suicide, and Marita does not, what remains is a certain assumption that she, somehow, intended or desired it. Beyond or beside this, 'her' supposed being-for-death might be re-supposed as an occlusion or occultation.

Antigone is seen at times as speaking on behalf of ancient, timeless, cthonic 'laws'. The spirit of this might be translated into the rhetoric of *Bones*. In Hove's text there are two sections that do not appear under the proper names of the dramatis personae, which engage in inner conversations with the departed, and these two sections are entitled: 'The Spirits Speak'. It is not completely clear who or what these spirits are. However, textual hints and local knowledge, or historical and anthropological research, would suggest that they are the Ancestral Spirits of the Shona. In the first spirit 'chorus' in *Bones*, we are given a date – 1897– and the incantatory refrain 'Arise all the bones. . .'. The date marks the suppression of the first *Chimurenga*, or uprising against the plague of white colonisers, and the refrain refers to the words of a female spirit medium of the spirit of Nehanda. As documented by David Lan, when this medium of Nehanda, whose name was Charwe, was captured and condemned to death, she prophesied that 'my bones will rise'.[15] In *Bones* the Spirits prophesy: 'The ribs of the graves will break when my bones rise/ and you stare in disbelief' (p. 47).

Whereas in pre-colonial and early colonial Shona society ancestral or guardian spirit possession was largely a male preserve, this altered with the increasing domination of European culture, education and religion. I. M. Lewis writes: 'A new morality, validated by the Christian faith, thus gradually replaced the old authority of the ancestor spirits which appear to have been relegated to the staus of mere peripheral spirits and left to plague women.'[16] That is, some women became the custodians of the 'old gods' in a process of increasing acculturation. When the second *Chimurenga*, or war of independence, began, ancestral spirit mediums not only acquired a revived popularity and respect, but were regarded as providing crucial guidance, political inspiration and ethical legitimacy to the liberators of Zimbabwe. The revival of the 'old gods' or re-invocation of the spirits has been seen as crucial in forging a necessary solidarity between the guerrilla armies and the peasant populace, and as forging a national consciousness during the war years, as Lan points out. When the new government came to power, it could be said to have re-imposed the concept of a civic state on that of a 'spirit nation', the former acquiring or requiring ascendancy. In addition, it could be argued that there was a need to re-establish the family unit within the nation, in some contradistinction to the war ideology of the family-nation. *Bones* addresses this legacy.

When the Spirits first speak in the text (in the year given as 1897) it is in a voice urging collective defiance, in the war-spirit of Nehanda. When they next speak, towards the close of the text (at a time after Independence) it is in a tone of lament. What they recount here is not a collective history, but just the stories of the three individual women, whom no one will remember. In particular, they reveal to us what none of the other characters in the novel can know, namely, how Marita was killed. They also tell us that this scandal will be suppressed and passed over by the new soldier-bureaucrats: 'They will talk . . . but nobody will mention the spirit of the woman who wanted to bury a woman they did not know. No, it is just a bad day' (p. 105).

The question is, then, to what extent can the spirits of the three women characters be related to the Spirits designated in the text as spirits of the ancestors? Although no explicit connection is made, the montage structure of the novel allows for a connection to be made in the mind of the reader: that Marita, the Unknown Woman and Janifa are discarded mediums who continue to preserve the now civilly-supressed fighting spirit and 'unwritten sacred laws' of the ancestors. If this is the case, to what extent are the female characters in possession of this knowledge? As fictional characters they cannot speak for themselves, but it can be said that Marita and the Unknown Women act in conscious accordance with their own desires. Like Antigone they appear to know just what they are doing. With Janifa, however, it is different. She, a daughter figure to Marita, does not seem to know exactly what possesses her, what precisely makes her so rebellious and restless. She says: 'Marita . . . I hear the bones inside me creaking with the spirit of walking which is in me' (p. 96). Without knowing it, she is repeating or enacting the prophesy of Nehanda: 'my bones will rise'. Janifa also says: 'yes, I hear you call for the rest of my body, Marita. But you died. . . . How can my soul rest?' (p. 103). Is it Marita's unburied spirit taking possession of Janifa? Is it madness? Rebellion? As far as her birth-mother and the local healer are concerned, she has been possessed by an evil spirit (*shave*): 'I do not understand how such a vicious evil spirit can enter the soul of such a young girl' (p. 96). This pronouncement would, in effect, indicate that the once familiar ancestral spirits have become alien to their own descendants. On the other hand, the text suggests, in another diagnosis, that Janifa has gone mad and gets interned, interred, buried alive, in 'the house where people with bad heads are kept' (p. 104), also refered to as 'the house of ghosts' (p. 110). Then, thirdly, Janifa emerges as one who will remove the 'chains' (of her confinement in the mental asylum, and, metaphorically, of oppression) that hold her down and sing the revolutionary song (pp. 112–13). As in Clément's and Cixous' cross-analyses, she is sorceress, hysteric, and potential 'newly born woman' all in one.

It would also be possible to say that, in terms of the psychoanalytic theories of Abraham and Torok, Janifa is the bearer of a 'phantom'. That is, Janifa might be posited as the unwitting recipient of a family secret, or parental 'crypt', something 'undead', not worked out through mourning – something that does not achieve symbolisation, and so is enigmatically and unconsciously transmitted without exorcism or catharsis.[17]

It could be claimed that, in a certain sense, Marita is killed by her son, her beloved soldier prodigal redeemer son. At the beginning of *Bones*, the rumoured nature of a terrorist is given, ending with:'a terrorist, a killer who kills his own mother' (p. 4). Later, we are told another rumour, of a man who sleeps with his own daughter in the city. They do not know each other because he has left his own name behind in the village. Also later, the Unknown Woman tells of how the supposed terrorists presented themselves to villagers as 'your children', and when she goes to the city she is addressed by a kind unknown official as 'Mother'. In the rhetoric of the war of independence, freedom fighters were 'sons of the soil' and the village women whose support they relied on were their 'mothers'. The war was fought in the name of the mother and son – until Independence.

Putting these hearsays together, a further rumour could be started. You have heard of how Marita wants to know what has become of her son, who left his own name behind in the village, who could be a terrorist-killer or filial-emancipator? 'The womb bears all sorts of people, thieves and priests. . . . This is why I also want to find him' (p. 39). Perhaps, odd as it may sound, Marita's unconscious destiny is the need to determine her son's desire, that is, whether he wants to kill her or, in piety, return to her. She needs to provoke this encounter, and when she does she is slain; by the soldier-son who cannot recognise his own mother in a woman like Marita, in Marita. The (father's) son turns out to be a mother-killer. However, the son is not only this sanctioned criminal, but the one who also lovingly returns to her always. Marita's true son does return, eventually. (He is just the same, according to Janifa, but he limps, like Oedipus.) He returns, his mother now dead, to claim . . . Janifa? By this stage of the narrative, we are not sure if Janifa is herself, so thoroughly possessed is she by the spirit of Marita. He claims the one who houses the spirit of his mother, an incestuous *liebestod*. To complicate things further, in the son's absence Janifa took his place, as the son admits when he calls her up (p. 109). He seems to say: you are me. He also says that he comes under the auspices of his mother's guiding desire – her desire for him. What looks like an innocent proposal seems founded on a web of incestuous longings.

According to George Steiner, Kierkegaard's reading of *Antigone* confirms that 'Tragedy is inherited guilt.'[18] Marita says: 'The sins of the fathers and mothers, the preachers say, /Show me someone whose father or mother did not commit sin' (p. 41). In Kierkegaard's cryptic reading, Antigone goes to the grave as the guardian of her father's secret, her father being Oedipus, and his secret being mother/son incest. Antigone's fidelity to her brother (Polyneices) is also a fidelity to the family secret she now alone possesses – a fidelity to her father-brother, Oedipus. It is for this brother she dies too, and thus for a mother-son love that cannot be further transmitted. However, from being the bearer of a secret, she becomes herself a crypt/tomb outside and within history, a history that will continue without her yet troubled or haunted by her: a 'living dead' for Kierkegaard, an already dead and death-bound, for Lacan. I will return to this daughter or brother thing.

In Shona society, bones are used for divination. They may be scattered to predict, tell all in advance, or spell out the unknown in incalculable permutations. *Bones* (as words or letters) begins: 'She asked me to read the letter again for her again today, Marita . . . "please read it, read it all the time. . ." ' (p. 1) [ellipses mine]. And, it ends: 'Marita . . . she asked me to read the letter for her again today, every day she comes to me, all pleading' (p. 113) [ellipses in the text]. The effects of this, Marita's repeated demand for the letter, are overwhelming. I will briefly try to contain or net a few:

1. The love-letter sent by the son to the daughter is, at the beginning (of the novel) requested by the mother. Write to me, remember me, love me. Does he write out of her imagined desire for him, and his to fulfil hers? Then, the daughter reading the son's letter sent to her is put in the son's place, repeating his words, the addressee, become addressor-in-effigy. Marita, occupying the place of the addressee, occupies Janifa's place. In short, but hardly to short-circuit this, they are caught up in a whirlwind of transferences. This transference motion of one ghosting for another is set up by the absence of the son and his letter in his absence.

2. We are not exempt from this. Every time the letter-text addresses Marita in her absence, as it continually does, we are there, reading, if not loud and clear, quietly and unclear. That is, we are put in the position of the one who is addressed with love. Janifa, Jennifer, Marita, My Reader.[19] We have been abandoned, we are loved. But, recall, it was Marita who started all this too, suggesting to him a letter (or a literature).

3. The fact that the text begins and ends inside Janifa's mind could suggest that the whole story has been something she imagined, projecting herself into every part, some hysteric's private theatre. Then again, she could just be the medium for the son, the writer son, using her in ventriloquist fashion. From this projection and ventriloquism, too, the reader is not exempt.

4. There has been no story at all. The son's letter is never read in the text, that 'dirty secret' (as Janifa's teacher perceives the letter) does not get its contents revealed to us. No story at all. It ends where it begins. With the demand for the letter. And that is all there is to it. Just the demand for a letter, but never yet the letter. It postpones itself infinitely, and the story will run forever.[20]

I suggested at the outset that *Bones* has literature as its subject and signature. As the above discussion indicates, *Bones* writes the writing of itself. George Steiner, drawing on Lévi-Strauss, interestingly proposes that Greek Tragedies, *Antigone* in particular, perpetually repeat themselves in our literature because they tell of the origins of writing – the myth is an encoding not only within language but of language.[21] Somewhat similarly, Lacan repeats an insight of Lévi-Strauss that: 'Antigone with relation to Creon finds herself in the place of synchrony in opposition to diachrony' (Lacan, *The Ethics of Psychoanalysis*, p. 285). It is a matter of the skeletal story of the history of writing, in which perhaps the mystery of the unwritten (what is pre-originary to writing) is locked up or locked out for the sake of conceptual life. As Derrida writes: 'Antigone . . . capable only of interrupting the conceptual life, of taking away the breath of the conceptual or, which comes to the same thing, of sustaining it from the outside or the inward of a crypt'.[22]

Some literature, such as *Bones*, returns or provokes the return of that twilight zone or horizon where ghost-stories are told or where graveside vigils are held.[23] *Bones* opposes a history of succession, son succeeding father, being his linear, historical substitute. It does this in its very textuality. Its structural movement is that of a spiral, ever going towards and returning away from its beginnings and endings, in defiance of a story or history. Its language, its very terms, terminology and conditions (a certain read-me-in-my-own-terms) resist to the limit and because of it any decidability or certainty. It is a question of a textuality of each-and-all, of irreplacable singularity and endless substitutability. Flora Veit-Wild writes: 'Lastly, Hove sees all the endeavours of the African writer fused in the ultimate goal of creating a world of human dignity and love.'[24] This creed or text of the imperative or vocation to create in the name of each-and-all would seem unthinkable, unrealisable and unwritable. Lacan suggests that the 'unwritten' that Antigone invokes is: 'of the order of the law, but which is not developed in any signifying chain or anything else' (p. 278). How would Antigone then serve to illustrate 'it'? If it is a matter of finding 'the words to say it', then a text such as *Bones* speaks a language that is not amenable to reason. Would not its relation to other discourses, those that would aim to make it see their respective senses, be something like that of an Antigone, who does not contest, who resists utterly, what 'they' say. None the less, it could be claimed that the novel's abiding image is that which serves to eclipse or displace the silhouette of the figure of the daughter, if that abiding image is one of a pacifying, immortalised love between mother and son, a configuration that is possibly Oedipal, Shona-spirited, and Christian all at once. Dangarembga's *Nervous Conditions* will be read so as to re-address the non-assimilation of the figure of the daughter, with reference to Antigone.

*Bones* is, as other readers have found, an hypnotic text, in its rhythms, syntax, rhetoric, and its suspensions of decidable meanings. It seems to be a text written in a trance, or that state of inspiration, and it is a text that can put its reader into a trance. But, at least for some lettered daughters, as opposed to lettered sons or unlettered mothers, it provokes a certain resistance. When you go into a trance, you are sometimes liable to be possessed. And what if you do not want to be possessed: 'My mind is not here any more' ('Janifa', *Bones*, p. 100). She, the one who takes breath away, where is her breathing space or her inspiration? She has no privacy left, not even the privacy of her own mind. In the story, she never wanted to carry out the demand to read out the son's love letter; perhaps she should have kept it to herself as something of her own. Filial concern for the non-literate mother may be a consoling memorisation, as long as it is not your destiny to take on her destiny at the expense of what would have been putatively your 'own.'

Chenjerai Hove tends to be characterised by those who read Zimbab-wean literature as the caring, true son, whereas his 'brother' writer, Dambudzo Marechera, is characterised as the uncaring, truant son.[25]

Tsitsi Dangarembga's novel *Nervous Conditions* can be situated between the novels of these two.[26] It was published in 1988, as was *Bones*, and Marechera died in 1987. There is another published Marechera, Dambudzo's brother, Nhamo, who paid tribute to the memory of his brother.[27] Dangarembga's novel begins: 'I was not sorry when my brother died.' The female narrator has two brothers. The first one, the elder brother who dies, is called Nhamo (a name which can mean either 'problems' or 'mourning' depending on how it is pronounced). When he dies, his sister, the narrator, Tambudzai (meaning 'to create problems') takes his place. That is, Nhamo had been taken into the privileged household of the uncle, Babamukuru, in order to be educated. He, a boy, was destined for glorious achievements, whereas she, Tambu, the sister, had to face the threat that her female destiny was to remain at home. Nhamo's death enables her to take up his privileges: a guaranteed education and entry into a middle-class Europeanised world. At the end of the novel when Tambu is secure in her educational achievements and greater prospects, she pays a visit to her original rural home. There she meets, and we are introduced to, her baby brother born in her absence. His name is Dambudzo. However, my edition of the novel at one point renders this name as Dumbudzo (p. 85). Thus, a Dam-brother becomes Dumb. Whoever's slip or 'literal' it is, it is telling. The infant brother is dumb – stupid (as yet) and/or speechless. In one earlier episode in the novel, Tambu accuses her arrogant, boasting brother of making too much 'noise'. He makes too much noise, and too much noise is made about him. As for Tambu, she is both wise and quiet and reserved.

Without wanting to over-force possibly groundless analogies, Dambudzo Marechera might be described as a noisy writer, about whom much noise was or is made. Is *Nervous Conditions* in some respects a response to his writing or his name? In *Black Sunlight*, Marechera writes of: 'Terrorizing the neighbourhood with quotes from Fanon's psychiatric notebooks.'[28] The title of Dangarembga's novel is taken from a translated paraphrase of Fanon,[29] indicated by the novel's epigraph. She cites, perhaps even mis-quotes or re-paraphrases, Sartre's paraphrase of Fanon but neither Fanon's nor Sartre's name is given. 'Nervous Conditions' is henceforth under the signature of Dangarembga, a 'clandestine translation' to re-phrase a phrase from the novel. 'Clandestine Translations' could well be another name for the novel.

*Nervous Conditions* is, like its narrator, quite a reserved text, but also a very knowledgeable one, one that can tell us a lot, if not everything. It does not have to be told things. It already knows, like Tambu who can both pose and answer her own questions (pp. 25–6). Apart from being able to figure things out for itself, it is learned and can remember things. If the idiom of *Bones* is Shona-(in)-English,[30] *Nervous Conditions* is carefully and perfectly bi-lingual. It uses Shona words for Shona things, it remembers the mother-tongue: *magrosa, dara, dare, nhodo, mahewu* (and so on). And then it is well-versed in academic terminologies, particularly those pertaining to clinical diagnoses: aphasic; sublimation; bacterium-infested; *post-partum*; hysterical; masochistic (and so on). Aphasia, or a faking of it, is diagnosed as Nhamo's problem. What is puzzling then, is why the text gives us no clinical diagnosis of his death. What exactly did he die of?

*Nervous Conditions* deals then with cultural transition, as does *Bones*, from a Shona world to the world of the white man that the black man partially inherits. However, there is seemingly little, if anything, that is haunting or magical about Tambu's rural lifestyle, represented as a life of hard labour, especially for women, and as one of monotonous poverty. It would seem that there are worlds of difference between the misty or mystic spirit-ringed environment or ambience of *Bones* and the factual, sharp-edged, self-contained materiality of the world in *Nervous Conditions*, both with respect to the material realities of rural poverty and with respect to the middle-class culture of consumerist material-ism. However, I wish to perform something of a clandestine translation between these texts that seem so unrelated.

In *Nervous Conditions* magic is associated with the world of the white people. It begins with the story told by the grandmother, Tambu's *ambuya*, of how her son, Babamukuru, was sent away to learn the white man's 'wizardry'. The young Tambu thinks of her uncle's success story as being the most captivating, entrancing fairy-tale or family romance. She and her brother aspire to this magic fortune of their Babamukuru, beyond the mundanities of existence. Tambu's first visit in a car to a town is presented as spell-binding. When she moves into her uncle's white-like, middle-class household, the full force of this magic hits her. However, this dream come true occasions all sorts of anxieties. In particular, Tambu fears being taken over, possessed, something she has to be ever careful or ceaselessly vigilant about. She speaks of having been 'disinterred' (p. 85) from her home soil, and 'reincarnated' (p. 92) in god-uncle's, or the good-father's Heaven. But was it not Nhamo who died and was buried? That is to say, if she has been reincarnated, is it not as the potential receptacle for Nhamo's restless, self-aggrandising spririt – Nhamo's home-foresaking ghost, an *ngozi* of sorts? Put differently, it is the Nhamo she has buried within herself, without mourning him (which is to say, not burying him) that she fears will take her over. Tambu, or the narrator Tambu who analyses the young Tambu, is well aware of this. It is said that the young Tambu suffered from feelings of inferiority and inadequacy and the narrator comments of herself: 'I was a bit masochistic at that age' (p. 89). Immediately after this diagnosis we are told of a dream that Tambu has in which her brother reproaches her for being over-ambitious, too sophisticated for her own good, and for having deserted her home and familial duties. One could read this masochistic dream in terms of either her internalised Nhamo-self, functioning as a superego, punishing and cautioning her; or, in terms of her reproaching Nhamo for making himself ill with his ambitious greed for white things (in the dream he is eating white-coated mealies that will make him ill) and coming to a 'bad end' (p. 90). That is, the accusations directed at herself could also be seen as her accusations against her brother-enemy who left her behind and came to a bad end. Tambu, desiring 'white' acculturation, fears her brother's fate, the inheritance of his destiny, that of falling into a trance and getting dangerously possessed: 'Some strategy had to be devised to prevent all this splendour from distracting me in the way my brother had been distracted' (p. 69). Tambu asserts: 'I would not go the same way as my brother' (p. 71).

But in what way did her brother go, pass away? His death, as said, received no certain medical diagnosis. His physical symptom is 'pain in the neck', maybe mumps, from which he seems to have recovered when suddenly he dies. There are no rational explanations, all Babamukuru can do is to say it was God's will, fate, necessity, just the ways things are. Less rational explanations need to be attempted for this death with no reason. As far as Tambu is concerned, Nhamo is 'a pain in the neck' and swollen up with his own male snobbery (mumps, swollen glands, his 'budding élitism' p. 49, his being so 'puffed up' p. 47). The few symptoms he shows before his death are symptomatic of his character. Thus, he dies for being what he is. Nhamo's father's conclusion is that it was 'jealous spirits' that took the boy away. A little earlier in the narrative, Tambu says of her feelings towards her brother: 'a little jealousy was permissible. . . . I was more than healthily jealous' (p. 48). Their mother regards the rivalrous war between brother and sister as not their own madness, within their control, but a question of 'evil spirits'. Just as Tambu's concern for her brother can die a sudden death, so can the brother die a sudden death. Her jealous spirit, her wishing him dead kills him. While such suggestions may sound like animistic 'mumbo-jumbo', it can be put quite commonsensically. The narrator has to wish her brother dead, even if in retrospect, or only in retrospect, because if he had not died she would have had no story of her own, or rather, no chance to tell her story as if he had never existed.[31] Just as Nhamo fakes aphasia, loss of his mother-tongue, his death may be read in terms of a faked aphanasis, fading away or death in language. At one point, Tambu finds herself literally unable to speak to her brother: he is beyond spoken language or even linguistic address. This is signalled at the outset of the text: 'my brother died', it begins, and continues: 'For though the event of my brother's passing and the events of my story cannot be separated, my story is not after all about death' (p. 1). It will instead be a story of women's lives and stories, their living (on) stories. The death of the brother had to be willed retrospectively, that is: because he died, I could then want his death; I could recreate his death, despatch him, in order to begin re-creating myself, re-presenting myself, writing. Perhaps this could be re-construed of the son's 'death drive' or death wish. Nhamo dies on the brink of a visit to his home. Mother and daughter are prophetic about this: ' "That son of mine," she sighed. "If he could avoid it, he would never come home." Spitefully, I agreed' (p. 53). He would rather die than come home? Nhamo's mother attributes her son's death to his loss of voice, Shona tongue, and bewitchment by the European world and its words: 'First you took his tongue. . . . You bewitched him. . . . You and your education have killed my son' (p. 54). Babamukuru, the familiar of white wizards, those *shave*, alien spirits, has, in this diagnosis, word-killed the son. Or, he is thought-to-death?[32]

Tambu, to avoid her brother's fate, his seduction, practises a tense self-possession. She is careful about what she takes in, careful not to be taken in. She is vigilant of her behaviour and that of others. Everything needs to be strictly monitored and regulated, an activity self-consciously profiled in the novel. She believes in discipline and self-control. She does this because she knows of some pre-inclination in herself: 'I was meeting outside of myself . . . things I had known always existed in other worlds although the knowledge was vague; things that made my mother wonder if I was quite myself, or whether I was carrying some other presence in me' (p. 93). Would this be a foreign body, or an alien spirit, a *shave*?

Fritz Kramer documents cases of spirit possession in which it appears that the spirit or charismatic or fascinating traits of a stranger to the community are identified with.[33] While a European is only one of such strangers, Kramer evidences a spirit possession cult among the

Shona, traceable to pre-colonisation, in which it is the white man who is identified with and imitated. The ritual of acting oneself out as the fascinating (or frightening) other seems to effect, I would argue, a cathartic ownership of the symptoms of wanting to be different or other. The community recognise a *shave* affinity as something special to a person, marking the truth, say, of his or her desire, or 'genius', and ritual conventicles allow the community as a whole to give a non-pathologised space to this desire to introject, become the alien.

As far as the character of Tambu is concerned the colonial mandate is to initiate the African person into white civilisation, and this accords with what Tambu wants for herself, as an imagined form of glorious emancipation. But this transformation within the bourgeois capitalist nuclear family household and mission school becomes a nervous condition insofar as it brings problematic contradictions or inner conflicts into play. On the one hand, within this environment, individual growth, broadening of the mind, self-cultivation are encouraged, with the implied goal of becoming what you dream to be, while simultaneously there is the injunction to keep a close check on these very aspirations, desires, appetites. They are stimulated to be checked, and checked in order to be stimulated.

Once Tambu has entered into the middle-class household, the traditional Shona methods of regulating transgressive desires, for example the introjection of otherness, no longer apply. Or, the desire to be other to one's supposed self is transposed into a different regulating economy. Here, the desire to be of the exotic civilisation coincides with the injunction to conform (be like the whites). Transforming is conforming, and yet this conforming involves, in turn, its own nego-tiation with transgressive limits or self-excesses. It is difficult to unravel the confusions of this, as Tambu finds in the long section devoted to the moment of her arrival at Babamukuru's house in the precincts of the mission school. She is assailed on all sides by a cacophony of 'sounds/voices' (appeals, alarms, hymns, wails): 'Nhamo's chorus sang in my head and now it sounded ominous' (p. 64); 'My finely tuned survival system set off its alarm at once' (p. 65); 'I would not go the same way as my brother. A shrill, shuddering wail pulled me abruptly out of my thoughts ... images of witches on hyena's backs, both laughing hellishly flitted through my mind. This was no time to be frightened, when I needed all my wits about me' (p. 71).

The school siren is, for a moment, demonic eerie laughter. Among other things, it serves to pin-point a momentary identification of the exotic European(ised) culture with 'primitive witchcraft'. Tambu, in order to survive, has to decide which is 'witch'. She opts for reason over superstition, education over primitivism. In accommodating herself to European transforming conformities, she comes to act in perfect accordance with colonial, middle-class and patriarchal 'technologies of the self'.[34] She swiftly comes to police herself, as the head of the household requires, as indeed he is socially and culturally required to police himself ('his nerves were bad' p. 102). In part, 'anorexia' should be the perfect, ever self-controlling, patriarchal daughter's symptom, whereas it becomes the nervous complaint of the self-pleasing rebellious daughter, Nyasha, Tambu's cousin.

Although set in the war years of liberation, *Nervous Conditions* makes little reference to this, choosing to address issues of women's emancipation. The war areas in the novel are within the patriarchal family. If *Nervous Conditions* is critically angled as a response to *Bones* or to *The Wretched of the Earth*, then it contrastingly deflects attention from national appeals to the question of inequalities between families (the élite and non-élite) and especially to the question of the inequalities and tyrannies within the 'model' middle-class family. If charity begins at home (and *Nervous Conditions* is about familial charity), then so, perhaps, does war.

*Antigone*, in Hegelian terms, is read as dramatising a conflict between the laws and ethics of the state and family values. Such a reading does not quite work here.[35] If *Nervous Conditions* is read in terms of an analytic of the Antigone scenario, then Tambu would be an Ismene figure, the resigned and compliant daughter, and her cousin, Nyasha, an Antigone figure, the untamed, undomesticated daughter. It is Nyasha who, for the patriarchal and household law, is the limit. All in the family agree, she goes too far. She is the limit to what can be reasonably tolerated on the home front. The struggle to re-domesticate Nyasha, the woman who has been given too much of a taste of freedom or independence, prefigures the programme of the re-domestication of women in the newly post-colonial Zimbabwe:

> During the war people were spoilt – everyone was behaving in the same way – married women, single women, men and boys. . . . Everyone said they were fighting, everyone was a guerilla. . . . You see the comrades told us this because we were all fighting for the country.
>
> But now people are still behaving in the same way. So the village and district committees were formed to teach people, especially mothers, to behave like mothers. The young women were the most affected. . . . The war caused people to behave wildly.[36]

This policing of women also took the form of rounding up women on the streets, designated as prostitutes whether they were or not, who were then sent to rehabilitation camps.[37] In *Bones*, the Unknown Woman is called a 'prostitute', for no good reason, other than the fact that she is perceived as non-submissive. In *Nervous Conditions*, Nyasha is called a whore by her father, not because she is one, but because she stands up to male authority. Such women are 'prostitutes' in that they will not give up on their desires, which are not subject to the desires of men.

What Nyasha does is to push her father and all that he would represent (the enlightened, Anglicised, law-abiding consumer-capitalist middle-class family) to a point of intolerable self-contradiction. For instance, when Tambu first arrives Babamukuru gives her his position on her which she summarises: 'I was an intelligent girl but I had also to develop into a good woman, he said, stressing both qualities equally and not seeing any contradiction in this' (p. 88). It is really Nyasha who sees the contradiction in this logic and flaunts it. The first fight we witness between her and her parents is over the fact that she is reading *Lady Chatterley's Lover*. In Babamukuru's logic, books are supposed to be on the side of pure civilisation, as opposed to dirt and poverty. But his daughter flaunts the fact that she is reading a 'dirty book', although it is one, she points out, written by someone judged to be a 'good writer' (p. 75). While Tambu rigidly tries to keep distinctions between the supposedly pure and the impure, Nyasha symbolises a contamination produced by the family in terms of its enabling limits, would-be exclusions. Nyasha, knowing that the family figures its limit in the silhouette of the unbridled woman, derisively mimics the whore, plays at being her without being her: 'it's only a book and I'm only reading it' (p. 75).

Tambu, at first split between her African self and the proto-English stranger within her, is, in relation to Nyasha, faced with a split between her educated-Anglicised persona and what threatens it:

> From what I had seen of my cousin, I was intrigued and fascinated with one part of my mind, the adventurous explorative part. But this was a very small part. Most of me sought order. . . . There was something about her that was too intangible to be comfortable with (p. 75).

Is there something of the return of the 'African' (or the African Nyasha has never really been) about this threatening intangibility? I will return to this question of cultural splitting. Firstly, there is the question of a split allegiance within the daughter.

Nyasha and Tambu, presented as very different characters, seem very similar at times and could be regarded as one and the same character (as hinted at in the text, e.g., pp. 173, 199, 202). Nyasha's spectacular fights with her father (a Creon figure of justice provoked to lose his cool) recall Tambu's violent fights with her brother, Nhamo. Strikingly, in one physical fight with her brother, Tambu incurs a wound and a trickle of blood runs down her thigh. After one physical wrestling match between Nyasha and her father: 'Her period came the next day, which was nine days early' (p. 119). What seems to be implied is a 'second castration', when a woman must be violently forced to remember she is just a woman (something Nhamo and Babamukuru do insist on in these battles). The fact that Nhamo and Babamukuru occupy substitutable positions in the drama is also interesting. Certainly fathers and sons inherit the same position of privilege relative to the women of the family, but beyond this, there is a conflation between father and brother. Derrida points out that Antigone is also her brother's enemy[38] (enemy to the proper heir and hero). Tambu hates Nhamo, the rival brother, but loves Babamukuru, the man she idealises as the beloved person she would like to become, in fact be heir to, while Nyasha hates this petty tyrant. What emerges from this is an ambivalence within the figure of the daughter towards the father figure and an ambivalence within the father. The father is the kind and good man, as Tambu sees him, and the inflexible representative of the law, as Nyasha sees him, to be loved as one and violently hated as the other. Or, the incompatible faces of the father produce ambivalence within the daughter. What also emerges is that there can only be one son at a time, that there can only be one man in the house (p. 115).[39]

Nyasha eventually gives up trying to make her father question himself, since the intolerable cracks in his self-image that she provokes only rebound on her.[40] This unwitting, non-self-originating self-destructiveness (which I think it would be dubious to dismiss as mere daughterly masochism) is something that Nyasha makes a final spectacle-statement of. The father's need to preserve himself becomes 'her' need to make herself disappear, played out all too literally in her hunger-strike. The symptom of anorexia (but whose exactly, is the question that circulates in this fictional text) is played out in the form of the daughter's exaggerated obedience to the father. Or, Nyasha silences herself and enacts her live burial within the stifling family prison, forcing her parents to watch the daily process of flesh becoming bone (p. 199).

No one knows what possesses her. When Nyasha finally breaks down she says that she does not hate her father and that 'They want me to, but I won't' (p. 201). 'They', in the most immediate interpretation, refers to the 'fucking liars' of British colonial history. That is, Babamukuru is but a product of this history, a 'good kaffir' as Nyasha sarcastically puts it, and that it is not he who should be hated but them. The place for this war is not within the family, but against the white government with all its lies. Nyasha shreds her history book to pieces with her teeth, and her hunger-strike in this context can be seen as refusal to consume their lies and their education and 'civilisation'.[41]

The question also arises: why would 'they', whites, want her to hate their faithful 'good kaffir'? Tambu's mother, a few pages on, gives her diagnosis: 'you could not expect the ancestors to stomach so much Englishness' (p. 203). In this reading, 'They' might be read as the ancestors, and what was African in her compels Nyasha to vomit out all the Englishness she has been fed. Her bones will rise again? It would seem too late, for what were once ancestral family spirits are something entirely foreign to the Anglicised Nyasha – not even *shave*, not even spirits anymore. Nyasha asks to be sent away for psychiatric treatment of her condition for there is nowhere else for her to go: 'So where do you break out to? You're just one person and it's everywhere' (p. 174).

If *Nervous Conditions* is a reply to Fanon, it would seem that it adds another case history to those of the traumas of brutal Algerian history. It is one of everyday terrorism within the Western lie of the model family. It might also be conceived of as a reply to Sartre. Sartre writes: 'If I were them, you may say, I'd prefer my mumbo-jumbo [Shona philosophies?] to their Acropolois [house of stone; their Hellenism[42]]. Very good: you've grasped the situation. But not altogether, because you aren't them – or not yet. . . . Two worlds: that makes two bewitchings; they dance all night and at dawn they crowd into the churches . . . each day the split widens' (*The Wretched of the Earth*, p. 17). *Nervous Conditions* treats bewitchments neither with rational scepticism, nor with credulity. There is a 'bewitchment' by white culture that is 'brain-washing' (p. 204), in which daughters still get treated as witches, literally so. Superstition towards and suspiciousness of this education is in order here. Moreover, what gets posited as 'spirit beliefs' are not merely superstition, or someone else's religion, but another mode of reasoning or working things out, another language.[43] This is of the order of canniness, not uncanniness.

What by some is seen as a limit, might also be seen as escape over the horizon. Attention can be drawn to such disappearing tricks, as opposed to Nyasha's literal withering away in the novel. When Tambu does not want to go her parents' Christian wedding, she performs, or fakes, an hysterical paralysis. Her body lies immobile in bed, while she exits from this body. All Babamukuru can see when he enters the room is a prostrate body: 'Meanwhile the mobile, alert me, the one at the foot of the bed, smiled smugly, thinking that I had gone somewhere he could not reach me, and I congratulated myself on being so clever' (p. 166). In the text's terms, this is neither madness, nor spiritual 'mumbo jumbo', but artful feminine wit and wile. The text ends with another stunning escape: '(S)omething in my mind began to assert itself . . . bringing me to this time when I can set down this story. . . . It was a process whose events would fill another volume but the story I have told here is my own story'. The book ends abruptly; it is as if we have been having a long long-distance conversation and the narrator, virtually without warning, hangs up, becoming suddenly unreachable, or showing that she always was. We may hang on . . . but silence. We are at the last possible moment jolted into an awareness that the 'person' who has been telling us the story, telling us so much, is not who we thought she was, was never there, has been a stranger all along. We are left asking the question of: but who and where are you? when there is no one there to reply. The answer is many silent, unwritten volumes, volumes of silence. We have got the story, but we are not to be told the story of the story, the escape which escapes us, the unwritten which makes for further writing, further departures – the story begins with departures, ends with further depatures – she being a step ahead of us or surpassing herself. All that is occult knowledge, and there is nothing uncanny about it,

> not in right now, But if you'd like to leave a message, please speak after the dots and the long dash: . . . ——

## Notes

1. Certainly, it is important to register that the critical 'I' is by no means neutral and this essay (but not only this essay) has its autobiographical, cultural and political investments and biases. Part of the reluctance lies in a self-promotion that could interfere with a listening to the texts in question. (It is also necessary to forget yourself.) Beyond this, the reluctance is one of a resistance to inquisitorial and inquistive demands for confession and self-declaration, where the demand is, often, posed as neutral or distanced, and its targets are, often, the woman, the homosexual, the immigrant, the native informant, and so on. ('Tell us who you are'.) One further consideration is that it is not always possible to name what haunts us.

2. Chenjerai Hove, *Bones* (1988; London: Heinemann, 1990). Further references will be to this edition and will be included in the text.

3. Marie Cardinale, *The Words To Say It: An Autobiographical Novel*, trans. Pat Goodheart (1975; London: The Women's Press, 1993), p. 38.

4. Hélène Cixous and Catherine Clément, *The Newly Born Woman*, trans. Betsy Wing (1975; Minneapolis: University of Minnesota Press, 1986) p. 70. In Cardinale's remark the response is one of internalisation and in Cixous' one of politicisation, which is not to say that these types of responses are distinctly separable. This essay contains a web of allusions to the French–Algerian intellectual environment, a post-colonial subtext of what we call 'theory'.

5. Both *Bones* and *Nervous Conditions* (London: The Women's Press, 1988) raise questions of madness or neurosis, particularly with reference to the figure of the daughter. It is, though, a question of a madness that could also be read in terms of 'possession' or rebellious outrage. Beyond this, or together with this, the texts are to be read as literary texts (and not just fictionalised 'case histories') in which the terms of psychoanalysis and anthropology are put into question. With respect to some of these issues, see my essay, 'Dangerous Knowledge and the Poetics of Survival' in *Motherlands*, ed. Susheila Nasta, London: The Women's Press, 1991. See also, Jacqueline Rose, 'On the "Universality" of Madness: Bessie Head's *A Question of Power*' in *Critical Inquiry*, Vol. 20, No. 3 (Spring, 1994) pp. 401–18.

6. These citations are taken from *Mothers of the Revolution*, ed. Irene Staunton, Harare: Baobab Books, 1990. Page references are included in the text.

7. The four citations are taken from interviews with, respectively: Sosana Marange, Margaret Viki, Erica Ziumbwa, Dainah Giori.

8. Chenjerai Hove, *Shadows*, Harare: Baobab Books, 1991, p. 9.

9. The context of this discussion is to an extent that of Derrida's speculations on the writing of Freud's *Beyond the Pleasure Principle*. See, for example, Derrida, 'Coming Into One's Own' in *Psychoanalysis and the Question of the Text*, ed. G. Hartman, Baltimore: Johns Hopkins University Press, 1978.

10. This is to pre-figure indirectly a consideration of Freud's proposition of a 'death drive'. The discussion, however, will not be in Freud's terms, or psychonanalytic terms, but will veer in the direction of a literary and political reading.

11. Since, in the text, 'Jennifer' is heard and pronounced as 'Janifa', Hitler/Hikila may be heard as 'her-killer', one of the text's preoccupations.

12. Samuel Weber, 'Breaching the Gap: On Lacan's Ethics of Psychoanalysis' in *Politics Theory and Contemporary Culture*, ed. Mark Poster, New York: Columbia University Press, 1993, p. 146. Weber argues this on the side of Antigone, whereas I would suggest the same may be said of the law she is confronted by.

13. 'Heroes Acre' was built after Independence as a national burial ground for the heroes of the war, and future heroes. There is a tomb for 'The Unknown Soldier'. So far, the only woman to have been buried there is Sally Mugabe. *Bones*, though, implies that a collective mourning (as opposed to triumphant national monumentalism) has yet to happen: it is, in a sense, mourning itself that has gone unmourned or been forgotten.

14. See Jacques Lacan, *The Ethics of Psychoanalysis*, ed. Jacques-Alain Miller, trans. Dennis Porter, London: Routledge, 1992. I say 'not disinterested' since Lacan read pages of his manuscript to his step-daughter, Laurence, when she was in prison for her participation in the Algerian resistance movement. I am grateful to Julia Borossa for alerting me to this point and its source in Elisabeth Roudinesco, *Généalogies*, Paris: Fayard, 1944, pp. 88–9. I have explored this further in 'Post-Colonial Antigones: Lawless and Unlawful Subjects' (due for publication). Slavoj Zizek in *The Sublime Object of Ideology* (London: Verso, 1991) insists on Antigone's 'death drive' aspect, while Weber (above) explores more of the ethical ambiguities raised by Lacan.

15. David Lan, *Guns and Rain: Guerrillas and Spirit Mediums in Zimbabwe*, London: James Currey, 1985, p. 6.

16. I. M. Lewis, *Ecstatic Religion: A Study of Shamanism and Spirit Possession*, 2nd edn; London: Routledge, 1989, p. 126.

17. See Abraham and Torok, *The Wolf Man's Magic Word*, and Nicolas Abraham, 'Notes on the Phantom: A Complement to Freud's Metaphyschoiogy', trans. Nicholas Rand in *Critical Inquiry* Vol. 13, No. 2 (Winter, 1987). See also, Nicholas Royle, *Telepathy: Essays on the Reading Mind* (Oxford: Blackwell, 1991).

18. George Steiner, *Antigones* (Oxford: Oxford University Press, 1984) p. 57. Kierkegaard's reading broadly anticipates a reading along the lines of Abraham and Torok. Steiner draws attention to the autobiographical aspects of Kierkegaard's reading.

19. Again, 'Marita' may be played on as a Shona pronunciaton of 'My Reader'. Marita is not a Shona name, as far as I have been able to ascertain – 'mariita', however, could translate as 'she will do it'.

20. These considerations are readily derived from the text itself. However, interesting cross-references could be made with writings by Derrida, which have influenced some of the considerations raised here. With respect to textual borders or edges, see 'La loi du genre/The Law of Genre', in *Glyph: Textual Studies*, 7, Baltimore: Johns Hopkins University Press, 1980.

21. Steiner, *Antigones*, p. 135. Steiner, however, is talking of a transition from speech to writing. While *Bones* supposedly transcribes orature and an oral Shona culture, this is not my emphasis. I am interested in the leap from the non-verbal to language. This 'unwritten' realm may subsequently, *after* this writing event, be associated with the oral.

22. Derrida, *Glas*, Paris: Editions Galilee, 1974, p. 187. Derrida is here engaged with Hegel's reading of *Antigone*. I have used Steiner's translation.

23. This is to speculate on possible literary 'repetition compulsion' or 'eternal return'. Flora Veit-Wild finds *Bones* (too) traditionalist in its African provenance and also (too) 'Western romantic' in its appeal (Flora Veit-Wild, *Teachers, Preachers, Non-Believers: A Social History of Zimbabwean Literature*, Harare: Baobab Books, 1993, pp. 314–20. I find this coincidence interesting and have addressed the issue in several unpublished conference papers on ' "Animisn" and the cross-cultural imagination'.

24. Veit-Wild, *Teachers, Preachers, Non-Believers*, p. 314. Veit-Wild draws on Hove's acceptance speech for the Noma award.

25. Ibid., p. 316; also Barbara Makhalisa, 'Weep Not', in Norma Kitson, *Zimbabwe Women Writers Anthology* No. 1, Harare: Zimbabwe Women Writers, 1994).

26. 1988 was also the year in which I submitted my doctoral thesis on 'The Androgyne and the Double in Literature, 1890–1940'.

27. Nhamo Marechera, 'To the Memory of My Beloved Brother, Dambudzo Marechera' in *Matatu: Journal of African Culture and Society*, 10 (1993), p. 138.

28. Dambudzo Marechera, *Black Sunlight*, London: Heinemann, 1980, p. 113.

29. In the preface to the Penguin edition of Fanon's *The Wretched of the Earth*, trans. Constance Farrington (1990), Sartre is translated as writing: 'The status of "native" is a nervous condition introduced by the settler among colonised people *with their consent*' p. 17. Dangarembga's epigraph is: 'The condition of native is a nervous condition.'

30. *Bones* is regarded as a faithful rendition of the Shona language in English. However, *Bones* is a prose poem and its technique is comparable to the so-called 'stream of consciousness' method of Modernist writers.

31. '. . . as if he had never existed' is a re-phrasing of Freud's comment on the death of his daughter, Sophie, in a letter to Ferenczi, 20 March 1924. Cited by Jacques Derrida in *The Post Card: From Socrates to Freud and Beyond*, trans. Alan Bass, Chicago: University of Chicago Press, 1987, p. 334.

32. With respect to some of the 'intellectual autobiography' which runs through the notes, I have in mind this century's interrogation of humanism and phallocentrism, in which it may be said that 'man' has been 'thought to death'. This can be juxtaposed with Antigone's status (in the critiques of Lacan and Derrida) as representing what is death to thought.

33. See Fritz Kramer, *The Red Fez: Art and Spirit Possession in Africa*, trans. Malcolm R. Green, London and New York: Verso, 1993, pp. 72–87. I have paraphrased Kramer's material, whilst also re-interpreting it.

34. See Michel Foucault, *Technologies of the Self*, ed. Luther M. Martin, Huck Gutman and Patrick H. Hutton, London: Tavistock Publications, 1988.

35. It also does not work in *Bones*, and is variously contested by Lacan and Derrida in their respective readings of an Hegelian reading of *Antigone*.

36. Meggi Zingani, *Mothers of the Revolution* Harare: Baobab Books, 1990 p. 134.

37. See Simukeliso Bhule, *Prostitution and the Law in Zimbabwe*, LLB dissertation, 1992, Law Department, University of Zimbabwe.

38. A phonemic reading of the names in *Nervous Conditions* suggests two lineages: an 'am' and a 'ny/sh'. There is the sequence of: Nhamo, Tambu, Babamukuru, Dambudzo. Then there is the sequence of: Nyamarira (the river where women have their own bathing spots), Nyari (a best friend of Tambu's), Nyarandzo (a friend, whose name sounds beautiful to Tambu), Nyasha. There is also Nyasha/Lucia (with the 'sh' sound), Lucia being a rebellious woman who escapes. The former lineage could signify the daughter's insertion into a male line. The latter seems to represent female friendship, or what takes place between women.

39. Derrida, *Glas*, p. 197. Derrida writes: 'Antigone est aussi le frère ennemi d'Eteocle'; see also ibid., p. 198.

40. Ibid., p. 211. Derrida suggests that woman (if that is possible) is the divisive irony or disquiet within 'God' or deity in the masculine.

41. This can be cross-referenced with Ama Ata Aidoo's novel *Our Sister Killjoy*, in which issues of cultural assimilation are figured and literalised in terms of the consumption or rejection of food. In addition, Sartre in *L'être et le néant* speaks of eating and the refusal to eat in terms of a choice of a mode of being.

42. 'Zimbabwe' means 'House of Stone'. Western culture affiliates itself with classical Greek culture ('our Acropolis'). A certain Western fascination with Hellenism may also be allied with a fascination with primitivism.

43. Western Thought? '. . . [M]irrors that had once been reliable but had now grown so cloudy with age that they threatened to show you images of artful and ancient spirits when you looked into them, instead of your own face' (*Nervous Conditions*, p. 62).

# Esoteric Webwork as Nervous System: Reading the Fantastic in Ben Okri's Writing

## ATO QUAYSON

Ben Okri's experiments with esoteric and ghostly narrative from his short stories through to *The Famished Road* and *Songs of Enchantment* exemplify a longstanding concern in African literature with non-realist forms of representation. The career of the best-known African writers has often traced a trajectory spanning a tendency towards realism followed by a bent towards alternative forms of representation. Chinua Achebe, Ngũgĩ wa Thiong'o and Ayi Kwei Armah all began with realism and later moved on to experiment with alternative forms of representation. In other writers published more recently such as Kojo Laing and Biyi Bandele-Thomas, there has been an early interest in non-realist modes of representation.

Ben Okri's writing is particularly relevant for assessing non-realist narrative modes in African writing because he focalises several aspects of narrative through a prism of indigenous beliefs. His ghostly writing raises fundamental questions about narrativity as well as about the relationship between literature and what it purports to represent. A good way of grappling with his non-realist discourse is to compare it with the fantastic in the work of other African writers. Kojo Laing's work offers an interesting point for comparison because of his consistent experiments with non-realist protocols of representation from his very first novel in 1986. Laing's first novel *Search Sweet Country* can be used for such an exercise because not only is it highly poetic and surreal, as is Okri's writing, it also draws on indigenous beliefs for aspects of the narrative. Furthermore, it manages a careful balance between fantasy and reality. While it is clear that the writing is meant to subvert dominant modes of realism, there is also the awareness that it is rooted in concerns with the real world. In *Search Sweet Country* the sociogeography of Accra forms the dominant background to the characters' quest for an authentic mode of existence. In *Search Sweet Country*, as in Okri's work, there is a suggestion of the radical intersubstantiation of things. However, the mode of representing this intuition throws up quite different implications in the work of the two writers.

M.E. Kropp-Dakubu has written an elegant analysis of the language of authenticity in *Search Sweet Country*. Proceeding from a socio-linguistic perspective she points out that the novel creates a special literary sociolect that draws elements from various Ghanaian languages.[1] Furthermore, she notes, Laing achieves a peculiar poeticised idiom for the novel through a careful patterning of alliterations, puns and other poetic devices. She argues that this type of language is a transposition of the language of Laing's poetry which is itself influenced by the work of the Concrete Poetry Movement of Scotland in the 1960s as well as Akan proverbial usage. It is necessary, however, to extend the terms by which to assess the narrative discourse of the novel from an examination of discrete linguistic elements to an analysis of the discursive interplay of the effects of language with other dimensions of the narrative. Even though it is not possible in this short piece to fully outline these terms, I hope to identify some ways in which the narrative discourse of *Search Sweet Country* operates as a means by which ultimately to compare Laing's work with Ben Okri's writing in terms of broader literary strategies. By touching on Laing and moving on to Okri, I hope to indicate some fruitful ways in which non-realist African writing may be read.

As an example of Laing's mode of interweaving fantasy with the real or recognisable consider a telling passage in the novel in which Kofi Loww, one of the central characters, is walking through the centre of Accra:

> Passing Ussher Fort by Sraha Market where the Pentecostal church clapped its walls, Loww saw how clearly everything – from fresh water and churches to governments and castles – could fit easily in reflection in gutters. This city could not satisfy the hunger of gutters, for there was nothing yet which had not been reflected in them. The Bukom building gaped through its small windows at the ancient coconut tree . . . which danced with the rhythm of his own heartbeats. The old fisherman mending his nets had hair the same colour as the passing clouds; and this same colour was thrown down in different shades onto the buildings, buildings sharing among themselves the poverty and richness of different decades, different centuries. (*Search Sweet Country*, p. 7)

As the passage shows, the narrative has a surreal texture to it. This emerges in a series of discursive moves in the narration of events. The first move involves the partial humanisation of setting. The Pentecostal Church 'clapped its walls', the Bukom building 'gaped through its small windows' while the coconut tree is seen as dancing the odd rhythm of Kofi Loww's heart. In all these, there is an investment of human qualities in some aspects of the setting described. However, this is restricted to local details only. The setting is not shown as being capable of agency or action. A suggestion of such agency would immediately strip the setting of all innocence and make it a potential character interacting with the other characters in the novel.

Another discursive move involves the metaphorical transfer of qualities from one item to another and the suggestion that everything partakes of the qualities of everything else. In this passage the metaphorical transfers are partly focused in the reflection of images in the gutters of the city. When the hair of the old fisherman is described as of 'the same colour as the passing clouds' and the ancient buildings are said to borrow the same hue, their being reflected in the gutters encloses them in the same fluid space to show how easy it is to perceive the interrelationships of different qualities with the shift in perspective. Significantly, however, there is also the suggestion that the inter-relationships are a more pervasive and nebulous part of existence and that it is not just physical attributes that are continually circulated among things but also more intangible essences. This can be gleaned from the hint that the buildings shared among themselves 'the richness and poverty of different periods' as if there is a continual interchange of agedness and youth among the buildings. The observations made here about the passage by no means exhaust the rich and varied ways in which the surreal texture of the novel is sustained. The notion of metaphorical transfers is a pervasive part of the novel's discourse and quite often one item, be it a tree, a human being or a wall is described in a simultaneous relationship with the qualities of other items.

Drawing on Roman Jakobson's typology of linguistic discourse, we can say that items in the narrative are described in a metaphoric discursive mode.[2] Things are defined in a metaphoric relationship to other things so that it is not just their physical positioning in relation to other things that matters but their metaphoric relationships as well. So when early in the novel the tree under which Kofi Loww and his father stand is said to 'shine' their souls, the tree is being described in relation to the activity of shoe shining. But, as Kropp-Dakubu points out, this depends for its effectiveness on a prior pun of 'soul' with 'sole' which, however, is not made an explicit part of the text. We may expand the range of potential referents and add that the tree might be a vantage point from which shoe-shine boys ply their customers. Or it could be shining their souls due to the emotional effects of the peace it is capable of generating. Alternatively, could it not also be shining in terms of 'polishing' as is done with knives? Would this not be a pointer rather to contentiousness instead of peace? This might explain the fact that the two men express their different personalities and disagreements under the tree. The point of all these analogies is to show how each described item often exceeds its material location in the text because of the metaphorical transfers that are seen to go on at all times. Thus the description of any one item requires careful unravelling by the reader with recourse to the subtle and often concealed metaphoric relationships in the text.

It must be noted, however, that the surreal quality of the narrative is largely a function of the narrator's perspective on events and the language used to describe them. The novel adopts a third-person mode of narration and this is not identified with any particular character in the novel. The narrator shifts liberally from describing one character to another. Because of this aspect of the narrative's discourse, the surreal quality of the descriptions has little impact on the ways in which the characters perceive setting or the events in which they are involved. Rather, the special quality is a function of the narrator's attitude to what is being described. The poetic quality of the writing is aimed at disrupting the reading process and presenting the narrative representation as problematic in the face of the language in which it is couched. As language affects setting, it renders it surreal and partly humanised but neutral in terms of the course of the action. Furthermore, it remains strictly discrete and coherent from the limited perspective of the characters. In relation to characterisation, the characters are themselves presented to us as partaking in the surreal exchanges of the narrative's discourse, but this is not evident to them. Because of this dichotomy between how the narrator describes things and how the characters perceive their world, the narrative institutes a subtle level of irony into the unfolding of events. Though the characters are all bent on seeking an authentic mode of social existence and perceive this as a vague possibility, they are frustrated from achieving any such goal because, in fact, the goal cannot be consolidated within the surreal texture of things, something which they are largely unaware of. Thus Beni Baidoo struggles to communicate by talking to everyone but ends up talking to himself. And the characters often shout at each other and talk across each other instead of to each other. The play of the language, then, props up the staging of the deracination of the central characters amidst bureaucratic corruption which is the thematic concern of the novel.

There is a significant dimension of the narrative, however, where it can be seen that the surreal perspective of the narrator coalesces with the perspective of certain characters in the novel even though this is not shown to have a direct effect on the course of the action. This dimension is that of the esoteric within the narrative. The esoteric is introduced in direct relation to the characterisation of Adwoa Ade who we are shown flying across the face of the city. This defines her clearly as a witch in popular belief. Interestingly, however, she is not an evil force but rather a 'witch for Christ', since she balances the witchcraft bequeathed to her by her grandmother with a strong belief in God. When she flies across the city, her itinerary is over the lives of ordinary work-a-day people burdened with their petty worries and confusions. These people 'pray' to her and address her as an agony aunt, telling her all their personal problems as she flies across at night (*Search Sweet Country*, pp. 28–34, 124–34).

The thing to note about Adwoa's characterisation is that she is the only character defined in terms of indigenous spiritual beliefs. The notion that witches are bequeathed their craft by others and that they can fly is widespread not only among the Akan but also among several African peoples. But Laing is not so much interested in reflecting indigenous beliefs as in getting a surrogate for spiritual beliefs in general, be they indigenous or Christian. Filiating Adwoa's spiritual potential to a Christian basis ensures that the whole issue of spiritualism becomes relativised and problematic. The fact that her spiritual potential is projected outwards, and that she is perceived by people, disrupts the unity and coherence of the world for them. However, this disruption is beneficial rather than traumatic as they are allowed to momentarily escape their problems and enter into a dialogue with the spirit-realm represented in the flying Adwoa Ade. Irony attends this particular form of quest for spiritual solace, partly because Adwoa herself has unresolved problems when she descends into the flesh. From the point of view of the narrative's discourse, the significant thing is that Adwoa's characterisation hints at the potential sources of indigenous beliefs upon which the experiments with form may be grounded as a way of problematising narrative representation. But, because this potential is shown to be peripheral in terms of the course of the action, the force of the non-realist experiment resides largely within the play of the highly aestheticised language of the novel.

It is in the implications deriving from this aesthetisation of language, used here as a means of foregrounding the intersubstantiation of things in *Search Sweet Country*, that Okri's work can be differentiated from Laing's. Okri's work throws up different challenges. From the short stories onwards, when he began experimenting with non-realist modes of representation, there has been an effort to problematise protocols of representation by routeing several aspects of narrative discourse through a prism of indigenous beliefs about spirits and their relationship to the real world. The area of setting, for instance, is progressively de-neutralised so that it takes on a hallucinatory potential and has a direct impact on the structure of narrative events. The contours of the city in particular are conceptually re-mapped so as to carry a load of hallucinatory potential. But this re-mapping goes hand in hand with an increasing decentring of characterisation as well. Character is based on indigenous beliefs about the spirit potential of human beings. These intuitions are expressed differently from story to story, with 'Stars of the New Curfew', 'Incidents at the Shrine' and 'When the Lights Return' all giving different perspectives on the spiritual and decentred foundations of characterisation.[3]

Yet, perhaps the most innovative in terms of both the conceptual re-mapping of the city-scape as well as the decentring of character is 'When the Lights Return'. In this story, involving the strained love relationship between Ede and Maria, the characterisation of Maria relies on beliefs to do with spiritual vitality and witchcraft. Maria's character depends on a dual movement in which she is shown as the potential victim of evil forces as well as one who is capable of projecting her spiritual vitality outwards on to the environment as witches are believed to be able to. As the story unfolds, her essence is shown to be projected on to several features of the city. Her face is seen by Ede on the faces of goats, cats and dogs, and blind beggars seem momentarily to take on her appearance. Whole crowds are shown to be pervaded by her essence, and she finally manifests herself to her boyfriend in a tangle at the market as a 'midget-girl with an old body, a young face, and a weird growth of beard'. The point of her continual reflection in aspects of the urban setting is to show that the hallucinatory potential of spirituality no longer resides solely in the breasts of 'evil' people, but, rather, that the city itself harbours terror as it produces the squalor and dispossession of urban life. This idea is further grounded in the fact that Ede walks through an urban 'hell' in his journey to Maria's place. All the evidence of squalor and brutality that he encounters is meant to register this dimension of the urban setting.

In 'When the Lights Return', setting as well as characterisation rely on mythopoeic indigenous beliefs to problematise the question of narrative representation. It must be noted that Maria shares some affinities with Adwoa Ade in *Search Sweet Country*. Like Adwoa Ade, her spiritual potential is projected outwards. The difference, however, is in the hallucinatory effect that this projection is shown to have on setting. The esoteric disruptions of the narrative are shown to have material correlatives in the squalor and terrible brutality of the urban environment. In Okri's short story, not only is the hallucinatory potential of Maria's character coalesced with aspects of the urban setting, this is made manifest to Ede and has a decidedly tragic effect on him. In Okri's writing indigenous spiritual beliefs are increasingly centralised till they become the very basis by which narrative events are to be explained.

The experiments carried out in the short stories are further elaborated in *The Famished Road* and its sequel *Songs of Enchantment*.[4] In these novels not only are setting and characterisation shown to be decentred and fractured, but narratorial agency itself is surrendered to a character who is not unified in terms of our ordinary knowledge of human beings. All the events in the novel are narrated in the first person by Azaro, an *abiku* child who retains ties with his spirit companions and has access to both the real world and that of spirits. Belief in the *abiku* phenomenon is widespread in southern Nigeria and refers to a child who is trapped in a cycle of births, deaths and re-births. The phenomenon has already had literary treatment in the writings of Wole Soyinka, J. Bekederemo-Clark and Chinua Achebe.[5] For Azaro the problem is that he does not always enter or exit these realms through acts of his own volition. The matter is often entirely out of his control. Rather, a spirit potential is posited as inhering in all things and this potential is shown to be able to manifest itself arbitrarily. Because the narrative is focalised through the consciousness of the *abiku* child who is himself radically decentred, the whole work has a shifting and unsettling quality.

Two examples may serve to illustrate this. Once, early in the novel, Azaro goes to the market-place where he sees spirit-figures who have come to the market. Curious about them, he follows a baby-spirit 'with the face of a squirrel' out of the market. He follows it into the forest where he notices a clearing, apparently for road construction. He is fascinated by a 'gash' in the earth. He stares at the gash and suddenly hears a tearing sound. He shuts his eyes and on opening them finds to his amazement that he has been transferred into the 'belly of the Road'. He has moved along the real-world-spirit-world axis without any act of volition on his part. A gigantic turtle questions him to find out his purpose there. Not satisfied with his answers, the irate turtle lumbers off and leaves Azaro to cry himself to sleep. On waking he finds that he is lying on an excavated sand-pit being used for the construction of the road (*The Famished Road*, pp. 15–17). The implication of this episode is that the 'same' geographical space is simultaneously in the real world as well as that of spirits and that each dimension is manifested to Azaro without any act of volition on his part.

In another incident, Azaro decides to depart to the spirit world with a three-headed spirit in protest at being flogged by his father. He refuses all food and falls progressively into a trance till it is impossible to wake him up. He journeys with the three-headed spirit in a spirit world in which they encounter people building a highway. They finally come to a river on which there is a canoe guarded by an old woman with the feet of a lioness. However, his parents are desperate to revive him and after a few days solicit the help of a fetish priestess. The whole episode is striking in that every gesture of his parents and the priestess is simultaneously calibrated with events in the spirit world. The ending of the section is significant in this respect:

> The weapon of the old woman with the feet of a lioness had become golden-red. One of the heads of the spirit had rolled onto the river of mirrors and its eyes stared at the eternity of reflections in a bad-tempered astonishment. Dad's knife, full of reflections, was lifted above me, as if I were to be the sacrificial victim of my own birth. I screamed. The knife in Dad's hand descended swiftly, slashed the air twice. The herbalist released a piercing cry. The old woman struck the spirit at the same moment, with a mighty swipe of her weapon. Dad slashed the chicken's throat. The old woman severed the spirit's last head. The spirit fought vainly in the canoe as the chicken twitched. Its blood dripped on my forehead. The herbalist fell silent. The spirit's head, landing on silver, looked around, saw itself separated from its body, and let out its final scream of horror, cracking the surface of the river. The mirror shattered. It became dark. Splinters and reflections caught in my eyes. (*The Famished Road*, p. 339)

In this section, there is a rapid translation of events between the spirit world and the real world and the reader is orientated to the two simultaneously. There is a dream-like quality to the whole incident, and it seems to be an interesting adumbration of the relationship between dream stimuli and dream work. The implications of this episode exceed such an explanation however. Here readers are placed in a position where they can perceive the operations in both realms simultaneously, almost giving them a visionary privilege in having access to dimensions of the incident unavailable to Azaro's parents. But this also implies that there is a continual intersubstantiation of the two dimensions of existence that is not always evident to the senses. The implication of this is that Azaro, and by extension the whole of nature, is located on a kaleidoscopically moving space in which the same space can be arbitrarily re-located in either world at any point in time. In *The Famished Road*, the potential intersubstantiation of things derives from a postulation of a spiritual/physical duality in all things. The expression of the arbitrary interplay of this duality is what gives the novel its peculiar surreal texture, unlike what was observed in Laing's work where the implications of intersubstantiation derive mainly from effects of language.

Because of the varying interplay of the real world with that of spirits even when Okri seems to be striking a note of mere surrealism, the implications are quite different from other surrealist narrative discourses. Consider a passage which is remarkably full of colour and a gentle play of essences:

> I ran through the night forests, where all forms are mutable, where all things exchange their identities, and where everything dances in an exultation of flame and wisdom. I ran till I came to the Atlantic, silver and blue under the night of forests. Birds flew in the aquamarine sky. Feathers gyrated onto the waves. The sky was full of dense white clouds moving like invading armies of mist and ghosts over the deep serene blue and under the regenerative skies. (*The Famished Road*, p. 457)

The sense of an infinite potential for transformations is conjured in the various shifting images of colour, water, clouds and birds and there is a feeling of stillness as well as motion because we are encouraged to dwell on the images while being aware of movement in verbs like 'exchange', 'dance' and 'gyrate'. The whole effect is much like a surreal painting of a seascape with a hint of hidden potentialities in the contours of the various images playing on the surface of the canvas. Significantly, the narrator himself foregrounds his sense of perceiving the intersubstantiation of things from the very first sentence in the passage when he notes that this is a place 'where all forms are mutable' and 'all things exchange their identities'. But, because this sense is presented as part of a general knowledge of the interrelationships between the real and the spirit worlds, which have demonstrated their capacity for arbitrary manifestation, we know that the surreal potentialities in such a passage have a material effect on the turn of events themselves. Here lies a significant difference between the non-realist experiments in Okri's work and those by other African writers.

Part of the arbitrariness in the interplay between real and esoteric derives from the diminution in the stature of the mythopoeic hero in *The Famished Road*. Critics have already noted how the novel recalls the discursive schema of Amos Tutuola's work.[6] But in Tutuola's narratives the protagonists all had heroic potential which was continually re-affirmed in the course of their adventures in the spirit realms. They have an epochal quality because they are partial inscriptions of communal values. The mythopoeic character derives strength from being a representative of a communal ethos. Azaro has none of that energetic stature. His is the existential condition of being (in the sense of living the essence of) *abiku*. He resides more in the mode of 'once and the repeated time' which the *abiku* in Soyinka's poem of the same title articulates. Azaro himself offers a key to understanding his condition, when, in describing the attack of thugs on his neighbourhood, he says he perceived 'in the crack of a moment, the recurrence of things unresolved – histories, dreams, a vanished world of great old spirits, wild jungles, tigers with eyes of diamonds roaming the dense foliage' (*The Famished Road*, p. 176). His peculiar condition is to see the recurrence of things within the flux of existence. Azaro cannot consolidate a form of action in the partial framework of the mythopoeia in which he resides. It is other characters in the novel such as Madame Koto and Dad who manage to grow from one position to another even though in both cases this is also rendered problematic given the choices they exercise. Whereas Dad moves to a greater grasp of the reality of spiritual realities in his re-dreaming of the world at the end of the novel, the mode of social action he aspires to is shown to be severely limited in the light of the conditions of squalor and dispossession within which he has to exercise his visions. And Madame Koto's attainment of wealth and spiritual power is shown to be limited in value precisely because she moves towards separating the amassing of wealth and influence from questions of morality by filiating herself with the Party of the Rich.[7]

In many ways Okri's experiments with narrative form harbour ambiguous meanings for working out the relationship between literature and the real-life conditions which it is meant to be engaging with. *The Famished Road* has been described as 'snake biting its tail'.[8] This might be taken to point to tragedy and potential non-being. However, it can also be interpreted as an image of fertility and liberation. The duality of the image is a good marker of the ambiguousness of the structure of non-realist discourse in Ben Okri's work. If, as is suggested in *The Famished Road*, the whole of reality is sited on a continually shifting conceptual space, is it not to suggest the impossibility of consolidating a sense of self and identity within such an arena? The novel attempts a partial resolution of such a conundrum in its narrative structure by drawing on mythopoeia and continually gesturing to the sense of completion available in it, even if this is not completely available in the text. But a total location in mythopoeia would have altered the relationship between a recognisable condition of post-colonial dispossession and the strength to be drawn from indigenous beliefs by sundering the novel completely from reality so that it would have to be read solely as allegory or other symbolic discourse. So an uneasy balance is maintained in the novel between a concern with reality and a reliance on mythopoeia.

This particular formula is abandoned in *Songs of Enchantment* in which the whole narrative takes a complete turn to mythopoeia. The object of the novel is to stage the elemental struggle between the forces of Good, represented by Azaro's Dad, and those of Evil, represented by Madame Koto and the Jackal-headed Masquerade. The lineaments of this elemental struggle are sharpened around a set of moral choices presented to Azaro's neighbourhood when it is faced with the question of whether to bury Ade's father against the expressed wishes of the two political parties which threaten a reign of terror if they are disobeyed. Ade is killed in a fight over who covered Madame Koto's car with snails and his father is killed in a subsequent brawl. As the two parties forbid the burial of the father's corpse in a strange evocation of the sanctions of a perverted Greek tragedy the moral tension in the novel tightens until Azaro's father decides to dare damnation and bury the corpse. He immediately becomes the target of the evil forces led by Madame Koto, and there is an extended and colourful stand-off between the forces of Good and Evil played out in exuberant esoteric images.

Colourful though all this is, it restricts the novel to the closures of mythology in terms of the outcome of elemental struggles. This formula dissolves the fine balance between the real world and the esoteric that was problematically maintained in *The Famished Road*. *Songs of Enchant-ment* is not only narrated through the consciousness of Azaro, who, as was noted, has access to both the real world and that of spirits, but all characters have equal access to the world of spirits. There is thus a loss of the irony that often attended the relationships between Azaro and other characters in the earlier novel. Secondly, there is a certain portentousness involved in the characters' actions because of their equal access to spiritual resources and the configuration of the struggle for ascendancy between the forces of Good and those of Evil. There is an implied moralism in the novel that derives directly from the socialising and morally affirmative tone of myth and folktale. However, it is a moralism that is not easy to identify with because of the positing of moral particularities taken to define the characters' mode of action from beginning to end. The conflict in the narrative is delimited mainly within the ethos of folklore and mythology, making not only the outcome of the conflict predictable from the very beginning of the novel but also rendering characterisation a function solely of moral codes. The novel depends for its message on a simple manichean polarisation which is difficult to accept without reservations because of the distance this implies from social reality. Such simple moral oppositions are impossible to sustain when read against the complexities of social reality.

Does this mean that the mythopoeic and/or the fantastic cannot remain sources for non-realist narrative discourse without contingently narrowing the moral positions available to the text? Or that indigenous beliefs such as those to do with spirits cannot be transferred into literature without carrying with them the moral particularities of the belief-systems which were their foundations in the first place? Perhaps this is to ask imponderable and irrelevant questions of literature. To grope towards an answer, it is better to see non-realist writing in Africa as part of a broader field of cultural endeavour in which the hybrid fusion of indigenous beliefs with more modern predilections defines a continual *movement of cultural transition*. What Okri's initiative demonstrates is the tensions and contradictions that inhere in every hybrid moment of cultural transition. Thus the tensions and contradictions in Okri's writing cannot be worked out solely in terms of the boundaries of the literary text. The full meaning of the contradictions in the experiments with narrative form lie simultaneously elsewhere, partly located in the relationship between literature and the real world it purports to address and partly dispersed within culture.

It is also important, for instance, to grasp the relationship of non-realist writing to the sense of the incoherence in the status of the post-colonial condition in Africa, political, social as well as cultural. Biodun Jeyifo traces an extensive genealogy in African writing for relating a sense of post-independence disillusionment. He points out that works from across the continent such as Achebe's *A Man of the People*, Soyinka's *The Interpreters*, Ayi Kwei Armah's *Fragments*, Ngũgĩ's *Petals of Blood* and Dambudzo Marechera's *The House of Hunger* share the same dissatisfactions:

> In all these works, with varying levels of technical self-assurance and competence, the narrative and stylistic organisation of the material is

informed by a problematic which assumes that the work of fiction can no longer complacently proffer a fictional 'reality' axiomatically at variance with the socio-historical reality of alienation, degradation, chaos and instability for the vast majority of its living generations.[9]

Jeyifo adds that the significance of these novels lies not just in the content which explores social malaise, but that there is an insinuation of the sense of social disjuncture into the very form and structure of the novels. The specific dissatisfactions with political and social malaise differ from country to country as do their literary expression in narrative discourse. In the particular case of Nigeria the euphoria of decolonisation was rapidly replaced by disillusionment and a questioning of the viability of the nation-state in its contemporary constitution. The events leading up to and including the Biafran secessionist bid from 1966 to 1970 is a clear indication of the extent to which the viability of the Nigerian state was questioned.

For Okri and his generation, growing up in a post-independence Nigeria, the euphoria of decolonisation was not available to fall back on. All that they inherited was a bewildering sense of absent opportunities. Furthermore, the pervasiveness of corruption and graft in social and political life deepened the sense of disillusionment even further. The stories that circulated in the 1970s and 1980s about embezzlements in the country have literary treatment in Okri's 'Disparities', a story which tells of the pauperised existence of the narrator in the painful knowledge that a Nigerian state official has 'forgotten' a quarter of a million pounds on a cab seat in London. Okri had a particularly bitter taste of the effects of the potential disruptiveness of corruption in Nigeria due to growing up in the ghettos of Lagos where social amenities were always uncertain and people were forever at the mercy of their landlords. In fact, his first bid at writing was to relate in fictional form some of the problems in the ghettos of Lagos. The state of corruption made it impossible to write about events using the same rationalism of prevailing protocols of representation.[10]

If *The Famished Road* is re-read in the light of these considerations, we can see that the radicalisation of narrative form is a means of rendering the acute sense of bewilderment at the incoherence of the socio-political domain. The experiments with form have a literary as well as socio-political dimension. It is not idle, therefore, that at certain moments in the novel the *abiku* motif becomes a trope by which the condition of the nation-state and other realities are to the understood:

Things that are not ready, not willing to be born or become, things for which adequate preparations have not been made to sustain their momentous births, things that are not resolved, things bound up with failure and with fear of being, they all keep coming back, and in themselves partake of the spirit-child's condition. They keep coming and going till their time is right. History itself demonstrates how things of the world partake of the condition of the abiku-child (*The Famished Road*, p. 487)

The pointer to improper preparations for momentous births links up with Soyinka's own reminder to his nation of the cyclicality of political irresponsibility in a *A Dance of the Forests*, a play which was commissioned specifically to mark Nigeria's independence celebrations in 1960. The nation is partly figured in that play as a half-bodied child, alluding suggestively to an *abiku* condition and also to the fact that the country's nation-status is not something to be taken for granted in euphoric celebrations of a new birth. By implying that the state partly shares the *abiku* condition thirty years on, Okri suggests that the cyclicality of arrested development can become endemic if it is not recognised for what it really is. That he chooses to pose the issue as a function of the potential relationships between the real world and that of spirits suggests that the condition of post-colonial arrested development cannot be adequately grasped within the rationality of Western discourses. The rationality of indigenous belief systems has a part to play in the understanding of the African condition.

## Notes

1. M. E. Kropp-Dakubu, 'Search Sweet Country and the Language of Authentic Being', *Research in African Literatures* 24, 1 (1993), pp. 19–35.

2. See Roman Jakobson, 'The Metonymic and Metaphoric Poles', in *Modern Criticism and Theory*, ed. David Lodge, London: Longman, 1988, pp. 57–61; and, for a fuller exploration of the implications of Jakobson's typology, see David Lodge, *The Modes of Modern Writing*, London: Routledge, 1977.

3. I take the liberty of referring to Okri's short stories without indicating the specific collection from which they come because of the fairly widespread thematic and formal connections between them. My focus, as can be seen, is on his second collection *Stars of the New Curfew*, London: Heinemann, 1988, from which I take 'When the Lights Return' for special comment. His first collection was *Incidents at the Shrine*, London: Heinemann, 1986.

4. *The Famished Road*, London: Cape, 1991; *Songs of Enchantment*, London: Cape, 1993. Page references will be included in the text.

5. See Chidi Maduka, 'African Religious Beliefs in the Literary Imagination:

Ogbanje and Abiku in Chinua Achebe, J. P. Clarke and Wole Soyinka', *Journal of Commonwealth Literature* 22, 1 (1987), pp. 17–30.

6. See, especially, Chidi Okonkwo, 'The Quest for Order in a Changing Order', *Cambridge Anthropology* 15, 3 (1991), pp. 41–52; and Kole Omotoso, 'No Poor Relation', review of *Songs of Enchantment*, the *Guardian* (Manchester) 23 March 1993.

7. For a fuller discussion of the shifting basis of heroic vocation in *The Famished Road*, see my 'Orality–(Theory)–Textuality: Tutuola, Okri and the relationship of literary practice to oral traditions', forthcoming in *The Pressures of the Text*, ed. Stewart Brown, Birmingham: African Studies Series.

8. Odia Ofeimun in a discussion generated by a paper entitled 'Literature and the crisis of the nation state in Africa' presented at the 20th Annual African Literature Conference held in Accra, 26 March to 1 April, 1994.

9. Biodun Jeyifo, 'The Voice of a Lost Generation: The Novels of Ben Okri', the *Guardian* (Lagos) 12 July 1986.

10. See his interview with Jane Wilkinson in *Talking With African Writers*, London: Heinemann, 1992.

# Mediating Origins: Moyez Vassanji and the Discursivities of Migrant Identity

> Break a vase, and the love that reassembles
> the fragments is stronger than that love that
> took its symmetry for granted when it was
> whole. The glue that fits the fragments, the
> cracked heirlooms whose restoration shows its
> white scars. This gathering of broken pieces
> is the care and the pain of the Antilles, and
> if the pieces are disparate, ill-fitting, they
> contain more pain than their original sculpture,
> those icons and sacred vessels taken for
> granted in their ancestral places. Antillean
> art is this restoration of our shattered
> histories, our shards of vocabulary, our
> archipelago becoming a synonym for pieces
> broken off from the original continent. (Derek Walcott)[1]

Walcott's metaphors carry the particular history of the Caribbean, its narratives of deracination, slavery, colonialism and survival. The history is one of fragmentation and then a piecing together by a glue that mediates that history's shape and dimensions even as it fixes it; it survives to locate the identity of the present in that past. But in their images of an Origin filtered through a history of diaspora, these metaphors go beyond the particular to speak eloquently of the discursive pressures and practices that attend all migrant experiences.

Moyez Vassanji's *The Gunny Sack, Uhuru Street* and *No New Land*[2] testify to the pervasive presence of origins – several origins, given the centrality in these works of members of a (fictional) Shamsi community from India, who, seeking their fortune in East Africa, first settle in Zanzibar, Mombasa, and Rukanga. Those in German-controlled African territory then flee to British Tanganyika after the First World War and set up business in Dar-es-Salaam. Finally, those who can, migrate to the West after Tanganyika's independence and Idi Amin's expulsion of Asians from Uganda. *The Gunny Sack* focuses on one family, beginning with the migration from Junapur in India to Zanzibar of Dhanji Govindji, the narrator's great-grandfather. The narrative features the lives of four generations of the Govindji family and spans almost a century (1885 to the 1970s). The catalyst and central metaphor of the novel is a gunny willed to the narrator by his grand aunt Ji Bai, which contains mementos from her past that enables him, Salim (nicknamed Kala because of his dark complexion), to imagine and probe his family history. As each object in the sack becomes a mnemonic device, Salim invests the gunny itself with a gender, a name – Sherbanoo – and personality which in turn seduces, teases, mesmerises, keeps watch and nags. There are echoes here of Padma the pickle-maker who, as companion to Saleem Sinai in Salman Rushdie's *Midnight's Children*, urges him on in his narration and keeps a check on his imagination. Such portrayals, and such a gendering of the gunny by Vassanji are not innocent and are constructed within patriarchy, for in *The Gunny Sack* Sherbanoo becomes the seductive partner that is the past, the Scheherazade-like 'woman' who, spinning tales, shares the basement flat with an otherwise lonely Salim in Toronto. There is nevertheless important recognition of the centrality of origins and the past in the formation of the migrant's sense of self, which is either a Rushdiesque pickle or a re-couperable history as in Vassanji's work (whose own trajectory as a Tanzanian of Indian origin who now lives in Canada mirrors that of Salim in *The Gunny Sack*).

Salim states in *The Gunny Sack*: 'The past is just this much beyond reach, you can reconstruct it only through the paraphernalia it leaves behind in your gunny sack . . . and then who would deny that what you manufacture is only a model' (p. 127). There is understanding here of the sense of loss and fragmentation of the past that Walcott referred to, the irretrievability of origins except through the imagination and therefore the past as something 'manufactured'. This resonates with yet another statement on the migrant's relationship with the past. Salman Rushdie comments that:

> if we do look back, we must also do so in the knowledge – which gives rise to profound uncertainties – that our own physical alienation from India almost inevitably means that we will not be capable of reclaiming precisely the thing that was lost; that we will, in short, create fictions, not actual cities or villages, but invisible ones, imaginary homelands, Indias of the mind.[3]

This imagining also engenders distortions, as is borne out in *Midnight's Children* in which Saleem Sinai is an unreliable narrator, making numerous errors when describing, in his inimitable fashion, life and history in India. At times he invents a topography of his own, mixes up dates and events and gets his mythology wrong. In remembering India, both the filter of memory and, as Rushdie explains, Saleem's desire 'to shape his material (so) that the reader will be forced to concede his central role' mediate in how the homeland is presented (*Imaginary Homelands*, p. 24). Nor are these 'mistakes' confined to the characters. As will be shown later on in this essay, it is possible to see in migrant literature the author's own anamorphosis in depicting the place of origin and its landscape.

What Walcott, Vassanji and Rushdie affirm then is that the migrant's reminiscence produces something both less than whole – which brings 'pain' in Walcott's sense, 'profound uncertainties' for Rushdie and to Vassanji is '*only a model*' – while at the same time being more valuable and enabling for freeing the mind to create imaginary homelands. This imagining, as Walcott implies, elevates signifiers of the past to the status of heirlooms and icons which re-invest the migrant with a sense of wholeness. It is this nexus of loss and gain that is constructed and negotiated in the discourse of migrant writing, albeit with varying emphases and different narrative strategies. The recouping of the past and origins becomes then always a fresh production of identity. It is the ideology underpinning this process and the discursive practices by means of which it occurs that will be the focus of this essay.

The need to re-visualise and record the past is a strong impulse that is given voice to in many registers throughout Vassanji's work. At one level is the author's own 'Adamic' yearning to chronicle the collective history of his community.[4] In an interview Vassanji stated of the Asian community in East Africa:

> That life . . . has never been written about. It's something that's slowly being wiped out, and as the people who've experienced that life die . . . there's no more record of that life. I think all people should have a sense of themselves, a sense of where they come from and it just happens that people in East Africa – I think Indians as well as Africans and especially in Tanzania – don't have that sense, a historical sense, of where they come from. There is a vague kind of oral history telling them where they come from but it's not something that you read about; it's something that's constantly changing, and if you just compare it with what goes on in the West where everything is recorded you can see that our lives have not been recorded and that's what I set out to do when I wrote the novel.[5]

The construction of this archive is an ambitious project, both full of creative possibilities and fraught with dangers. The recognition of the importance of a *recorded* collective history to a community's identity echoes Nuruddin Farah's statement that: 'To write is to claim a text of one's own; textuality is an instrument of territorial repossession; because the other confers on us an identity that alienates us from ourselves, narrative is crucial to the discovery of our selfhood.'[6] While in the African context this was a pragmatic strategy in cultural de-colonisation, the legitimising of orature through the written word is none the less *classed*, for a written history is accessible only to the educated. Moreover, it carries a hegemony which 'fixes' a certain history as the authoritative one. But within this, transcribing a collective history allowed Vassanji a creative space in which, with sensitivity, he redresses certain imbalances to include disparate voices that would otherwise never have been the subject of history, and recoup from the margins incidents in the lives of ordinary citizens to relate them as grand narrative.

Thus one of the most moving episodes in *The Gunny Sack* describes how, when British–German tensions of the First World War spill over to East Africa and Tanganyika threatens to become a theatre of war, the Asian community in Matamu decides to flee into exile. The implemen-tation of that decision is precise and accepted stoically. The men take what they can – gunny bags stuffed with one-rupee notes and their wives' jewellery tied to their waists, for 'If they did not return they could start again, elsewhere':

> At every junction where two trails crossed, two families would leave the caravan and take the cross-trail to the nearest village. They used a simple device to select the two families whose turn had come. A woman would sing a line from a song; the next one would sing one from another song, beginning with the last word sung. And so the game was played as the singing caravan proceeded deeper inland, until at a junction one of the guides called a halt, selecting the woman with a song on her lips, and her predecessor. The two families would then start their farewells to the rest of the caravan . . . Ji Bai had always been good at the game, and she often won. The trick, she would say, was to take the cue quickly, without a moment's hesitation, and to pick a short line to sing – no matter how silly it sounded. This time it was important she should win . . . (*The Gunny Sack*, p. 49)

The understatement, the unsentimentality of this move belies the anxieties and upheavals experienced by the community. Vassanji's superbly controlled description of the diaspora makes it the stuff of epic narrative.

On the other hand, the pressure of constructing a collective history produces a certain essentialism through a homogenising of the community which illustrates the dangers involved in such an Adamic venture. In Vassanji's work, the emphasis on an Islamic sect sidelines the heterogeneity of the Asians in Tanzania comprising Ismailis, Bohras, Sikhs, Punjabis, Hindus, Jains and Goanese, and faiths such as Buddhism, Roman Catholicism and Zoroastrianism. In focusing on a period that begins in the latter decades of the nineteenth century, Vassanji gives the impression in *The Gunny Sack* that the Indian presence in East Africa is a recent one when in fact its involvement there has a long history. For instance it was an Indian who piloted Vasco da Gama from Malindi to Calicut in 1501, while both the caravan and slave trades in East Africa relied on the pivotal role played by Indian bankers.[7] Later, the British colonial enterprise relied on Indian labour to run its bureaucracy as well as to build and run its railways. Despite Indian involvement in these fields, it is the stereotype of the Indian migrant as a trader that abounds in Vassanji's work. Nor are Indians in other professions such as the medical, legal, administrative and clerical services particularly visible. It is not that communal diversity is never given voice in Vassanji's stories. The Hindu Mrs Daya, and 'Uncle Goa' enjoy an important presence in *The Gunny Sack*. At election time, Salim is aware that where TANU, the Governor, the Africans, in short everyone else, saw 'Asian', the Asians saw 'Shamsi, Bohra, Ismaili, Hindu', conscious of themselves as distinct ethnic and religious groups competing for the same votes (*The Gunny Sack*, p. 146). But Vassanji's (wholly expected) failure to give equal weight throughout his work to the experiences of all these groups and the diverse histories of Asian migrancy in East Africa means that the aspirations, insecurities and customs of the Shamsis he selects for detailed portrayal are read as metonymic for the larger collective experience.

Thus it is through the common spaces, codes of behaviour and intimacies shared by the Shamsis, as depicted for instance in the short stories that comprise *Uhuru Street*, that Vassanji delineates the impact of the history of migration on the particular as individual families settle into new landscapes or face the poignancy of departure. Uhuru Street, beginning at the hinterland with its African settlements, running through Dar-es-Salaam with its Indian stores, homes and mosque and ending on the sea front is the link between these disparate worlds. It is where mistrust between Indian and African spill over in the taunting of an African beggar by Indian schoolboys ('The Beggar'), the London-returned parade their latest fashions and sightseeing foreigners stroll through. It is also where, indoors, vignettes of family life are created by Vassanji to illuminate a larger collective communal identity through the foregrounding of common family aspirations, hypocrisies and oppressions.[8]

A reading of the subtly nuanced first story in the collection, 'The Quiet of a Sunday Afternoon', illustrates how, in the tale of a man (the narrator) at the cross-roads, Vassanji foregrounds selected histories of origin, colonialism and family custom as cornerstones of the communal identity. The setting is the ubiquitous Indian store minded in turn by members of the family. The narrator, a 'half-caste' because his mother was African, is given an offer he cannot refuse in a proposal that makes him the husband of Baby, the fat and lethargic daughter of Hussein, the owner of the store. The 'impurity' that he is marked with because of his mixed parentage and the unequal status accorded to him because of his underclass background, says much about the rigidity of caste and class conventions the Indian migrants preserve even when settled in localities outside India, and their refusal to integrate with the native population. Thus the narrator's choice in 'The Quiet of a Sunday Afternoon' is between his wife and the extended family pressures she brings – a domineering father-in-law, the necessity to father a son and conversely, a feeling of emasculation – and Zarina, a woman he is attracted to, admires for her industry and pities for her poverty. It becomes a choice between orthodoxy and a rebellion which, although it still remains within patriarchy, carries a smarting critique of the rules and regulations he has lived by.

There is a suggestion in the story that these orthodoxies are most rigidly guarded by the older generation. The father-in-law's queries on meeting Zarina are made to locate her in terms of class, caste and family history:

> 'You are the daughter of Jamal Meghji,' he said at length.
> 'Yes,' said Zarina.
>     . . .
> 'I knew your father . . . What town was he from?'
> 'Mbinga,' she answered.
> 'I know that! Where in India?'
> 'I don't know. In Cutch or Gujarat somewhere.'
> 'Mudra,' he said, nodding at me. 'I remember when he came to Africa.'
> (*Uhuru Street*, p. 6)

That Zarina names an African town as her point of origin, is not sure which part of India her father came from and has to be corrected by

Hussein (who declares her a member of a 'third class family' to his son-in-law), hints at the Tanzanian-born second generation's lack of interest in fetishising their Indian origins. At the same time however, the open-endedness of the story as the narrator realises that the ever-watching Hussein prevents him from leaving the family domain for Zarina with anything but the 'clothes on (his) body and the few shillings jingling in (his) pocket', so that his very going becomes an 'If', suggests that the power of orthodoxy and materialism are not easily shaken off.

In Hussein's story of how Zarina's father made and lost his money is a powerful parable of the structures of colonialism and migrant experience within it. In selling the Germans stolen commodities, Jamal Meghji's wealth was built on a business acumen and complicity with both the local population and the colonial power that rehearses the stereotype of the Indian migrant as one who always 'plays both sides' to best economic advantage. It is then in a cultural space that his vulnerability is really shown to lie. With tension in the air following rumours of German defeat in the First World War, the Indian migrants hide their cash and jewellery from possible German looters. Some bury their wealth, others stuff their mattresses with it. Meghji chooses to hide his money in the several beehives he keeps in front of his house. This is because, according to African custom, stealing other people's beehives is taboo. The Germans however, subscribing to no such code, shoot them down while foraging for food. Meghji dies a pauper.

Through this one anecdote, Vassanji underscores the pressures on the migrant whose survival requires striking a delicate balance, in this instance, between the native African population and the colonial power even if this means collusion with both parties. That Meghji reaps the economic benefits of an expanded market thanks to the colonial presence on the one hand, but falls between two cultural stools with tragic consequences on the other, shows the process of survival to be a tense and insecure one, and points to a fundamental insight that it is at times of crisis that identity comes most undone. For at such moments the migrant's knowledge of cultural practices or business acumen prove shallow and inadequate. S/he remains isolated, foreign and rootless, and apart from the support of his/her own community enjoys no other protection. Nor can integration with the native population and land-scape ever be fully achieved by the Indian migrant in East Africa, as Vassanji's work testifies. Given his/her colonial conditioning and business interests, the migrant is always shown to prefer affiliation to the colonial power, singling out the native in most instances for scorn.

But assimilation with the native population is a much more complex reality than being merely a matter of individual choice over integration. For identity is a reactive discursivity and in the case of a minority, forged in response to its political and cultural marginalisation and the economic pressure of having to compete with other communities for the same resources. Under these circumstances, there are very few options available to the migrant. Either s/he has to subsume his/her identity, belligerently assert it or migrate elsewhere. Two examples from *The Gunny Sack* poignantly capture migrant identity as always such a site of tension.

> Then there were of course the demagogues out to provoke reaction against the Asians. 'The Asians are not integrating enough!' thundered one. 'If you want to stay in Africa, you must learn to live with Africans . . . the days of your dukas are numbered!'
>
> 'Foul!' murmured the gathering of shopkeepers at Diamond Jubilee Hall. 'Didn't we only recently give a gift of four sewing machines to the women's movement?'
>
> 'They have their eyes on our daughters, mind you,' Hassan Uncle gravely muttered.
>
> 'This flag,' roared the commissioner, 'it has the colours of Africa! This black and green and yellow flag – what does the black signify, eh jamani?' He held up his arm and pinched his black skin for all to see. 'This. And the green is the beautiful land of Africa. Eh? And what is this yellow stripe in the middle? Eh?'
>
> 'The Indians! The Mhindis!' shouts an unknown voice.
>
> Uproar. Laughter. Gleeful self-congratulation. And an angry commissioner . . . The commissioner was escorted to his car.
>
> 'Never invite him again. First he eats our food, then he lambasts us!' (pp. 162–3)

The second example is that of Nuru Poni, who writes to the authorities complaining against the public call to Muslim prayer as disturbing the neighbourhood. The narrator's comment is that 'A.A.Raghavji – Nuru Poni – who in his younger days had been one of the first to wake up and walk to mosque at four . . . now preferred to sleep through the night, having been taken over – relatively speaking – by an agnostic phase not unrelated to the changes taking place in the country' (p. 163).

The laughter of the Indian migrants in the first example clearly carries a defensiveness. That the African politicians who accuse them of resisting assimilation are derided as demagogues shows that this familiar charge always rankles. The Indians' contribution to society in the form of sewing machines to the women's movement is at best fragile for being such a token, and only reinforces the commissioner's complaint. In their counter-accusation that their women are not safe from Africans is the ancient dread of the contamination of a race and culture, fiercely guarded when most vulnerable. The joke about the flag may be good humoured but the laughter carries a *yearning* to be represented in the national iconography. This aspiration is however met with anger by the commissioner. It is clear that under the new political forces he represents the Indian migrant will be even more insecure.

It is this changing political reality that also pressures Nuru Poni to subsume his identity and dilute his sense of difference, for as the narrator claims his 'agnostic phase (is) not unrelated to the changes taking place in the country'. It is also in keeping with this suppression of identity that participation at the Tanzanian Independence ceremony is not actively sought by the Indians but followed from the safety and seclusion of their homes through a radio commentary (*The Gunny Sack*, p. 156). Others, however, belligerently assert their identity in a rhetoric that defies integration. They are of course shown to suffer for their self-exclusion. At times of political and economic crisis these Indians, perceived as a wealthy minority, become the target of nationalisation and expulsion, or, as in the case of Meghji, the victims of looters and violence. If then, as Rosemary George writes in her essay 'Traveling Light': 'Immigration *unwrites* nation and national projects because it flagrantly displays a rejection of one national space for another more desirable location, albeit with some luggage carried over' so that at times, 'there may be no desire on the part of immigrants to write themselves into a national discourse *except* as aliens',[9] it is important to acknowledge the price paid, in material and epistemic terms, for such Otherness.

For George this refusal to integrate emanates from a sense of superiority and position of strength which comes from the migrant being 'more multi-faceted a figure than . . . the equation that delivers a subject who is marginal and who therefore yearns for assimilation into the mainstream' ('Traveling Light, p. 79). It is because of this that George takes issue in her essay with Homi Bhabha's account in 'DissemiNation'[10] of how those at the margins constantly disturb, problematise and so supplement the constructs of a homogenised and cohesive national identity conjured by the hegemonic majority and officialdom. For Bhabha these marginal voices, whether those of the migrant, women or the colonised, are always subaltern. For George on the other hand, the margins need not encompass subalterneity. Of the migrant for instance she states: 'The immigrant who opts out of national projects such as liberation day euphoria is *not* always subaltern. Especially not the immigrant who speaks her story through collections of luggage – spiritual, material, linguistic, written, or oral' ('Traveling Light', p. 85).

Rosemary George reads Kulsum's tale about God's creation of mankind in *The Gunny Sack* as an example of 'those at the margins (who) may read their marginality as a positive, even superior stance from which to experience the modern nation' ('Traveling Light', p. 86). According to Kulsum, the white man came out of the oven under-done, the African over-done. Success came only with the Asian – golden brown and perfect. It is certainly the case that Kulsum insists on her family's sense of 'Asianness' (the 'golden brown' of course carries another hegemony for privileging only the fairer Indian), and particularly its knowledge of India. At night, her bed-time stories are from the Indian epics. She is superstitious and has great faith in all manner of purification rituals shown to have their roots in Indian customs. But it is important to bear in mind that these assertions are insisted upon when her sense of identity is most swamped. Her tales from *The Mahabharata* for instance are narrated for her children's 'edification' as *interventions* to Begum's stories of Wellington, Nelson and Portia which have her siblings enthralled (*The Gunny Sack*, pp. 120–1). Her sense of pride in being an Indian then is a self-determination that is not born from a position of strength but rather a feeling of racial vulnerability. Being at ease as an alien is a privilege afforded, if at all, by a tiny minority who are in a position of hegemony and therefore in complete control of their surroundings. The richness of Vassanji's work is that most of his characters are realistically shown to be outside this hegemony.

What of the migrant who decides to emigrate yet again? An unpacking of the discursive framing of homelands in Vassanji's work itself illustrates that the paradoxes and ambivalences that attend this site are not momentary ruptures or lapses but organising principles in migrant experience. In recording the life of the community there are certain spaces which Vassanji refuses to romanticise. Several stories in *Uhuru Street* which deal with characters and incidents that have their echoes in *The Gunny Sack* as well, expose the hypocrisies and abuses prevalent in these migrants' lives. Apart from rigid caste, class and racial orthodoxies which make falling in love across racial lines, as an Indian girl Yasmin does with an African Professor, something that calls for an act of 'Breaking Loose' (*The Gunny Sack*, pp. 79–90), there are businessmen/politicians who are corrupt and vindictive ('Ebrahim and the Businessman'), the rich who treat their poor relatives with utter contempt ('The Driver'), and a community that is ruthless in its extra-judicial punishments as when the narrator's own grandfather Dhanji Govindji is murdered for stealing from Shamsi community funds (*The Gunny Sack*, pp. 54–5). A particularly chilling story in *Uhuru Street*, retold by Salim as part of his adolescent experiences in *The Gunny Sack*, reveals the dark secrets of child abuse ('For a Shilling').

Most of all, Vassanji is mindful of the oppression wrought on women by patriarchy buttressed by cultural codes. Each of the stories in *Uhuru Street* reveal young women married off to husbands who become drunkards, womanisers and wife-beaters. At times such women are driven to suicide, as Nurmohammed's daughter is in 'The Driver'. In *The Gunny Sack*, seemingly confident women like the narrator's Aunt Gula – 'big, fat, strong and quarrelsome' – are shown to crack under the humiliations heaped upon them by unfaithful husbands. Gula douses herself with kerosene and sets herself aflame (*The Gunny Sack*, p. 75). Elsewhere the narrator's widowed mother shoulders the burden of bringing up her family at the expense of other personal fulfilments:

> She had been thirty-three when Father died, and she had refused several offers of marriage because they would all have entailed one thing: sending us all to the 'boarding' – the orphanage. Pictures of her before his death showed her smiling and in full bloom: . . . I had never seen her like that. All I had seen of her was the stern face getting sterner with time as the lines set permanently and the hair thinned, the body turned squat, the voice thickened. (*Uhuru Street*, p. 77)

When, in *The Gunny Sack*, the three parts of the book emphasise the lives of three women – Ji-Bai, Kulsum and Amina – it is Vassanji's acknowledgement of the strong influence of women on their respective communities. This uncovering of what patriarchy normally subsumes coincides with the author's project of centering marginal voices.

This is not to say that Vassanji's stories consist only of the darkest textures and are devoid of humour. There are many delightful comic cameo roles in them, moments of good humoured self-awareness on the part of the characters and achievement of personal aspirations. But it is significant that the verbal and physical violence, corruption, hypocrisy and decay these stories carry, make every tale in *Uhuru Street* end in rupture and fragmentation. The only exception is 'Breaking Loose' but even here, Yasmin's rebellion is tentative and fragile.

If these conclusions in which resolution is impossible or endlessly deferred reflect a conscious effort on Vassanji's part not to romanticise his land of birth, it is also possible to read them as symptomatic of the ambivalence that informs the migrant writer's narrativisation of his/her native land. At the matrix of this ambivalence is the writer's own alienation from the landscape and its people, a distancing produced by factors of class, cultural conditioning and migrancy itself, which almost always precludes a complete integration with the new homeland. Under these circumstances the land is strange and terrifying and is often framed, rather in keeping with Orientalist paradigms, as eternally violent, dark and irrational. It is the accentuating of the shadowy and grotesque that feature in the description for instance of a sultry night in Dar:

> Outside was a thick darkness, a black, menacing universe, with faces occasionally illuminated by moving kerosene lamps, and eerie, momentary shadows, gigantic, cast by passing cars against building walls: a darkness that rang with shouts and cackles and squeals of laughter. (*The Gunny Sack*, p. 87)

Again, it is the arduous and uncanny that Vassanji emphasises when describing the city:

> The image of quiet, leafy suburbia impressed on the mind, of Nairobi's Desai Road, cracked in the heat of Dar into a myriad refracting fragments, each a world unto its own. One of which was grotesque and mysterious, always threatening, that never failed to leave a chill in your heart every time you encountered it. (*The Gunny Sack*, p. 86)

Of the many facets of Dar then, the one selected for foregrounding, is the world in which terrain and climate are difficult, and which misshapen beggars and sinister old people inhabit. These larger-than-life images are, of course, those that strike the imagination of Salim the child. Much more significant is the emphasis in the novel by Vassanji the migrant writer on the deterioration that has taken place in the lands of origin – both India and Tanzania – which makes them unstable and untenable and therefore *justifies* departure.

A similar framing of the native land is to be seen in Romesh Gunesekera's collection of short stories *Monkfish Moon* and Chandani Lokugé's *Moth and Other Stories*,[11] which point to common discursivities in migrant writing. Both Gunesekera and Lokugé are Sri Lanka-born writers now domiciled in England and Australia respectively. Gunesekera describes re-connections with the native land that are always painful and awkward. Sri Lanka is no longer the idyllic place of childhood, of uncomplicated, sensuous countryside, but of violence in which curfews are a way of life and family mansions are in decay. The emphasis in the stories is on an ambience which, because many of them are set at night, in isolated places, when the 'flexing' of the jungle or the ominous cry of a gecko are the only sounds heard, makes the land itself appear menacing and sinister.

While the central characters in Gunesekera's stories are portrayed with a subtlety and skill that foregrounds their sensitivity to both their environment and inner conflicts, the peripheral characters often feature only as disquieting voices that intrude in the night, mysterious forms that cast shadows on the landscape. 'Ranvali' is a story about a woman who, after many years, visits her father's beach bungalow. As childhood memories are recalled, different images and perspectives on who her father really was strike the now grown-up daughter. Implied in the story through the juxtaposition of the father's communist idealism and the present-day state of insurrection are the wasted and misdirected opportunities for political stability in the country. The scene in which the woman encounters the revolutionaries is carefully evoked:

> The trees lining the road became silhouettes. A gilt line divided the sky from the edge of the sea: everything else was turning black. Then I came around a bend and a fire flared on the road ahead. I touched the brakes and slowed down. There was a make-shift roadblock of oil-drums and logs laid across. A red flag was up.
>
> Some figures moved at the edge of the road and two young men came slowly towards the car. I wound down my window. 'What's the matter?'
>
> The man in front, the leader, looked hard at me. He had a wispy beard and a long thin throat. When he swallowed I could see his Adam's apple plummet. He was dressed in a jungle shirt and blue trousers. He shone a torch on me. There was some whispering in the dark. Someone climbed on to one of the oil-drums on the road. He cupped his hand and lit a cigarette. A red glowing face floated in the air. (p. 101)

One finds similar portrayals in Lokugé's stories. Apart from 'A Pair of Birds', which charts the rupture of a friendship when Sinhala–Tamil communal tensions spill over into the burning and looting of Tamil houses, the cause and agents of such violence, whether Sinhala or Tamil assailants, are shown to penetrate public and private places, but are faceless. In the story 'The Man Within', the Tamil terrorist who blackmails Sunil into carrying a bomb into the Central Telegraph Office is one with 'unblinking, pitiless eyes ferreting into him, exploring, exposing his soul' (p. 62), known only by a serial number. Each story in the collection maps the impact violence has on the people and the landscape through the different perceptions that form their narrative structures, none however from the terrorist's point of view. What we have then in both Gunesekera and Lokugé is an effacing of the individuality of the agents of violence which allows a subsuming of the cause of their violence for effect. This in turn permits a sense of the native land as an ontological space that is perpetually violent and ruptured.

In the interview with Susheila Nasta referred to above (see note 5), Vassanji acknowledged this notion of instability in the native land by saying that Tanzania 'seems to me at least to have degenerated in many ways. I think if the Asians had remained there and been allowed to maintain the structures that they had set up – the educational system, the health system, business – then the country would have been in a much better shape than it is now' (p. 21). The regret these words carry at the loss of a certain privilege by Indian professionals points to an important justification of departure, which also has its roots in the author's own alienation from the landscape and its people.

But in order to highlight the extent of the deterioration that has taken place in the lands of origin, there is a move in *The Gunny Sack* to present an originary moment that is mythic and utopian. The inauguration of the Shamsi community is one such instance and the metaphors and images carried in the descriptive language itself support this mythic moment as magic. The night is quiet, starry and leisured. A cool wind rustles the leaves, crickets chirp and insects weave 'dances around the solitary lamp hanging from a tree' (*The Gunny Sack*, p. 7). It is on such a tranquil night that, as legend has it, a tall, bearded man called Shamas arrives in the village of Junapur, begins a dance and sings in a ritual that mesmerises the villagers into joining him. He initiates them into a new sect of Islam that ushers a complementarity that is nourishing. For a cornerstone of this new faith is its syncretism. The Junapur Shamsis consider 'thundering Allah as simply a form of reposing Vishnu' (p. 7). Later, when members of the community migrate to Dar-es-Salaam, they live harmoniously together with Hindu migrants, celebrating Diwali and Id jointly. We are shown such syncretism in practice when Ji-Bai administers medicine to a sick Sona. Hers is an art of healing handed down to women in her Indian home town 'on the eve of Hindu Diwali . . . yet the prayers were all ayats from the Quran' (p. 142). Names themselves are described as carrying such multiplicity, with that of Dhanji Govindji being 'Banya in its aspiration for wealth as Hindu: yet gloriously, unabashedly, Muslim' (p. 10). Salim's comment is that this hybridity is as 'surely, a sign, as any, of prosperity and stability' (p. 41).

Current African self-determination makes independent Tanzania on the other hand a place hostile to migrants in its call for an essentialist nationalism, while modern India is no longer an innocent and accommodating site of heterogeneity. In *The Gunny Sack*, three centuries after the first Shamsi conversion, failed economic prosperity produces strife and confusion amongst the community 'that was (once) both Hindu and Muslim' (p. 8). 'India (begins) to feel its seams' and it is suggested that Dhanji Govindji's migration to Zanzibar and murder at the hands of other Shamsis are consequences of these conflicts. In Junapur the Shamsi community no longer exists and fundamentalists hold sway.

It is important to bear in mind however that a 'seamless' India is a sentimental construct in the first place which ignores the reality of caste and communal hegemonies and conflicts that have always existed.[12] But here it is a necessary invention for Vassanji's mapping of the rupture of that utopia which makes contemporary India no longer tenable. Similarly, the notion of different cultural traditions existing in *equal* measure within the migrant is another discursive construct that incidents in *The Gunny Sack* themselves challenge. For if we understand migrant identity as a fluid site which implies a constant negotiation *vis-à-vis* assimilation or self-determination, signifiers of Hindu, Muslim and African identity cannot possibly be forwarded equally but as *contesting* forces depending on the exigencies of the moment. This is amply illustrated in *The Gunny Sack* when Salim registers himself at school.

'Grandfather's name first,' said the application form, and Uncle Goa asked me.

'Huseni,' I said, naming my renegade half-caste ancestor, and became Huseni Salim Juma for ever after.

The rest of my family ignored the whole question and became Dhanji, even the more classy Dhanjee, a name invoking wealth and respect, while I, under the auspices of Uncle Goa and Mrs. Schwering's glaring eye, became: anybody. No trace of tribe, caste, colour, even continent of origin. How much in a name? Salim Juma, the name chose me, and it chose my future and this basement in which I hide myself with my gunny.' (*The Gunny Sack*, p. 108)

Salim is of course aware that such a tabula rasa – 'no trace of tribe, caste, colour' – can never be, and perceptively locates his biography in the history and identity his name carries. It is then in this disjuncture between Salim's self-awareness and Vassanji the migrant author's construct of homeland that the competing, incompatible and contradictory structures of migrant discourse are most effectively seen.

The distinct topography of No. 69 Rosecliff Park Drive with which *No New Land* begins is in counterpoint to the sense of alienation and flux the emigrants who inhabit the block experience. The first steps in the migration of Nurdin Lalani and his family to Canada are humiliating and unexpected. They suffer the indignity of contemptuous service on the airline they travel with and are refused a visa to Britain. In Toronto, they move into the flat of Zera's sister only to find that the extended-family situations that were a way of life in Dar don't work in the spaces and cultures of the West. The jobs that come their way are menial and their sense of inadequacy becomes pronounced. Once again, present life is made meaningful only with constant reference to the past and the extent to which the migrants embrace it. The past impinges on the lives of the Lalanis mainly through two figures from Dar – Nurdin's father Haji Lalani and 'Missionary', the head of the Shamsi sect, also known as 'Master'. It is both intruding and benevolent. Haji Lalani was the autocratic patriarch whose photograph hangs on his son's wall. But depicting a man 'relentless in his judgement here as the real person had been in Africa' (p. 83), it is a gaze from the past that Nurdin flinches from. For Zera however, the photograph is a prize possession, an icon to which she holds incense sticks, 'giving it a real presence in the home' (p. 83). Missionary on the other hand comes through as wise, dignified and reliable[13] although here too, Zera's total reliance on him for spiritual and practical guidance shows her to be in complete harmony with this past, albeit in an absurdly naive fashion:

> For Zera, such questions of modesty were referred to the Master himself, Missionary, who reflected on values and tradition, and sent his verdict: If you wear pants, cover your behinds. An ardent request was submitted by Zera and his other former pupils, begging him to emigrate. We are desperate for guidance they said. Life here is full of pitfalls. Children come home from school with questions we can't answer. And want to celebrate Christmas. They sent him a long list of innocent-looking items that contained pork by-products, from bread to toothpaste. What is a by-product? Please come. (pp. 67–8)

*No New Land* is one work which offers a resolution at its end to the turmoils of migrant life, and Zera's relationship with her past is a pivotal factor in this closure. Her adulation of Missionary invests him with an aura and a power that is shown automatically to soothe their troubled lives. With his arrival in Canada, charges of rape against Nurdin are dropped (this is coincidental for it is Jamal's spadework that achieves this solution, but the timing is significant). Nanji finds personal fulfilment with his marriage to Missionary's daughter, and Zera, as principal devotee, has a role in life that she once again cherishes.

There is a narrative price paid however for such resolution. For the beneficial impact of the past in *No New Land* is entirely dependent on a particular stasis. Vassanji does give voice in the novel to gradations of change in the migrants brought about by their new environment. The younger generation – the Lalani children and lawyer Jamal – are shown to have assimilated well to Canadian life and as a result fetishise the past less than Nurdin and Zera. There are times when Nurdin too strains to break with the past. An act of eating pork or his sexual attraction to Sushila mark these moments. Zera on the other hand, despite the fact that she lives in a radically different environment to what she knew in Dar, and is the bread-winner of the family, remains unchanged. Here is the woman – and particularly the mother figure – as static cultural signifier who becomes the vehicle through which past values are handed out, redeemed and made authentic. If dislocation and contradiction are the underlying bases of migrant experience, it is also the imperative need for a resolution which irons out these tensions that is reflected in the way closure is mediated and made possible in *No New Land*.

Vassanji's work is a dynamic site which lays bare the paradoxes, incompatibilities and ambivalences that are central paradigms of migrant experience and discourse. How the homeland is discursively mediated and imagined through narrative strategies, selection and construction of a communal archive gives us fundamental insights into the very nature of migrant discourse itself. It is in the 'textual resistances', as in the moments of disjuncture between the fictional characters and the author's construction of a collective consciousness and homeland, that the discursive pressures that attend the recording of migrant life are most fruitfully to be seen. A reading of these gaps then points to important suppositions that can form the bases of a theoretical framework for our understanding of the production of migrant identity. Of these suppositions, the challenges to notions of migrant hybridity as something automatically acquired or unanchored to socio-cultural privilege, and something which is also a point of reconciliation that is always nourishing (in Han Suyin's words, 'a benevolent coalition of fragments'[14]), are the most pathbreaking. The value of Vassanji's work lies precisely in the projections of how such hybridity, if at all, can never comprise an equal mixing of disparate strands. For identity is a site of negotiation which depends on the exigencies of situation, is always anchored to political, economic and cultural hegemony, and comes most unstuck at moments of crisis.

## Notes

I am grateful to Dr Arjuna Parakrama for his suggestions on this essay and his insights on 'hybridity as hegemony' (work in progress) which have clarified my own thoughts on the subject considerably.

1. Derek Walcott, 'The Antilles: Fragments of Epic Memory', (Nobel Prize lecture) *The New Republic*, 28 December 1992, pp. 26–32.

2. Moyez Vassanji, *The Gunny Sack*, Oxford: Heinemann, 1989; *Uhuru Street*, Oxford: Heinemann, 1991; *No New Land*, New Delhi: Penguin, 1992. Page references will be to these editions and will be included in the text.

3. Salman Rushdie, *Imaginary Homelands*, New Delhi: Granta and Viking Penguin, 1991, p. 10.

4. I use the term 'Adamic' after Walcott, whose enterprise has been to 'give' the Caribbean a history by an act of naming – naming the topography, flora, fauna and people of the archipelago.

5. Vassanji, 'Interview with Susheila Nasta', *Wasafiri*, No. 13 (Spring 1991), p. 19.

6. Nuruddin Farah in *From Commonwealth to Post-Colonial*, ed. Anna Rutherford, Sydney: Dangaroo Press, 1992, p. 375.

7. See for example Abdul Sheriff, *Slaves, Spices & Ivory in Zanzibar*, London: James Currey, 1987.

8. In the interview with Susheila Nasta, Vassanji stated: 'In the midst of writing *The Gunny Sack* I wrote a collection of short stories which deals with a view to recreate Dar-es-Salaam where I grew up, during a specific period. And what I thought of doing was just to basically turn off and turn on lights . . . so each story would be a flicker of light and then you would have a whole street emerging', *Wasafiri*, No. 13 (Spring 1991), p. 21.

9. Rosemary Marangoly George, 'Traveling Light: Of Immigration, Invisible Suitcases, and Gunny Sacks', *Differences*, Vol. 4, No. 2 (1992), p. 83 and p. 86 respectively.

10. Homi Bhabha, 'DissemiNation,' *Nation and Narration*, ed. Homi Bhabha, London & New York: Routledge, 1990, pp. 291–322.

11. Romesh Gunesekera, *Monkfish Moon*, London: Granta, 1992; Chandani Lokugé, *Moth and Other Stories*, Sydney: Dangaroo, 1993.

12. See Romila Thapar, *Interpreting Early India*, Delhi: Oxford University Press, 1992. In Chapter 5 entitled 'Early India: an Overview' Thapar, analysing methodologies of historical narrative to show how they are not arbitrary but ideologically informed, illustrates the political and economic manouverings and conflicts between various groups based on religious, caste, class and professional distinctions that existed from Vedic times.

13. In an interview Vassanji stated of Missionary that 'he is not presented as a kind of Ayatollah type of figure', a comment that also points to Vassanji's need to counteract the stereotype of the fanatical Islamic mullah which has gained

currency in the West. See ' "Broadening the Substrata": An Interview with M.G. Vassanji' by Chelvakanaganayakam, *World Literature Written in English* 31, No. 2 (1991), p. 28.
14.  Han Suyin, keynote address at EACLALS conference on 'Nationalism vs Internationalism', Graz, Austria, May 1993.

# Biographical Notes

STEWART BROWN lectured for three years at Bayero Univerity, Kano, Nigeria, and since 1988 has been lecturer in African and Caribbean Literature at the Centre for West African Studies, University of Birmingham. He has published two collections of his own poetry, *Zinder* (1986) and *Lugard's Bridge* (1989), both from Seren Books, and has edited three poetry anthologies, *Caribbean Poetry Now* (Hodder & Stoughton, 1985), *Voiceprint* (Longman, 1989) with Mervyn Morris and Gordon Rohlehr, and *The Heinemann Book of Caribbean Poetry*, with Ian McDonald.

ABDULRAZAK GURNAH was born in Zanzibar, Tanzania. He was educated there and in England and now teaches literature at the University of Kent at Canterbury, England. He is the author of four novels, *Memory of Departure* (1987), *Pilgrims Way* (1988), *Dottie* (1990) and *Paradise* (1994), which was short-listed for the Booker Prize 1994.

LYNN INNES is Professor of Post-Colonial Literatures at the University of Kent, Canterbury, England. Her recent books include *The Devil's Own Mirror: The Irishman and the African in Modern Literature* (1990), *Chinua Achebe* (1990), and *Woman and Nation in Irish Literature and Society, 1880–1935* (1993). She is an Associate Editor for *Wasafiri*, a journal of African, Asian and Caribbean Literature.

BELINDA JACK is Lecturer in French at Christ Church, University of Oxford, and also British Academy Post-doctoral Research Fellow at the newly established European Humanities Research Centre, Oxford. She read French with African and Caribbean Studies at the University of Kent, England, and took her doctorate at the University of Oxford, where she submitted a thesis on Black Francophone Literatures and Criticism (to be published by Greenwood, Connecticut). Her *Introduction to Francophone Literatures* is forthcoming from Oxford University Press. She has contributed several articles on African and Indian Ocean writing in French for the forthcoming *Oxford Companion to Literature in French* and writes for a number of journals.

LUCY STONE MCNEECE teaches Francophone Literature, Comparative Literature and Film at the University of Connecticut, where she is Chair of French and Francophone Studies. She has published on Khatibi, Ben Jelloun, Kateb and Meddeb, among others, and her book on the politics of representation in Duras, *Shadows of Empire*, is to be published by the University of Florida Press.

NELOUFER DE MEL teaches literature at the University of Colombo, Sri Lanka. She wrote her doctorate on the plays of Wole Soyinka and Derek Walcott, and has written on Nationalism and the Sinhala Theatre, Sri Lankan Drama in English, and women's writing. She sits on the panel of the annual

State Drama Festival in Sri Lanka and is an active participant in university theatre, recently working on an adaptation of Wole Soyinka's *Opera Wonyosi* into an experimental trilingual (Sinhala, Tamil, English) production, and directing Harold Pinter's *Party Time*. She is the editor of *Options*, a quarterly focusing on women's issues in the context of the Indian sub-continent. She is currently editing a book of essays on Sri Lankan poetry in English, and working on a book on Soyinka and Walcott.

MPALIVE-HANGSON MSISKA is a Lecturer in the Department of English at Birkbeck College, University of London. He has previously taught at Bath College of Higher Education and the University of Malawi. He is co-author of *The Quiet Chameleon: Modern Poetry from Central Africa* (Hans Zell, 1992) and co-editor of *Writing and Africa* (Longman, forthcoming 1995).

ATO QUAYSON completed a PhD for the Faculty of English, University of Cambridge, on oral traditions and their strategic transformations in the works of the Rev. Samuel Johnson, Amos Tutuola, Wole Soyinka and Ben Okri. He is now Junior Research Fellow in the African Humanities at Wolfson College, Oxford and his current work centres on the links between drama, democracy and development with particular reference to Ghana, Nigeria, South Africa and Zimbabwe. He is also interested in the spread of amateur video films in Africa and how indigenous theatrical traditions are affected by the new visual technologies.

CAROLINE ROONEY was born and educated in Zimbabwe. She took her first two degrees at the University of Cape Town before going on to do a D.Phil. at Oxford University. She has held lectureships at Cape Town and at Oxford and is currently a lecturer at the University of Kent. She has published a number of articles on African literature and continues to do research in this area. Her book on 'The Androgyne and the Double' is due to be published by Routledge.

# Index